UNLOCKING THE MYSTERIES

OF

DANIEL

by
Wallace L. Emerson

PROMISE PUBLISHING CO.
Orange, California 92668

Cover Design by Mary Chapeau

UNLOCKING THE MYSTERIES OF DANIEL

1988 by Promise Publishing Company

Published by Promise Publishing Company

Orange, California 92668

Printed in the United States of America

Library of Congress

Cataloging-in-Publication Data

Emerson, Wallace L.

Unlocking the Mysteries of Daniel

ISBN 0-939497-07-7

FOREWORD

Understanding prophetic events is not a simple task! It requires diligent and careful study of the Bible, awareness of history and language and a confidence in the inerrancy and inspiration of the Word of God. This book reflects all three essentials.

The prophecy of Daniel was written about 2500 years ago, several hundred years before the Apostle John received his vision on the Isle of Patmos which we now possess as the Book of Revelation. Daniel and Revelation must be studied together. It is difficult to understand the teachings, visions and events of Revelation without a thorough knowledge of the prophecy of Daniel. Daniel's words are quoted frequently in the New Testament and Jesus supported its reliability and inspiration by quoting from its message in His own prophetic discourses.

There are available fine commentaries on the Book of Daniel. The question might be, "Why print another one?" Wallace Emerson has produced a unique book on Daniel in that it describes historical situations and events in such detail. With extensive experience as a librarian, Dr. Emerson shows careful scholarship in his documentation as well as mature and spiritual insights in his commentary. He will answer questions for you that other books do not deal with as thoroughly as this one does. You will be glad that this volume is a part of your prophetic library.

The reader should be aware of the fact that this is not an exegetical commentary in the sense of verse by verse analysis. It was not written for the scholar but for the average lay person. It gives an overall picture and is written with a style that keeps you interested and fascinated with ancient history as well as its relationship to our prophetic future.

I have never read a book like this one - it is a refreshing approach and a delight to read. It is the king of books which I will refer to again and again when wanting to understand the historical backgrounds of this great prophecy of Daniel. I pray that the Lord will use this volume to deepen our spiritual commitment as well as our biblical understanding and most of all, to build our anticipation for that great day when our Lord Jesus Christ shall return!

David Hocking
Speaker, BIOLA HOUR
Pastor, CALVARY CHURCH
Santa Ana, California

PREFACE

It is well known that commentaries on the Book of Daniel abound both from Jewish and Christian authorities. Among the noted interpreters have been Jerome, Aquinas, Luther, Calvin and Sir Isaac Newton, to name but a few. But every generation has an obligation to re-study this work which ranks politically and spiritually as one of the greatest documents of all time.

Dr. Wallace L. Emerson who has given a lifetime of service to Christian instruction (an important segment of it as a college dean and president), has lent his erudition and spiritual insight to the task of the exposition of Daniel's strategic prophecy. His work reveals breadth of research, depth of spiritual comprehension, exemplary Christian courtesy for those from whom he differs and a keen sense of the comprehensive issues involved. Through it all, there is exhibited a love for the Lord and His Word. The exposition is admittedly orthodox and premillennial and as such, is a genuine contribution to the literature on the subject. Dr. Emerson has placed us all in his debt for this exacting labor of love.

Charles Lee Feinberg, Dean Emeritus
Talbot Theological Seminary
La Mirada, California

ACKNOWLEDGEMENTS

To all of those many commentators of Scripture, past and present, whose labors have entered into the making of this book, may I express grateful acknowledgement.

My more immediate indebtedness to my contemporaries, not all of whom are included in the bibliography and citations, is here acknowledged. These have in many ways contributed to my knowledge and have given needed encouragement.

Special thanks are due Dr. Charles Lee Feinberg, Dean Emeritus of Talbot Seminary, whose lectures and classes I have been privileged to attend, whose sound scholarship, whose reverence for the Word, whose gracious spirit of helpfulness have been an inspiration.

I am grateful to Dr. Nicholas Kurtanek and to Dr. Harry Sturz, both formerly of the Bible Department of Biola College, for suggestions and to Gerald Gooden, head of the Biola College library for his constant helpfulness and counsel. Reverend Homer P. Emerson contributed by proofreading the manuscript. Thanks to Fred Emerson and Timothy Kurtanek for their help.

I shall be eternally grateful to Miss Esther Turrell whose selfless and constant cooperation over many months was largely responsible for bringing this work to its present conclusion.

And, a special acknowledgement to James Bardwell who has been a great encouragement to me in bringing this book to print. His personal friendship and care have been a practical expression of his love and commitment to Christ, which overflows. I'm deeply grateful.

Dr. Wallace L. Emerson

To my wife,

Eve,

who has given so generously

of her time and strength

to make this book possible.

TABLE OF CONTENTS

PROLOGUE

As a brief overview of the format, the purpose, and the thrust of the book, may we suggest the following: Daniel's first six chapters (except for part of Chapter 2) are historical, the Babylonian and Persian scenes of Daniel's own experience. There is not the slightest hint that Daniel ever again visited his native land. The last six chapters concern prophetic visions vouchsafed to Daniel and are meticulous as to the time, place and circumstances of his visions. Seemingly, the prophecy is mostly concerned with the Times of the Gentiles and gentile affairs. As we shall try to show in the interpretation of Nebuchadnezzar's dream, there were to be four great world empires - Babylon, Persia, Greece (Macedonia), Rome, following one another in order, with whom Israel would have to deal as a subject people. During the dominion of the last world power (Rome), Messiah's first advent would take place but He would have nothing which was His. The old Roman Empire would finally disappear and, after a hiatus, would reappear but the horizons of the old and new empires are blended. The interval of fifteen centuries has to be inferred. We now see that there was a long lacuna between parts of the prophetic picture symbolized by the feet of the image.

After this gap, as we interpret Chapter 7, there would again be four great powers, one of which would be a revived Rome; the others, as we interpret it, would be England, Russia and an Arab hegemony. These again, would be nations with whom Israel must be concerned either as friends or foes and will be on earth at Messiah's second advent at the end of the age. Israel is not pictured as subject to any of these but somehow involved with her own destiny summed up in the seventy weeks of Daniel Chapter 9. Most of the pages of Daniel, therefore, are filled with doings of persons and events distinctly non-Jewish because Israel's fate is, according to divine purpose, largely bound up with the gentiles.

The book of Daniel begins with the captivity of the Jewish nation in a strange land. Daniel is a prophet of the Exile. We might therefore expect the whole purpose of the book to be the promise of a gradual emancipation of Israel from her past sins and difficulties coming to a crescendo in the glorious restoration of Israel under Messiah's reign. In Ezekiel, for example, the factor of hope is especially evident for while Ezekiel enumerates at length Israel's sins and the reason for God's heavy hand upon a backsliding nation, there is a final and far-distant picture of Israel's glory and restoration to divine favor. But encouragement and hope do not comprise the most obvious messages of Daniel's book. There is, in Daniel 9, a confession of national sin and God's justice in the discipline meted out (Daniel 9:1-19) but we look in vain for any hope of national restoration or glory in the near future or even a deliverance to former

i

independence. Even Messiah, when He comes, "shall be cut off and have nothing" and the city will again be destroyed (Daniel 9:26). Instead of a vision for universal peace, wars and desolations are determined to the end. Furthermore, in the five verses of Daniel 11:31-35 probably referring in part to Israel's struggle during the Maccabean revolt, they are only promised that "when they fall they shall be helped with a little help." Out of the 357 verses in the book most of which are preoccupied with gentile affairs, fewer than fifteen seem to offer comfort for the near future. Many of the others provide long lists of suffering for Israel. Not only human adversaries but even supernatural ones are arrayed against Israel. Nowhere in Old Testament Scripture do we have such definite hints of the demonic forces working against the Chosen People. The great deliverances vouchsafed to Daniel and his companions are personal, not national. Even the great promise of a resurrection from the dead at the end of the age is accompanied by the prediction of a time of trouble for Israel " such as never was since there was a nation."

We could sum up Daniel's message by saying there is:

(a) no picture of a delivered and glorified Israel as in Ezekiel except by implication (Daniel 2:44, 7:13-14, 27);

(b) no picture of a conquering Messiah who would speedily restore all things;

(c) no confirmation of divine support for a Maccabean[2] uprising except "they shall be helped with a little help";

(d) no reminder of the divine mission of Israel;

(e) no call to national action to deliver them from persecution.

Instead, there is a series of descriptions of an individual, or individuals, in deadly enmity against the truth, against Israel and against God. While these individuals are finally destroyed "without hand," they are allowed to "wear out the saints of the most high."

Time and again, the prophetic writer reminds us that the prophecy is for the "end time" which was small comfort for a people needing the promise of immediate relief and deliverance. Instead of a message concerned with deliverance of the temple, the city and the land, in reality the book is much more concerned with the Times of the Gentiles than with present affairs of Israel. But whether implied or stated, Israel is the focal point.

Listen to a prophet's word of hope:

In that day will I seek to destroy all the nations that come against Jerusalem. And I will pour out upon the House of David and upon the inhabitants of Jerusalem the spirit of grace and of supplications; and they shall look upon me whom they have pierced and they shall mourn for him,

*as one mourneth for his only son, and shall be in bitterness for him, as
one is in bitterness for his firstborn. In that day there shall be a fountain
opened to the house of David and to the inhabitants of Jerusalem for sin
and uncleanness.*[3]

But these words are from Zechariah, not Daniel. Daniel ends with the
announcement "of a time of trouble such as never was since there was a
nation" and a national survival only with the help of Michael, the archangel. This time of trouble, to be sure, is accompanied by a resurrection of
those that sleep in the dust but again, there is no sign of Messiah's
kingdom. If we turn to the middle of the book (Chapter 7), however, we
are given the vision of the Son of Man and His saints possessing a kingdom
that shall never be superseded. But otherwise, there is persecution,
frustration and defeat for the People of God. It may be said that the book
of Daniel was not written for the immediate situation and need but for the
distant scene, "the end of days, the time of the end." It is a book of hope
only for those Israelites who, by faith could with the prophet, see through
the tumult of the Times of the Gentiles to the end of the age and to the
resurrection of the just.

INTRODUCTION

As to the critical problems alleged to be so prominent in the prophecy of Daniel, it is not our purpose to deal with them since this is not intended to be a critical study of the book.[1] However, we must notice the problem of the time element; in other words, whether it was written as alleged by some, approximately 165 B.C. or whether there is reason to think that the account given by the book itself of its own origin, namely a date somewhere between 605 B.C. and 534 B.C., is to be taken as correct. Basic to all other problems is the date of its writing for dependent upon this date are its authorship and authenticity.

If written when, where and by whom it professes to have been written, it is obvious that the book (especially Chapters 7 to 12) is a book of prophecy - apocalyptic, prophetic. On the other hand, if written as is claimed by many theologians, in the Maccabean era (ca. 165 B.C.), then at least some of the alleged prophetic portion is largely not prophecy but history (or fiction). The pious purpose for this line of thought, namely, to encourage Israel during the time of persecution by Antiochus Epiphanes while admirable in its intent, is dishonest in its method. To those who are unalterably opposed to the miraculous and to supernatural manifestations of God in the affairs of men, the late dating is not only preferable but necessary in support of their viewpoint. But in the place of the prophetic problem and an understanding of the supernatural element in it, we have been presented with literary, historical and moral problems equally difficult.

The theory that Daniel was written by an unknown author in Maccabean times is, of course, a denial of its inspiration by the Holy Spirit unless we subscribe to a very loose theory of inspiration. It would be therefore, in plain English, a pious fraud. For whatever good intentions and pious purposes may have motivated the alleged Maccabean author, one can hardly believe that the Holy Spirit, the Spirit of truth, could be a party to such a transaction[2] It is equally impossible that our Lord, Himself, could put His imprimatur on Daniel as a prophet were there no Daniel or prophetic inspiration. To say that He was merely repeating the thought of the times is to forget that our Lord was quick to challenge erroneous religious beliefs. Their theory, with all due deference, tells us more about the viewpoint of the minds producing this theory than it does about the prophet or the book. It carries an aura of wishful thinking in the interest of an unprofitable theory.

The following questions regarding date, authorship, and purpose of the book are pertinent to our discussion:

DATE

If Daniel were written 165 B.C. or thereabouts, how could a literary and religious writer have achieved complete anonymity among a people suffering persecution when any encouragement alleged to come from Jehovah would have been like a ray of light on a dark night? If such a book achieved its purpose, someone (its author or its alleged discoverer) must certainly come to popular attention. The Maccabees were not in the least anonymous. Therefore why would the author of Daniel be, if he professed to have discovered a prophecy or to have written one?

We might ask ourselves what kind of a book should we expect from the exile period. The two books of the Maccabees would be the types of books one naturally would expect to come out of the great persecution of Antiochus Epiphanes. But Daniel shows sufficient evidence of belonging to the Babylonian Exile. It has been rightly said:

"If the Exile has that importance in relation to the development as already described, then the whole progressive development of the divine revelation as it lies before us in the Old and New Testaments, warrants us to expect from the period of the Exile, a book containing records such as are found in the book of Daniel. Since miracles and prophecies essentially belong not only in general to the realization of the divine plan of salvation but have also been especially manifested in all the critical periods of the history of the kingdom of God neither the miracles in the historical parts of the book nor its prophecies, consisting of singular predictions, can in any respect seem strange to us.".[3]

As we compare First Maccabees with the book of Daniel, we have in the former, the kind of book that embodies most of the elements that the book of Daniel should have had, had it been written in the Maccabean period. To be more specific, Daniel should have been anti-Hellenic and shown zeal for the temple and temple worship and a holy indignation for those profaning it. The book should have been full of zeal for the law and denunciation of those not so zealous. First Maccabees is full of Palestinian places, names, local color and glorification of the Hasmonean exploits. This we do not find in Daniel. Even Montgomery says, "Further, the historical background of these chapters is Babylonian. Again their sumptuous barbaric scenery is obviously not that of Palestine: one need only compare the arid scenery of the later chapters."[4]

Since 400 years had elapsed between the Babylon of Nebuchadnezzar's reign and the Babylon of the Maccabean period, conditions utterly different had come into being with reference to the whole city and area. The city had lost its preeminent position and was under Greek control. What a wonderful research staff and what a wonderful source library the pseudo Daniel must have had. He seems to have avoided the pitfalls into which Herodotus fell only a century after the events about which he wrote.

vi

How could the Jewish high priest in 332 B.C. have shown Alexander the Great the prophecy of Daniel as pertaining to his own conquests when, according to the theory, the book was not (to have been) written for another 164 years? Josephus could hardly have imagined the dream that Alexander related to the high priest. How also do we explain Jerusalem's escape from destruction after its refusal to surrender? And how do we explain its switch in loyalty from a nearly monotheistic Persia under which the Jewish people had peace, prosperity and governmental friendliness, to a polytheistic Macedonia?[5]

How could a book with such uncertain antecedents have ever become a part of the Canon of Scripture? It was not the Jewish custom to select the canonical books carelessly or at random.[6] Even though Daniel is listed in the "writings" rather than in the "prophets," we have no record of any hesitancy of including his book in the sacred Scripture until the time of Porphyry (233-304 A.D.). It was the Jewish belief and criterion that all Scripture had a prophetic authorship[7]

If the Maccabean authorship and the date of 165 B.C. for Daniel are rejected, when was it written? If we were to accept the internal evidence aside from the evident familiarity of the author with the life and time of Nebuchadnezzar, we have two hints in the book, itself. The first chapter ends with the words "And Daniel continued even unto the first year of king Cyrus." If this is to be taken at face value, this chapter at least, may have been written 537-536 B.C.; i.e., in the first year of Cyrus.[8] On the other hand, Daniel's final vision (Daniel 10:1) dates the vision in the third year of Cyrus; that is 534-533 B.C., which would also be the dating of the last three chapters since they all are a part of the same vision. The problem would thus be simple if we could be sure that all of the remaining chapters were written in the intervening two years. We note that each chapter has a unity of style - in fact, all of the chapters together have a unity of style that would suggest that they were at least taken from notes put down on the spot at the time of the occurrence. Since these were all written under inspiration and since the Holy Spirit brings to our minds not only from our own human experience but beyond our experience the things which he wills, there is nothing to prevent our dating the actual writing from 537-533 B.C.   After all, if John could write another apocalypse during a comparatively brief stay on Patmos, Daniel might well have written his prophecy in what could have been the last few years of his life. Both books are the product of a long walk with God, and both are swan songs.

AUTHORSHIP

How did a fictitious Daniel ever get mentioned in Ezekiel 14:14 and 20 as having a righteousness as Job and Noah? We must be utterly incredulous that any such person otherwise not even mentioned in Scripture and therefore having no religious renown, could be given such eminence. To evoke a Ugaritic Daniel, mentioned in Ugaritic literature centuries before, as being the Daniel of the book is as preposterous as trying to identify George III with St. George just because they have the same name. Since the Ugaritic Daniel of fourteenth century B.C. has no known record of righteousness outside of his own country, how could he possibly be borrowed for the highest purposes centuries later as having a righteousness equal to Noah and Job (especially as Ugaritic ideas of righteousness were greatly at variance with Hebrew standards)?

Furthermore, at a time when national instincts were likely to give predominance to such names as Moses, the great deliverer, Joshua, the great conqueror and other Jews of great biblical eminence sent as warriors and deliverers, are we to introduce two biblical kings of great renown coupled with the name of Daniel neither of whom was a deliverer nor a Jew? The point of reference with Moses and Joshua is personal righteousness. And who of all people, linked these names? It was Ezekiel, a priest and a prophet. Until Ezekiel can be discredited and until Daniel can be shown to have a righteousness fit for such company and a righteous renown among the Jews of Ezekiel's day, we must humbly confess our lack of faith in such an interpretation of these verses in Ezekiel.

LANGUAGE

Why are there two languages used in the book of Daniel? Approximately half of the book (from Daniel 2:4 to 7:28 - 200 verses out of a total of 357 for the book) is in Aramaic, the language of the Chaldean court and later the official language of the whole Persian empire; a language which gradually superseded the everyday language of Palestine itself. The second half of the book (from 8:1 to the end of the book - 158 verses) is written in Hebrew. This will be discussed later and somewhat more at length but with Daniel's position as a civil servant, familiar with both Hebrew and Aramaic (the latter being learned after he came to Babylon), we ought not to be greatly surprised that both languages should be used in his prophetic work if there was a valid reason for doing so. His ability to use them is not in question. Our only surprise might well be the absence of more Persian words (there are only fourteen) in light of the close diplomatic and political ties of Babylon with Persia. We have the same bilingual problem in Ezra on a somewhat different basis, where parts of four chapters are in Aramaic (Ezra 4:8-16-18, 7:12-26) and include official Aramaic documents. Otherwise, Ezra is written in Hebrew. This does not seem to be the reason for Daniel's bilingual usage. (The presence of Greek words in Chapter 3 will be discussed in that chapter.)

It can finally be said that the bilingual form of the book is perfectly consistent with the Babylonian setting of the book and is explained rationally. The following may be pertinent:

(1) The book of Ezra, for example, is often bilingual when quoting official documents. They are quoted in the original language, Aramaic, which had become the official language of the Persian Empire. We would also expect Daniel in Chapter 4, which is an official document, to quote in the language in which it was written, again Aramaic.

(2) Having said this, we have not answered the question as to why the other chapters of Daniel (from 2:4 to 7:28) are also in Aramaic since they are not official documents. Briefly, the following are some of the reasons offered:

(a) That he, Daniel, might give the prophecy regarding the world power in the language of the world power which, for the Chaldean dynasty was native in Babylon, the eastern Aramaic.[9]

(b) The author of Daniel had two related but distinct kinds of messages to deliver. One was a message of judgment and final defeat to the gentile world of whom the chief representatives of the time were Nebuchadnezzar, Belshazzar, Darius and Cyrus. The other was a message of hope and deliverance for God's oppressed but precious holy people, the Hebrews. The appropriate language for the first was Aramaic, the appropriate language for the second was Hebrew.[10]

(c) As a resident of Babylon, the Jew would doubtless use both languages; Aramaic for everyday business and Hebrew for synagogue worship, but the prophecy of his hope for the future would appropriately be in the language of past prophecy.

(d) The device of enclosing the main body of a composition within the linguistic form of a contrasting style so as to heighten the effect of the work was commonly employed in the construction of single, integrated writing in the corpus of Mesopotamian literature.[11] Interestingly the language of Israel at Christ's first Advent was the secular Aramaic; that of His predicted second Advent, Hebrew, the pure language.

As we see, these views are not mutually exclusive and may perhaps be summed as does Dr. Culver when he points out that the part of Daniel which is "slanted" to the gentiles is in Aramaic and that which is "slanted" to the future of Israel is in Hebrew. It should be remembered that Aramaic was not only the court language of the Chaldean Empire but, upon its dissolution, as we have indicated, became the official language of the Persian Empire.

PURPOSE

Why do most of Daniel's prophetic chapters avowedly point toward the end time and not primarily to the intervals between his own time and the end of the age? Certainly, they do not deal principally with the

Maccabean situation. This does not mean that Chapter 11 does not have areas already fulfilled (i.e., the immediate scene) but it has such language and such form as to make it a background to the real purpose of the chapters. Otherwise, why do we have such statements as Daniel 8:17, "Understand O son of man for at the time of the end shall be the vision"? This is in answer to Daniel's desire for an interpretation of what had gone before. In verse 19 of the same chapter, the angel says, "Behold, I will make thee know what shall be in the last end of the indignation: for at the time appointed the end shall be." Again, in verse 23 there is a hint of later fulfillment at the end time. And we have the same, far-distant view in Daniel 10:1, "The time appointed was long," and in verse 14 , "Now I am come to make thee understand what shall befall thy people in the latter days" while the whole of Chapter 7 leads into a Messianic denouement. Similar statements are made in Daniel 11:6, 11:35 and 12:1. It is therefore impossible to think of the prophetic portions of Daniel as largely related to what was happening in the Maccabean period. As to the areas of prophecy which have since had fulfillment, even they seem to have double horizons. Our guiding philosophy for the interpretation of the prophetic portion should be:

Unless otherwise indicated, it is the end time that is constantly in view. But whether we are concerned with the historical section or with the prophetic portions of Daniel, we should do well to consider the following assumptions:

(1) Whether we are dealing with history or predictions, it is not the purpose of Daniel to write a brief world history per se though he deals with historical facts.

(2) The total biblical focus is Israel - from Abraham to Christ, from Genesis to Malachi. Of Israel, it is said,

To whom pertaineth the adoption and the glory and the covenants and the giving of the law and the service of God and the promises, whose are the fathers, and of whom concerning the flesh Christ came, who is over all, God blessed forever.[12]

While the Christian church and in general the Times of the Gentiles are in the interval between the sixty-ninth and seventieth week, Daniel tells us nothing of the church. We do learn from Daniel that in the latter days, Israel will again be the focal point of God's dealings with mankind. So then, whether history or prophecy, it is there because it relates significantly to Israel. Therefore, in Daniel we may well expect that prophecy involving other nations and people are there because they are friends or foes of Israel and are significant because of God's purposes through and in Israel.

Israel once was, and again will be both a witness and a warning:

a witness when faithful; a warning when unfaithful.

From a literary standpoint, we come to realize that Daniel has not given us a set of lay figures on which to drape certain pious ideas of encouragement. We see here a spiritual and moral purpose, a historical reality and a consistency with all other Scripture. We realize that, from a literary standpoint, it would take far more than the genius even of a Daniel to portray the personalities, the dramatic scenes and the unity of perspective that we find in this book.

STRUCTURE

As to the organization of the prophecy of Daniel, we may observe the following:

Chapters 1 to 6 seem to be in chronological sequence (ca. 604 B.C. to 538 B.C.); Chapters 1 to 5 are Babylonian in background and locale; Chapter 6, Medo-Persian. These chapters are historical with the exception of a part of Chapter 2 (Nebuchadnezzar's dream).

The last six chapters (7 to 12) are Daniel's own visions and are prophetic. These visions are given in the chronological order of their reception but do not necessarily provide a chronological sequence as to the events they foretell. They occur from the first year of Belshazzar (553 B.C.)[13] to the third year of Cyrus (534 B.C.).

The language of the book is Hebrew; i.e., Chapters 1-2:4 and Chapters 8:1-12:13. The Aramaic chapters (2:4-7:28) seem to be those having greatest significance for the gentile world; the Hebrew language chapters are those with the greatest significance for the Hebrew people.

Daniel purports to be the author of all of the chapters except Chapter 4 which is Nebuchadnezzar's own proclamation.

Since Daniel was a very old man, ninety years or more when the last chapter was written, the book could not have been written much later than 534 B.C., the third year of Cyrus. Since the first chapter ends with this statement, "And Daniel continued even unto the first year of king Cyrus," it would seem plausible to think of the book as whole as assembled late in Daniel's life. But since the chapters have the freshness of a day-by-day account, they may have been written as they occurred. In the main, Daniel is meticulous as to time, place and circumstance. The whole effect of the book is that of an on-the-spot record.

We get very little biography except as it is incidental to the events which Daniel portrays. We do not know when he was born or where, nor do we know his father, his mother, his social status (whether royal or noble) or his age when he came to Babylon. For events that took place in the magnificence and the glory of the most splendid court of ancient times and at a time when that court was the focal point of history, we get a sober and matter-of-fact recital - no glamor, no false values.

Since there are so many, and such excellent commentaries on the book of Daniel, it smacks of presumption for one whose training has been in other fields to attempt to add to them. This book, however, is not intended as a verse-by-verse commentary in the ordinary sense of the word but as a brief interpretive examination of persons and events, of human motives and of the reasons for these events; in other words, an overall picture. It is an attempt to present a viewpoint with the necessary factual material with which one can begin the study of Daniel. If the book can present to the reader, especially the lay reader, the overall purpose and meaning of the book, leaving to the many excellent commentaries item-by-item considerations, it wil l have fulfilled its purpose.

There is a definite attempt to maintain a historical perspective, as well as the psychological probabilities. The miraculous facts of the book are accepted at full face value for to evade them would make Daniel meaningless. Admittedly, they are not everyday occurrences. The reader will discover that the interpretation offered is premillennial and, while to the writer this view is the only one that can give full meaning and consistency to much Old Testament prophecy, the valuable insights of amillennial authorities have been most helpful.

CHAPTER I

THE JUDGMENT ON THE NATIONS AND ON ISRAEL

The book of Daniel opens with the siege of Jerusalem by Nebuchadnezzar. There is no statement that the city was actually taken. The temple treasures, however, were partially expropriated and hostages were taken from among the nobility and from the royal family. Three times the army of the King of Babylon ultimately appeared before Jerusalem. On each of these occasions, additional parts of the population were taken into exile and on the third occasion, the city was destroyed. At each appearance of the Chaldean army, the city should have taken warning that the words of Jeremiah were about to be fulfilled. Each time, the warning was disregarded. Each time, the prophetic words of Jeremiah, of Zephaniah, of Habakkuk and of Hulda, the Prophetess, fell upon deaf ears. Finally, Jeremiah - a voice that could not otherwise be silenced - was imprisoned and threatened with death. The optimists of the nation appeared to trust in the protecting presence of the temple, repeating the shibboleth "The temple of the Lord, the temple of the Lord" not knowing that the Shekinah glory of the Presence had departed the temple, no more to return until Messiah's reign.

It was not enough that the Exile of the nation had been proclaimed from the time of Moses to Jeremiah's own warnings. There were even other signs of danger if the nation had had ears to hear and eyes to see. For one hundred years, one after another, judgment had fallen on most of the famous cities of the ancient world. As each judgment came closer in time and in nearer proximity, Israel was not only deaf to prophetic warnings but blind to the signs of the times, not realizing that the protective hedge that Jehovah had placed around His choice vineyard had been taken away to permit the wild beasts of the forest to enter and to trample it down.

Before each city and nation was itself judged, it was used as an instrument in Jehovah's hand to carry out judgment on others: Assyria on Babylon, Egypt and Elam; Babylon on Assyria, Egypt, Tyre and Israel; Medo-Persia on Babylon; Greece on Medo-Persia, in unending series. There is a built-in moral order, a spiritual cause and effect, most obviously seen only when judgment finally comes due.

Nations rise and fall, appear on the world stage and either go into oblivion or are relegated to the wings. What the historians speak of as a cyclical process wherein nations appear, develop and decay, the Psalmist describes differently, going back of the appearances to the cause:

"The wicked shall be turned into Sheol and all the nations that forget God."[1]

"The nations are sunk down in the pit that they made; in the net which they hid is their own foot taken."[2]

Including Israel? Especially Israel; since their light and their privileges were so great. God is the God not only of Israel but of the nations. If Israel is to be exiled, her temple with its Shekinah presence departed destroyed, her beautiful city devastated, what shall we say about the nations morally and spiritually even more guilty than Israel? Because they had less light, are they then to escape? Do individuals who sin escape the built-in consequences of sin? And since nations are but individuals in the aggregate, are they allowed to evade the same laws of cause and effect? If we are tempted to come to this conclusion, we have to examine the history of the sixth and seventh centuries B.C. for light on the subject. It was Jeremiah the prophet to whom the Lord spoke:

See, I have this day set thee over the nations and over the kingdoms, to root out, and to pull down, and to destroy, and to throw down, to build, and to plant.

For thus saith the Lord God of Israel unto me, Take the wine cup of this fury at my hand, and cause all the nations to whom I send thee, to drink it. And they shall drink, and be moved and be mad, because of the sword that I will send among them.[3]

Jeremiah then lists those nations and cities upon whom judgment fell or will fall even as Isaiah and Nahum had prophesied before him. Among them are Egypt, Tyre, Elam, Babylon and Nineveh. And what if they hope to escape? Hear the word of the Lord as He answers:

Therefore, thou shalt say unto them, Thus saith the Lord of hosts, the God of Israel, Drink and be drunk, and vomit and fall, and rise no more, because of the sword which I will send among you. And it shall be, if they refuse to take the cup at thine hand to drink, then shalt thou say unto them, Thus saith the Lord of hosts, ye shall certainly drink.

For, lo, I begin to bring evil on the city which is called by my name, and should ye be utterly unpunished; for I will call a sword upon all the inhabitants of the earth, saith the Lord of hosts.[4]

What Jeremiah was commissioned to prophesy, he was to see fulfilled on many nations. Some judgment had already been fulfilled before his day according to the warnings prophesied by earlier prophets. What he is telling Israel is that, *"God is not mocked,"* that *"whatsoever a (nation) soweth that shall it also reap."* *"The wages of (national) sin is national death."[5]* Let us examine a few of these national judgments:

JUDGMENT ON EGYPT

The city of Thebes (called by the Egyptians "No" or "No Amon"), according to Diodorus, had a circumference of 100 stadia (12 miles). It was one of the richest cities of ancient times and was adorned with magnificent temples, stately public buildings and was said to be the most beautiful and most imposing city, not only of Egypt but of the whole world. It was adorned with numerous monuments of gold, silver and ivory, with obelisks and colossal statues of the gods. It was so exceedingly wealthy that the forecourt of the temple of Amenhotep III was partly paved with sheets of silver. The invasion of Thebes by Ashurbanipal (661 B.C.) was prophesied by Isaiah, the son of Amoz, a generation before, saying:

Go and loose the sackcloth from off thy loins, and put off thy shoe from thy foot. And he did so, walking naked and barefoot. And the Lord said, Like as my servant Isaiah hath walked naked and barefoot three years for a sign and wonder upon Egypt and upon Ethiopia; so shall the king of Assyria lead away the Egyptians prisoners, and the Ethiopians captives, young and old, naked and barefoot, even with their buttocks uncovered, to the shame of Egypt. And they shall be afraid and ashamed of Ethiopia their expectation, and of Egypt their glory. And the inhabitant of this isle shall say in that day, Behold, such is our expectation, whether we flee for help to be delivered from the king of Assyria; and how shall we escape?

And, again, we read in Nahum 3:8-10 (comparing Thebes with Nineveh):

Art thou better than populous No (Thebes), that was situate among the rivers, that had the waters round about it, whose rampart was the sea (river), and her wall was from the sea (river)? Ethiopia and Egypt were her strength, and it was infinite; Put and Lubim were thy helpers. Yet was she carried away, she went into captivity: her young children also were dashed in pieces at the top of all the streets: and they cast lots for her honorable men, and all her great men were bound in chains.

We have Ashurbanipal's own statement of his invasion of Thebes:

"In my second campaign, I directed the march to Egypt and Ethiopia. Urdamani (the king) heard of the approach of my campaign and when I trod upon the border of Egypt he abandoned Memphis and fled to Thebes in order to save his life. I took up the march after Urdamani and came to Thebes, his fortress. He saw the advance of my mighty battle array, abandoned Thebes and fled to Kipkip. That entire city, under the protection of Ashur and Ishtar, my hands captured.

"(I seized) silver, gold, precious stones, the contents of his palace - all that there was: party-colored raiment, cloth, great horses and people, male and female. Two tall obelisks made of bright bronze, whose weight was twenty-five hundred talents which stood before the gate of the temple, I removed from their place, and took to Assyria. Heavy spoils without number I carried off from Thebes. Over Egypt and Ethiopia, I made my weapons rage and established my might. With full hands I returned in safety to Nineveh, my capital."

JUDGMENT ON NINEVEH (612 B.C.)

Just before the final decade of the seventh century (612 B.C.), Nabopolasar with the help of Astyages, King of the Medes, captured and burned the great city of Nineveh. So thorough was the destruction that Xenophon, two centuries later when passing the site, had no idea that there had been a great city there. The final end of the Assyrian empire came seven years later (605 B.C.) at the great battle of Carchemish in which the Babylonian forces under Nebuchadnezzar completely defeated the Assyrians and their Egyptian allies and thus ended forever the empire that had terrorized the nations from the Tigris to the Mediterranean, among them the Hebrew kingdoms of Israel and Judah. Nineveh had occupied the center of the world stage for three centuries. It was one of the most famous cities of the ancient East and was the capital and center of the warrior kingdom of Assyria.[8] Let us quote a particularly apt description of her reason for being:

"Assyria was preeminently a nation of soldiers, a warrior state whose monarch was the head of a great general staff, whose ministers were field marshals. It toiled not, neither did it spin. Its necessities, its food supply and even its play things, were wrenched and looted from the unhappy peoples who surrounded it. Its builders and laborers were prisoners of war. Its rulers transplanted entire tribes and nations from one part of their dominions to another uprooting them as they uprooted the cedars of Lebanon for transplantation in the avenues of their wonderful metropolis. Every Assyrian was a soldier. Behind this ruthlessness lurked the sinister shape of Ashur the tutelary deity of the soil. So that vast temples might be raised to the glory of Ashur, continual war was waged and tribute levied; so that his fanes might be filled with magnificence, the bodies of countless slaves in many a distant province were bastinadoed into intensive production. Asia Minor groaned beneath the rod of Ashur."[9]

The cruelty and wickedness of Nineveh cried to heaven in the days of Jonah in the eighth century B.C. and at Jonah's preaching, it repented in sackcloth and ashes. But it returned to its old ways and, as we have indicated, in the next century (612 B.C.) the armies of Astyges, the Mede, and Nabopolasar, the Babylonian (possibly aided by the Scythians), destroyed the city forever. Nineveh had been used of God to scourge other nations as wicked as herself and was in turn expunged from the record by nations whose turn had not yet come.

JUDGMENT ON SUSA AND ELAM

Susa was called the eternal city of the East. Its origin was lost in the mists of antiquity. For much of its existence, because of its military might and its aggressive spirit, it was a terror to the neighboring nations. Civilized, rich, proud, predatory and given to conquest and plunder, it was ripe for punishment when it was conquered by Ashurbanipal in 645 B.C. Ezekiel gives her obituary in two verses:

There is Elam, and all her multitude round about her grace, all of them slain fallen by the sword, who are gone down uncircumcised in the lower parts of the earth, who caused their terror in the land of the living; yet they have borne their shame with those who go down to the pit.

They have set her a bed in the midst of the slain, with all her multitude; her graves are round about her all of them uncircumcised, slain by the sword; though their terror was caused in the land of the living, yet have they borne their shame with those who go down to the pit; he is put in the midst of those who are slain.[10]

And, again, Jeremiah prophesied:

And upon Elam will I bring the four winds from the four quarters of heaven, and will scatter them toward all those winds; and there shall be no nation whither the outcasts of Elam shall not come. For I will cause Elam to be dismayed before their enemies, and before them that seek their life: and I will bring evil upon them, til I have consumed them: And I will set my throne in Elam, and will destroy from thence the king and the princes, saith the Lord.[11]

Ashurbanipal's record of conquest of Susa is as follows:

"On my return, when Ashur and Ishtar enabled me to stand against my foes, I conquered Susa, a great city, the abode of their gods, the seat of their oracles. By the command of Ashur and Ishtar I entered his palaces and sat down with joy. I opened their treasure-houses, wherein was stored up silver, gold, property and possessions which the former kings of Elam and the kings who ruled even up to these days had gathered and stored away, and on which no other enemy besides me had laid his hand, and I brought it out and counted it as spoil. I carried away to Assyria as spoil silver, gold, property and possessions of Sumer, Akkan and Karduniash - everything which the former kings of Elam had carried away as spoil in seven times and had brought to Elam - splendid cariru-metal, shining eshmaru-metal, precious stones (which were) a costly ornament, fit for kings, which the former kings of Akkad and Shamash-shum-ukin had paid to Elam for the purpose of a league with them; clothing (which was) fitting decoration for kings, weapons of war, trophies, everything used in battle such as were fit for his hand; all the portable furniture of his palaces; that whereon he had sat and slept, that from which he had eaten and drunk and poured libations and anointed himself; chariots, state carriages, wagons covered with cariru and zahala-metal, horses and large mules whose harness was of gold and silver. I destroyed the temple tower of Susa which was made with an encasement of ukn-stone and I broke off its turrets, which were made of shining copper. I took to Assyria thirty-two statues of kings which were made of silver, gold, copper, and alabaster. I threw down the bull-colossi and the guardian gods and all the other watchers of the temple and I tore down the fierce wild oxen which decorated the door. I overthrew the temples of Elam until there were no more. I gave its gods and goddesses to the winds. My soldiers entered into their secret forests into which no stranger had ever pressed and whose borders no stranger had ever trod; they saw their secret places and burned them with fire. The mausoleums of their kings, the earlier and later ones, who had not feared Ashur and Ishtar my lords but had been hostile to the king, my father, I destroyed and laid waste and exposed them to the sun. I took their bones to Assyria; I gave their shades no repose and deprived them of their food and drink offerings."[12]

We gather here something of the destructive fury of an Assyrian king who found the land a garden and left it a desert. He is not satisfied with the destruction of the physical properties of the nation, the plundering of all its wealth, but even carries his venom into the hereafter and renders the souls of the departed (shades) as miserable as he is capable of doing, depriving them of their votive offerings.

JUDGMENT ON CARCHEMISH

Scripture mentions the city of Carchemish but three times (II Chronicles 35:20; Isaiah 10:9; Jeremiah 46:2) and gives us no information good or bad, about its manners, morals or its religious worship. The city was located at one of the few fords of the Euphrates, at the point where the river approaches closest to the Mediterranean. It was thus strategically located on the great caravan route from the Euphrates valley to the city of Tyre. The city grew rich and important from tolls levied on passing caravans. Whether it was destroyed for its wickedness or because it associated itself with Egypt, a nation devoted to punishment by Jehovah, we cannot know. This we can know: God had given all the nations of the Near East into the hands of Nebuchadnezzar, king of Babylon, with the warning that whosoever resisted would be consumed. They resisted.

And it shall come to pass, that the nation and kingdom that will not serve the same Nebuchadnezzar, the king of Babylon, and that will not put their neck under the yoke of the king of Babylon, that nation will I punish, saith the Lord, with the sword, and with famine, and with the pestilence, until I have consumed them by his hand.[13]

Nebuchadnezzar destroyed the city and the army of its Egyptian allies in 605 B.C. The last of the Hittite cities, it was later replaced by non-Hittite towns.

JUDGMENT ON TYRE

The great city of Tyre, the maritime commercial center of the ancient world, was at first built upon the mainland (Paleotyre) but later extended its borders to a rocky island offshore (on which was located the palace of its kings). It was noted for its citadel, the temple of Agenor Baal, the temple of Astarte (the female goddess of lust) and more magnificent than these, the temple of Melkart in which were two pillars, one of gold and one of emerald, with an appropriate magnificence of the temple as a whole. Both cities, the old and the new, had massive walls that had resisted siege by three great Assyrian conquerors: Ashurnasirpal, Esarhaddon and Ashurbanipal. This city, famous throughout the ancient world for its glassware, its artifacts of gold and silver and above all, the works of its weavers whose famous purple dye was often reserved for kings, sucked up wealth wherever ships could go or caravans travel. Its sailors circumnavigated Africa. Its artisans were used to build Solomon's temple. The city was unusually wise in the ways of navigation and commerce and incredibly rich, as we read in the 27th chapter of Ezekiel 14, a city of luxury, pleasure and sin. Its very worship was an abomination, involving sex orgies, human sacrifice and on the part of its priests, self-mutilation. She was a city long ripe for the judgment that Ezekiel predicted (Ezekiel Chapter 26). One judgment was to come up on her through Nebuchadnezzar. Three hundred years later, final destruction overtook her under Alexander the Great. Both judgments are included in Ezekiel's prophecy.

ISRAEL

If God waited four hundred years for judgment on the Amorites because the cup of their iniquity was not yet full, must we not assume that all of these ancient cities and nations met judgment because their cup was full? We do not even have to assume this in the case of the two kingdoms of Israel and Judah. Every prophet from Joel to Jeremiah reiterated the warnings. In 722 B.C., judgment finally came due to the northern kingdom when Shalmaneser, king of Assyria destroyed its cities, carried away and scattered its people in "Halah and In Habor by the river of Gozan and in the cities of the Medes."[15] This permanently ended the northern kingdom of Israel even though many individuals from the ten tribes later on drifted back into Palestine. Of the history of the ten tribes of the northern kingdom, little good can be said of the nation as a whole. Not one of its kings was righteous and as to the people, the Lord could count only seven thousand righteous in the time of Elijah.

JUDAH

Of the kingdom of Judah in the south, only five or six of its kings could be said to be truly righteous. With the apostasy of two-thirds of its kings, there was usually apostasy of the people at large.

Jewish kings of the Southern Kingdom, sitting upon the throne of David, had been given privileges and promises not given to any other royal family in history nor to any other people. But, in spite of unheard-of blessings to king and people, the general progress of Judah was downhill. They would return to the Lord after the Exile but to a limited independence. Theirs also is the record of every great gentile nation of the past. It seems to be the human record.

Twenty years before the capture of Jerusalem, the great and pious king, Josiah, celebrated the greatest Passover in the history of Israel. Of him it was said, "He neither turned to the right hand nor to the left, but followed the Lord wholly." Furthermore, when the Book of the Law was read to him and he heard, apparently for the first time, the judgments pending against his people, he not only carried out a thoroughgoing reform, cleansed the Temple and restored the worship of Jehovah, but we have the statement that "he caused all that were present in Jerusalem and Benjamin to stand to it and the inhabitants of Jerusalem did according to the covenant of God, the God of their fathers."[16]

Why then, within twenty years, has judgment fallen upon a nation that has committed herself to a righteous return to the Law? We get the answer in Jeremiah 3:10,

And yet for all this her treacherous sister Judah hath not turned unto me with her whole heart, but feignedly, saith the Lord.

Of the successors of Josiah (Jehoahaz who reigned three months, Jehoiakim eleven years, Jehoiakin three months and ten days and Zedekiah who reigned eleven years), all are apostate to Jehovah. The reforms under Josiah could not touch the moral and spiritual decay of Israel. We have only lip service, not a change of heart. The prophet, Jeremiah, who represented Jehovah, spoke not to a spiritual but to an apostate people, a people who were no longer willing to permit even the testimony of Jeremiah. At last, God, responsible for the moral order of the universe, can no longer delay punishment.

But herein is the righteousness and the love of Jehovah toward a wayward people. Heaven is not silent and Israel is not allowed to go into captivity with no word from Jehovah.

Not one prophet, but five are contemporary with the Babylon captivity: Jeremiah, Zephaniah and Habakkuk remaining in the land; Ezekiel among the captives by the Khebar Canal; Daniel in the king's palace. At a time when Israel is under discipline, demoralized and captive, Jehovah speaks through Daniel of the coming Messiah; through Ezekiel of a restored temple, of Messiah's reign, the return of the tribes to Palestine and a full occupancy of the land promised Moses (from the sea to the Euphrates, from Egypt to Hamath), with kingdom blessing to Israel and the forecast doom to all of those nations that oppressed Israel; Zephaniah speaks of the Day of the Lord and judgment of gentiles; Jeremiah foretells Israel's spiritual restoration in the latter days when the law of the Lord shall be written in their hearts and when a new covenant will be made with Israel; Habakkuk reminds his people of the justice of the Exile because God is just and holy. Jehovah has not left His people without comfort and guidance even in the time of their Exile.

For the present, however, Jehovah's hand is heavy upon Israel. The beautiful temple is to be destroyed. The ark of the covenant, its cherubim and Mercy Seat, the furniture of the Holy Place, the Altar of Incense, the Golden Lampstand - all are lost.[17] The Shikinah glory of God has left the temple and the city.[18] The city is to be reduced to a heap of stones and will be desolate for seventy years according to the prophecy of Jeremiah. Of course, while Israel is in Exile, there will be no Temple, no sacrifices and no king. When at the end of seventy years, she returns, there will still be no king of the lineage of David. Later, in the time of the Maccabees, there will be a brief dynasty of the Maccabean line but it will have no divine legitimacy for the Maccabees sprang from the priestly tribe of Levi and not from the royal tribe of Judah. We remember the words of Ezekiel which both the Jewish rabbi and the Christian commentator have applied to the Messiah,

I will overturn, overturn, overturn it: and it shall be no more until he comes whose right it is; and I will give it him.[19]

And again, Hosea prophesies,

For the children of Israel shall abide many days without a king and without a prince, and without a sacrifice, and without an image, without an ephod, and without terephim; Afterward shall the children of Israel return, and seek the Lord their God, and David their king, and shall fear the Lord and his goodness in the latter days.[20]

This prophecy began to be fulfilled at the time of the Exile and continues to this day. Of the Exile itself, Jeremiah prophesies time and circumstance,

And this whole land shall be a desolation and an horror; and these nations shall serve the king of Babylon seventy years, and it shall come to pass, when seventy years are accomplished, that I will punish the king of Babylon, and that nation, saith the Lord, for their iniquity, and the land of the Chaldeans, and will make it perpetual desolation. And I will bring upon that land all my words which I have pronounced against it, even all that is written in this book, which Jeremiah hath prophesied against all the nations. For many nations and great kings shall make slaves of them also, and I will recompence them according to their deeds, and according to the works of their own hands.[21]

CHAPTER II
KING NEBUCHADNEZZAR AND FOUR NOBLE CAPTIVES

(Daniel 1; Language, Hebrew)

O that there were such an heart in them, that they would fear me, and keep all my commandments always, that it might be well with them, and with their children forever. Deuteronomy 5:29

To orient ourselves chronologically, the Book of Daniel opens in 605 B.C. According to Greek timing, it was in the forty-second Olympiad, shortly after the archonship of Solon; by Roman reckoning, 148 years after the founding of Rome (A.U.C.) during the reign of the the Etruscan Tarquins; by Jewish chronology, the year 3,225 from the creation of the world. It is the year previous to the first regnal year of Nebuchadnezzar and the third year of the reign of Jehoiakim in Jerusalem. The kingdom of Judah is just beginning her servitude to Nebuchadnezzar.

A portion of the vessels of the temple have been expropriated and are being taken to Babylon though the city has not yet been thoroughly plundered. Hostages have been taken to insure the good behavior of King Jehoiakim, among them members of the royal family and of the nobility. Daniel and his companions, probably of the king's family, are among the first to be sent to Babylon.

Thus begins a confrontation and association of two of the most notable characters mentioned in Scripture: Daniel, of the royal house of David (according to tradition) and Nebuchadnezzar, about to become king of Babylon. Daniel is the representative of a kingly house that for nearly half a millennium has ruled on the throne of David. He is representative of a people to whom "pertaineth the adoption, and the glory, and the covenants, and the giving of the law, and the service of God, and the promises."[1] They are a people to whom the oracles of God came and through whom will come the Messiah. Because of national sin, Daniel and his companions have been carried to a strange city to become servants of a pagan monarch and who, as Josephus hints, may have been made eunuchs,[2] though this is somewhat doubtful as these young men are "without blemish." Whatever their physical condition, they appear before us in the book of Daniel with no hint of bitterness or resentment or loss of self-respect or the demoralization that would ordinarily accompany a transition from honor and affluence to one of dependence and servitude. Daniel, himself, maintains not only courage and morale but is himself, in every respect, a kingly figure.

And who is Nebuchadnezzar to dictate the terms of this servitude? He is the son of Nabopolassar, his royal ancestry going back but one generation. The dynasty will endure for eighty-seven years and Nebuchadnezzar, himself, will reign forty-three years.[3] (Daniel will outlive his master by at least twenty-eight years.)

Bersos, as quoted by Josephus, says, "When Nabopolassar, his father (i.e., of Nebuchadnezzar), had heard that the satrap whom he had set over Egypt and over the regions of Coele-Syria and Phoenicia, had revolted from him, being unable himself to endure the fatigue, committed certain parts of his forces to his son, Nebuchadnezzar, who was still a young man and sent him against the rebel. Nebuchadnezzar joined battle with him, conquered him and reduced the land at once to his dominion. It so happened at this time that his father fell ill in the city of Babylon and died, having reigned twenty-one years. When Nebuchadnezzar heard not long afterward of his father's end, he set in order the affairs of Egypt and the rest of the district and committed the captives which he had taken from the Jews, Phoenicians and Syrians and from the nations belonging to Egypt to some of his friends that they might conduct the heavy armed troops and the baggage to Babylonia while he, himself, pushed over the desert with but a few to Babylonia. When he arrived there, he found that public affairs had been managed by the Chaldeans and the kingdom preserved by the principal persons among them so that he was now ruler of all his father's dominions and ordered the captives, when they arrived, to be assigned dwelling places'[4]

Nebuchadnezzar, himself, now stands out in history as a genius whose intelligence, abilities and drive are far beyond the ordinary endowments of royalty; boundless in ambition and with restless energy, he is a conqueror who is apparently unimpressed by his own military conquests. His main ambitions and energies are directed to the rehabilitation of agriculture in his kingdom of Babylonia, the rebuilding of its ruined cities and temples and especially, as a restorer and builder of the greatest city of the ancient world, Babylon. He is a man whose fervent piety to his pagan gods apparently motivated all his great accomplishments.

For forty-three years, Nebuchadnezzar and Daniel are associated as master and honored servant. Nebuchadnezzar occupies center stage because of his royal position, his kingly power, his genius but, most of all (so far as the Book of Daniel is concerned), because God has chosen him as a special tool. Daniel is presented to us as a person of intelligence, righteousness, having skill in interpreting dreams, an excellent spirit and above all, he is a man determined to be true to the God of his Fathers. These are but two of the outstanding characters in the Old Testament Scriptures.

To understand Nebuchadnezzar's activities, it is necessary to remember that Nabopolassar, his father and the the founder of the dynasty, had only begun to rebuild Babylon. The city had been thoroughly demolished by Sennacherib in 690 B.C. It had been somewhat restored by his son, Esarhaddon. Nabopolassar had begun to rebuild it, apparently on a more magnificent scale but even so, it was largely unfinished and relatively unimpressive in terms of its future splendor.[5]

We must remember also that Nebuchadnezzar's future building enterprises were not done in an era of peace. He did not inherit a really stable empire but only the beginnings of one. In the annals of the first eleven years of his reign, only one year is recorded in which he is not in a military campaign at the head of his army. In that year (really eighteen months), he is refitting the army for further campaigns. Nebuchadnezzar seems to have been something of a military genius but in spite of his military conquests, he is at heart a builder. When Nebuchadnezzar has finished the city of Babylon, it contains two of the ancient wonders of the world; namely, its mighty walls and its Hanging Gardens.[6] From a series of conquests begun by his father, Nebuchadnezzar built an empire extending from the Tigris to Egypt. The former kingdoms of Assyria, the Aramean kingdom of Syria, Palestine, Paleo-Tyre, Carchemish and later Egypt were consolidated into the first world empire of Dan II. He was given, by Jehovah Himself, sovereignty over mankind wherever he cared to exercise it.

Whom he would he slew; and whom he would he kept alive..[7]

This man, moreover, is not just a successful leader of armies for he is a dreamer who is permitted to see his dreams come true. We stand in awe at the vast building achievements, all finished in forty-three years and wonder if all other labor ceased to accomplish this, until we remember that all this was done by slave labor.

As in the case of vast, ancient, oriental monarchies, conquests meant a vast supply of slave labor, the unlimited use of men's bodies, a supply of the most beautiful women for the harem and the expropriation of their possessions. However, this man, Nebuchadnezzar, knows how to capture and utilize the minds of men as well as their bodies. We are given the picture of the careful selection of captive youths - young men in whom there was no blemish; well favored and skillful in all wisdom and knowledge and understanding in science.[8] When he trains these young men, he does so royally. They are fed with the best of food from the king's table. Their health and appearance is a matter of concern. When the time comes for the examination of the results of their three years of study, the king himself conducts the examination. Unless we misinterpret these hints that are given us from this chapter, here is a man who recognizes the importance of the minds and spirits of those who are to serve him and treats them in a manner calculated to enlist their loyalty and devotion. The results are amply rewarding to him in the loyalty and service which he receives and in the spirit of courage and self-respect which has been fostered in them.

It might be proper at this point to sum up the main facts of Nebuchadnezzar's record from secular history. He was the son of Nabopolasar who reigned twenty-one years (626-605 B.C.). He had a twin brother named Nabushumlisher. He was brought up in pious and humble worship of Marduk, married Amytius, a median princess, possibly in 614 B.C. or 612 B.C. and was in charge of his father's army in Egypt at his father's death (605 B.C.). He crossed the desert to claim the throne and was apparently aided by one that was the "principal of the Chaldeans."[9] He conquered Syria, Egypt, Palestine, Paleo-Tyre (besieging Tyre thirteen years), Carchemish, Jerusalem ("Laid 'our' temple desolate in the eighteenth year of his reign."[10] He rebuilt Babylon and its great walls, rebuilt Borsippa and built The Hanging Gardens for his queen. He rebuilt and adorned the temple and shrines of the gods of Babylon in a most lavish manner.[11] An eleven-mile-square flood control reservoir was built on the Euphrates and he built quays and embankments on the Euphrates and Tigris, the remains of which are there to this day. He was a faithful and enthusiastic worshiper of Maduk, chief of the Babylonian gods. He had an architect named Labashi and a friend, the Greek Antimenidas. Nebuchadnezzar reigned forty-three years, "fell sick, and died." He was succeeded by his son Avil Marduk.

Josephus quotes Megisthenes as saying that the king exceeded Hercules in fortitude and the greatness of his actions.[12] And we ought not to overlook the prominence given Nebuchadnezzar in Scripture,[13] mainly by Jeremiah and Ezekiel and, of course, Daniel. The following are the names of a few important biblical characters with the number of times they are mentioned and the number of chapters in which their names appear:

	Number of chapters	Number of references
Cyrus	22	11
Uzziah	29	13
Josiah	54	24
Noah	56	20
Job	57	23
Daniel	80	14
Nebuchadnezzar	91	39

As for Daniel,[14] we are assured by Ezekiel that he not only belongs in the class of Noah and Job as to his righteousness but in the first chapter, we learn that his skill and learning, the training that he has been given together with his companions, transcend all wisdom and understanding of his contemporaries.[15] In verse 20, we read:

And in all matters of wisdom and understanding, that the king enquired of them, he found them ten times better than all the magicians and astrologers that were in all his realm.

And in verse 17:

Daniel had understanding in all visions and dreams.

Servitude is not good for the servant nor for the master. Masters become arrogant and callous and slaves, ordinarily, since they come from a defeated people, are crushed in spirit, lose morale, are either futilely defiant and exist in sullen enmity or there may be a desertion of the former ideals, religious beliefs and hopes and an accommodation to their conditions. When there is a loss of cultural framework which supports any people, there almost inevitably comes demoralization. But not so here. Daniel and his companions seem neither to be overawed nor fearful; they are steadfast and faithful. They adapt without conformity. There is no sin of self-pity. They are beloved of the immediate officials who have charge of them. The episodes in the first chapter are significant not only in terms of the immediate faithfulness of these Jewish youths to the demands of their sacred Scriptures but are indicative of the general self-control of spirit and body characteristic of them through out. For four healthy young men, who may be somewhere in the neighborhood of seventeen or eighteen years of age, to give up the luxurious food and drink of the king's own table for a simple fare, would have been a courageous act of conscience if, in their eyes, the king's food had been of a forbidden kind or contaminated by having first been offered to pagan gods. But why the vegetable diet? Their own law permitted many kinds of meat, fish, fowl and flesh, and wine as well was permitted. These young men might have had these foods prepared in a kosher manner upon request, one might think. In some way, their diet was a matter of conscience and not necessarily an argument of vegetarianism. It may have been that they observed the better mental results of a spare diet. On the other hand, they may have imposed upon themselves a voluntary restriction for religious reasons.[16]

Chapter 1 closes: *"And Daniel continued even unto the first year of king Cyrus."* This would lead one to think that this chapter, at least, had been written at this time, namely, the first year of Cyrus (537 B.C.). As for the life and circumstances of the four Hebrew youths in the court of Babylon's greatest king, it is the purpose of Nebuchadnezzar to absorb these young men into the service of the court and to make them efficient Babylonian servants. As a first step, they are given Babylonian names. They will be treated honorably, will be given food from the king's own table, will have the benefit of tutors and will finally be examined as to their proficiency by the king himself. These young men know, through the prophecy of Jeremiah , that their captivity will last seventy years and that in all probability they will never see Jerusalem again.

They are subject, then, to the seduction of preferred treatment, to the pressures of a luxurious court life, to the knowledge that their own contemporaries are largely apostate, to separation from a social order and a religious setting that made life meaningful and to the knowledge that, for better or worse, they must make lifelong adjustments to this new environment. A whole new culture must be absorbed, a new, spoken and written language learned and a body of knowledge, not at all meager, must be assimilated in the three years given them before they are to appear before the king.

We cannot entirely know what kind of knowledge these four kinsmen of Zedekiah are expected to acquire but, lest anyone consider that their curriculum consisted only of magical incantations, modes of divination and lists of pagan gods and their proper worship together with the acquisition of the related Semitic language of Babylon and its cuneiform writing, consider the following:

There is, first, the code of Hammurabi, one of the earliest codified legal systems, which prescribed adequate regulations for a highly civilized society;[17] in addition to an unscientific astrology, there had come into being a highly accurate astronomy with an ability to predict solar and lunar eclipses. Schools taught arithmetic[18] with a sexagesimal system, with fractions, surveying, elements of algebra, geometry and calculus; scientific grammars and dictionaries were used; on the practical side, they had scientific irrigation and flood control.

"Commerce, literature, art and science flourished during this age. The Chaldeans were the founders of astronomy as a science. Careful astronomical observations were continuously kept for over 360 years and these calculations form the longest study ever made. One great Chaldean astronomer, living shortly after the completion of this period of observation was able to calculate the length of the year as 365 days, 6 hours, 15 mintues and 41 seconds - a measurement which the modern telescope has shown to be only 26 minutes, 26 seconds too long! His calculations on the diameter of the face of the moon were far more accurate than those of Copernicus. Certain measurements of celestial motions by another Chaldean astronomer actually surpass in accuracy the figures long in practical use among modern astronomers.[19]

In manufacturing and technology, these young men could learn that Babylon was famous all over the ancient world for its luxurious garments of wool, cotton and silk, its jewel manufacture, its carpet industry and its manufacture of terra cotta and glazed brick.[20] Whether or not they were introduced to the medical knowledge of the day, they could have learned the names and usages of over five hundred medicinal drugs,[21] and that Babylonian surgeons performed amputations and removed cataracts.[22] In addition to this, there was extensive literature in theology, astronomy and some of the sciences to which they might have been introduced.

Since Babylon was the business center of the east, a highly sophisticated and efficient banking system grew up with its written contracts, bills of sale, deeds, mortgages and banking procedures of all kinds. We even have the name of one of the great banking houses of the day: Engebi and Sons. With caravans from China, Tyre, Egypt, Arabia, India and Asia Minor coming and going, these young men would certainly be expected to know something about the commerce of these countries and the geography involved since even members of the royal house might be involved in commerce. Later on, the Jews became entrenched in their new home and developed a banking business of their own probably under the leadership of Marashi and Sons.

Whether or not the fourth verse of Chapter 1 of Daniel is to be taken as comprehensively as we have indicated, at least the three-year curriculum could have been a busy one in addition to which we read (in verse 17): *"God gave them knowledge and skill in all learning and wisdom: and Daniel had understanding in all visions and dreams."*

As to the land of their captivity, when we examine the map of southern Babylonia, we see that the city was a natural point of confluence of caravan routes. Caravans from China, India, Lydia, Tyre, Egypt and the goods of many kingdoms met here. Through the Euphrates River, Babylon had access to the sea and in every way was strategically located for commerce or for war.

If ever a city had right to think of itself as eternal, Babylon was that city. The fertility of the Babylonian alluvial plain, famous throughout the world, made possible the support of a dense population.[23] Its water supply was inexhaustible. The mighty Euphrates flowed through the city itself and, through its systems of canals, it could tap waters of the great Tigris. The climate was that of hot days and cool nights and the massive walls of its buildings were thoroughly adapted to the climate, being suitable for a maximum coolness in the summer and an equal comfort in the winter. Through its river traffic, it could draw upon the forests of Lebanon, the vineyards of Armenia and, through its access to the sea, the cotton, rice, and precious stones of India; in fact, all of the traffic of the Indian Ocean and the riches of east Africa. Through its caravan routes, it tapped the land resources of all Asia. Through its conquest of Tyre, it absorbed the riches of the Mediterannean and the western seas. The city, itself, was a manufacturing center possibly the greatest in the ancient world.

As to its fertility, the basis of its food supply, we have the eyewitness report of Herodotus:

"But little rain falls in Assyria, enough, however, to make the corn begin to sprout, after which the plant is nourished and the ears formed by means of irrigation from the river. For the river does not, as in Egypt, overflow the corn-lands of its own accord but is spread over them by the hand or by the help of engines. The whole of Babylonia is, like Egypt, intersected with canals. The largest of them all which runs towards the winter sun and is impassible except in boats, is carried from the Euphrates into another stream called the Tigris, the river upon which the town of Nineveh formerly stood.

"Of all the countries that we know there is none which is so fruitful in grain. It makes no pretension, indeed, of growing the fig, the olive, the vine or any other tree of the kind but in grain, it is so fruitful as to yield commonly two-hundred-fold, and, when the production is the greatest, even three-hundred-fold. The blade of the wheat-plant and barley- plant is often four fingers in breadth. As for the millet and the sesame, I shall not say to what height they grow, though it is within my own knowledge; for I am not ignorant that what I have already written concerning the fruitfulness of Babylonia must seem incredible to those who have never visited the country. The only oil they use is made from the sesame plant. Palm trees grow in great numbers over the whole of the flat country mostly of the kind that bears fruit and this fruit supplies them with bread, wine and honey.

"They are cultivated like the fig tree in all respects, among others in this. The natives tie the fruit of the male palms, as they are called by the Greeks, to the branches of the date-bearing palm to let the gallfly enter the dates and ripen them and to prevent the fruit from falling off. The male palms, like the wild fig trees, have usually the gallfly in their fruit."[24]

When Daniel came to Babylon (607-606 B.C.), the city had not yet achieved its new look and its tremendous size. In truth, the city of Babylon became a city that Nebuchadnezzar built. Most of the bricks found in the ruins bear his signature.[25]

Babylon, under Nebuchadnezzar, was to conquer a large part of the civilized Middle East. One of the purposes of conquest, besides plunder and tribute and the control of trade routes, was the huge reservoir of slave labor that could be drawn upon from conquered countries. When we think of the ancient cities of Nineveh, Babylon and probably many other important capitols, we must think of them as slave-built.

Drawing on conquered countries for slaves does two things: It provides an almost unlimited labor force that is cheap and often skilled and it so weakens the conquered country by its drain upon manpower that further rebellion becomes difficult. For the Babylon that was yet to be, the sources of slave labor could have been the populations of Nineveh, Carchemish, Israel, Tyre, Syria and Egypt.[26] Daniel was to see the tremendous human slave resources of these countries put to work to raise the mighty walls of Babylon, its Hanging Gardens, its villas and temples, to pave its streets, dig its canals and to build its palaces.[27]

Israel must have played its part in this gigantic accomplishment, all in the forty-three-year reign of one man. Because of its apostasy, Israel had exchanged the brickyards of Egypt for the brickyards of Babylon.

THE CAPTIVITY

When we come to ask why the kingdom of Judah is captive and desolate, its temple destroyed, its palaces burned, its people transported to a
foreign land, we have the biblical answer that this has been building up
for half a millennium and that God's patience with Israel has finally ceased
to be consistent with His holiness and His justice. Of all nineteen kings
of Judah, at the most fewer than one-half could be considered righteous
and of these, two, Amaziah and Joash, could hardly be called ideal.

With the kings, there was usually a general apostasy of the people,
with their persistent tendency to worship the gods of the nations round
about and with this worship to indulge in the accompanying moral
abominations.

But we ask, "Was there not soundness somewhere in the nation?" Perhaps the nobles could in some way neutralize the delinquency of the royal
house. Ezekiel gives us, in one pungent verse, the moral stature of Israel's
nobles, "Her princes in her midst are like wolves ravening the prey, to
shed blood, and to destroy souls, and to get dishonest gain."[28] Evidently, there is no help for Israel here.

Surely, the priests, with their whole livelihood dependent upon the
freewill offerings of the temple and their better knowledge of the law and
their tradition of conservatism, will be on the side of righteousness.
Again, let us hear Ezekiel's pronouncement:

*Her priests have violated my law, and have profaned my holy things;
they have put no difference between the holy and profane, neither have
they shown difference between the unclean and the clean, and have hidden their eyes from my sabbath, and I am profaned among them.*[29]

When those of the priesthood, with all of their privileges and supposed
knowledge of the law, are the lawbreakers and the sabbathbreakers of the
nation, what may we expect from the people? Possibly, there is hope from
prophetic sources. Again, Ezekiel gives us a biting summary of the
prophets of his day:

*There is a conspiracy of her prophets in the midst of her; like a roar-
ing lion ravening the prey, they have devoured souls; they have taken the
treasure and the precious things; they have made her many widows in the
midst of her. And her prophets have daubed them untempered mortar,
seeing vanity, and divining lies unto them, saying Thus saith the Lord God,
when the Lord hath not spoken.*[30]

There were righteous prophets but their voices were drowned in the
clamor of the charlatans and they themselves met, ofttimes, undeserved
persecution and death. According to tradition, Isaiah was sawed in two;
Jeremiah was threatened with death, imprisoned in a cistern full of muck

and finally shanghaied to Egypt; Ezekiel was assassinated by a Jew in Babylon whom he had rebuked for idolatry.

What hope for a people whose leaders lead them astray and prey upon them?

Again, Ezekiel gives a picture of a people, themselves as wicked as their leaders,

The people of the land have used oppression, and exercised robbery and have vexed the poor and needy; yea, they have oppressed the sojourner wrongfully. And I sought for a man among them, that should make up the hedge, and stand in the gap before me for the land, that I should not destroy it; but I found none. Therefore have I poured out my indignation upon them; I have consumed them with the fire of my wrath; their own way have I recompensed upon their heads, saith the Lord God.[21]

The prophet Jeremiah summed up the situation even more succinctly,

An appalling and horrible thing is committed in the land: The prophets prophesy falsely, and the priests bear rule by their means, and my people love to have it so; and what will ye do in the end of it all? Shall I not punish them for these things? Saith the Lord. Shall not my soul be avenged on such a nation as this?[32]

So the kingdom of Judah has been taken to Babylon where the people can no longer oppress the poor, the needy and the stranger, where they in turn may learn what it means to be themselves oppressed.

There the prophets may be relegated to the brickyards of Babylon where, if they still prophesy falsely, they may meet the fate of Zedekiah and Ahab *"whom the king of Babylon roasted in the fire."*[33]

There the priests can no longer profane the temple and the land can once more keep her sabbaths.

There the nobles, bereft of their ill-gotten gain, can no longer shed blood and destroy souls with impunity.

King Zedekiah's sightless eyes will not see the land to which he has been taken.

Jehoiachin, considered by Nebuchadnezzar the rightful king, remains under custody until the death of the king, himself, with his curse ringing in his ears,

O, earth, earth, earth, hear the word of the Lord. Thus saith the Lord, Write ye this man childless, a man that shall not prosper in his days: for no man of his seed shall prosper, sitting upon the throne of David, and ruling any more in Judah.[34]

When Messiah comes, He will be of the line of Nathan, son of David, not of the line of Solomon and Jehoiachin.

For seventy years, Israel will be back in the land of Mesopotamia from which her father Abraham came to escape idolatry. They have been sent back to get their fill of it.

CHAPTER III

A KING DREAMS OF
THE TIMES OF THE GENTILES

(Daniel 2:1-4; Language, Hebrew; Verse 4 On, Aramaic)

The time is the third year of Nebuchadnezzar's accession to the throne of Babylon (603 B.C.), his second regnal year. It is the same year in which Daniel and his three companions took their final examination before the king.

Chapter 2 is concerned with a dream which greatly troubled the king, even to the point of continued sleeplessness. As we see later, it is given to this gentile king to give, in general outline, the Times of the Gentiles; from his own time to the end of the age, to the second coming of Messiah.

Dreams are one of the means by which in Old Testament times God spoke to men, especially in the absence of written Scripture or without the presence of a prophet of God. Sometimes dreams were given to one of God's own people, usually a prophet, in which case, they were understood by the persons themselves as in the case of Abraham (Genesis 15:1-6). Abraham was promised not only an heir but a multitude of descendants. Where the dream was sent by god to a gentile, the interpretation was usually given by a Jew as in the case of Pharaoh's dream in Genesis 41.

Modern psychology has given much attention to dreams and their meanings, usually without attempting to inquire into their spiritual significance (certainly not assigning them to divine source).

Of the various types of dreams, the following are general categories:

(1) prodromic (dreams caused by, or signifying some bodily condition or disease);

(2) kinesthetic (dreams of levitation or soaring);

(3) paralytic (dreams in which the individual feels that he cannot move or speak - often a part of a horror situation);

(4) collective (two or more people having the same dream);

(5) premonitory (dreams of foreboding);

(6) prophetic (dreams that clearly, or symbolically, anticipate some future event).

Biblical dreams are both premonitory (e.g., Herod's wife's dream, Matthew 27:19) and prophetic (as in the case of Nebuchadnezzar's own dream). We might add to this list what might be called dreams of guidance; e.g., Joseph's being warned in a dream to escape into Egypt.

While Freud (wish fullfillment, symbolically expressed) and especially Jung (archetypical memories) have attempted to give dream interpretation great scientific significance, some modern psychologists regard dreams as a sort of safety valve, releasing the tensions of the day; involving a carryover of the pressures of the day, making them a sort of clearing house of unresolved experiences. Perhaps, all of the psychological theories have some elements of truth. Certainly, none are complete explanations, especially with reference to biblical dreams. In them (i.e., biblical dreams), we have an exact correlation between the dream and its fulfillment. They are of such a nature as not to be explainable by natural, psychological causes. Nebuchadnezzar's dream, however, has this peculiarity: While the content of the dream itself is forgotten, the emotional impact of it has left the king shaken and foreboding. This is not at all uncommon to some of us. We have had experiences with dreams which left a distinct mood or emotional reaction without being able to recall their ideational elements, only remembering that we dreamed. This is Nebuchadnezzar's situation. The king does the usual thing under the circumstances (Daniel 2:2-6),

Then the king commanded to summon the magicians, and the astrologers, and the sorcerers, and the Chaldeans, to show the king his dreams. So they came and stood before the king.[1] (2) And the king said unto them, I have dreamed a dream, and my spirit was troubled to know the dream.(3) Then spoke the Chaldeans[2] to the king in Aramaic, O king, live forever; tell thy servants the dream, and we will show the interpretation. (4) The king answered and said to the Chaldeans, The thing has gone from me. If ye will not make known unto me the dream, with the interpretation of it, ye shall be cut in pieces, and your houses shall be made a refuse heap. (5) But if ye show the dream, and its interpretation, ye shall receive from me gifts and rewards and great honor; therefore, show me the dream, and the interpretation. (6)

Here we have an example of a dream with a surviving, emotional impact but without any content that can be recalled.

In the king's speech to his wise men, there is first a threat and then a promise of a reward - certainly, a very strange way of dealing with a group whose place in Babylonian society was one of honor and prestige. Threats are usually reserved for enemies.

To digress a moment, the whole prophetic message of the book of Daniel is given by dreams and visions. Nebuchadnezzar's dream, as we shall see, is an overall account of a succession of empires that will appear from the time of Nebuchadnezzar until the time of Messiah's kingdom, the Times of the Gentiles.

The four visions of Daniel himself, coming after an interval of nearly half a century of service as a civil servant, will not be concerned with Babylon or Nebuchadnezzar (the latter having died at least eight years before the first of these visions). They are, otherwise, largely amplifications of Chapter 2 and Chapter 7.

Beginning with certain, selected kings of the Persian empire, Daniel amplifies this dream Nebuchadnezzar in his own, later visions, putting flesh onto its bony framework, as follows:

The first vision (Chapter 7), seen by Daniel in the first year of Belshazzar, carries us directly to the time of the end, as we interpret it. It exhibits to our eyes four empires that will occupy the world stage at the end of the age. Out of one of them appears the Antichrist. In Daniel 8, we are given a description of Antichrist's coadjutor, the False Prophet, who is given equal billing with Antichrist in Daniel, as he is in Revelation 13.

Daniel then gives us (Chapter 9) the Jewish place in this gentile setting, the Seventy Weeks, during which Messiah will come "and have nothing" and the city will again be destroyed by the "people of the prince that shall come" (Antichrist). He tells us that wars and desolations shall continue until the end. Men will cry, "Peace, peace; when there is no peace."[3]

In Chapter 10, we are given insight into some of the dynamics of history. Principalities, powers and rulers of darkness of this world are its sources. And finally (Chapters 11 and 12), we are given an amplification of the gentile times with Antichrist featured in type and antitype, and the final consummation of gentile dominion in the judgment of the Great Tribulation. Both Jew and gentile alike will face this judgment but though it is a time of Jacob's trouble, it is also the time of the great Resurrection of Jewish saints.

Returning to Nebuchadnezzar's dream, this dream vouchsafed to Nebuchadnezzar was a divine and cosmic answer to his smaller, personal desire to know the future of his own dynasty. He was instead, through divine foreknowledge, given a vignette of world history (on a selective basis), from the standpoint of God's standard of values and purposes. As all roads lead to Rome so all of Daniel's visions lead to the End Times. While very little overt mention is made of Israel (except Chapter 9), Israel, her Messiah and Messiah's kingdom are the hidden themes that give meaning to all the rest. Nebuchadnezzar's dream has this orientation, also. His dream seems to have been the divine answer to Nebuchadnezzar's ambitious purpose of building an abiding empire, a world empire and for his own dynasty, perpetual rule.

Thy dream, and the visions of thy head upon thy bed, are these; (28) As for thee, O king, thy thoughts came into thy mind upon thy bed, what should come to pass hereafter; and he that revealeth secrets maketh known to thee what shall come to pass. (29)

We get some clue to these thoughts in the following inscriptions of Nebuchadnezzar in which he prays that his descendants may rule forever:

> "A firm throne do thou grant me!
> May my sway be long and Extend forever!
> Adorn my kingdom Forever With a righteous sceptre,
> With goodly rule, and With a staff of justice,
> For the welfare of my people! Protect my people
> With strong weapons and With the onslaught of battle!
> Do thou, O Shamash, Truly answer me
> In judgment and in dream!
> At thy noble command, Which cannot be altered,
> May my weapons be drawn, May they wound,
> May they overthrow the weapons of the enemies!"[4]

And again, the petition, written apparently after his building operations were advanced:

> "O lord of countries! Marduk!
> Hearken unto the word of my mouth!
> May I enjoy the splendor of the house which I have built!
> May I attain therein, In Babylon, old age!
> May I be sated with offspring!
> May I receive therein The heavy tribute
> Of the kings of the four quarters of the world, Of all mankind!
> May my descendants Rule therein Forever
> Over the Black-headed races!"[5]

The king's waking purposes are clear and conscious but not his dream. The dream cannot be recalled:

They answered again and said, Let the king tell his servants the dream, and we will show the interpretation of it. (7) The king answered and said, I know of certainty that ye would gain time, because ye see that the thing has gone from me. (8) But if ye will not make known unto me the dream, there is one decree for you; for ye have prepared lying and corrupt words to speak before me, til the time is changed; therefore tell me the dream, and I shall know that ye can show me its interpretation. (9)

Is the king demanding that these Chaldeans live up to a reputation for omniscience - claims that they themselves have made over the years? The Chaldeans may have inherited a class reputation for infallibility in the interpretation of dreams, omens and unusual occurrences. Their system had an answer for almost every contingency but not for this one. Nothing in their training or their knowledge provided for the interpretation of a dream that could not be remembered by the dreamer himself.

The Chaldeans answered before the king, and said, There is not a man

*on the earth that can reveal the king's matter; therefore, there is no king,
lord, nor ruler that can ask such things of any magician, or astrologer, or
Chaldean. (10) It is a rare thing that the king requireth, and there is no
other that can reveal it before the king, except the gods, whose dwelling
is not with flesh. (11) For this cause the king was angry and very furious,
and commanded to destroy all the wise men of Babylon. (12) And the
decree went forth that the wise men should be slain; and they sought
Daniel and his fellows to be slain. (13)*

That Daniel and his fellows should be slain would assume that they
had been incorporated in the fellowship of the wise men and, as a matter
of course, would suffer the same penalty.

There are two questions that come to us when we consider the king's
threat. The first is its legality, the second its propriety. With reference to
the lawfulness of Nebuchadnezzar's action in threatening (and almost
consummating) the death penalty, we ask whether or not there were legal
restrictions on the authority of a Babylonian king which would prevent
such arbitrary and apparently unjust action. The answer would seem to
be that such parts of the Code of Hammurabi as have survived speak of
the king as father, shepherd and law giver, and the direct channel through
whom the god speaks but with no provision whatever for limiting the
king's authority or action. Apparently, he is responsible only to the gods.
He is not under the law; he is the human source of the law, the divine
source being especially Shamash though other gods are invoked. Custom, expediency and religion (not law) would be the restraining force and
custom was on the side of royal authority. However, public sentiment for
or against, the dynasty, the personal qualities of the monarch and the
presence (or absence) of antagonistic political forces within the kingdom;
in other words, expediency, would undoubtedly play a part, as would the
religious factor.

From the standpoint of the propriety of the king's action, we have more
than the normal problem. This pronouncement of the king may be considered arbitrary, childish and irresponsible unless we consider carefully
the latter part of the ninth verse : "... for ye have prepared lying and corrupt words to speak before me, til the time be changed..." Of what "time"
is the king speaking? It seems that there are several possibilites, any of
which might be significant:

(1) If we remember that the Babylonians and the Assyrians were su-
persititious to a degree with reference to the fortunate and unfortunate
days to initiate and carry on business, we see that the king may be referring to the fact that if the particular time be passed, the fortunate moment
will also have passed for whatever good (or evil) may be impending.

(2) It may be that Nebuchadnezzar is testing the priesthood and only
pretends not to remember. This seems, in my opinion, to be inconsistent

with his known devotion to priestly things and even so, the death penalty is hardly consistent with this view.

(3)Nebuchadnezzar could feel that members of the priesthood (that is, the Chaldeans, astrologers, etc.) are playing for concessions and that they are refusing to answer until the rewards are sufficient to meet their larger expectations. However, the rewards, though unspecified, are open to very ample interpretations.

(4) Nebuchadnezzar, knowing his people and knowing the gift of the priesthood for intrigue, may feel that there is a conspiracy brewing, that this dream is a warning and that the Chaldeans, etc., may either know of the conspiracy and are withholding information or, indeed, may be part of it. This, in my opinion, is the real reason. Anyone thinking this view to be farfetched need only remember that Nebuchadnezzar's own son, Avil Marduk, was assassinated after ruling for only two years and that his grandson, Labashi Marduk, was also done to death after ruling but nine months.

It must be remembered that Nebuchadnezzar himself has only recently been crowned and must not be thought to be firmly established in his kingdom. If some such thought as this were not in the king's mind, it is difficult to understand the reason for the extreme urgency of his command and the widespread punishment that was threatened. Even a despot does not wipe out a whole order of society except under extreme fear of danger to himself.

Regardless of which reason, the significant part of this verse is the phrase *"til the time be changed."*

The Chaldeans make it very clear that it is one thing to interpret a remembered dream with an interpretation according to the prescribed formula and quite another thing to reproduce another man's forgotten dream.

Then Daniel answered with counsel and wisdom to Arioch, the captain of the king's guard, who was gone forth to slay the wise men of Babylon. (14) He answered and said to Arioch, the king's captain, Why is the decree so hasty from the king? Then Arioch made the thing known to Daniel. (15)

We gather from the fourteenth verse something of Daniel's interpersonal relationship with the people around him. The impact he had had upon the Prince of the Eunuchs (Chapter 1), upon the melzar and now upon Arioch, Captain of the Guards, makes it evident that these relations were of the best and that his sincerity and courage had impressed these members of the king's household. When Daniel goes to Arioch and asks for a respite apparently there is a favorable reception even though a risk to Arioch, himself, is involved. The petition that Daniel made of the king for time does not necessarily indicate that he saw him personally but at least there is respite granted.

Then Daniel went to his house, and made the thing known to Hananiah, Mishael, and Azariah, his companions; (17) That they would desire mercies of the God of heaven[6] concerning this secret; that Daniel and his fellows should not perish with the rest of the wise men of Babylon. (18)

The result of the meeting of four young Jews is that the king's dream and its interpretation were revealed to Daniel in a night vision. In verse 19 through 23, we have Daniel's prayer of thanksgiving and gratitude:

Then was the secret revealed unto Daniel in a night vision. Then Daniel blessed the God of heaven. (19)

Daniel answered and said, Blessed be the name of God for ever and ever: for wisdom and might are His: (20) And He changeth the times and the seasons: he removeth kings, and setteth up kings: He giveth wisdom unto the wise, and knowledge to them that know understanding: (21) He revealeth the deep and secret things: He knoweth what is in the darkness, and the light dwelleth with Him. (22)

I thank thee, and praise thee, O thou God of my fathers, who hast given me wisdom and might, and hast made known unto me now what we desired of thee: for thou hast now made known unto us the king's matter. (23)

When we remember that Daniel had received all that the wisdom of Babylon could give him and that he had a special understanding in all visions and dreams (verse 17), we are glad to find that his secular learning does not interfere with his understanding that it is God who reveals the deep and secret things. (Science sometimes helps us discover and formulate the questions but does not always give answers.)

Therefore Daniel went in unto Arioch, whom the king had ordained to destroy the wise men of Babylon: he went and said thus unto him; Destroy not the wise men of Babylon: bring me in before the king, and I will shew unto the king the interpretation . (24)

Then Arioch brought in Daniel before the king in haste, and said thus unto him, I have found a man of the captives of Judah, that will make known unto the king the interpretation.(25)

Daniel's answer to the king, the revelation of the dream and its interpretation, is more than just the satisfaction of the royal demand. It is the first of a series of revelations to the heathen world, to each of the world empires represented in the dream. Each of these revelations is calculated to impress each empire with the omnipotence, omniscience and the concern of the one true God to civilizations unaware of Him. Paul, in his sermon on Mars Hill, stated that God had not left Himself without witness and certainly, here is an example.

WITNESS TO BABYLON

There are four revelations and manifestations of God's power given to Nebuchadnezzar himself and his family line through him, to the people of Babylon:

(1) this dream,

(2) the rescue of the three young Jews from the fiery furnace,

(3) Nebuchadnezzar's own madness (this witness was not in vain to Nebuchadnezzar nor to his family but there is no record that the city of Babylon responded to this witness as Nineveh did to the preaching of Jonah) and

(4) to the last king of the Chaldeans, Belshazzar, the handwriting on the wall and the prediction accompanying it. This last witness was one of judgment because of the neglect of the previous warnings and was final.

WITNESS TO PERSIA

In Chapter 6, Darius the Mede was given an understanding of the keeping power of Jehovah in the miraculous rescue in the lion's den, a witness that was heeded by the king and may have been effective in the life of his successor, Cyrus the Great.

WITNESS TO THE GREEK WORLD

As to the Macedonian Empire of Alexander the Great, the witness was of a different kind but apparently, nonetheless effective. Josephus tells that when Alexander the Great approached Jerusalem with the intent to destroy it, Jaddua, the high priest , met him in his priestly robe, accompanied by his fellow priests and that Alexander, instead of destroying the priests and the city, bowed down to him because of a dream. This premonitory dream pictured the high priest in his high priestly robes exactly as he appeared in person. Josephus tell us also that the high priest pointed out to Alexander the prophecy of Daniel concerning his own successful conquest of Persia. (This would seem to make the dating of the book of Daniel in the Maccabean period absurd.)

WITNESS TO THE ROMAN EMPIRE

The fourth kingdom mentioned in the dream was that of the Roman Empire which was given an even greater witness though perhaps more obscure and less spectacular in its beginnings. The Messiah, Himself, His miracles, His crucifixion and His resurrection were all under Roman auspices. More widespread and almost as miraculous, was the growth of the Christian church, the willing death of the martyrs and the witness of

Christian lives. *("Behold these Christians how they love one another.")* Therefore, God witnessed to each of these world monarchies in turn and in ways that should have been convincing. Daniel begins his discourse to Nebuchadnezzar by disclaiming any wisdom of his own, saying,

There is a God in heaven that revealeth secrets, and maketh known to the king, Nebuchadnezzar, what shall be in the latter days. Thy dream, and the visions of thy head upon thy bed, are these (2:28).

THE VISION OF THE AGE OF MAN

THE TIMES OF THE GENTILES

Then follows the revelation of the dream itself:

Thou, O king, sawest, and behold a great image. This great image, whose brightness was excellent, stood before thee; and the form thereof was terrible. (31) This image's head was of fine gold, his breast and his arms of silver, his belly and his thighs of brass. (32) His legs of iron, his feet part of iron and part of clay. (33) Thou sawest til that a stone was cut out without hands, which smote the image upon his feet that were of iron and clay, and brake them to pieces. (34)

How could one better describe the succession of gentile empires than by the analogy of the image of a man? It will be man's day, his works, his phony glory, his futile dreams. The excellent brightness of the image would surely be descriptive of the outward forms of the civilization represented by great Babylon, the Persian empire, Alexander's empire and his successors, and the great Roman empire but it is equally true that the form has been terrible. All of these empires while maintaining order and all of the outward pertinences of civilization, were based on conquest, slavery and force. Of none of them could it be said that "thy scepter is a scepter of righteousness." Several things are noticeable in this dream:

(1) The head of the image is not a nation but a man, Nebuchadnezzar.

(2) The succeeding parts (three) of the images are kingdoms not persons.

(3) The head of gold, Nebuchadnezzar, is identified to us; the three kingdoms are not.

(4) There is a decreasing value to each of the succeeding parts of the body, that is, kingdoms.

(5) There is an increasing strength as we go downward from the head but while the legs are iron, the feet are a composite of iron and clay, partly strong, partly broken (that is, brittle in nature).

(6) The smiting stone strikes the last part described, the feet, breaking them in pieces (i.e., the time of the destruction of the image, the world

system, is at the end time).

(7) The whole image (i.e., the world system) dissolves into chaff and is blown away and lost. The stone that smites the image becomes a great mountain, filling the whole earth. The stone that smites is the Messiah.

(8) If we assume, for the present, that the parts of the body (or the kingdoms) are the Babylonian, the Persian, the Macedonian and the Roman empires and roughly approximate their lengths of existence as empires, we have the following:

	B.C.	Years	Percentage
Head and neck (Nebuchadnezzar successors)	605-539	66	.6+
Breast and arms (Persia)	539-332	207	9.0+
Belly and thighs (Greco-Macedonian)	332-63	269	25.0-
Legs (Rome)	63 B.C.- 476 A.D.	539	9.5+
Feet (Revived Roman Empire)	?	7	.5

If we compare these measurements with the lengths of the divisions of the body of a six-foot man, we have, very roughly, the following:

Head, 8 inches (+11% of body height).

Shoulders and chest, 12 inches (+17% of body height).

Belly and thighs, 24 inches (+33% of body height).

Legs, 21 inches (+29% of body height).

Feet, 7 inches (+10% of body height).

From the above tables, we see that, as to the time factor, these four empires approximate, very roughly, the proportion of the parts of the body that they represent and that the feet (7 inches from the ankle forward) approximate the length in body percentage of the seventieth week of Daniel; i.e., seven years. We also note that just as there are two arms (one for Media and one for Persia) and two legs representing a bifurcated Roman empire (the eastern half and the western half), we again have an apt analogy. There is no account taken for the continuation of the Eastern Empire or, at least the remnants of it, a thousand years after the dissolution of the western half though the Eastern Empire as a distinct division, really came into being with Diocletian, 285 A.D., and really ceased to be an empire long before the fall of Contstantinople in 1453 A.D.

It is, of course, not demanded of an analogy or of a parable that it should be carried out in nonessential items; however, in this dream, we have remarkable conformity in all salient points. In verse 37, we begin the interpretation of the dream and are at once given the source of

Nebuchadnezzar's power.

Thou, O king, art a king of kings; for the God of heaven hath given thee a kingdom, power, and strength, and glory. (37) And wheresoever the children of men dwell, the beasts of the field and the fowls of the heaven hath He given unto thine hand, and hath made thee ruler over them all. Thou art this head of gold. (38)

Jeremiah's prediction agrees with this statement:

And now have I given all these lands into the hand of Nebuchadnezzar, the king of Babylon, my servant; and the beasts of the field have I given him also to serve him. And all nations shall serve him, and his son, and his son's son, until the very time of his land come; and then many nations and great kings shall serve themselves of him. And it shall come to pass, that the nation and kingdom which will not serve the same Nebuchadnezzar, the king of Babylon, and that will not put their neck under the yoke of the king of Babylon, that nation will I punish, saith the Lord, with the sword, and with the famine, and with the pestilence, until I have consumed them by his hand. Therefore, hearken not ye to your prophets, nor to your diviners, nor to your dreamers, nor to your enchanters, nor to your sorcerers, which speak unto you, saying, Ye shall not serve the king of Babylon; For they prophesy a lie unto you, to remove you far from your land, and that I should drive you out, and ye should perish.[8]

Compared with the succeeding kingdoms interpreted by Daniel, apparently God has put a value upon Nebuchadnezzar's rule superior to any kingdoms that follow after. The statement is not that Babylon is the head of gold but the king himself is that head. As a part of the significance of the prophecy, there is as we have indicated, a descending quality represented by metals in the image; the head of gold, the breast and arms of silver, the belly and thighs of brass, his legs of iron and the feet part of iron and part of clay.[9] This is expressed definitely in verse 39: "And after thee shall arise another kingdom inferior to thee, and another third kingdom of brass, which shall bear rule over all the earth."

We may ask why only the head of gold is identified as to nationality. The best interpretation seems to be that the second kingdom of silver is the Medo-Persian kingdom; the third, that of Alexander and his successors; and the fourth kingdom, that of Rome. All of these kingdoms, and no others, have had undisputed rule over the civilized earth. Perhaps, we have here a prophetic principle: Nebuchadnezzar is given insight into that which concerns him alone but later, when Daniel in his own visions has had revealed to himself the significance of these other kingdoms and is given their names, it is because these will have a significance to the people of God, the Jews.

One of the difficulties of this thirty-ninth verse is that statement: *"after thee shall arise another kingdom inferior to thee."* At first glance, we see no inferiority in the Persian empire over the Babylonian; in fact, quite the contrary. If we accept the continuing lesser value of the metals as a guide then each subsequent kingdom is inferior to the preceding one. From the Jewish viewpoint, Babylon was a persecutor or, at least, a desolator of their city, had removed them from their land and had kept them in servitude. From a religious point of view, Babylon was the ancient center of polytheism and all that went with it but was nonetheless the mother of Western Civilization. Contrariwise, Persia was their liberator, was kindly in its rule and religiously not far from monotheism. Of course, the vision and interpretation represents God's viewpoint, not Israel's.

There are several answers to this apparent difficulty but perhaps we should pinpoint more clearly the possible areas of inferiority. Is it in the size or extent of area controlled? No it is not, for each of the succeeding empires is larger in extent than its predecessor. Is the inferiority moral or ethical? Again, not entirely provable. Has it anything to do with ethnic traits, physical or moral vigor, love of truth, outstanding national gifts, contributions to civilization?

It would be hard, indeed, to equate these things one by one. But certainly Babylon, the mother of civilization as we now believe, was inferior to no one in its gifts to future generations, neither to Persia nor to Greece, who borrowed so largely from her. Keil holds that the inferiority lay in their lack of inner unity. This could be so, both religiously and politically: religiously, since Babylon, a polytheistic people ruled over people similarly polytheistic while Persia, a non-polytheistic nation, governed and probably despised the religious confusion of these same nations over which she ruled. Politically, both Babylon and Persia were conglomerates but Babylon had a more autocratic and centralized authority, lacking the effective Persian satrapal system. There is another way of looking at this inferiority. It is not Babylon but Nebuchadnezzar who is the head of gold. It could be that Daniel is comparing a man with a kingdom, not a kingdom with a kingdom. And who shall say that Nebuchadnezzar, the greatest gentile king of antiquity by biblical standards (Daniel 4:20-22) was not in God's sight superior to any government that Persia produced? If this is a comparison between Nebuchadnezzar and the Persian kingdom, not between Nebuchadnezzar and Cyrus the Great, this would be an acceptable interpretation.

While not specifically stated, the third kingdom by implication is inferior to the second, not intellectually nor artistically to be sure but perhaps morally or spiritually. The Greeks had certain moral traits that God might rightly consider decidedly inferior - individualism gone to seed, lack of interpersonal loyalties and moral instability. The Persian youth, according to Xenophon, were taught to ride, to shoot the bow and to tell the truth. To the Greek, truth was abstract. The Greek mind was subtle and devious neither was it remarkable for veracit, and Herodotus tells us that the Greeks taught Asia unnatural lust. As for the last nation, Rome, with its tenacity of purpose, its ability to absorb and use the results of Greek genius and its gift for law and order, did not hide the fact that it became parasitic upon the East for its material prosperity, its very food, its art, its literature and even its religion. In the latter years of the empire, it became dependent upon tributary nations for the greatest of its emperors: Diocletian, Theodosius, Constantine, Justinian - all except Theodosius were Illyrians (Jugoslavs). Theodosius was a Spaniard.

To those who find it difficult on so-called scientific grounds, to believe in the supernatural especially as it relates to prophetic foreknowledge, let us follow the interpretation of this dream with a little historical perspective. If, as is somewhat commonly believed by conservatives, the facts of history demand interpretation of Nebuchadnezzar's dream as the neo-Babylonian, the Medo-Persian, the Graeco-Macedonian and the Roman Empires, what Gallup poll of intelligent contemporaries (605 to 535 B.C.) could have predicted the rise of any of these to dominion over the Near East?

Nebuchadnezzar had yet to consolidate his empire against various coalitions especially against a resurgent Egypt. The Medes and Persians were on the move but had not yet completed their empire even though they would have been party to destroying two (first, Assyria, 614 B.C.; later Lydia, 546 B.C.). Greece was an unorganized group of city states with a genius for non-cooperation and Macedonia had hardly been heard of in international affairs. As for Rome, it was under Etruscan rule and could not by any stretch of the imagination, have been thought of as a future empire. It was just another town.

The usual answer to this list of impossibilities is, of course, to place the writing of Daniel after the event, say, at the time of the Maccabean revolt, about 165 B.C. This leaves us with at least two unsolved problems. First, it would have been still too early to predict a Roman Empire especially a bifurcated one as symbolized by the two legs. Second, how could Alexander the Great,[10] 332 B.C., have been shown the prophecy of Daniel and its application to himself as we have already indicated in the introduction when as yet it had not been written and was not to be written for 167 years?

Beginning with the fortieth verse of Chapter 2 which we understand is concerned with the Roman Empire, we have a symbolism that fits perfectly with the Roman Empire as it finally developed. The two legs, of course, are the western half of the empire centered in Milan, the eastern part of the empire centered first in Nicomeda then in Constantinople. Even as the ankles form a break in the continuity in the direction of the legs so we may assume that this also has significance in the future of the Roman Empire, and later prophecy will lead us to believe that it will be a revived Roman Empire from which will spring ten toes; i.e., ten kings.

While verses 40-43 make no overt provision for the two horizons involved, the old Roman Empire and the Roman Empire in its revived form are implicit as stated. Two horizons are not uncommon in Scripture. But it would be entirely out of character to describe the old Roman Empire as a mixture of iron and clay even though it could be said that the iron of the Roman Imperium was mixed with the clay of human slavery. It would hardly be appropriate to consider the later mixture of barbaric tribes as answering this description. Human slavery has been the basis of all ancient civilizations, more or less, and the absorption of other nations or tribes could, in itself, be a source of strength. The Scofield notes rightly assess these verses:

"This passage fixes, in relation to other predicted events, the time when the millenial kingdom will be established. It will be 'in the days of these kings,' i.e., the days of the ten kings (cp. 7:24-27) symbolized by the toes of the image. The ten kings did not exist at the advent of Messiah, nor was the federation even possible until the dissolution of the Roman Empire and the rise of the present nationalistic world system."[11]

Obviously, the God of heaven has not set up a kingdom either in the days of these kings or at all, as yet. And this kingdom of God and heaven has not yet broken in pieces and consumed all these ten kingdoms. Surely, no one seeing all this contemporary wickedness and anarchy and the exceedingly imperfect church can think that we either are in this condition or are arriving at this state. Rather, we are more like the days of Noah when the earth was filled with violence and all flesh had corrupted itself.

The forty-third verse of this chapter is a very strange one and reads as follows:

And whereas thou sawest iron mixed with miry clay, they shall mingle themselves with the seed of men; but they shall not adhere one to another, even as iron is not mixed with clay.

In this verse, we ask, Who are "they"? "Mingled" in what way? Apparently, "they" are the seed of men, and at least they are persons. Keil says:

"As in the three preceding kingdoms, gold, silver and brass represent the material of these kingdoms; i.e., their peoples and their culture, so also in the fourth kingdom iron and clay represent the kingdoms arising out of the division of this kingdom; i.e., the national elements out of which they are constituted and which will and must mingle together in them. If then, the 'mixing themselves with the seed of men,' points to marriages, it is only of the mixing of different tribes brought together by external force in the kingdom using marriages as a means of amalgamating diversified nationalities. But the expression is not limited to this for in Ezra IX 2, occurs mention of the mixing of the Holy nation with the heathen by marriage. The peculiar expression, 'the seed of men,' is not of the same import as, but is obviously chosen with reference to the following contrast to the divine ruler, vss. 44f., so as to place (Kran.) the vain human endeavor of the human rulers in contrast with the doings of the God of heaven, as the reference in Jeremiah XXXI.27, is occasioned by the contrast. The figure of mixing by seed is derived from the sowing of the field with mingled seed, and denotes all the means employed by the rulers to combine the different nationalities, among which the Connubium is only spoken of as the most important and successful means. But this mixing together will succeed just as little as will the effort to bind into one firm coherent mass iron and clay. The parts mixed together will not cling to each other.[12]

Keil wrote these words long before the worldwide communist movement was dreamed of. If the words "communist infiltration" had been known in Keil's day, I feel sure he would have considered this an option and perhaps a preferable one to the idea of tribal mixing in one nation. Today there is no nation earth where the clay of communism is not mingled with the iron of nationality. Whereas most modern nations are of mixed ethnic origin, this would hardly distinguish any modern nation and very few ancient ones.

There are questions which commentators frequently fail to answer, which are:

(1) Will the revived Roman Empire consist of two parts (an eastern and a western)? Or will they be reunited as a single unit?

(2) Will the ten kings, represented by the ten toes, rule over all of the territory previously controlled by eastern and western Rome? Or, in fact, are they political rulers?

(3) Will the revived empire consist of ten separate unrelated kingdoms? Will they be grouped into two hegemonies?

The above questions, perhaps, cannot be satisfactorily answered but would be significant in this day when we see the scenery being moved into place for the great last act of mankind's final revolt against God. We cannot answer these questions with assurance nor with the full significance of the meaning of the iron and clay in the feet. The forty-second verse is descriptive of a combined strength and weakness (the feet of the revived empire), the strength of the iron and brittleness of the combination with clay. Whatever is meant, certainly one cannot leave out the possibility that the symbolism of the miry clay may apply very appropriately to the presence in every country of some element that weakens the iron; communsim or perhaps a general anarchy. How significant it is that the clay of communism does not adhere to the iron of national governemnt armed to the teeth and how symbolic and descriptive clay is for communism which is of the earth earthy and knows nothing of anything spiritual. A man, according to communism, is clay; he has no soul, he has no God, there is no hereafter and the legitimate governments of the world are to be infiltrated and, if possible, overthrown by force, subversion, treachery, and specious promises of an earthly paradise. This is the philosophy of dialectic materialism. Communist leaders are apt pupils of Machiavelli. The interpretation continues:

Thou sawest till that a stone was cut out without hands, which smote the image upon his feet that were of iron and clay, and break them to pieces. (34) Then was the iron, the clay, the brass, the silver, and the gold, broken to pieces together, and became like the chaff of the summer threshing floors; and the wind carried them away, that no place was found for them; and the stone that smote the image became a great mountain, and filled the whole earth.13 (35)

There are varied interpretations of the stone but it can hardly be other than Christ. The forty-fourth verse says:

And in the days of these kings shall the God of heaven set up a kingdom, which shall never be destroyed; and the kingdom shall not be left to other people, but it shall break in pieces and consume all these kingdoms, and it shall stand forever.

This is Messiah's kingdom of which Ezekiel gives us certain, definite descriptions[14] and which many of the prophets foresaw.

As we see, Nebuchadnezzar is given the substance of the dream and the meaning of it insofar as it concerns him, not that which does not concern him. He falls on his face and worships Daniel and confesses that the God of Daniel is a God of gods and a Lord of kings and a revealer of secrets.

It is not to be supposed that Nebuchadnezzar will give up his pagan gods because the language he uses merely includes the preeminence of Jehovah with reference to the revelation of secrets. He must learn, through other means and in other ways, the power of God and the helplessness of his own gods. For that purpose, he will be given the witness of the fiery furnace and the witness of his own mental breakdown and restoration.

The chapter ends with the promotion of Daniel to the governorship of the whole province of Babylon and to his elevation as chief of the governors over the wise men.

How this promotion will set with the Chaldeans who have been helpless in the performance of their function while Daniel, a foreigner and a captive, is given preeminence over them, we will see in the following chapters. A group, with pride of office and prestige in the community, made to look foolish by someone whose social standing is inferior, may have several ways of responding but their emotional reaction is hate. An entrenched priesthood does not give up easily especially when assured of popular backing. This group, whose capacity for intelligent intrigue was notorious, would not necessarily feel that this defeat was permanent and it would be very interesting, indeed, to know what the relationship was between this new head of the Chaldeans with the rank and file of the group and with his fellow governors.

The chapter closes with Daniel's elevation to a position of great honor and, at his request, minor honors for Shadrach, Meshach and Abednego. "But Daniel sat in the gate of the king." Here begins a civil and prophetic career that continues for seventy years, even to the third year of Cyrus, the Persian.

CHAPTER IV

THE GOLDEN IMAGE AND THE FIERY FURNACE

(Daniel 3; Language, Aramaic)

The scene of this chapter is on the plain of Dura in the province of Babylon probably just outside the city walls. The time is not indicated but for reasons which will appear later, it is possibly about 595 B.C. The chapter begins with a most arbitrary act on the part of Nebuchadnezzar.

Nebuchadnezzar, the king, made an image of gold whose height was threescore cubits and the breadth of it six cubits; he set it up in the plain of Dura in the province of Babylon. (1) Then Nebuchadnezzar, the king, sent to gather together the princes, the governors, the captains, the judges, the treasurers, the counselors, the sheriffs, and all the rulers of the provinces, to come to the dedication of the image which Nebuchadnezzar, the king, had set up. (2)

Whatever is to happen in the following verses will take place before all the officialdom of all the provinces so that the happenings described will not be done in a corner. Whether Nebuchadnezzar knows it or not, this thing which he had planned will be used as a divine occasion for a witness to the "God of heaven."

Then the princes, the governors and captains, the judges, the treasurers, the counselors, the sheriffs and all the rulers of the provinces were gathered together unto the dedication of the image that Nebuchadnezzar, the king, had set up; and they stood before the image that Nebuchadnezzar had set up. (3) Then a herald cried aloud, To you it is commanded, O people, nations, and languages, (4) That at the time that ye hear the sound of the horn, pipe, lyre, sackbut, psaltery, dulcimer, and all kinds of music, ye fall down and worship the golden image that Nebuchadnezzar, the king, hath set up; (6) And whoever falleth not down and worshipeth, shall the same hour be cast into the midst of a burning fiery furnace. (6) Therefore, at that time when all the people heard the sound of the horn, pipe, lyre, sackbut, psaltery, and all kinds of music, all the people, the nations, and the languages fell down and worshipped the golden image that Nebuchadnezzar, the king, had set up. (7)

Of the seven names of dignitaries in verse 2, four are Persian titles, not Babylonian which is strange since it will be possibly half a century before Persia will take over the Babylonian Empire. It is not at all strange, however, if the book was written as we have suggested in the prologue, between the first and third years of Cyrus the Persian and Daniel used terms then in use, the equivalents of former Babylonian official positions. Young, quoting the archeologist Oppert, offers the following suggestion as to the location of the plain of Dura:

"The archeologist Oppert (Expedition Scientifique en Mesopotamia, 1:238 ff.) declared that S.S.E. of Hillah, at a distance of about 12 miles, there are some mounds called Tolul Dura (the mounds of Dura). One of these, known as el-Mokhattat, consists of a rectangular brick structure 45' square and 20' in height, which according to Oppert, may have formed the pedestal of a colossal image. If this is a mere legend, composed in the second century B.C. as a 'polemic against the heathen worship and in particular against idolatry' (Bevin), how account for the presence of this word Dura? The appearance of the word is in reality an evidence of genuineness in that it seems to presuppose some knowledge of the Babylonian Geography."

As to the presence of the furnace, we quote Herodotus:

"And here I may not omit to tell the use to which the mould dug out of the great moat was turned, nor the manner wherein the wall was wrought. As fast as they dug the moat the soil which they got from the cutting was made into bricks, and when a sufficient number were completed they baked the bricks in kilns. Then they set to building, and began with bricking the border of the moat, after which they proceeded to construct the wall itself, using throughout for their cement hot bitumen, and interposing a layer of wattled reeds at every thirtieth course of the bricks. On the top, along the edges of the wall, they constructed buildings of a single chamber facing one another, leaving between them room for a four-horse chariot to turn. In the circuit of the wall are a hundred gates, all of brass, with brazen lintels and sideposts. The bitumen used in the work was brought to Babylon from the Is, a small stream which flows into the Euphrates at the point where the city of the same name stands, eight days' journey from Babylon. Lumps of bitumen are found in great abundance in this river."

If we could know the chronology of this chapter, it is possible that we might more easily understand Nebuchadnezzar's reason for demanding universal worship for the image of gold. We can guess, though it is only a guess, that it might have taken place soon after the tenth year of his reign (594-593 B.C.) and was the psychological cause, and his reaction to a revolt of a portion of his army. We could conceive of this act of unusual religious urgency as an attempt to stabilize an unsettled situation in the army and in the city by a spectacular religious act and a dramatic appeal to the religiosity of Babylon.

It would be most helpful also to know more about the identity of the golden image. Was it Marduk, the favorite god of Nebuchadnezzar, whose preeminence was being proclaimed? Some conservative scholars have assumed that Nebuchadnezzar was setting up an image of himself for deification, a device used before and since to give authority and sanctity to a king. This would be most reasonable if it were not for the king's own statements relative to his devotion to Marduk. Another possibility might well be the introduction of a syncretist god after the analogy of the Serapis of the Egyptian Ptolemies. Just how all of the priesthoods of the various gods of Babylon would welcome such a newcomer - one with no place or a minor one to the Babylonian pantheon - is open to question. Daniel does not enlighten us so we cannot be sure. One thing seems to be a reasonable assumption: A man who could rule Babylon for forty-three years in a city noted for intrigue, could not possibly be a stupid politician and whatever other motives may have been involved, the political motive must have been as important as the religious one. The appeal for popular loyalty would be "for God and king."

The setting of this chapter, as even Montgomery concedes, is Babylonian[3] as are the first five chapters so the background is not fictitious and it has "a sumptuous, barbaric scenery." The theory of pious fraud basically rests upon two major assumptions:

(1) That the supernatural, as pictured in Scripture, has not, cannot and does not occur. Since prophecy involves the supernatural, if it conforms to later historical fact, it must therefore have been written after the event, not before. This view is qualified by the admission that trends may be discovered in the social, political, moral and spiritual fields and conclusions drawn, but drawn on purely natural and understood principle - logical conclusions based upon logical reasoning. This deistic viewpoint is contrary to the whole spirit of Scripture and the logical outcome of this viewpoint is to reject all Scripture not understood in terms of present knowledge. This viewpoint leaves out faith, for the definition of faith, given in Hebrews, "as the substance of things hoped for and the evidence of things not seen" definitely adds another dimension to knowledge.

(2) The second assumption, as far as the book of Daniel is concerned, rests on the now discredited view that the alleged Greek names of the musical instruments listed in Daniel 3:5, 7 and 10 are anachronisms and could not have been so named in the Babylon of the sixth century B.C.; hence, if data in the third chapter is spurious so is the chapter and so is the book. It seems that here we have just a matter of common sense. The Greeks and their artifacts were found all over western Asia by 600 B. C. Greek mercenaries served in the Assyrian armies and in the army of Nebuchadnezzar. Greeks were as ubiquitous in the Near East as the Phoenicians were farther west in the Mediterranean. When we remember that wherever a musical instrument goes, its name is apt to go with it and with the added fact that the Babylonians were a trading nation, quite as likely to borrow artifacts as to distribute them, we should need to know much more than we do now to rest any generalization, large or small, on

the names of musical instruments. The real question is not whether the instruments have Greek names but whether they might reasonably be found in use in Babylon.

We have the following common sense, scholarly reactions to this former stumbling block:

"The names of the three Greek musical instruments mentioned in Daniel III as forming a part of Nebuchadnezzar's band are as follows: kitheros; Greek, the lyre. R.V. Harp. pesanterin; Greek; Italian, salerio; Italian, sampogna; bagpipe. R.V. Dulcimer. The possibility of these musical instruments reaching Babylon and carrying their Greek names with them may, as we have seen, be taken for granted on *a priori* grounds but the question as to the precise channel by which they came is doubtful, and forms a very fascinating theme without in any way weakening the argument."[4]

Pusey, with his usual common sense, is more explicit:

"The Greek names are but another instance of the old recognized fact, that the name of an import travels with the thing. When we speak of tea, sugar, coffee, chocolate, cocoa, cassia, cinnamon, tobacco, myrrh, citrons, rice, potatoes, cotton, chintz, shawls, we do not stop to think that we are using Chinese, Malay, Arabic, Mexican, Hebrew, Malabar, South American, Bengalle, Persian words and we shall continue to use them, even though they were originally misapplied, and we know the word tobacco was the name, not of the plant but of the vessel out of which the natives smoked it. When Solomon's ship brought him the peacocks, apes, ivory, almug, or algumwood, they brought with them also the Sanskrit and Malabar names of the ape (which passed thence into Greek and our European languages), and of the algumwood; the Tamul name of a peacock and the Sanskrit of the elephant. There is nothing stranger in our finding Greek instruments of music in Nebuchadnezzar's time at Babylon, than in the Indian names of Indian animals and of an Indian tree, having reached Jerusalem under Solomon."[5]

On the supposition that these instruments were Greek, there were sufficient Greek influences in Babylon and in fact, all over the Near East which would amply account for the use of such names and such instruments. Greek artifacts have been found all over the areas involving Assyria, Babylonia and in Scythian burial mounds. When it is remembered that Antimenidas, a Greek of Mytilene, was a friend of Nebuchadnezzar, that there was a Greek theater and a Greek quarter in Babylon and that Greek mercenaries served in both Assyrian and Babylonian armies and, as Pusey indicates, that musical instruments usually carry the names given them at their place of origin even where there may only be slight cultural contact otherwise, one wonders why this argument was ever expected to carry any weight. There is another view of the origin of these instruments, equally fatal to the liberal theory. Harrison sums up this view:

"Furthermore, while the names of the instruments mentioned may appear to be Greek, the instruments themselves are of Mesopotamian origin. The 'harp' can probably be identified according to Werner with one of the many Asiatic precursors of the classical Greek Kithara, and being a strictly secular instrument it fitted quite well into the picture of the banquet of Nebuchadnezzar. The antiquity of the 'lyre' in the Near East has been amply demonstrated by the work of Wooley at Ur, precluding the necessity of positing a Greek original for this type of instrument. The 'sackbut' or 'trigon' was another variety of chordophone, which may have been similar to, or derived from the sabitu or seven stringed lyre of the Accadians. Among the Greeks the sambuke was of ill repute as the instrument played by vulgar musicians and prostitutes and of such general character as to earn its rejection from Plato's ideal republic. The psaltry, also translated harp, was the old dulcimer the Persian-Arabic santir, and its occurrence both on Assyrian reliefs and in the eastern Mediterranean culture in the first millenium B.C. generally amply attested. [6]

Before we continue in the discussion of this event on the plain of Dura, it might do well to take into account the theory that this whole occasion was a somewhat inaccurate account of the traditional Akitu New Year's festival which took place yearly in Babylon in the spring month of Nisan. It was the greatest religious celebration of the Babylonian year and continued for twelve days, the festival ending on 12 Nisan. For the common people, it was supposed to celebrate the marriage of the god Marduk to the goddess Sarpanitum. To the initiated, it probably had a cosmic significance of some sort, going back to the dim past. The highlight of the occasion was a great procession which started at the beautiful Ishtar gate and moved down the processional street first to the temple of Marduk, Esagila, and then beyond the city walls to a special building erected for the occasion where the goddess Sarpanitum awaited her husband.

The king not only played a leading part in this New Year's festival from the standpoint of his duties as the religious head of the kingdom but in a sense, it also confirmed his own legitimacy as its ruler. The king rode in a carriage with his hand clasping that of the image of Marduk so that he literally "took the hand of Bel." Beek tells us:

"The king played a most significant part in the New Year's festival for he is the mediator between the gods and the people of Babylon and atones for the sins of the people. The sceptre is taken from his hands, the crown is taken from his head, and the king confesses his innocence or guilt and the guilt of the people, and atones for the sins of the community." [7]

We do not have any complete account of this most important celebration in the Babylonian religious year nor do we know all the details of this parade but, human nature being what it is, all of the resources of the city and empire would have been used to make this a most spectacular affair. It might be likened to a Russian May Day procession in Red Square, combined with a coronation of an English queen, in the spirit of a great Papal holy year presided over by the Pontiff himself plus the Pasadena Rose Parade. A parade is a parade, in any language, at any time, with any people. With an opulent sophisticated society, it must have been a sight to behold. The sacred image of the god, Marduk, in the sacred carriage with the king himself clasping the hands of the image, the high priest (the urigallu) accompanied by thirty classes of subordinate priests was there in his glory, followed by the chief priestess (the entu), bride of the gods, with her twenty order of priestesses. With the magicians, astrologers and the soothsayers all in festal robes, it must have been a glittering and splendid sacred part of the procession. All of this was accompanied by the odor of incense and the sound of music.

These religious orders would have been followed by hundreds of the nobles each in magnificent dress and retinues. There would, of course, follow the military might of the empire: the armored chariots, the Assyrian, Scythian and Arabian horse archers, the Greek mercenaries (heavily armed Hoplites) marching in step to the music of pipes and phalanx after phalanx of Babylonian infantry.

In this procession, all of the religious, aesthetic and patriotic emotions of the people were consummated in this great yearly event. The hymns of the priests and priestesses and of the worshiper were undoubtedly accompanied by instruments mentioned in Daniel 3:5, 7; the horn, the pipe, the sackbut, the psaltery, the dulcimer and the harp. As the procession moved through the Ishtar gate, down the mile-long processional street (the sacred way), the battlements on either side thronged with participating worshippers. The picture must have partaken of a splendor and glamour the equal of anything that we have today, all in honor of the gods of Babylon but in particular of Marduk.

The scene before us, however, does not seem to be this famous festival, though possibly partaking of its pomp and circumstance. The Akitu (New Year's) festival has its culmination in the marriage of Marduk with his wife, Sarpanit. The one in Daniel 3 is merely the worship of the golden image.

The circumstances portrayed in this chapter were after the events in Chapter 2 and before the completion of the walls, almost certainly before the midpoint of Nebuchadnezzar's reign. This is one of two undated chapters in the book with only scanty clues as to the time element. Since Daniel, as a good civil servant, is meticulous about times, places and circumstances in his visions, we can only assume that he felt that matters of such public note needed no date line. Or are the events undated because of his own lack of personal participation? Or is the event coupled with other events, making it too painful to recall (for example, the great rebellion in the city, 595 B.C., which was somehow connected with these events)?

The chapter opens with a description of an image of gold (probably plates of gold over a framework of wood), tremendous in size (threescore cubits high and six cubits broad; i.e., ninety feet high by nine feet thick.) It is not necessary to discuss Nebuchadnezzar's ability to employ this much gold whether we think of the height as involving both the image and its pedestal or regard the dimensions as referring to the image alone. To a conqueror who has the wealth of Babylon to draw on (e.g., the plunder of Nineveh which in turn had plundered Egyptian Thebes), the problem of a gold supply presents no problem. The thing that chiefly concerns us is the "Why?" not the "How?"

Why is Nebuchadnezzar insistent that this particular image should be worshipped by all of his subjects, regardless of their own gods? And why is this worship made so mandatory that the death penalty was punishment for refusal? We are told that in the tenth year, Nebuchadnezzar remained in Babylon to deal with a local rebellion involving a revolt in the army which was quickly suppressed by the king, personally.

"Nebuchadnezzar remained at home for the greater part of his tenth year, for during the month of Kislev and Tebet (c. December 595 - January 594 B.C.) there was a revolt in the country which was only suppressed by the slaughter of many of his troops (?) and by the capture of the rebel leader. Order must soon have been restored, for the king was able to go in person to Syria before the end of the year to receive the tribute brought by the vassal kings and other officials and to bring it back to the capital. . .. There is no direct indication of the internal dissension in this year apart from that given in this Chronicle.

"Its brief duration and suppression probably place it among those frequent intrigues which any Babylonian or oriental monarch had to face. The opponent does not appear to have claimed the royal title in Babylonia as did a number of later rebels who, ironically enough, proclaimed themselves king with the very name of Nebuchadnezzar. The strain put on the standing army by the frequent and lengthy campaigns in the west may have been a factor contributing to the disturbances. What may be an indirect indication of the revolt is given by a contract tablet from Babylon dated in the eleventh year of Nebuchadnezzar. This tablet tells of the confiscation and disposal of the property of Baba-ahu-iddina, the son of Nabu-ahhe-bullit, who had been tried by court martial and , on being found guilty of breaking the royal oath and of insurrection, had been condemned to death and executed.

"The actual reading of the tablets is: 'In the tenth year the king of Akkad (was) in his own land; from the month of Kislev to the month of Tebet there was rebellion in Akkad; with arms he slew many of his own army. His own hand captured his enemy. In one month, he marched to the Hatti-land, where kings and officials (came before him) and he (received) their heavy tribute and then returned (to Babylon).'"[8]

After suppressing the rebellion, Nebuchadnezzar left Babylon for a campaign in the west. When we realize that the Neo-Babylonian Empire was new and beset within and without with enemies, it is not hard to believe that Nebuchadnezzar would use every device of government, secular and religious, to bring stability. As to the identity of this object of worship, we are given no light in Scripture. We sense several possibilities here:

(1) The image may have been erected to the honor of Marduk to emphasize his preeminence.

(2) Some other god of the Babylonian pantheon, possibly Nabu or Shamash.

(3) Some composite deity after the analogy of the Serapis of the Ptolemies.

(4) As some suggest, Nebuchadnezzar may have erected the image in his own honor.

It seems that the first option is the most likely, in view of Nebuchadnezzar's intense devotion to Marduk, and the last option the least likely (for the same reason). To a man of Nebuchadnezzar's background as we know it, would he not consider it to be sacrilege to claim deity? The purpose, regardless of the god involved, remains obvious. A monolithic state needs a unifying, common god.

Nebuchadnezzar spake and said unto them, Is it true, O Shadrach, Meshach, and Abednego, do not ye serve my gods, nor worship the golden image which I have set up? (14) Now if ye be ready that at what time ye hear the sound of the cornet, flute, harp, sackbut, psaltery, and dulcimer, and all kinds of music, ye fall down and worship the image which I have made; well: but if ye worship not, ye shall be cast the same hour into the midst of a burning fiery furnace; and who is that god that shall deliver you out of my hands? (15) Shadrach, Meshach, and Abednego, answered and said to the king, O Nebuchadnezzar, we are not careful to answer thee in this matter. (16) If it be so, our God whom we serve is able to deliver us from the burning fiery furnace, and He will deliver us out of thine hand, O king. (17) But if not, be it known unto thee, O king, that we will not serve thy gods, nor worship the golden image which thou hast set up. (18)

In the previous chapter, we have indicated the possible thoughts of Nebuchadnezzar upon his bed involving the perpetuity and universality of his kingdom and we must not suppose that a man of his largeness of mind and tenacity of purpose had given up his hope for a universal kingdom - if not for eternity, then for whatever length of time might be ordained of the gods.

In the interpretation of his dream by Daniel, he is given no perpetuity but the certainty of a succession of kingdoms which shall follow; they in turn, to be overthrown by a universal kingdom which shall continue forever.

Seemingly, he is not the man to fail to make use of the time he has, and so he uses a device which undoubtedly was used before and certainly has been used since to ensure control over the hearts and minds of the subject races by creating a unity of government guaranteed by a religious unity. The people of various provinces are not asked to give up their own gods but to acknowledge a common god. This thing would not be basically repugnant to polytheistic thinking.

The local pride and local interests among the various peoples might naturally give a preference for the chief, local god. Such local preference, however, might easily be overcome by sufficient threat of punishment and Nebuchadnezzar is seemingly surprised when this threat does not sufficiently intimidate the three Jewish youths.

Some have supposed, as we have said, that the image Nebuchadnezzar has set up was an image of himself and that he is trying to claim deity. This I find hard to believe, for reasons previously mentioned. In addition, we have the statement of verse 18 where the three youths, through their spokesman, say:

But if not, be it known unto thee, O king, that we will not serve thy gods, nor worship the golden image which thou hast set up.

What gods were they being asked to worship? None, unless it be this golden image.

There is a second reason, previously stated, that appeals to me with an even stronger force, namely, that of Nebuchadnezzar's intense devotion to Marduk, the chief god of Babylon. This devotion which began in youth was fostered by his father. It is a devotion that is shown by one of the most beautiful prayers that have come down to us from pagan sources:

"From the time that the lord my god, Marduk, had created me and had formed my embryo in the womb, at the time I was born, at the time I was created, I sought out the shrines of the god, the path of the god I followed. As for Marduk, the great lord, the god my creator, his clever deeds I held in high esteem. As for Nabu, his true son, the beloved of my royalty, the lofty path of his divinity I steadfastly followed; with all my faithful heart I loved the worship of their divinity, I reverenced their lordship.

"At the time that Marduk, the great lord, lifted up my royal head and entrusted me with the rule of all people; and Nabu, the ruler of the host of heaven and earth, gave into my hands a righteous sceptre for the governing of the people; then, as for me, I stood in awe of them and sought out their divinity, for the renown of their famous name I reverenced both god and goddess. To Marduk my lord I made supplication; I read his prayers, and the word of my heart reached up to him. To him I spoke:

"O eternal prince! Lord of all being!
To the king whom thou lovest, and
Whose name thou hast proclaimed.
As was pleasing to thee,
Do thou lead aright his name,
Guide him in a straight path.
I am the prince, thy favorite,
The creature of thy hand;
Thou hast created me, and
With dominion over all people
Thou has entrusted me.
According to thy favor, O lord,
Which thou dost bestow on All people,
Cause me to love thy exalted lordship,
And create in my heart The worship of thy divinity,
And grant whatever is pleasing to thee,
Because thou hast fashioned my life."[9]

This prayer would not be entirely inappropriate for a Jew if the name "Jehovah" were to be substituted for "Marduk." A Hebrew king could have prayed this same prayer with few changes. The following excerpt from an inscription of Nabopolassar, his father, will further illustrate the point:

"An image of my royalty carrying a dupshikku I constructed; in the platform-foundation I placed it. Unto Marduk, my lord, I bowed my neck; I arrayed myself in my gown, the robe of my royalty. Bricks and mortar I carried on my head, a dupshikku of gold and silver I wore; and Nebuchadnezzar the first-born, the chief son, beloved of my heart, I caused to carry mortar mixed with wine, oil, and (other) products along with my workmen. Nabushumlisher, his twin brother, the offspring of my own flesh, the junior, my darling, I ordered to take a basket and spade (?); a dupshikku of gold and silver I placed (on him). Unto Marduk, my lord, as a gift, I dedicated him. I built the temple in front of Esharra with joy and rejoicing, and like a mountain I raised its tower aloft; to Marduk, my lord, as in days of old, I dedicated it for a sight to be gazed at.

"O Marduk, my lord, look with favor upon my goodly deeds! At thy exalted command, which cannot be altered, let the performance of my hands endure forever!

Like the bricks of Etemenanki, which are to remain firm forever, do thou establish the foundation of my throne for all time!

O Etemenanki, grant blessing to the king who has restored thee! When Marduk with joy takes up his abode in thee,

O temple, recall to Marduk, my lord, my gracious deeds!"[10]

The piety of the father is an example to the son.

There is a second question of motive. Are the accusers of the Jewish youths motivated by a pure love of Marduk and his worship (if indeed the image was one of Marduk)? Or are they motivated by jealousy and the memory of defeat in the matter of the king's dream and its interpretation by Daniel?

Wherefore at that time certain Chaldeans came near, and accused the Jews (8). They spoke and said to the king, Nebuchadnezzar, O king, live forever. (9) Thou, O king, hast made a decree, that every man that shall hear the sound of the horn, pipe, lyre, sackbut, psaltery, and dulcimer, and all kinds of music, shall fall down and worship the golden image. (10) And whoever falleth not down and worshippeth, that he should be cast into the midst of a burning fiery furnace. (11) There are certain Jews whom thou hast set over the affairs of the province of Babylon, Shadrach, Meshach, and Abednego; these men, O king, have not regarded thee; they serve not the gods, nor worship the golden image which thou hast set up. (12) Then Nebuchadnezzar in his rage and fury commanded to bring Shadrach, Meshach, and Abednego. Then they brought these men before the king. (13) Nebuchadnezar spoke and said unto them, Is it true, O Shadrach, Meshach, and Abednego, do not ye serve my gods, nor worship the golden image which I have set up? (14)

There is some confusion about the phrase "do not ye serve my gods?" since no other gods are in the picture and they have not been asked to worship anything but the golden image. It would seem that we might think of the phrase as reading "do you not serve my gods, even the golden image?" in which case, there is the implication that it is not an image of himself that Nebuchadnezzar has set up. Moreover, we are somewhat surprised that he gives these young men another chance rather than visiting condign punishment upon them.

Nebuchadnezzar here casts down the gauntlet to any and all gods other than his own. And why not? He does not know that his invincibility is from Jehovah. Hitherto, he has not seen what Jehovah, the God of Gods can and will do when it is His purpose to give a witness of Himself and to protect His chosen servants. The only question is whether or not these young men by their faith and courage will give God the occasion to so reveal Himself.

Then was Nebuchadnezzar full of fury, and the form of his visage was changed against Shadrach, Meshach, and Abednego; therefore, he spoke and commanded that they should heat the furnace seven times more than it was usually heated. (19) Then he commanded the most mighty men that were in his army to bind Shadrach, Meshach, and Abednego, and to cast them into the burning fiery furnace. (20) Then these men were bound in their coats, their stockings, and their turbans, and their other garments, and were cast into the midst of the burning fiery furnace. (21)

It is entirely characteristic that Nebuchadnezzar should react with rage and fury at the public resistance of these men. After all, these very men have been promoted by him and ought above all others to remember that they were picked even though foreigners and captives for promotion to high office, and they owed their preeminence to Nebuchadnezzar alone. Their refusal to worship is not only a public affront to the authority of a powerful king but is an insult to his god and a challenge to the very stability of his empire. This would be especially true if the event were related to the time or circumstances of the rebellion of the tenth year. At any rate, this appeal to the Jehovah whom they serve, to deliver them not only from the king but from the gods of Babylon on whom the king depends, would be infuriating to him. We must regard the miracle that follows not only as a rescue of faithful witnesses for which there are many examples before and afterwards in Hebrew history but significantly above all, as a second witness to the heathen world, a witness so public and so complete that even Nebuchadnezzar is obliged to say that there is no other god that can deliver after this sort. After all, there were many ways by which these youths could be delivered, if that were the sole purpose.

Let us remember that Israel was in exile. It had ceased to be a witness as a nation and had been removed out of its place. But God had not left Himself without witness even to the heathen world and even as His first witness, the king's dream was a matter of public knowledge to the Chaldean group. This miracle is to the officialdom of the whole kingdom.[11]

Now there is a more extensive witness of an even more marvelous kind. These three youths furnish the steadfastness and the purpose. The faithful God revealed Himself in power on their behalf. God was saying to the heathen world that Israel was still His people even though the nation was in disgrace, in servitude and in exile.

Really, the astonishing thing about this tremendous occurrence is the apparent hesitancy that Nebuchadnezzar had in immediately punishing the three rebels. He gives them another chance for they are picked servants and loyal to him in all other matters. There is a manifest reluctance to carry out the punishment that he had threatened.

However, with the steadfastness of these three young men along with the fact that this is a public occurrence, the king cannot afford to be outfaced and, above all, his religious instincts involving the preeminence of his god are challenged. There is only one thing that he can do and as a result, he seems to have determined not only to carry out the threatened execution but to do it in a most spectacular way. This is shown in the heating of the brick kiln *"seven times more than it was wont to be heated."*

Anyone who has even seen a brick kiln in operation realizes that under ordinary circumstances, no human being could live in it for thirty seconds and therefore, there would be no necessity for any super heating.[12]

Therefore because the king's commandment was urgent, and the furnace exceedingly hot, the flame of the fire slew those men that took up Shadrach, Meshach, and Abednego. (22) And these three men, Shadrach, Meshach, and Abednego, fell down bound into the midst of the burning fiery furnace. (23)

The servants of despots must suffer the dangers as well as the rewards of their service and the heat of the furnace possibly was fueled by asphalt or even petroleum. This miracle of the fiery furnace has no precedent in Scripture. It is *sui generis*. The other two miracles are nearly so, namely, the handwriting on the wall at Belshazzar's feast and the deliverance from the den of lions at Darius' court. In the same category, we have the first dream of Nebuchadnezzar and the unique setting for the theophanies of Chapters 10, 11 and 12. If the writer of Daniel was engaged in the manufacture of a pseudo-prophecy,[13] it would seem to have been the better part of wisdom to follow precedent. To produce an aura of authenticity, it might seem that an ounce of similarity would be worth a pound of innovation. If the author was going to imitate Scripture, should it not have been like previous Scripture? If miracles are introduced, should they not bear the union label? But in Daniel, they do so only in that they are consistent with the principle that God not only responds to faith and in His own way, meets the needs of the moment but above all, that He has not left Himself without witness in the gentile world. These miracles differ from pseudo miracles in their moral tone, their purposefulness in promoting a spiritual impact upon Babylon and their fitness.

We have the following options not only with the account of miracles in Daniel but in all other Scripture:

(1) The account is true as stated. "The right of the book of Daniel to canonicity was never called in question in the ancient synagogue."[14]

(2) It is partially true but the account has been garbled. It is based on an actual occurrence but with the miraculous element interpolated.

(3) The account is wholly ficticious - a pious fraud: in the case of Daniel, a pseudo-prophecy written to boost morale during the Maccabean persecutions. Involved, of course, is the whole question of divine inspiration. Is God speaking to man? Are men moved by the Holy Ghost? Or is Scripture entirely man-made?

The miracle of the fiery furnace is particularly obnoxious to any person who thoroughly believes that God has never in the past nor will He ever act except through natural law, that regularities and relative certainties that obtain in the field of physics and chemistry (to a lesser degree in biology and to an even lesser degree in psychology) shall never be disturbed by the unexpected or by divine expressions of power. Many will admit that a man's family does not have to run on the same rigid basis that the same man's factory does nor do his inter-personal relations within the family have to be limited to the inter-personal relations obtained in the business world. But somehow, it seems difficult to apply to the divine-human relationships these interpolations which we usually speak of as miracles if they are no more miraculous than the so-called laws of nature.

In truth, miracles are of relatively rare occurrence in both the Old and New Testaments and full centuries pass in the divine-human relationship with no hint of a miracle. In fact, miracles center about Moses, Elijah, Elisha, Hezekiah and the Exile. So far as we can read, miracles are never pictured as something that God forgot nor are they puposeless, spectacular evidences of power.[15] They are expressions of eternal, divine purpose expressed in an inter-personal relationship almost exclusively through Israel and through an individual Jew. The particular miracle under discussion is unique in Scripture and would be susceptible of no natural explanation, unless we are willing to regard the report as due to mass hypnosis or suggestion (a most unlikely explanation)[16] or to pious fraud (at least equally improbable). We must accept it for what is is; namely, a tremendous public witness to the fact of three Jewish young men answering the challenge of a heathen king and through him, a heathen priesthood, given as a testimony to a heathen world at a time when the nation Israel had no testimony. The time came when Babylon was no longer a sovereign nation but when that time came, Babylonians would never be able to say, "We had no witness of the truth and no knowledge of a true God." Four times Babylon will have been able to see the power of Jehovah:

    (1) the interpretation of the dream in Chapter 2,

    (2) the miracle of the fiery furnace in Chapter 3,

    (3) Nebuchadnezzar's predicted madness and restoration in 4 and

    (4) the handwriting at Belshazzar's feast in Chapter 5.

As the apostle Paul said on Mars Hill, *God has not left Himself without witness.* One of the questions that we may ask is, Why was there no hint of this or any of these events included in any of Nebuchadnezzar's inscriptions, which are now in our possession (i.e., extra-biblical testimony)? All of Babylon knew of the interpretation of the dream; representatives from all over the Babylonian empire saw the miracle of the fiery furnace and everyone knew or could have known, of Nebuchadnezzar's madness and of the prediction that preceded it and his own testimony which accompanied his recovery. A thousand people saw the handwriting on the wall. Why has not some hint of this other miracle come down to us from contemporary, pagan sources? The obvious answer might be that which is so adequately expressed by E.M. Yamauchi in his article entitled "Stones, Scripts and Scholars":

"If one could by an overly optimistic estimate reckon that one-fourth of our materials and inscriptions survived, that one-fourth of the available sites have been surveyed, that one-fourth of those sites have been excavated, that one-fourth of the excavated sites have been examined, that one-fourth of the materials and inscriptions excavated have been published, one would still have less than one one-thousandth of the possible evidence (i.e., 1/4x1/4x1/4x1/4x1/4). [17]

Kings come, and kings go. Priesthoods continue. In Babylon, national records were kept by, or at least subjected to scrutiny and possible control by the priesthood. Since their prestige and power, as vested authority, would have been forever challenged by such records, the most obvious thing for them to do would be to destroy any such public records upon the death of Nebuchadnezzar.

Even at that, there are hints that the witness of Jehovah to His own power and purpose may have found a following in Babylon, even in the royal palace. In our own day and age, we have seen Russian history written and rewritten at least three times with men and events deleted, reinterpreted and misinterpreted. Vested interests and most especially, prieshoods or any self-perpetuating group in control of intellectual resources whether in Babylon, in Egypt, in Medieval Europe or even in modern America, have seen to it that public events were interpreted, changed or suppressed for their own interests, their publicity being carefully, and favorably, edited.

To return to the theme, verse 24 states that Nebuchadnezzar was astonished (and well he might be):

Did we not cast three men, bound, into the midst of the fire? Lo, I see four men loose, walking in the midst of the fire, and they have no hurt; and the form of the fourth is like the Son of God.

Of all the beautiful and precious statements in Scripture relative to God's identification with His people, it seems to me that this is one of the most unique and meaningful. Are we dealing here with the presence of an angel (which seems most likely since, until the incarnation of the Son of God, it is not recorded that a gentile was ever given a vision involving deity)? Nebuchadnezzar's claim that he is like a son of God would not necessarily make it so. Whether angel or pre-existent Christ, Jehovah was represented.

It seems to be very difficult for mankind to realize how closely a faithful God and men can be identified, even though under most circumstances, this identification is invisible to human eyes. [18] These three young men are summoned from the fire and come forth, *"upon whose bodies the fire had no power, nor was the hair of their heads singed, neither were their coats changed, nor the smell of fire had passed on them"* [19] The fourth Presence in the midst of the fire does not come forth.

We have one final view of this occasion in which Nebuchadnezzar rightly interpets the situation and blesses the God of Shadrach, Meshach, and Abednego who had sent His angel and who delivered His servants who had trusted in Him. Nebuchadnezzar ungrudgingly acknowledges defeat and admits that a higher power than his *"has changed the king's word."* We may remember that when Jesus later authenticates Daniel as a prophet, He is verifying an occurrence in which He, Himself, might possibly have been a fourth, visible participant. There may be objection to this view (e.g., that here we have a theophany) on the ground that it is contrary to biblical precedent that a theophany should have been experienced by a gentile, but it is also contrary to any biblical precedent that an angel should have shared such an experience as the fiery furnace. In Nebuchadnezzar's use of the words *"the most high God"* and his acknowledgment that *"no other God can deliver after this sort,"* are we to infer that the truth of the omnipotence of Jehovah, the true God, is beginning to cast doubts upon his previous worship of Marduk? If not, what would it take to convince him? The chapter ends with a public declaration and a decree of acknowledgment:

That every people, nation, and language which speak anything amiss against the God of Shadrach, Meshach and Abednego, shall be cut in pieces and their houses shall be made a dunghill; because there is no other God that can deliver after this sort . (29)

As for Shadrach, Meshach and Abednego, instead of death: promotion.

The pious-fraud theory does not at all fit the picture given in this chapter for Daniel, the hero of the supposedly fictitious tale, is not even present at the greatest miracle of all. This is perhaps the most spectacular and inexplicable (in natural terms) of all biblical miracles. But if we take into account the sorcercy, the pseudo-miracles that usually accompany sophisticated, pagan worship, we realize the necessity of something stupendous to call attention of pagan people in some completely unequivocal manner; something that Satan's lying wonders could not fake.

It was a great miracle to accomplish a great end. Babylon's long history as the mother of civilization and holy center of pagan worship is to come to an end in a matter of fifty or sixty years. God's justice is about to be visited upon her though there will be no physical destruction. This miracle is given so that Babylon may have a final warning and final witness and repent as did Nineveh seventy years before by the witness of Jonah. She is given four miraculous manifestations of the power and goodness of Israel's God, the God of all the earth who is not willing that any should perish.

If God wished to call attention to His own truth and power and to give through His servants a witness to Himself, how would He best do it in such an utterly alien and polytheistic setting? Not by the ordinary circumstances, not by something explainable by the ordinary course of events which pass almost unnoticed. Certainly not by devices that could be easily imitated by religious charlatans; something that with adequate staging could be made equally impressive. There is more than a little evidence as we have indicated, that pagan priesthoods have known and used slight of hand, hypnosis, mass suggestion, ventriloquism, as well as necromancy and have known the uses of various drugs about manic states (e.g., the haoma of the Persians). Truth ought not to be put forth through these means which are an imitation of true miracles.

God's witness then might best be carried out when the setting was entirely outside of the power of human witnesses and where the environmental circumstances were under the control of the opposition - something that could not possibly be staged; something not explainable by suggestion, fraud, illusion of any sort or of any known device of an intelligent opposition; something in an unfriendly setting; something inconceivable in natural terms. This is what this chapter is about. The purpose of the miracle of the fiery furnace is indeed a rescue of three faithful youths but far more than that, it is Jehovah's witness of the truth of Himself.

C. S. Lewis, in commenting on Hume's denial of the possibility of miracles, quotes Sir Arthur Eddington, as follows:

"We sometimes have convictions which we cherish but cannot justify; we are influenced by the innate sense of the fitness of things. This may sound a perilously subjective and aesthetic criterion; but can one doubt that it is a principal source of our belief in uniformity? A Universe in which unprecedented and unpredictable events were at every moment flung into nature would not merely be inconvenient to us; it would be profoundly repugnant. We will not accept such a universe on any terms whatever. It is utterly detestable to us. It shocks our sense of the fitness of things but if we admit God, must we admit miracles ? Indeed, indeed, you have no security against it. That is the bargain.

"Theology says to you, in effect, 'Admit God and with Him the risk of a few miracles, and I in turn will ratify your faith in uniformity as regards the overwhelming majority of events.' The philosophy which forbids you to make uniformity absolute is also the philosophy which offers you solid ground for believing it to be general, to be almost absolute. The being which threatens nature's claims to omnipotence confirms her in her lawful occasions . . . The alternative is really much worse. Try to make nature absolute and you find that her uniformity is not even probable. By claiming too much you get nothing.

"You get the deadlock as in Hume. Theology offers you a working arrangement which leaves the scientist free to continue his experiments and the Christian to continue his prayers. We have also, I suggest, found what we are looking for; a criterion whereby to judge the intrinsic probability of an alleged miracle. We must judge it by our 'innate sense of the fitness of things,' that same sense of fitness which led us to anticipate that the universe would be orderly. I do not mean of course, that we are to use this sense in deciding whether miracles in general are possible; we know that they are on philosophical grounds. Nor do I mean that a sense of fitness will do instead of close inquiry into historical evidence. As I have repeatedly pointed out, the historical evidence cannot be estimated unless we have first estimated the intrinsic probability of recorded events. It is in making that estimate as regards each story of the miraculous that our sense of fitness comes into play."[20]

In this miracle of deliverance from the fiery furnace, it is easy to misapply the criterion of fitness. If the purpose back of the miracle was only the deliverance of the three Hebrew youths, there were certainly other, more appropriate ways by which this might have been done; ways perhaps unusual but not involving the miraculous: a defense by the youths, appealing to the magnanimity of the king; a reminder by a counselor that there were other issues involved; rescue by friends; an appeal by Daniel based on former services to the king. But if the purpose of the miracle was to give a witness of Jehovah to the king, a city and a people for centuries steeped in polytheism and bound up in concomitant ways of thinking that made then almost impervious to monotheistic truth, how else could an effective witness be given?

Polytheism is not only a way of worship, it is a way of thinking, of living. It is also a system of values out of which a people's moral sensitivities proceed. How then shall the kingdom of darkness be given light? The difficulties were great, the witness must needs be inescapable. The means used, as we see it, were necessary, and it appeals to our sense of fitness.

What we are saying is that a stupendous miracle is not used to solve a small problem for, as Lewis implied, the regularities of nature do not stir us, we are used to them and we must be stirred by something unusual. The basic questions we have to face are two, therefore: Is there a God? and, Does He have a right (i.e., is it fitting?) to supersede or interpolate, for His own purposes, the regularities of nature? If He has made nature, are we obliged to believe He is bound, hand and foot by the nature He has made?

In this ancient world center of error, it was necessary to bring home God's truth to Babylon in a way inexplicable by any trickery, legerdemain or mass suggestion; all of which were well-known to the priests of Babylon. The means used to persuade them needed to be, and was, overwhelming.

CHAPTER V

A KING'S PRIDE BROUGHT LOW
SEVEN-YEAR INTERIM

(Daniel 4; Place, Babylon: Date, Toward the End of
Nebuchadnezzar's Reign; Author Nebuchadnezzar;
Language, Aramaic)

The locale of this chapter is Babylon, a completed Babylon, with its
sixty miles of outer wall, its hundred gates of shining bronze, each gate
with its wild bull and erect serpent of bronze; its temples enriched and
beautified lavishly; a city with villas and gardens, with canals reopened.[1]

We have no way of knowing the total population but as the greatest
city of antiquity in area, it must also have been the most heavily popu-
lated. A list of the temples and shrines restored and rebuilt would make
us guess that the population requiring such an outlay must have been
several million.[2] The king's own fortress palace is completed, as are the
hanging gardens (one of the wonders of the ancient world) erected for the
delight of his Median queen, Amytis. Likewise, the sacred processional
street leading from the great Ishtar gate, has been raised and repaved. The
driving, restless spirit of Nebuchadnezzar has rest, his Herculean projects
are finished, his conqeusts have been completed, his ambitions satisfied.
He says in Daniel 4:4,

*I Nebuchadnezzar was at rest in my house, and flourishing in my
palace.*

This would seemingly be near the latter part of his reign. The rest of
the chapter is the king's own proclamation to *"all people, nations, and
languages that dwell in all the earth,"* and he gives us, at the same time,
his purpose for the proclamation.

*I thought it good to show the signs and wonders that the high God hath
wrought toward me. (2) How great are His signs! And how mighty are
His wonders! His kingdom is an everlasting kingdom, and His dominion
is from generation to generation. (3)*

What under heaven has brought Nebuchadnezzar to a knowledge of
the Most High God rather than his familiar praise to Marduk? For the
second time, Nebuchadnezzar dreams a dream, a premonitory dream that
fills him with apprehension and again he does what might be expected;
that which is part of the public life of any monarch, he appeals to the established forecasters: the magicians, the astrologers, the Chaldeans and
the soothsayers. One wonders why, after the experiences at the beginning
of his reign, he should again make a futile appeal for interpretation to men

who had previously failed so signally. However, a king is bound by custom and tradition and, after all, these men are a part of the establishmnet. We are disappointed in that after that he has acknowledged the High God as eternal, he should revert to polytheistic language when he speaks of Daniel: *"Whose name was Belteshazzar, according to the name of my god, in whom is the spirit of the holy gods"* (8).

Is Nebuchadnezzar still a polytheist in spite of his acknowledgment of Jehovah's pre-eminence? Or is he proclaiming his message to the world in the kind of language that they can understand? Since Daniel is the reporter, the language has not been edited by the Chaldeans. However, if we remember Nebuchadnezzar's childhood and the fact that every aspect of life was interwoven with polytheistic concepts and language, we may either consider his reference to his polytheistic gods as a way of speaking or as a still lingering belief in these gods, no longer pre-eminent but still existing. It is difficult to escape ideas inculcated in childhood. It would be very interesting and strange if this same proclamation should ever be recovered on some cuneiform tablets and if recovered, how differently it might read after having been edited by the priests of Marduk.

In verses 10 to 18, we have the dream and again we have God's estimate of Nebuchadnezzar in this God-given, premonitory dream:

> *Thus were the visions of mine head upon my bed; I saw, and behold, a tree in the midst of the earth, and the height of it was great. (10) The tree grew, and was strong, and its height reached unto heaven, and the sight of it to the end of all the earth. (11) Its leaves were fair, and its fruit much, and in it was food for all; the beasts of the field had shadow under it, and the fowls of the heaven dwelt in its bows, and all flesh was fed from it. (12)*

Of what gentile ruler could more be said? Phrases such as *"its fruit much and in it was food for all"* and *"all flesh was fed from it"* give a description of prosperity and abundance for all the nations under his control, an acknowledgment that Nebuchadnezzar is the human source of it. There are few kings of history having achieved success in war as a path to glory, who have had continued military successes and who, at the same time that they were creating an empire, brought widespread abundance and order in a world as potentially unstable as that of the sixth century B.C.

We could wish that the phrase *"all flesh"* could have included the multitudes of slaves who built his walls, erected his palace, adorned his temples. It is greatly to be questioned that it did, in view of Jeremiah's statement,

> *Israel is a scattered sheep; the lions have driven him away: first the king of Assyria hath devoured him; and last this Nebuchadnezzar king of Babylon hath broken his bones.*[3]

Isaiah, one hundred years before had foreseen Israel's captivity and speaking of the Chaldeans, had said,

I was angry with my people; I have polluted mine inheritance and given them into thine hand: thou didst show them no mercy; upon the ancient hast thou very heavily laid thy yoke.[4]

Human slavery and its misery did not begin south of the Mason-Dixon Line and most certainly did not end there. In one form or another, it has never left the human scene. But in the ancient world, slave hordes were the machines with which cities were built.

To return to the dream, the description of the tree does not end on a happy note. We read,

I saw in the visions of my head upon my bed, and, behold, a watcher and a holy one came down from heaven; (13) He cried aloud, and said thus: Hew down the tree, and cut off its branches; shake off its leaves, and scatter its fruit; let the beasts get away from under it, and the fowls from its branches. (14)

Whatever the tree may symbolize, here is disaster, not only for the tree but for all the creatures dependent upon it. When a tree is hewn down, normally that is the end of it. The story does not end here.

Nevertheless, leave the stump of its roots in the earth, even with a band of iron and bronze, in the tender grass of the field; and let him be wet with the dew of heaven, and let his portion be with the beasts in the grass of the earth.(15 Let his heart be changed from man's, and let a beast's heart be given unto him; and let seven times pass over him.(16)

In these verses, we have a transition from *"it"* to *"he"*, from the tree to a person and we learn that the disaster is not irreparable.[5] The term *"watcher"* is not a theological term commonly used in the Old Testament. In fact, it appears only here in the prophecy of Daniel in this sense and certainly is not a term that should have been used by someone inditing a fictitious prophecy. However, it is most descriptive as is the more appropriate *"holy ones"* used with it.

We remember that while the dream is from God, the description is Nebuchadnezzar's. "Watchers" and *"holy ones"* are concepts within his pagan theological terminology. The idea of a *"most high"* as alone ruling the universe and the affairs of men is something else again. A preeminent *"god among gods,"* the *"first among equals"* is already a part of his religious background, the preeminent one being Marduk but the Hebrew Jehovah alone is God. As Isaiah tells us, *"I am the Lord and there is none else there is no God beside me."* This concept is strange to his thinking.

Sometimes, it is necessary for God to shake up completely and disorganize a mind so that the pieces may be reassembled into a truer pattern.

Sorrow, despair, failure, sickness, mental illness; all are a part of His plan to draw upon when other, more gentle methods fail.

So when we think of Nebuchadnezzar's madness as punitive, a judging of pride of heart and a rebuke for his harshness to Israel, there may be another purpose: that God may put together a mind that is conformed to the truth (made possible by a more tractable spirit) that he might come to a conviction of his own complete powerlessness to control his own destiny and even his own mind.

This dream I, king Nebuchadnezzar, have seen. Now thou, O Belteshazzar, declare the interpretation of it, forasmuch as all the wise men of my kingdom are not able to make known unto me the interpretation; but thou art able; for the spirit of the holy gods is in thee.(18)

This is, again a public occasion and again publicly, the powerlessness of the Chaldeans is openly contrasted with the God-given insight of Daniel. Even though Daniel is *"master of the magicians" (rab chartumim)* and in a sense, one of them, their efforts without him (verse 7) are futile and the whole court is aware of it. This must have been a bitter pill to swallow, the more so since Daniel had once saved them from death (which they were powerless to prevent) and their efforts to railroad Daniel's companions to their death had not only failed but had magnified the power of Daniel's God against whom they were powerless. These are the men in whom was reposed all the learning of the Chaldeans, the ancient wisdom.

In the face of truth or error, men have an option: either they love the truth and hate the error or ultimately they cling to the error and hate the truth. We have no record that any of these men were convinced of the truth of Jehovah and of the error of their own theological system. Their political futility may last during the reign of Nebuchadnezzar who has ceased to be one of them; but in the reactionary reigns of Neriglissar, Nabonidus and Belshazzar, they may have had something to do with Daniel's non-presence in Babylon (Daniel 8:2) and more certainly, with the conspiracy against him under Darius (Daniel 6:4). They acted as men so often act when their very reason for being was at stake, their very livelihood. Self-interest is usually worshipped by the natural man, no matter what other gods he may profess.

When Daniel is called in to interpret, he is astonished and his thoughts trouble him, and well they might. Daniel sees at once that the dream spells disaster for the king.[5] But how could such disaster befall a king to whom God had given everything? Given dominion over mankind and dominion over the beasts of the field, he was a conqueror who so far as we know, knew few defeats but who does not boast of his conquests; a monarch with nations to serve him; slaves innumerable to build his city; unlimited gold and resources to embellish his temples; possessed of an impregnable fortress; able in every respect to impose his will on his fellow man; a man who found a kingdom dilapidated and has made it an empire and who has raised it to a zenith of power and glory unheard of so that it is the greatest city of antiquity; how could such a one in the midst of prosperity and power, be cast down? He was the *"head of gold,"* the man to whom Jehovah had given power and glory, who had conquered and plundered Nineveh and Jerusalem and Tyre and Carchemish and had even conquered Egypt. How could such prosperity and power be suddenly stricken from a man's hand and by what means? No external power was visible and no internal power sufficient. No wonder that Daniel was astonished and that his heart was troubled. We sense here also a real affection on Daniel's part for this gentile king. The tone of his reply is reluctant acknowledgment of God's decree and a warning in which there is the element of personal concern. The interpretation is given reluctantly.

This is the interpretation, O king, and this is the decree of the most High, which is come upon my lord the king: (24) That they shall drive thee from men, and thy dwelling shall be with the beasts of the field, and they shall make thee to eat grass as oxen, and they shall wet thee with the dew of heaven, and seven times shall pass over thee, till thou know that the most High ruleth in the kingdom of men, and giveth it to whomsoever He will. (25) And whereas they commanded to leave the stump of the tree roots; thy kingdom shall be sure unto thee, after that thou shalt have known that the heavens do rule.(26) Wherefore, O king, let my counsel be acceptable unto thee, and break off thy sins by righteousness, and thine iniquities by shewing mercy to the poor; if it may be a lengthening of thy tranquility. (27)

Two things stand out in this prediction. The first has to do with the mental problem. King Nebuchadnezzar is to be stricken in his reason. The very mind that has envisioned and produced the walls of Babylon, the magnificence of the sacred street, the conquest of strong nations is to become the mind of a beast. Today, we would call this mental abnormality boanthropy, a type of paranoia. The strange thing about this visitation is that, instead of being a grandiose delusion (which would be entirely consistent with the proud and arrogant attitude Nebuchadnezzar is taxed with), we have the unexpected opposite in which he not only does not consider himself a god or invincible or a superman but he thinks and acts as a beast of the field.

Again God has many ways of disciplining men and mental illness is one part of he resources that He may command.

There is a second question in this passage that needs to be answered. When Daniel says, *"Wherefore, O king, let my counsel be acceptable unto thee, and break off thy sins by righteousness, and thine iniquities by shewing mercy to the poor, "* we are inclined to ask, What particular sins other than those incidental to the exercise of authority, is Daniel speaking of? There is then this sin of pride which the chapter specifies but we have another hint in Jeremiah's prophecy where Jehovah speaks of the punishment that Israel is receiving through exile but the comment *"this man Nebuchadnezzar has broken his bones"* (i.e., Israel's) would lead us to think that there had been a period of harshness in dealing with Israel.[6] Even though Israel is under discipline and out of the land and is Jehovah's unfaithful wife, she is still loved with an everlasting love and may not be dealt with unjustly, without retribution upon him who is guilty. So has it been throughout history.[7] King Nebuchadnezzar, apparently does not heed Daniel's warning. At the end of twelve months, he is walking in his fortress-palace and says, *"Is not this great Babylon, that I have built for the house of the kingdom by the might of my power, and for the honor of my majesty?"*(4:30).

Shall we pause here to enumerate what the king had done exactly? What he says, in spite of the spirit of pride and arrogance without any acknowledgment of the Jehovah who had freely made possible all of the things he had done, is a true statement.

The Babylon of King Nebuchadnezzar was the mightiest city that had ever existed up to that time. The wealth of the world flowed into it; through conquest, through caravan trade and through the skills and commercial know-how of its citizens. It contained two of the seven wonders of the world; the great walls and Hanging Gardens and his own palace which was completed in fifteen days. The River Euphrates had been harnessed and the great flood-control reservoir, eleven miles square, had been constructed up the river from Babylon. (All along the Tigris and Euphrates in modern Iraq, there are remains of brick quays built by Nebuchadnezzar.) The old irrigation canals had been restored, the natural fertility of the land had been exploited, the Babylonian Empire had peace and protection. It is not that Nebuchadnezzar is not telling the truth. It is that he is neglecting the source of all his power.

While the word was in the king's mouth, there fell a voice from heaven, saying king Nebuchadnezzar, to thee it is spoken; The kingdom is departed from thee. 31) And they shall drive thee from men, and thy dwelling shall be with the beasts of the field: they shall make thee to eat grass as oxen, and seven times shall pass over thee, until thou shalt know that the most High ruleth in the kingdom of men, and giveth it to whomsoever He will. (32)

We do not know where Nebuchadnezzar spent the seven years of his insanity. Nor do we know the nature of the interim government. We do know that:

At the end of the days I Nebuchadnezzar lifted up mine eyes into heaven, and mine understanding returned unto me, and I blessed the most High, and I praised and honored Him that liveth for ever, whose dominion is an everlasting dominion, and His kingdom is from generation to generation: (34) And all the inhabitants of the earth are reputed as nothing: and He doeth according to His will in the army of heaven, and among the inhabitants of the earth: and none can stay his hand, or say unto Him, What doest thou? (35) At the same time my reason returned unto me; and for the glory of my kingdom, mine honor and brightness returned unto me; and my counsellors and my lords sought unto me; and I was established in my kingdom, and excellent majesty was added unto me. (36)

The normal procedure might well have been the deposition of the insane king and his succession by his son or possibly some strong contender among the nobility. What part Daniel had in securing proper care for the king and a stable interim government, we cannot know but Daniel's standing as man and as a prophet and his stability and trustworthiness must have played an important part. Sometimes, one man of character and integrity can be the factor that stabilizes an unstable situation. Since his prophetic interpretation of Nebuchadnezzar's dream was known to the court, who among them would dare to act against the certainty that the mightiest king of antiquity would after a lapse of time, resume power and authority to reward the faithful and punish the rebellious?

One of the strange and unexpected stories that comes down to us from Herodotus who visited Babylon about eighty years after the death of Nebuchadnezzar, is the story of the building exploits of two queens: Semiramis and Nitocris. This story was, of course, hearsay told him by the priests of Bel-Marduk:

"Many sovereigns have ruled over this city of Babylon and lent their aid to the buildings of its walls and the adornment of its temples, of whom I shall make mention in my Assyrian history. Among them two were women. Of these, the earlier, called Semiramis, held the throne five generations before the later princess. She raised certain embankments well worthy of inspection, in the plain near Babylon, to control the river, which, till then, used to overflow, and flood the whole country round about.

"The later of the two queens, whose name was Nitocris, a wiser princess than her predecessor, not only left behind her, as memorials of her occupancy of the throne, the works which I shall presently describe, but also, observing the great power and restless enterprises of the Medes, who had taken so large a number of cities, and among them Nineveh, and expecting to be attacked in her turn, made all possible exertions to increase the defenses of her empire. And first, with a straight course to Babylon, she, by certain excavations which she made at some distance up the stream, rendered it so winding that it comes there several times in sight of the same village, a village in Assyria, which is called Ardericca; and to this day, they who would go from our sea to Babylon, on descending to the river touch three times, and on three different days, at this very place. She also made an embankment along each side of the Euphrates, wonderful both for breadth and height, and dug a basin for a lake a great way above Babylon, close alongside of the stream, which was sunk everywhere to the point where they came to water, and was of such breadth that the whole circuit measured four hundred and twenty furlongs. The soil dug out of this basin was made use of in the embankments along the waterside. When the excavation was finished, she had stones brought, and bordered with them the entire margin of the reservoir. These two things were done, the river made to wind, and the lake excavated, that the stream might be slacker by reason of the number of curves, and the voyage be rendered circuitous, and that at the end of the voyage it might be necessary to skirt the lake and so make a long round. All these works were on that side of Babylon where the passes lay, and the roads into Media were the straightest, and the aim of the queen in making them was to prevent the Medes from holding intercourse with the Babylonians, and so to keep them in ignorance of her affairs."[9]

Just why should a cock-and-bull yarn like this have been given to Herodotus when the very stones and bricks of Babylon cried out against it? The Babylonia that Herodotus saw was almost in it entirely built by Nebuchadnezzar and on most of the bricks, his name was stamped. The very items mentioned as the work of these queens are his works. The temple of Bel-Marduk, itself, was restored and enriched by him.

Why a priesthood should be so ungrateful as to falsify such historical occurrences is utterly without reason unless and until we read Nebuchadnezzar's proclamation in this chapter. If Nebuchadnezzar forsakes Marduk, Marduk's priests will forsake Nebuchadnezzar and blot out his remembrance. This also explains certain historical references concerning Nebuchadnezzar's successors. Berosus included Nebuchadnezzar in his king list but in no way does justice to the greatness of his reign. The priests of Marduk transmitted a more accurate account in their own archives upon which Berosus draws for his history but he compounds Herodotus' error in ascribing the walls of Babylon to Nabonidus; again, priestly propaganda in favor of a polytheistic king and against a greater who was infected with Jehovah worship. One suspects that this is how history is sometimes made or unmade and what we now know to be true may have been largely half truths that have filtered through spiteful and biased minds.

Josephus comments, in part,

". . . in the third book of his Chaldean history wherein he (Berosus) complains of the Grecian writers for supposing without foundation that Babylon was built by Semiramis. After his death (i.e., Labashi Marduk's) the conspirators got together and by common consent put the crown on the head of Nabonidus a man of Babylon and one who belonged to that insurrection; in his reign it was that the walls of the city of Babylon were curiously built with burnt brick and bitumen."

Here Josephus has fallen for the same propaganda. To return to our theme: Nebuchadnezzar's mental syndrome would probably be called boanthropy, a form of paranoia and similar in dynamics to another very rare form of paranoia, lycanthropy, where the individual imagines himself to be a wolf. This type of mental disease is so extremely rare that many psychiatrists have never seen a case in a lifetime of practice. It is a delusional condition that develops slowly and over a period of years, becomes organized into an unassailable system of thinking in which the individual's actions, habits and traits are consistent with the central delusion. Most paranoid states are usually delusions of grandeur or persecution. Coleman sums it up:

"Paranoia is an intricate, logical, systematized and slowly developing delusional system centering primarily around delusions of persecution and or grandeur. Aside from the delusions, the patient's personality remains relatively intact, with no evidence of serious personality disorganization."[10]

It seems evident that Nebuchadnezzar's condition does not conform to this definition in several particulars. While the delusion is systematized in Nebuchadnezzar's case (i.e., he thinks of himself as an ox), it does not seem to have been of slow growth but came upon him suddenly. It was characterized neither by feelings of persecution nor of grandeur and involves serious personality disorganization. In fact, it is an inversion of his feelings of pride and accomplishment which were tangible and obvious realities.

Furthermore, again quoting Coleman:

". . we find that in the great majority of cases the dynamic core of the disorder centers around unbearable feelings of inferiority and inadequacy, growing out of a failure to achieve the aspirations and goals which the individual has adopted and considers his just due."[11]

Of course, this does not fit Nebuchadnezzar's case at all. Nor does his diseased mental pattern conform any more closely to the delusions of the schizophrenic (unsystematized and inconsistent delusions) or to depressive delusions. Concerning the latter, Rosen and Gregory write:

"Acute depressives suffer from delusional distortions of reality. Characteristically, the delusions consist of false self accusation, a conviction of worthlessness, and nihilism, the belief that the self and external reality have ceased to exist."[12]

The mood or affect, not the delusion, is the important factor here. It will be seen then that this madness does not conform to the definition of any paranoid state neither does it seem to fit into any description of New Testament cases of demon possession. It is not possible, in our limited space, to give all the possibilities or variations from the norm that might be thought of; there are so few cases of boanthropy, that comparisons are difficult to make. R.K. Harrison describes a case of boanthropy that came under his observation in a British mental institution in 1946. This individual's only food was grass but otherwise there was nothing particularly animal-like in his behavior.[13]

William Blake, the English artist, has given us a most dramatic picture of Nebuchadnezzar. The king is on all fours, his hair and beard long and matted, his nails like bird's claws but instead of a bovine expression on his face, it is the face of one tormented and unable to comprehend the thing that has happened to him. For dramatic effect and it truly is dramatic, the artist has chosen to give us the aspect of one possessed. Verisimilitude has been sacrificed for dramatic effect, though the effect is truly dramatic.

Nebuchadnezzar's insanity, if it can be called such, does not follow the usual mental dynamics and is obviously an "act of God" and unique. It has no affinity with Saul's madness with its murderous overtones nor with any Old or New Testament pattern of demon possession though it more closely resembles the latter than it does ordinary paranoid conditions. Daniel tells us that Nebuchadnezzar's madness was a direct visitation from God and Nebuchadnezzar, in this most unusual, original document confirms this.

Whether Nebuchadnezzar roamed free or was confined during his madness,[14] he undoubtedly was seen by many of the court. How anyone, observing the groveling, demented creature, stripped of all dignity and humanity could ever again see in him the majestic lord of empire, arbiter of life and death, determiner of destiny would indeed seem to be an impossibility. A fallen idol or a deposed and dehumanized king must seemingly dispense with future glory and majesty. Not so here. What God ·gave and then took away He has abundantly restored. We read,

At the same time my reason returned to me; and for the glory of my kingdom, mine honor and brightness returned to me; and my counselors and my lords sought unto me; and I was established in my kingdom, and excellent majesty was added unto me. (4:36)

Nebuchadnezzar has, moreover, come to a knowledge and acceptance of Jehovah. The disciplines of God are curative for those He loves. For those who accept Him, there is always a tomorrow. For He says, *"Now I Nebuchadnezzar praise and extol and honor the King of heaven, all whose works are truth, and His ways justice; and those that walk in pride He is able to abase" (4:37).*

Jehovah, King of heaven, has supplanted Marduk, *"lord of the gods."*

According to Daniel 4:4 and 4:30, Nebuchadnezzar's insanity must have come near the end of his reign, at least after his building exploits were complete. Therefore, we need to find a gap of seven years in his schedule where his presence was not otherwise demanded. There is a gap of seven or eight years between his eleventh and nineteenth years (594-597) but he could hardly have finished his building projects so early in his reign. There is a similar gap of six years from his thirty-seventh to his forty- third year (568-562) but this does not give us the seven years we need. The most likely solution would seem to be to find the seven year period during the siege of Tyre (585-573 B.C.) assuming that a siege of that length against a weaker antagonist would be carried on by a competent field commander with Nebuchadnezar in absentia. His presence at the beginning and end of the siege would be much more important than it would be during a long drawn-out stalemate of thirteen years. It is even possible that Neriglissar (Nergal Sharezar), his son-in-law, was the general in charge during this period (or Nebuzaraden perhaps). All this explanation, of course, is needed on the assumption that "the seven times" are seven years, as we would expect, rather than seven months or any other period of seven. We should reject the interpretation that would make this period to be months or weeks on the ground that his physical changes described in verse 33 could hardly have taken place in weeks or months; i.e., "til his hairs were grown like eagle's feathers and his nails like bird's claws." Furthermore, elsewhere in Daniel, the term "times" is most reasonably interpreted as "years" and we would hardly expect a prophet to change horses in midstream.

We must call attention to another aspect of Nebuchadnezzar's insanity and humiliation: the effect upon his family, his wife, his sons and daughter.

In the face of so disastrous but so impressive, a witness of Jehovah's power and mercy following upon the witness of Nebuchadnezzar's dream and the rescue of the three youths from the fiery furnace, could anyone doubt that his wife and children would be profoundly affected? There could be no emotional indifference on their part. These events must be either the beginning of a greater spiritual understanding or on the other hand, must be rejected and resented. The God who performs these miracles must be believed in and accepted or He must be hated. Nebuchadnezzar himself witnesses to his own belief. His son Avil Marduk, "lifted up the head of the captive Jehoiachin" and "spoke kindly to him, and set his throne above the thrones of the kings that were with him in Babylon." Would this not indicate that the son's reaction partook of the same faith? If the queen mother of Daniel 5 is Amytis then she, too, witnesses for Jehovah and for His prophet. As to Labashi Marduk, son of Neriglissar and Nebuchadnezzar's daughter, who was assassinated after nine months of reign, was he too a believer through the witness of a faithful mother?

Both Avil Marduk and Labashi Marduk, scions of the prestigious house of Nebuchadnezzar, were done to death by assassins, with the alibi that "they knew not how to reign," an alibi which is neither specific nor convincing. If we add to this the putative assassination of Belshazzar, the last of the family line, there is at least a hint that the family of Nebuchadnezzar might have been marked for extinction by the Marduk priesthood and to add insult to injury, the name of Nebuchadnezzar, himself, and his successors would insofar as possible, be blotted out from official remembrance as per the story told Herodotus concerning the exploits of two queens otherwise of no renown.

When we come to assess the life of Nebuchadnezzar, we may have an ambivalent reaction. If we are looking for his faults, this great monarch may seem to present a bad profile. Is he after all, a typical oriental monarch, using unlimited power in an entirely arbitrary way without regard to justice and devoid of mercy? The evidence for this view is impressive; (1) He captured Jerusalem, burned the temple and the king's palace to the ground, leveled the city walls and carried a large part of the population into captivity and slavery. (Jeremiah 39:6, 50:17.) (2) When he captured Jerusalem, Jeremiah states that he slew all the Jewish nobles. (3) He killed King Zedekiah's sons before his face then put out the king's eyes and carried him off to prison in Babylon where he remained during Nebuchadnezzar's lifetime. (Jeremiah 52:10, 31.)

All of this in addition to the things we have discussed here.

Having said all this, we find that there is another Nebuchadnezzar. We find a man who:

(1) Inherited an unstable kingdom and founded an empire, who, though for the first part of his reign, was continually at war and usually successful, did not love war for its own sake and apparently took no pride in his conquests. Scripture says that he was an instrument in God's hands to chastise the wicked nations of Egypt, Tyre, and Israel and to bring order and peace.

(2) While it is very true that many of the common people of the nations that he carried to Babylon lived a life of slavery (burning his brick, raising his walls, building his palaces, his temples, his quays, his great flood control reservoirs), it must be remembered that these nationals were in Babylon because of iniquity and apostasy. After all, we read of his committing no barbarities on these unfortunates comparable with the cruelties of the Assyrians.

(3) He was in no way the luxurious and indolent king whose life was one of self-gratification. He seems to have been a man of ceaseless energy who not only reconquered an empire and built two wonders of the world but restored agriculture, opened canals for irrigation, rebuilt temples and brought peace, order and prosperity to his empire.

(4) His training (and treatment) of the four young Jews who were educated in his palace, was generous and altogether kingly. Daniel 1:5.

(5) In his own pagan way, he showed not only piety but moral and spiritual understanding, and he acknowledges sin and mistakes. Daniel 4.

(6) He seems to have changed from an ardent polytheist to a true recognition and worship of Jehovah. Daniel 4.

(7) His hanging gardens were built for his queen, Amytis. This might seem to indicate that, instead of the more or less numberless concubines by which an oriental monarch satisfied his lust, he may have been monogamous. There is no mention of other wives or concubines as there is in the case of Belshazzar (i.e., Daniel 5:2).

(8) Nebuchadnezzar is disciplined by God but not destroyed and he responds to that discipline in a way not unworthy of a pious Jew or a modern Christian. Apparently, God thought it possible to deal with this man for the salvation of his soul.

(9) How can we avoid God's assessment of him when he speaks of him as *"my servant"* (Jeremiah 27:6) and *"head of gold"* (Daniel 2:38)? This is language that goes beyond Jehovah's characterization of the Assyrian in Isaiah, Chapter 10. When we consider that Jehovah has given him rule over the nations of men, the birds of the heaven and the beasts of the field (Daniel 2:38) and that God Himself gives him *"a kingdom, power, strength and glory"* (Daniel 2:37), we must give Nebuchadnezzar an exceptional rating.

(10) His cruelties to Zedekiah and his nobles were to men who persecuted their own prophets, who made treaties and broke them; his proposed destruction of the *"wise men"* may be partly excused as fear of assassination and revolt; his punishment of the three Hebrew youths may have been psychologically related to the revolt in his army.

Rawlinson, quoting Eusebius, says:

"The Chaldeans relate, says Abydenus, that after this Nebuchadnezzar went up to his palace, and being seized with a divine afflatus, prophesied to the Babylonians the destruction of their city by the Medes and Persians after which he suddenly disappeared from among them."

The character of Nebuchadnezzar, the length of his reign, the fact of his having uttered prophecies, are points in which there is a remarkable agreement between the sacred and profane authorities. The splendor and magnificence which this prince displayed, his military successes, his devotion to his gods, and the pride which he took in adorning Babylon with great buildings, are noted by Berosus and Abydenus.

Rawlinson goes on to say, with reference to the passage of Abydenus,

"The details are incorrect but it is at least that the particular prince, who alone of all the heathen monarchs with whom the Jews were brought in contact is said in Scripture to have had the future made known to him by God, is also the only one of those persons who is declared to have had the prophetic gift by a profane writer."[15]

Goodspeed has summed up something of the material accomplishments of Nebuchadnezzar:

"If the knowledge of Nebuchadnezzar's wars and the administration of his empire must be derived largely from others than himself, the case is different with respect to his activity in Babylonia. To this long inscriptions are devoted, and small tablets, stamps, and bricks from many famous sites add their testimony. He describes, particularly, his building operations in the city of Babylon, the fortifications, the palaces, and the temples reared by him. Utility and adornment were his guiding principles, but not without the deeper motives of piety and patriotism. In Babylonia at large, he labored at the restoration of the canal system, so important for agriculture, commerce and defense. One canal which was restored by him led from the Euphrates south of Hit directly to the gulf through the centre of Babylonia: another on the west of the Euphrates opened up to irrigation and agriculture the edge of the Arabian desert.

"The river as it passed along before Babylon, was lined with bricks laid with bitumen, which at low water are visible today. The city canals were similarly treated. Those connecting the two rivers and extending through the land between them were reopened. A system of basins, dykes, and dams guarded and guided the waters of the rivers, works so various and colossal as to excite the admiration of the Greeks who saw or heard of them.

"A system of defenses was planned by the erection of a great wall in north Babylonia stretching from the Euphrates to the Tigris; it was flanked east and west by a series of ramparts of earth and moats filled with water, and extended southward as far as Nippur. It was called the Median wall. Restorations of temples were made in Borsippa, Sippar, Ur, Uruk, Larsa, Dilbat and Baz. More than forty temples and shrines are mentioned in the inscriptions as receiving attention. Bricks bearing the king's name are said to come from every site in Babylonia, from Bagdad to the mouth of the rivers. He may well stand as the greatest builder of all the kings of the Mesopotamian valley."[16]

CHRONOLOGY OF NEBUCHADNEZZAR'S LIFE

635-630 (?), Possible date of Nebuchadnezzar's birth.

614 --, Capture of Assur and possible betrothal to Amytis, daughter of Astyages, King of Media.

612 --, Capture of Nineveh and possible marriage with Amytis.

605 --, Capture of Carchemish and defeat of Egypt; invasion of Judah, taking of some of the vessels of the temple and taking hostage Daniel, Mishael, Hananiah, and Azariah.

605 - 8th Ab., Nabopolassar dies after reign of twenty-one years.

605 --, Elul, Nebuchadnezzar returns to Babylon and ascends to the throne.

604 --, Accession year; Nebuchadnezzar takes the hands of Bel and Nabu and in Nisan, celebrates New Year festival.

604 --, Sivan, Nebuchadnezzar and army in Syria; Kislev, Nebuchadnezzar sacks Ashkelon; Sebat, Nebuchadnezzar returns to Babylon.

603 --, Iyyar, second year with army in Syria and the dream of Chapter 2.

602 --, Third year with army in Syria.

601 --, Kislev, fourth year, great battle with Egypt, inconclusive; Necho II exacted tribute from Jehoiakim.

600 --, Fifth year, rebuilding the army and assembling horses and chariots.

599 --, Kislev, sixth year, army in Syria and Arabia.

598 --, Kislev, siege of Jerusalem.

597 --, Second Adar, capture of Jerusalem, Zedekiah made king, Nebuchadnezzar took tribute and captives.

596 --, Eighth year, marches to Syria and returns.

596 --, Ninth year, against the Elamites on the Tigris.

595 --, Kislev, tenth year, rebellion in the army, leader killed and rebels also.

594 --, Eleventh year, army in Syria.

587--, Eighteenth year, Nebuzaradan, with no mention of Nebuchadnezzar's presence in siege of Jerusalem.

587 --, Nineteenth year, destruction of Jerusalem, beginning of Desolations.

582 --, Twenty-third year, Nebuzaradan carried captive; final group of Jews.

585-573 --, Thirty-third year, siege and capture of Paleotyre and possible interval of insanity, seven years in a period of twelve or thirteen years' siege.

572 --, Thirty-fourth year, invasion; Syria, Ammon, Moab; killed Apries (Hophra, king of Egypt).

568-567 --, Thirty-seventh year, invasion of Egypt.

562 --, Forty-second or forty-third year, Nebuchadnezzar's death.[17]

CHAPTER VI
THE END OF A DYNASTY
BELSHAZZAR'S FEAST

(Daniel 5; Place, Babylon; Date, Month of Tammuz, June,
539 B.C.; Language, Aramaic)

Twenty-three years have elapsed since the death of Nebuchadnezzar in 562 or 561 B.C. Upon his death, Nebuchadnezzar was succeeded by his son, Avil Marduk (Evil-Merodach of Scripture) who after a reign of two years, was murdered by his brother-in-law, Neriglissar. This Neriglissar may be the same person as Nergalsharezer mentioned in Jeremiah 39:3. The later comment made by Nabonidus that Avil Marduk was not fit to rule, is made without explaining why. Here we may have a further indication that Avil Marduk may have been "infected" with Jehovah worship or sympathies at least, to the point where priests of Marduk were being neglected. We have indicated elsewhere that those who write the history or who are the custodians of it, may have the last word. Scripture does not refer to Avil Marduk in a derogatory way but on the contrary, speaks of his having lifted up the head of Jehoiachin, King of Judah, out of a prison (II Kings 25:27-29). Why? Why should he have reversed his father's policy of repression and neglect?

And it came to pass in the seven and thirtieth year of the captivity of Jehoiachin king of Judah, in the twelfth month, on the seven and twentieth day of the month, that Evil-Merodach king of Babylon in the year that he began to reign did lift up the head of Jehoiachin king of Judah out of prison; And he spake kindly to him, and set his throne above the throne of the kings that were with him in Babylon; And changed his prison garments: and he did eat bread continually before him all the days of his life.

Whether he was an unfit king or not (and we may well doubt that he was not), he at least attempted to undo the severity of his father, Nebuchadnezzar toward Jehoiachin and even more, honored him above all captive monarchs. As we have indicated, Avil Marduk was murdered by his brother-in-law after a reign of two years. We have a brief record of Neriglissor's reign, showing him to have been an able general in his campaign in Cilicia, Asia Minor, in the years 557-556 B.C.

Neriglissar was apparently acceptable to the priesthood but died after four years and was succeeded by his young son, Labashi Marduk, who after nine months of reign was himself deposed and murdered by Nabonidus (son of the priest, Nabu-balat-su-iqbi and of a high priestess of the god, Sin, at Haran). He was not of the royal line or of Chaldean descent but evidently identified his family with the line by marriage to a relative of Nebuchadnezzar.

We quote:

"When the days were fulfilled and he had gone the way of fate, Labashi-Marduk, his younger son, who knew not how to rule, took his seat against the will of the gods upon the royal throne, and to the palace (?) they brought me, and all of them threw themselves at my feet and kissed them, doing homage to my royal rule. By command of Marduk, my Lord, I was raised to the rule over the land, while they cried out, 'Father of the land! He has no equal!'"[1]

Somewhere during this interval (i.e., between Nebuchadnezzar's death and Nabonidus' accession), the alliance with the Medes had gone by the board. The Medean treaty, cemented by the marriage of Nebuchadnezzar and Amytis, which had guaranteed Babylon's eastern boundaries and eastern caravan routes had been (apparently) not only abrogated but had been handled in such a way that the Medes had now become the chief enemies of the Babylonian empire. As the fifth chapter opens, though not stated in Scripture, the Medes and Persians had just defeated Belshazzar in battle at Opis and are now ready to begin the apparently hopeless task of capturing the impregnable city of Babylon, a city undoubtedly well provisioned with its water supply secure and its regent king, Belshazzar, though defeated in the open field, confident in its strong walls, its ancient gods, its prestige and its manifest destiny.

If we may go back seventeen years at this point, we find that the first seven years of the reign of Nabonidus (the time spent in Babylon, possibly) had been characterized by archaeological interests, the rebuilding of old temples and the identification of the royal family not with Marduk, the chief god of Babylon alone but with Shamash, the sun god (and possibly with the moon god, Sin). History is not very clear as to when King Nabonidus turned over the government of Babylonia to his son, Belshazzar. Whether he was deposed or abdicated voluntarily, he is still the titular king. When he captured Tema in Arabia and began to rebuild it, we do not exactly know. What we do know is that the records indicate that from the seventh year to the eleventh year of his reign, it is specifically stated that Nabonidus was in Tema (548-544 B.C.). We have the following,

"7th year. The king in Tema; the son of the king, the nobles and his soldiers in Akkad. (The king for Nisan) did not come to Babylon. Nabu did not come to Babylon; Bel was not brought forth and the akitu-festival (was not celebrated). They offered (gave) sacrifices in Esagila and Ezida to the gods of Babylon and Borsippa as is (right); the urigal poured out libations and guarded the house.

"8th year/9th year. Nabonidus, the king, in Tema; the son of the king, the nobles, and the soldiers in Akkad. The king did not come to Babylon for Nisan. Nabu did not come to Babylon; Bel was not brought forth, and the akitu-festival was not celebrated. They offered sacrifices in Esagila and Ezida to the gods of Babylon and Borsippa as is right.

"The month Nisan. The fifth day. The mother of the king died in Durkarashu, which is on the bank of the Euphrates above Sippar. The son of the king and his soldiers mourned three days. A lamentation was arranged. In Sivan, in Akkad, a lamentation for the mother of the king was arranged.

"In Nisan, Cyrus, King of Parsu, mustered his troops, and crossed over the Tigris below Arbela. He slew its king (and) took away its possessions. He stationed his own garrison there. After this time his garrison remained there with that of the king.

"10th year. The king in Tema; the son of the king, the nobles, and his troops in Akkad. (the king did not come to Babylon for Nisan.) Nabu did not come to Babylon; Bel was not brought forth, and the akitu-festival was not celebrated. In (Esaglia and Ezida) they offered sacrifices to the gods of Babylon and Borsippa, as is right. In Sivan, on the twenty-first day . . . of Elammiya in Akkad . . . the representative in Uruk . . .

"11th year. The king in Tema; the son of the king, the nobles, and his troops in Akkad. (The king did not come to Babylon for Nisan.) (Nabu did not come to) Babylon; Bel was not brought forth, and the akitu-festival was not celebrated. Sacrifices (in Esagila and Ezida.)"[2]

One of the former stumbling blocks to the Book of Daniel was this same Belshazzar who according to many critics, not only was not king but did not exist in the records. Harrison says succinctly,

"Yet another objection to the historicity of Daniel has involved the relationship between Belshazzar and Nabonidus. According to Daniel, the former was king, whereas in the cunieform records it was Nabonidus, father of Belshazzar, who was actually the ruler of the Neo-Babylonian Empire before it fell to Cyrus in 539 B.C.

"This difficulty has been resolved by archeological discoveries that have shown that for much of the reign of Nabonidus, his eldest son Belshazzar acted as co-regent. When Nabonidus took up residence in Tema, Belshazzar exercised sole rule in Babylonia and, for this reason, was represented as the last king of Babylon in Daniel (Daniel 5:30).

"The reference in Daniel 5:18 to Belshazzar as a son of Nebuchadnezzar is also correct according to Semitic usage where the term 'son' could also mean 'grandson' for which there was no separate word, or simply 'descendant' or 'offspring.' As far as ancient royalty was concerned, the interest was predominately in the succession itself, rather than in the actual lineal relationship of individuals. In any event, according to Dougherty, Nitocris, the mother of Belshazzar was apparently the daughter of Nebuchadnezzar which would make for lineal descent as represented in Daniel."[3]

The following text gives Belshazzar status as regent and co-king:

"He entrusted a camp to his eldest, first born son; the troops of the land he sent with him. He freed his hand; entrusted the kingship to him. Then he, himself, undertook a distant campaign, the power of the land of Akkad advanced with him; toward Tema in the midst of the Westland he set his face. He undertook a distant campaign on a road not within reach of the old. He slew the prince of Tema with the sword; the dwellers in his city and country, all of them they slaughtered. Then he, himself, his dwelling in Tema; the power of the land of Akkad ... that city he made glorious, he made . . .; they made it like the palace of Babylon . . ."[4]

From the eleventh year on, there is no record until we come to the year of the fall of Babylon in the seventeenth year of Nabonidus' reign (539 B.C.). Apparently, he has come back to aid, futilely, the defense of Babylon upon the invasion of the Medo-Persian forces and as we have said above, Belshazzar, his son, has just been defeated in the field.

The fifth chapter opens then with Belshazzar's feast for a thousand of his merchant princes and their wives and concubines. The wine flows freely and confident of the high walls and the impregnable defenses of Babylon, they do not neglect to praise Babylonian gods perhaps Shamash the sun god, especially. They are offering praise, not petition, for the city is accounted impregnable.

The second verse introduces for us a question. With all the temple plunder from Tyre and Thebes, from Carchemish and the other cities, why is the king moved to bring out the sacred temple vessels of Jehovah and not the captured trophies of other temples and other gods? We may only infer the answer but as we have indicated in the previous chapters, we may have here a priestly-inspired reaction against the last lingering memories of Jehovah's witness to Babylon through Daniel. Belshazzar is here throwing down the challenge: Babylonia's gods are greater than Jehovah since Babylon has conquered Israel and has left Israel's land desolate. In like manner, Babylonian gods will now smite the Persians.

The fifth verse of the chapter gives us God's answer to this pagan challenge,

In the same hour came forth fingers of a man's hand, and wrote over against the candlestick upon the plaster of the wall of the king's palace: and the king saw the part of the hand that wrote.

We have the following description by Robert Koldewey in his writings of the ruins of Babylon,

"To the south lies the largest chamber of the citadel (king's palace, the throne room of the Babylonian kings.) It is so clearly marked out for this purpose that no reasonable doubt can be felt as to its having been used as their principal audience chamber. If anyone should desire to localize the scene of Belshazzar's eventful banquet, he can surely place it with complete accuracy in this immense room. It is seventeen meters broad and fifty-two meters long. The walls on the longest side are six meters thick, considerably in excess of those at the ends, and lead us to suppose that they supported a barrel vaulting, of which, however, there is no proof. A great central door and two equally important side doors open on the court. Immediately opposite the main door in the back wall there is a doubly recessed niche in which doubtless the throne stood, so that the king could be visible to those who stood in the court, an arrangement similar to that of the Ninmach temple where the temple statue could be clearly seen from the court. The pavement does not consist in the usual manner of a single layer of brick but of at least six, which were laid in asphalt and thus formed a homogenious solid platform which rested on a projecting ledge built out from the walls. As we have aleady seen from the east gate, the walls of these chambers were washed over with gypsum."[5]

Kildeway goes on to say:

"The facade of the court was very strikingly decorated with richly ornamented enamel bricks. On a dark blue ground are yellow columns with bright blue capitals placed near together and connected by a series of palmettos. The capitals with the bold curves of their double volutes remind us of the forms long ago known to us in Cyprus.[6]

A floor plan of the throne room and courtyard is seen on the opposite page. Though written in a far different spirit, we are reminded of the quatrain of Omar, the tentmaker,

> "The moving finger writes, and having writ;
> Moves on nor all your piety nor wit
> Shall lure it back to cancel half a line
> Nor all your tears wash out a word of it."

In the sixth verse the bravado and the defiance of the king suddenly disappears.

The king's countenance was changed, and his thoughts troubled him, so that the joints of his loins were loosed, and his knees smote one against another.

The gods whom the king was extolling are now called upon, through their priesthood, to solve the mystery of the writing hand. And now the king brings in the forecasters to solve this strange and unwelcome, supernatural phenomenon.

The king cried aloud to bring in the astrologers, the Chaldeans, and the soothsayers. And the king spake, and said to the wise men of Babylon, Whosoever shall read this writing, and shew me the interpretation thereof, shall be clothed with scarlet, and have a chain of gold about his neck, and shall be the third ruler in the kingdom. (7)

There is very much significance in this verse which used to be a stumbling block to biblical interpreters. First, here is an acknowledgment that great honor, even the third rulership in the kingdom, shall be given to the one who can interpret. This unprecedented honor indicated the degree of fear and apprehension felt by the king. Secondly, it would seem to imply that his father, Nebonidus, has not yet been captured and is still in the city as titular king. Thirdly, a "third ruler" implies a first ruler, Nebonidus, and a second, Belshazzar.

Then came in all the king's wise men: but they could not read the writing, nor make known to the king the interpretation thereof (8).

As in all the other instances where Jehovah's hand is manifest in this book of Daniel, it is a Jew that must read and interpret. That Jew is Daniel. God does not commit the secret of His designs to the unbeliever, then as now, "The natural man receiveth not the things of the Spirit of God . . . neither can he know them."

Then was king Belshazzar greatly troubled, and his countenance was changed in him, and the lords were astonished. (9).

The tenth verse brings us to the question of the person of the queen. There are several women who come to mind as we read the clause "now the queen . . . came." The following are persons to whom the term could be appropriate:

(1) The wife of Belshazzar may be indicated though we are informed that the wives and the concubines of the king are already at the feast (v. 3). This person comes into the feast.

(2) The wife of Nabonidus may have left her husband's side for the safety of Babylon. Since she may have been a daughter or granddaughter of Nebuchadnezzar, she would also have known Daniel. If so, however, she would (at least in the absence of contrary evidence) have been in sympathy with the attitudes of her husband and her son, also she would doubtless have been at the feast.

(3) The wife of Neriglissar, as daughter of Nebuchadnezzar, is a possibility though in the absence of other evidence, not a probability since nothing indicates her survival of her husband's death or her outstanding faith (even though she is a daughter of Nebuchadnezzar).

(4)The wife of Avil Marduk, son of Nebuchadnezzar could be the one. We know nothing about her and there is nothing to suggest her importance or prestige even if she survived the murder of her husband.

(5) The wife of Labashi Marduk. Here, again, we are in the dark. But as the very young wife of a very young king who reigned only nine months before his murder, she seems out of the question. Her prestige could not have been great.

(6) Amytis, widow of Nebuchadnezzar, wife of the greatest monarch of antiquity and herself a king's daughter. If it were she, however, she

must have been of great age since it is twenty-four years since the death of Nebuchadnezzar who reigned forty-three years. If she was sixteen or eighteen at the time of her marriage, her present age would be from eighty-three to eighty-five. However, she most nearly meets the conditions of sufficient knowledge of Daniel's part and prestige in Nebuchadnezzar's reign and memories of the power of Daniel's God. She also most nearly fulfills Josephus' statement:

"Now when the king's grandmother saw him cast down at this accident, she began to encourage him and to say that there was a certain captive who came from Judea, a Jew by birth but brought away thence by Nebuchadnezzar when he had destroyed Jerusalem whose name was Daniel, a wise man, and one of great sagacity in finding out what was impossible for others to discover and what was known to God alone, who brought to light and answered such questions to Nebuchadnezzar as no one else was able to answer when they were consulted."[7]

According to Josephus, she was the King's grandmother, probably Amytis.[8]

Who then is the queen? Evidently someone who has not only a clear remembrance of the days when Daniel was governor of Babylon but one who had come to appreciate and to believe in him and whose prestige gave her an instant hearing. Whichever of these it may be, it still further seems to point to the fact that Jehovah's witness to the house of Nebuchadnezzar was not in vain. For this woman, in her speech to Belshazzar, is not at all equivocal in her testimony. When we consider that (1) she is not a part of the feast, (2) she at once refers to Daniel as a source of help and testifies as to his having the spirit of the holy God, and (3) speaks familiarly of Daniel's position as head of the magicians, Chaldeans, astrologers and soothsayers, all of these would confirm the feeling that two strong, antagonistic tendencies had been struggling within the royal dynasty: pressures to worship the old gods and the reactions against such worship because of the witness of Jehovah to Babylon.

Do we have here, also, a small straw in the wind that might explain why Nabonidus exalts the worship of Shamash above that of Marduk? Daniel's witness may have given rise to a general feeling that Marduk was not the all powerful god that his priesthood had claimed and rather than accept Jehovah, Nabonidus may have exalted Shamash to a position of preeminence. After all, reigning houses normally seek support from all the population and especially thoroughly established, priestly groups. Whatever the reason, the queen's words are significant:

There is a man in thy kingdom, in whom is the spirit of the holy gods and in the days of thy father, light and understanding and wisdom, like the wisdom of the gods, was found in him; whom the king Nebuchadnezzar, thy father, thy king, I say, thy father, made master of the magicians, astrologers, Chaldeans and soothsayers;(11) Forasmuch as an excellent spirit, and knowledge, and understanding, interpreting of dreams, and shewing of hard sentences, and dissolving of doubts, were found in the same Daniel, whom the king named Belteshazzar: now let Daniel be called, and he will shew the interpretation. (12)

We could hardly ask for a better testimony, not only on behalf of Daniel but on behalf of Daniel's God than that of this woman.[9] The narrative continues:

Then was Daniel brought in before the king. And the king spake and said unto Daniel, Art thou that Daniel, which art of the children of the captivity of Judah, whom the king my father brought out of Jewry? (13)

We are moved to ask why Daniel is unknown to Belshazzar.[10] If Daniel had continued as the head of the wise men of Babylon, it would hardly seem necessary for the king to ask who he was. As a matter of fact, we know that in the third year of the reign of Belshazzar, Daniel was at Susa which might indicate that he was no longer in favor though as indicated at the end of the eighth chapter, we know that he is still a part of the civil service (8:27). He may even have been permanently located at Susa. If so, we do not know how he may have gotten back through the Persian lines. In whatever way, we may account for his presence in verses 13 through 17. The king repeats in substance the information given him by the queen mother.

Then Daniel answered and said before the king, Let thy gifts be to thyself, and give thy rewards to another; yet I will read the writing unto the king, and make known to him the interpretation. (17)

If we will refer to the way in which Daniel, in each case, addressed Nebuchadnezzar, there seemed to be both respect and affection but we will see here by comparison, an entirely different tone employed. It is not, "O king live forever." Daniel's reply is straightforward and stern and in oriental terms, even discourteous. He is not speaking for himself but for Jehovah. His reply embodies his understanding of the offended majesty of Jehovah. He gives Jehovah's answer to the challenge and defiance of Belshazzar. His speech begins by reminding Belshazzar that God gave to Nebuchadnezzar, his father (probably his grandfather on his mother's side, which would be the appropriate oriental way of speaking), a kingdom and majesty and glory and honor.

And for the majesty that he gave him, all people, nations, and languages, trembled and feared before him: whom he would he slew; and whom he would he kept alive; and whom he would he set up; and whom he would he put down. (19) But when his heart was lifted up, and his mind hardened in pride, he was deposed from his kingly throne, and they took his glory from him: (20) And he was driven from the sons of men; and his heart was made like the beasts, and his dwelling was with the wild asses:

they fed him grass like oxen, and his body was wet with the dew of heaven; till he knew that the most high God ruled in the kingdom of men, and that he appointeth over it whomsoever he will. (21)

Then we come upon the significant statement in the twenty-second verse:

And thou his son, O Belshazzar, hast not humbled thine heart, though thou knewest all this.

The tradition had not died out. Men still living could easily remember the testimonies of Jehovah to the royal house and to the city of Babylon. After all, it was only twenty-three years since Nebuchadnezzar's death.

But hast lifted up thyself against the Lord of heaven; and they have brought the vessels of His house before thee, and thou, and thy lords, thy wives, and thy concubines, have drunk wine in them; and thou hast praised the gods of silver, and gold, of brass, iron, woods, and stone, which see not, nor hear, nor know: and the God in whose hand thy breath is, and whose are all thy ways, hast thou not glorified. (23)

Then begins the interpretation of the handwriting. The handwriting on the wall, as suggested by Young, would not only have consisted of consonants only but the characters used were unfamiliar and he quotes Charles as saying, "the writing may have consisted of ideograms; for according to the text even expert Babylonian scholars could not decipher it."[11] Whatever was the case, it was necessary that the text be both read and interpreted.

The usual translation of the words "Mene, Mene, Tekel, Peres" indicates that they are capable of double meaning and double interpretation, depending upon the Aramaic vowel points used. Translated and interpreted one way, the words would indicate the Hebrew coins: a mina, a shekel, and a half shekel. These are also names of weights. The interpretation could also mean that which is numbered (repeated for emphasis), that which is weighed and that which is divided. The "Peres," with slightly different vowel ("Paras"), points, could also have the meaning "Persian," so that there is a double play on this word. The word "Upharsin" is made up of the Aramaic word for "and" (U) and the plural for "Paras" (Persian); in other words, "Persians" (plural rather than singular).

In whatever way the consonants were given their vowel points in the translation by Daniel, the whole handwriting was mystifying and incomprehensible to these wise men who supposedly were the repositories of almost everything that was to be known. And even if they had been able to decipher the characters and to read the meaning of the words, they would have been in no position to decide who or what it was that was *"numbered,"* who it was that was *"weighed and found wanting"* and what part the Persians had in the division of somebody's kingdom.

When we come to the interpretation of the handwriting, it seems very simple and very clear when interpreted by Daniel:

This is the interpretation of the thing: MENE; God hath numbered thy kingdom and finished it. (26) TEKEL; Thou art weighed in the balances, and art found wanting. (27) PERES; Thy kingdom is divided, and given to the Medes and Persians. (28)

For eighty-seven years, the Neo-Babylonian kingdom has continued in a blaze of glory. It has had widespread dominion, victory in war, great prosperity and as far as physical resources are concerned, it has the potential of an everlasting existence. But it has been weighed in the balance. On one side of the scales have been demonstrations of Jehovah's power not heretofore given to any other pagan empire as far as we know. Nineveh repented on the mere preaching of Jonah; Babylon, apart from the royal family, has manifested defiance rather than repentance. And so the kingdom whose history goes back three milleniums passes into the hands of the Medes and Persians. For all the kingdom has been given, accountability has now been exacted .

Then commanded Belshazzar, and they clothed Daniel with scarlet, and put a chain of gold about his neck, and made a proclamation concerning him, that he should be the third ruler in the kingdom. (29)

It is sixty-six years since Daniel came to Babylon. He is an old man. We are not entirely clear how much of him went into the establishment and prosperity of the dynasty (probably very much in the days of Nebuchadnezzar and Avil Marduk, probably very little in the days of Neriglissar, Nabonidus and Belshazzar). This much is certain: Babylon had, in addition to the four great miracles, the steadfast, pure and holy life of one of the wisest men of antiquity; namely, Daniel.

In that night was Belshazzar the king of the Chaldeans slain. (30) And Darius, the Mede, took the kingdom, being about three score and two years old. (31)

And this is the end of the posterity of King Nebuchadnezzar as history informs us but when Babylon was taken by Darius and when he, with his kinsman Cyrus, had put an end to the dominion of the Babylonians he was 62 years old. He was the son of Astyages and had another name among the Greeks.[12]

Sit thou silent, and get thee into darkness, O daughter of the Chaldeans; for thou shalt no more be called The lady of kingdoms. I was angry with my people; I have polluted mine inheritance, and given them into thine hand; Thou didst show them no mercy; Upon the ancient hast thou very heavily laid thy yoke.(13) For thou hast trusted in thy wickedness;

*thou hast said, None seeth me. Thy wisdom and thy knowledge, it hath
perverted thee; and thou hast said in thy heart, I am, and none else beside me . . . Stand now with thine enchantments, and with the multitude of
thy sorceries, in which thou hast labored from thy youth, if so be thou shalt
be able to profit, if so be thou mayest prevail. Thou art wearied in the multitude of thy counsels. Let now the astrologers, the stargazers, the month-
ly prognosticators, stand up, and save thee from these things that shall
come upon thee.(14)*

There are several unanswered questions relative to the taking of
Babylon and with it, Belshazzar's death. The accounts in Daniel Chapter 5, the Cyrus cylinder and Nabonidus' annals seem clear enough or at
least, self-consistent when considered separately but are confusing when
evaluated together.

The biblical account in Daniel tells of Belshazzar's death and tells us
when; namely, the night of the banquet. It does not tell us how he died -
only that he was slain. It speaks of the transfer of the kingdom to Darius
the Mede but now how or when. This account speaks of no fighting. The
other two accounts, i.e., the Cyrus cylinder and Nabonidus' annals, very
distinctly say that the city was taken without fighting and that the Persian
troops entered peaceably. These two are in agreement with one another
and not contradictory to the Daniel account. But none mention the slaying of Belshazzar in battle which is very strange if he died defending his
palace, as some would have us believe.

The question for which we need answers are:

(1) Where in the picture do we place Belshazzar's banquet? It is inconceivable that a great state banquet would be given with the city taken
and occupied by Cyrus's troops. It would seem necessary to place the
banquet after the defeat of Belshazzar at Opis and before the taking
of the city. If this is correct, then Belshazzar could not have been
slain by Cyrus' troops. More probably, he was assassinated by the
Babylonians themselves. This would place the surrender of the city
after the assassination, not before.

(2) The second question relates to this: If Belshazzar had been killed
by the troops of Gobryas surely it would have received as much mention
as Nabonidus' capture. This is what the account of Xenophon alleges.
He pictures Belshazzar as being killed defending his palace (Cyropedia
VII, 5, 30). This would make for the renown of Gobryas and Cyrus. Perhaps Xenophon has again confused what happened in later revolts with
the original capture.

(3) We should very much like to know why there was a delay of nearly four months from the taking of the city to Cyrus' entry (16 Tammuz to
3 Marchesvan, Nabonidus's Annals).

(4) It would be of interest to know why, with Belshazzar dead,

Nabonidus failed to rally the army remaining in the city either to avenge his son's death or to defend the city. Was he, too, betrayed? Was he completely inept? Or was public confidence in him so low that people would not follow his leadership? That he was not present at Belshazzar's banquet makes it evident that he did not have his son's backing and had to act alone, if we may draw inferences from silence.

That Nabonidus was not popular with the Marduk priesthood is abundantly clear from the Cyrus cylinder. That he would hardly have been known to the population at large because of his long stay in Tema is also probable. However, a whole city does not refuse to defend itself ordinarily if it has a leadership that it respects and trusts.

The picture that seems to emerge is somewhat as follows:

(1) Belshazzar was defeated at Opis and returned to Babylon (Annals).

(2) Belshazzar gave a state banquet to reassure the nobles and the city at large that their city was impregnable.

(3) The handwriting on the wall predicted the end of the Chaldean kingdom.

(4) Somewhere in the picture, Nabonidus was defeated at Sippar and had already returned to Babylon. But whether it was before or after the banquet is in doubt. If before, why was he not at the banquet? The Cyrus cylinder seems to place his capture after the city was taken.

(5) The assassination of Belshazzar that night was contrived by the priests of Marduk who were possibly present at the banquet.

(6) The gates were opened by the conspirators who had previous contact with Gobryas or Cyrus.

(7) Gobryas entered the city and captured Nabonidus who was also undoubtedly betrayed into his hands.

(8) Gobryas quietly occupies the city, interfering as little as possible with its normal business activities and the Marduk priesthood aids with their influence and propaganda. In the absence of any royal leadership, no defense was attempted by the population.

(9) Cyrus entered the city four months later - a city going about its normal business, the Marduk priesthood re-established in its wonted preeminence and a people (not particularly devoted to its former rulers) ready to accept a conqueror who apparently had the approval of Marduk. Their acquiescence was easier because there were no battle scars, no casualties, no plundering of people or temple and no royal leadership with sufficient prestige to lead opposition. If it be objected that the view of treachery and assassination is not the proper answer, we would reply that implicit in the Cyrus cylinder, we have a defense of Marduk and by implication, his priesthood. Marduk was angry; therefore, the city fell. If

this is an insufficient hint as to the course of events or if the theory of assassination seems a little remote, we only need to recall the previous assassination of two others of the royal line; Avil Merodoch and Labashi Marduk as previously indicated.

Goodspead came to the same conclusions, when he said:

"Cyrus' attack on the great system of defenses was made at Upi (Opis) at the junction of the Tigris and the Turnat, where he broke through and stood on Babylonian soil in October 539 B.C. Belshazzar and his army were beaten back; Nabuna'id sought in vain to organize the people for defense. Sippar was taken early in October and the king fled to Babylon, closely pursued by a detachment of the Persians under Gubaru (Gobryas). It might be well thought that the broad and lofty walls of the capital would long withstand the assaults of an enemy; the narrative of Herodotus (I, 190, 191) tells how, after a tedious siege, Cyrus, in despair, set about diverting the main channel of the Euphrates and by marching his troops into the city through the river gates, thus laid open, took the defenders by surprise and captured the city. Nothing however, could have been further from the actual event. Gubaru found friends within the walls who opened the gates soon after his arrival; Babylon fell into the hands of the Persians without a struggle. So deeply had the feuds of parties, ecclesiastical and political, eaten into the body politic that the capital was betrayed by its own citizens."[13]

In examining our sources of information, we see immediately that they are in conflict to a greater or lesser degree. Of the three sources nearest the event (namely; Daniel Chapter 5, the Annals of Nabonidus and the Cyrus cylinder), all of which seem to be contemporary accounts by those who were eyewitnesses of the events described, there are differences as to detail. We are not quite sure, however, how soon after the events the latter two records were made. A lag of two or three years in transcribing them would remove some of our later difficulties with reference to the identity of Darius.

Of the later and secondary sources, Herodotus (484-425 B.C.) and Xenophon (435-355 B.C.) both of whom had to depend on hearsay from approximately similar types of sources, we find disagreement not only with one another but with the primary sources and they can be depended upon only when their account could be checked against primary sources. The same could be said about Berosus (260 B.C.), Abydenus (268 B.C.) and Ctesias (a contemporary of Xenophon) who had to depend upon sources much more remote than their own times.

When we see therefore, disagreements among competent, modern commentators, we realize that the differences between them are due to value judgments relative to their faith in the sources of evidence to which they had access. To what historian and to what evidence, shall greater weight be given?

To those of us who accept the prophecy of Daniel at face value as the completely true and inspired Word of God, we still have difficulty in equating with it contemporary evidence that is explicit even though it carries on its face evidence of bias. The prophecy of Daniel does not tell us all that we would like to know only because that was not the main thrust of the message. Taken separately, if we consult the biblical account of Belshazzar's last night, we have no problem; if we read the annals of Nabonidus alone, again no problem; but when we try to reconcile the two, we run into apparent difficulties.

The picture that we usually envision from Daniel's account is not necessarily that of a banquet given in the face of impending doom, recognized by all. The scene is one of seeming security. On the other hand, Nabonidus' annals quite definitely tell us that on the sixteenth of Tammuz (June, July), Gobryas and the troops of Cyrus entered Babylon without a battle; and on the third of Marchesvan, four months later (October, November), Cyrus himself entered Babylon.

Now if Belshazzar was slain by the Persians, it must have been sometime between the time that Gobryas entered and the entry of Cyrus when the troops of Cyrus would have been in the city nearly four months. In a city so vast, it might be argued that taking complete control could take weeks of fighting and even with the Persians in the city, the issue might long remain in doubt if the Babylonian troops and citizens chose to defend it, street by street and canal by canal. But the account distinctly says:

"On the third day of the month Marchesvan Cyrus entered Babylon. The harine (Babylonian troops) lay down before him. Peace was established for the city. Cyrus proclaimed peace to all Babylon."[16]

There is, we see, a mystery surrounding the death of Belshazzar that involves the questions, Why? When? By whom? Let us consider the last question first. The biblical account merely says, "that same night was Belshazzar king of the Chaldeans slain." When we realize that his father, Nabonidus, was not slain after his capture but sent to honorable retirement in Carmania, we wonder why the same mercy was not shown to the son; that is, if he were captured by the Persians. And, as we see, he could not have been slain fighting the Persians if there was no fighting. The question of when Belshazzar was slain not only involve the problem as a whole but there is an apparent contradiction between our two primary sources of information; i.e., the Daniel account and Nabonidus' annals.

This apparent contradiction exists only if we hold to a fallacious view of the last night, the night of Belshazzar's feast. Instead of a scene of security as Daniel implies, if we interrpret the feast as a final, last, desperate revel (after the analogy of Hitler's last days in his underground bunkers at the chancellory and the orgies of his followers as they faced the final capture of Berlin), we have a dramatic and plausible story. But if this is the picture, why is there no mention of so important a person as

Belshazzar, the king's son and why is there not so dramatic a scene given either in the Annals or the cylinder?

On the other hand, if we postulate an assassination of Belshazzar prior to the capture of the city or simultaneous with it, we have a reasonable explanation for the lack of resistance in the city and there being no mention of the name of Belshazzar as leading a defense. And if we take this view, there is no conflict among the Cyrus cylinder and the Annals and the biblical account. The only unsolved problem is a mutilated line in the Annals which cannot be used either for or against this view.

The situation would then be interpreted as follows,

(1) The banquet was given in a palace and in a city not yet taken.

(2) The handwriting on the wall was followed by the assassination of Belshazzar. The assassins may even have been encouraged to action by the prediction of the impending dissolution of the empire.

(3) On the news of the king's death and the capture of Nabonidus, the conspirators had a valid excuse for the surrender of the city. The city was entered by Gobryas and his troops on the eleventh of Tammuz. The Babylonian troops lay down their arms; there is no fighting.

(4) On the third of Marchesvan, nearly four months later, Cyrus enters the city.

If our clues are correct as to who killed the king, we also have by the same evidence, the reason for his death. If this seems inconsistent with the account in Daniel where we read, "they drank wine, and praised the gods of gold, and of silver, and of bronze, of iron, of wood, and of stone," Belshazzar is not neglecting the gods of Babylonia. His devotion to gods other than Marduk (namely, Shamash, etc.) can be entirely reconciled with the antipathy of Marduk's priesthood. It is in the nature of things and of what we know of the various orders of the Babylonian priesthood that there should be contention and fighting between them.

If we summarize the clues to the possible religious defection of Nebuchadnezzar and his family especially including his successors, Avil Marduk and Labashi Marduk, we have the following hints,

(1) After a series of Divine manifestations, we have Nebuchadnezzar's own testimony and proclamation (in Chapter 4), an original document preserved by Daniel but either suppressed by the Marduk priesthood or possibly lost for some other reason though we have many of Nebuchadnezzar's tablets and official pronouncements.

(2) We have the statement by Nabonidus that Avil Marduk was not fit to rule but there is no specific charge against him and the accusation is made by a reactionary rival (Nabonidus).

(3) The biblical testimony of the queen mother as to Daniel's character indicates not only a friendship for him but might also imply a faith in

his God.

(4) We need an explanation for the preposterous story told by Herodotus concerning the building exploits of Queen Nitocris. Why should the building exploits of Babylon's greatest king have been assigned to a woman who at the most, could have played only minor parts in the government of Babylon if indeed she is a historic character. Why this conspiracy of silence?

(5) Why were the vessels of Jehovah's temple selected out of all the captured spoil of Egypt, Tyre, Sidon and Carchemish for an act of defiance and mockery unless Belshazzar was trying to throw off the influence of a Jehovah tradition that somehow had attached itself to the house of Nebuchadnezzar? It is possible, of course, that sacred vessels of other nations were involved but not mentioned.

(6) The biblical account in Daniel calling Nebuchadnezzar the *"head of gold"* and *"my servant"* needs explanation. In giving him dominion and authority and empire (even over the beasts of the field), do we not have here a strong hint that Jehovah considers this man not only a tool to work His will but the implied possibility of an effective spiritual relationship involving Nebuchadnezzar and perhaps his family line? It seems evident that by three miraculous and prophetic events, by the warning given him and the subsequent events, we have an indication, not only of God's solicitude for Nebuchadnezzar but a foreknowledge of the outcome indicated in Nebuchadnezzar's confession of faith in Chapter 4.

(7) Perhaps it is not unreasonable to postulate that the cabal against Daniel under Darius, the Mede, may have been engineered by the Babylonian civil servants who were taken over by the Persians from the previous reign and who resented the Jehovah influence introduced by this man. This would give us a valid reason for an otherwise mysterious antagonism and is not inconsistent with other facts of the narrative.

I think too much credit has been given Herodotus when he tells us that Cyrus captured Astyages, his mother's father. After all, a historian that could omit Nebuchadnezzar, the greatest king of the ancient world, could from the same priestly sources, fail to mention the two-year reign of Astyages's son, Cyraxeres II (Darius), a king notoriously favorable to Daniel and hence responsible for the death of those who had conspired against him. Such a king would probably receive short shrift from any priestly chronicler if his priestly confreres had been involved in the conspiracy against Daniel. The omission of the king's name and filling the gap with fictitious history would be the best way to accomplish this. This is exactly what was done in the case of Nebuchadnezzar, the substitute in this case being a hitherto unknown queen, Nitocris. Where bias and fabrication can be proved in one case, it is not unreasonable to suspect it in another. The fact that Justin (1, 4, 7) repeats Herodotus (Book 1. 27-34) does not strengthen the case since the original source, Herodotus, so far as I know is the only authority of an early date that gives us this bit of questionable information.[17]

To recapitulate, the record concerning Belshazzar closes with his sudden death, "In that night was Belshazzar king of the Chaldeans slain."

It has been assumed, not unreasonably since there is a war situation, that he was slain defending his palace and the city from the Medo-Persian army. Actually however, this is contrary to our best evidence. Even the setting does not demand such interpretation. What is suggested by the evidence that we have is that the city was betrayed from within and that there was no actual resistance offered in the city by either Belshazzar or his father, Nabonidus. If we ask who might have an interest or a profit in a betrayal, we have to depend on inference. It could hardly have been the merchant princes of the city since for all we know, they were prospering under the present dynasty and, though they may have had grievances, a change of government especially to that of a foreign nation, could only have been accompanied by uncertainty from a business standpoint. Commercial interests, if prosperous, usually prefer a status quo. The great banquet given by Belshazzar to his merchant princes does not especially suggest an attempt to placate them.

When we look for other sources of betrayal, we have the army that has been twice defeated: once under Nabonidus and once under Belshazzar. But here again, there is no slightest hint of military disaffection. Nor do we have any hint of a conspiratorial group of common citizens or the common action of the many foreign groups within the city. This leaves the one group traditionally noted for conspiracy and specifically singled out in both the Cyrus cylinder and the Nabonidus annals; namely, the Marduk priesthood. So it is possible, even probable, that whoever opened the gates of Babylon to the Persian army would have had sufficient foresight to arrange the assassination of Belshazzar and thus remove any possible leadership for a counter coup. Intelligent conspirators would realize that even though the city itself were taken, Nebuchadnezzar's palace was a fortress within the city, capable of a prolonged defense and so long as Belshazzar was alive, a rallying point for a military upset. Treachery could be the only reasonable answer to the fall of the impregnable walls of the city and the equally impregnable fortress of the king's palace.

If assassination seems to be a somewhat farfetched solution to the problem, we should remember it was a solution applied to two other members of Nebuchadnezzar's descendants, Avil Marduk and Labashi Marduk. And we have the statement by Nabonidus' stele and the Cyrus cylinder that the city was taken peaceably and that it was taken because of Marduk's dissatisfaction with the reigning house. One thing more: traitors, then and now, would like to cover their tracks if possible or at least give their dirty work a patriotic, a religious or a moral aura.

CHAPTER VII
A CONSPIRACY AGAINST DANIEL
WHO WAS DARIUS?

(Daniel 6; Place, Probably Babylon; Date, 539 B.C.; Language, Aramaic)

We have departed the setting of the Neo-Babylonian court and are come into a wholly Persian framework. With the exception of the identity of the conspirators and of Daniel, himself, everything is Persian: the person and the powers of the king; the laws of the land; the religious implications. Nothing in the chapter is inconsistent with a monotheistic situation. This is in complete contrast with the preceding chapters. Here there is no mention of gods (plural) nor of a priestly hierarchy - Chaldeans, astrologers, magicians. The setting is entirely new.

Babylon has come under new management and a new master: Darius, the Mede, "being about three score and two years old." A Persian system of government is being established to replace the Neo-Babylonian period.

Being in Chapter 6, we read,

It pleased Darius to set over the kingdom a hundred and twenty princes (satraps, aghash-dar-p'nay-yah') who should be over the whole kingdom. (1) And over these three presidents (sah-r, cheen); of whom Daniel was first: that the princes might give accounts unto them, and the king should have no damage. (2) Then this Daniel was preferred above the presidents and princes, because an excellent spirit was in him; and the king thought to set him over the whole realm. (3)

While, according to Xenophon, Cyrus had the policy of placing over the provinces, the Persians and the other favorites who helped him win the empire, Darius may have had the policy of using, for the time being at least, part of the existing civil service, in order to disturb as little as possible the existing order until such time as the Persians could become oriented to the problems of their newly conquered territory.[1] As the Assyrians had already discovered, governing Babylon was a very touchy thing. As they were to find out later on two or three separate occasions, the Babylonians had the habit of revolt.

Even Cyrus two years later, seemed anxious to disturb as little as possible the status quo if we read Xenophon aright. These first verses tell us that Daniel who had just been given the empty honor of the third rulership of the Babylonian kingdom, is included in the new civil service. Because of an excellent spirit that was in him, he was preferred above all the others for first place in the new government. He owes his position to Darius. He would have lost an election in which the satraps were the electors, in all probability.

As to the Chaldeans, whom we have suggested betrayed the city to Cyrus, would it not have been appropriate to reward them with satrapies or even a place as one of the three presidents? Indeed, might it not have been part of the bargain when the city was betrayed?

Then the presidents and princes sought to find an occasion against Daniel concerning the kingdom; but they could find no occasion nor fault, forasmuch as he was faithful, neither was there any error or fault found in him. (4)

We have the feeling as we read these verses that we do not have a sufficient motive, either for the conspiracy itself or for its very sudden appearance. That a man of Daniel's probity and religious scruples might gradually build up an opposition to himself in an officialdom otherwise-minded would not be too strange. But here, supposedly at the beginning of a newly organized civil service, that a unanimous and bitter antagonism should suddenly develop is unusual to say the least and demands some sort of explanation. It is not enough to say that an unknown, newly-appointed official, the adherent of the unknown or poorly known God, is suddenly viewed with extreme distaste by his fellow officials to the point of attempted murder.

Fortunately, we are given a clue. The record especially points out the familiarity of the conspirators with Daniel's character and habits. Clearly, he was not unknown and he was hated to the point of attempted murder even though there was certainly not a sufficient period of time in which any possible, personal abrasiveness could furnish legitimate grounds for such hate.

What really motivated these conspirators? And who were they? If we place the locale in the court of Babylon and assume that most of these officials were part of the Babylonian civil service (which, together with Daniel, was taken over from the days of Belshazzar and who may even have had a hand in his murder) and if we remember that it is this Daniel who on three separate occasions has shown up their inability to meet their official function of interpreting the mysteries of the gods, we begin to see some light in the matter. When we add to this the possibility that Daniel may have been acquainted with or have suspected the conspiracy against Belshazzar by the same Chaldeans and the further fact that all through the years of his captivity, Daniel has been a fearless champion of Jehovah, victorious over the inabilities of Marduk and that this superiority has been shown by supernatural powers inexplicable by any possible trickery, we have a very strong case and apparently a very good explanation.

If we disallow the interpretation suggested for the previous chapters, this verse seems out of place but if we accept the hints that have been given us before (i.e., a priesthood discredited by God's witness to Babylon through miracles; Daniel's elevation to authority under Nebuchadnezzar; his final vindication of Jehovah's judgment under Belshazzar; his commanding rebuke of the king and his prediction of the speedy fall of Babylon) and if we can postulate as we have done in the previous chapters, a religious conflict in which the house of Nebuchadnezzar has been tremendously influenced by Daniel and Daniel's God and if we are right in assuming that there was a reactionary group centered in Belshazzar representing a powerful opposition to all such influence, perhaps we have a reason here for what seems otherwise to be merely a personal antipathy based on envy alone. These men (i.e., the conspirators in the group) are not strangers to Daniel and speak as if they know his characteristics. They recognize his righteousness and plainly say, "We shall not find any occasion against this Daniel, except we find it against him concerning the law of his God" (6:5). Then it would be reasonable to suppose that in this group we have many former civil servants and priestly leaders. At least all of them are motivated by a determination to rid themselves of this first president. Josephus says they were moved by envy. We lack a valid motive otherwise for this most venomous attack on a king's preferred civil servant. The intrigue which they initiate does credit to their intelligence if not to their moral standards and shows as well, that they have rightly evaluated Darius who is apparently vain and not too wise. But neither is he all evil.

Something of the flavor of the situation is contained in the Aramaic verb which is translated "assembled" in the King James version but having the connotation of "thronging in," "storming in," "coming in tumultuously".

The appeal came not alone to Darius' vanity but could easily be made to seem to be a means of emphasizing the power and authority of the new king. It is worth noting that these conspirators were not afraid to attempt to destroy a man who is manifestly in the king's favor. This gives us their estimate of the character of the king. In the seventh, eighth, and ninth verses, we read,

All the presidents of the kingdom, the governors, and the princes, the counsellors, and the captains, have consulted together to establish a royal statute, and to make a firm decree, that whosoever shall ask a petition of any God or man for thirty days, save of thee, O king, he shall be cast into the den of lions. (7) Now, O king, establish the decree, and sign the writing, that it be not changed, according to the law of the Medes and Persians, which altereth not. (8) Wherefore king Darius signed the writing and the decree. (9)

This is heady stuff for a newly enthroned king, whose authority is just beginning to be established and it seemed a heaven-sent opportunity to consolidate that authority in the minds of his new subjects. The statement that "all" the presidents, etc ., had counselled together is undoubtedly a lie.[2] It is entirely consistent with the intelligence, experience and insight of Daniel that he is not taken by surprise and he does not retreat. He is now a man at least eighty years old. Since his youth, he has put his faith in God, not in man. The tenth verse continues the story:

Now when Daniel knew that the writing was signed, he went into his house; and his windows being open in his chamber toward Jerusalem, he kneeled upon his knees three times a day, and prayed, and gave thanks before his God, as he did aforetime. (10)

It is apparently very easy for the conspirators to discover his prayer life since they undoubtedly know his habits. Whether this was accomplished through a suborned servant or through some other means, they now have their information and witnesses .[3] The twelfth verse describes their next move,

Then they came near, and spake before the king concerning the king's decree; Hast thou not signed a decree, that every man that shall ask a petition of any God or man within thirty days, save of thee, O king, shall be cast into the den of lions? The king answered and said, The thing is true, according to the law of the Medes and Persians, which altereth not. (12) Then answered they and said before the king, That Daniel, which is of the children of the captivity of Judah, regardeth not thee, O king, nor the decree that thou hast signed, but maketh his petition three times a day. (13)

The fourteenth verse gives us a favorable view of a king, if not from the standpoint of his governmental capacity, then from a personal standpoint, for he "was sore displeased with himself, and set his heart on Daniel to deliver him: and he labored til the going down of the sun to deliver him."

There are some implications here that can only be conjectured. If Nebuchadnezzar for failure to have a proper interpretation of a dream, could threaten and probably carry out the destruction of a whole powerful social group, why could not Darius since obviously this was a trap deliberately set for him as well as for Daniel? Nebuchadnezzar would have executed the conspirators. Why did not Darius? In the first place, Darius was not Nebuchadnezzar.

Secondly, he is bound by the Persian custom of placing a law, once made, above the human power to reverse even where it it obviously unjust. In some ways, this is not all bad since it does remove a source of governmental confusion should a king lightly change his mind especially where that king is responsible to no one but himself or to a subservient council of elders. There may be a hint here also of the doctrine of the infallibility of divinely appointed monarchs where the word once spoken and the law once given should be considered infallible because they come from an infallible source. However, it may be that this king is not strong enough nor shrewd enough to rescue Daniel from this dilemma.

In the book of Esther, we have an amendment to an infallible command by Xerxes. There the death penalty was not rescinded but the Jews were given permission to defend themselves. Darius does not discover a similar way out. In the sixteenth verse, the story continues with the execution of the edict but with the very human and humane aspect of the king brought out when he says, "Thy God whom thou servest continually, He will deliver thee."

And a stone was brought, and laid upon the mouth of the den; and the king sealed it with his own signet, and with the signet of his lords; that the purpose might not be changed concerning Daniel. (17) Then the king arose very early in the morning, and went in haste unto the den of lions. (19) And when he came to the den, he cried with a lamentable voice unto Daniel: and the king spake and said to Daniel, O Daniel, servant of the living God, is thy God, whom thou servest continually, able to deliver thee from the lions? (20) Then said Daniel unto the king, O king, live forever. (21)

What the king could not do, God had done. And in doing this, He had given to the Mede, Darius, a witness that, because of his deep concern over the injustice in which he had been a part, was the more significant to him.

Then was the king exceeding glad for him, and commanded that they should take Daniel up out of the den. So Daniel was taken up out of the den, and no manner of hurt was found upon him, because he believed in his God. (23)

King Darius may have been weak, he may have been used by these Babylonian conspirators but there is a revulsion of feeling and a swift justice that makes us understand that he was not entirely helpless. The twenty-fourth verse continues the story.

And the king commanded, and they brought those men which had accused Daniel, and they cast them into the den of lions, them, their children, and their wives; and the lions had the mastery of them, and break all their bones in pieces or ever they came at the bottom of the den.

Does the king, in his desire to do justice to these plotters, commit a greater injustice in sacrificing their children and their wives? We do not have to defend Persian justice. (It is not biblical justice after the admonition of Ezekiel 18:20.) It was the custom of the orient to assume a man's unity with his family and also to assume that if the husband and father was guilty, the wives and the children were implicated. This assumption might or might not be true but it can be said that children grow up with ideas of avenging their parents and wives can themselves foster their vengeance in their children and even take part in other conspiracies. This is not biblical justice, that everyone can be tried for his own sins and not his father's, but it was not Persian justice alone since there are numerous examples of this in the annals of all despotisms.[4]

Verses 25 and 26 are the words of a decree[5] proclaimed by Darius,

Then king Darius wrote unto all people, nations, and languages, that dwell in all the earth; Peace be multiplied unto you. (25) I make a decree, That in every dominion of my kingdom men tremble and fear before the God of Daniel; for He is the living God, and stedfast forever, and His kingdom that which shall not be destroyed, and His dominion shall be even unto the end. (26)

If we could know that this decree was published in Babylon, written probably by Babylonian scribes, we would not wonder that it has not come down to us as a part of a collection of Persian documents even if the vicissitudes of time had otherwise left them available. It would be strange indeed if any of the tablets contrary to the interests of the priestly establishment should ever have escaped their tender mercies. However, Josephus suggests Achmetha as the place to which Daniel was finally taken. What he purposed for Daniel in the first place he carries through to the end of his reign. Josephus adds:

"Now when Daniel was become so illustrious and famous, on account of the opinion men had that he was beloved of God, he built a tower at Ecbatana, in Media; it was a most elegant building, and wonderfully made, and is still remaining, and is preserved to this day; and as to such as see it, it appears to have been lately built, and to have been no older than that very day. When anyone looks upon it, it is so fresh flourishing and beautiful, and no way grown old in so long a time; for buildings suffer the same as men do, they grow old as well as they, and by numbers of years their strength is dissolved and their beauty withered. Now they bury the kings of Media, of Persia, and Parthia in this tower to this day, and he who was entrusted with the care of it was a Jewish priest; which thing is also observed to this day."[6]

Daniel's statement that "this Daniel prospered in the reign of Darius, and in the reign of Cyrus the Persian" should answer the claim that Darius, the Mede (5:31), is identical with Cyrus, the Persian. It does not help us in any way to translate the Aramaic conjunction "even" rather than "and," for Daniel specifically identifies Darius as a Mede (5:31) and of the seed of the Medes (9:1) and just as specifically speaks of Cyrus as the Persian.

As we examine sacred writ and try to evaluate the other authorities quoted, do we have something of the following sequence?

(1) The conquest of Babylon by Darius and Cyrus with Cyrus the actual conqueror and general in the field.

(2) Perhaps Xenophon is right in telling us that Cyrus turned over the

conquered kingdom to Darius who received it, being Cyrus' overlord.

(3) Darius incorporates Babylonia with the whole empire and reorganizes it under three presidents and 120 satraps, Daniel being the chief of the presidents.

(4) The conspiracy against Daniel takes place while Darius is still in Babylon. The circumstances seem to fit this setting best.

(5) The conspirators, (identical with or instigated by the Marduk priesthood) are discomfited and punished and Daniel is restored to his presidency.

(6) Darius returns to his old capital of Ecbatana (Achmetha) taking Daniel with him.

(7) Darius dies after two years. Cyrus succeeds him and appoints Cambyses as his vice-gerent and appoints Gabryas governor of Babylon.

According to the Cyropedia, the later Persian kings had three residences according to the seasons of the year: Ecbatana in the summer; Babylon in the winter; Susa (Shushan) in the spring. The Cyropedia (VII, VI, 22) tells us:

"Cyrus himself made his home in the center of his domain, and in the winter season he spent seven months in Babylon, for there the climate is warm, in the spring he spent three months in Susa, and in the height of summer two months in Ecbatana."

The record continues,

Then king Darius wrote unto all people, nations and languages, that dwell in all the earth: Peace be multiplied unto you.(25).

Here, again, Darius speaks as a universal sovereign. There is no apparent limit to his rule, no hint of joint sovereignty and no one to whom he is responsible. Again we must emphasize that unless Daniel has given us an inaccurate account, Darius is claiming complete dominion over an empire which since Babylon has been conquered, extends to the Mediterranean on the west and to India on the east. In thus quoting him, Daniel acquiesces tacitly at least, to Darius' claim of sovereignty. Darius' proclamation continues:

I make a decree, That in every dominion of my kingdom men tremble and fear before the God of Daniel: for He is the living God, and steadfast forever, and His kingdom that which shall not be destroyed, and His dominion shall be even unto the end. (26) He delivereth and rescueth, and He worketh signs and wonders in heaven and in earth, who hath delivered Daniel from the power of the lions. (27)

When we read this proclamation and recall Darius' perturbation at Daniel's plight, we begin to wonder if here again the statement that Darius (Cyaxeras II) was weak and sensual (Cyro. 1, 5, VIII, 7) may not have been a slander, at least as it assumed the exclusion of nobler motives. Weak he certainly was, in that the conspirators against Daniel considered it safe to engineer such a bold affront to the king in the matter of his favorite official. We can imagine the fury and effectiveness with which Nebuchadnezzar would have reacted under similar circumstances, even though Persian law was not Babylonian law. But Darius' proclamation could have appropriately been made by a pious Hebrew monarch without the change of even a word.

So this Daniel prospered in the reign of Darius, and in the reign of Cyrus the Persian.(28)

From this, we see that Darius' friendship for Daniel is a consistent and persistent thing. For two centuries, the Jewish people continued under the Medo-Persian rule; in the main, a kindly one so far as Israel was concerned. We hear of no bitterness, no revolt, no Persian persecution of Israel's religion.

The persecution pictured in the book of Esther was engineered by Haman, the Agagite, not by Persian hatred. Under Persian rule, Israel returned to her own land and rebuilt her own temple and her city walls. Opposition came from non-Persian sources. We do not know whether the religious reforms under Zoroaster had permeated Persian society or the royal court producing something like a religious like-mindedness with Israel's faith, reinforcing the witness of Daniel and possibly the Hebrew Scriptures. This is possible since we are assured by Haug that at its beginnings, Zoroaster's emphasis was monotheistic.[8] What we do know is that when confronted with Alexander's invasion, the Jews chose to remain loyal to Persia until it was impossible to escape the capture of the city.

This ends the historical section of Daniel without one hint of the Macedonian persecution (for which the book was presumably written), with no Palestinian local color and no slip of the pen betraying Israel's return to the land.

WHO WAS DARIUS THE MEDE?

The fifth chapter of Daniel ends with a statement, "And Darius the Median took (received) the kingdom, being about three score and two years old," and the sixth chapter begins, "It pleased Darius to set over the kingdom one hundred and twenty princes, who should be over the whole kingdom."

On the surface, this is a plain and simple statement: that one man, Darius, the Mede, succeeded Belshazzar, the Chaldean, as the ruler of the Babylonian empire. He not only is centerstage but alone, occupies it. This is further emphasized when later we read: *"In the first year of Darius, the son Ahesuerus, of the seed of the Medes, who was made king over the Chaldeans"* (9:1; also 11:1).

No mention at all is made of the part played by Cyrus, the Persian, until Daniel 10:1. Then the year of his reign is mentioned. No mention of the exploits of Cyrus who according to secular sources was the real conqueror of Babylon. The two contemporary, secular accounts (the Cyrus Cylinder and the Nabonidus Annals) make no mention of Darius. Cyrus is designated conqueror of Babylon and king.

In evaluating the conflicting testimony in the light of our present knowledge regarding these sources, we realize that, first, there are altogether four contemporary accounts of the fall of Babylon (three on-the-spot reports, if you will); Daniel the prophet, Jeremiah the prophet (especially Jeremiah 51), the Annals of Nabonidus and the Cyrus Cylinder. Jeremiah is the only one not actually in Babylon but being in communication with the exiles. But Boutflower quoting Olmstead, has this warning concerning official records:

"At first sight nothing would seem more certain than the accuracy of the contemporary annals. But we have to take into account that these records are official. 'In that fact,' as Olmstead points out, 'lies their strength and their weakness . . . Like all official records ancient or modern, these documents have been edited to a degree of which it is difficult to conceive.'"[9]

On the contrary, the reason that Scripture has spoken with the authority of truth to our race is precisely this lack of editing to serve national, royal or family pride and interest. It is unique among ancient or modern documents in that the failures, sins, mistakes and ignoble purposes of men and people have been set forth in stark reality, sparing no one, high or low. David's sin, Solomon's lapses, Rehoboam's foolishness, Uzziah's presumption, the ingratitude of Joash and the apostasy of two-thirds of Judah's kings and the depravity and idolatry characteristic of the people, are all set forth in unvarnished candor by men who risked their lives to tell the truth. Why should they not be believed above all ancient records? Why should not Scripture be the criterion by which ancient documents are judged when they speak of the same matters? Even so, we are not including the most important factor of all: the Holy Spirit's illumination.

The secondary sources are much more numerous; Herodotus, Ctesias, Abydenus quoting Megasthenes, Justin, Jospehus, Aeschylus, Diodorus, Strabo, Xenophon - all of whom had to depend on these or other primary sources not now known and perhaps of no greater validity.

As we shall try to show, two of the primary sources are tainted and show evidence of biased editing. One of the most quoted secondary sources, Herodotus, apparently was deliberately misled by his informants and many subsequent writers merely repeated these errors by depending upon Herodotus. On the other hand, there is no reason to suspect bias in Jeremiah or Daniel of a kind that would manufacture a non-existent king

and give preeminence to a subject people (i.e., the Medes) or feature a non
-existent kingdom as Aeschylus and Xenophon (especially the latter)
would, thereby being involved in a purposeless fabrication. Josephus
might possibly be accused of bias in favor of the sacred record but where
he does not fully understand or differs from biblical or secular sources, he
takes cognizance of it. In the case of Darius, he not only indicates no such
controversy but goes on to give non-biblical information showing his possession of sources independent of the Old Testament.

Xenophon's bias would naturally omit or soften any facts not con-
ducive to his hero's glory. To make Darius, as he does, even the nominal
superior of Cyrus could not serve such a purpose. Let us examine possible options suggested by a few modern, conservative commentators as
somewhat representative.

Relative to the identity of Darius, the Mede, Keil uses over eight pages
to explore the evidence for and against Darius as Cyaxares II. He quotes
extensively from the Cyropedia and from Herodotus with supporting
opinions from Hitzig and Kranichfeld . He comes out strongly for the
view that Darius is Cyaxares II.

Albert Barnes gives us a short (pp. 6;10, vol. 2) but clear account of
the various theories from the time of Jerome to his own day. They include
identifying Darius with Neriglissar as the fourth Chaldean monarch, with
Astyages the Mede, with the brother of Astyages, with Darius Hystaspes,
finally with Cyaxeres II which is his own view. He quotes Josephus and
Jerome as supporting his own view.[10]

Kliefoth supports the Cyaxares identification also. Leupold quotes
Keil and Kliefoth disapprovingly and R.D. Wilson and Charles with approval (pp. 246-248). He makes Darius and Gubaru of the Annalistic
Tables of Cyrus. Albright seems to concur in this view. Walvoord mentions six scholars who favor the Gubaru view but is himself uncommitted.
He gives an excellent, brief discussion of the matter (pp. 132-134).
Young is equally non-committal. In his pamphlet, Whitcomb has given a
thoroughly researched and up-to-date study from the standpoint of Darius
as Gubaru. In a pamphlet of seventy-two pages, he seemingly gives all
the evidence possible in favor of this thesis. (Darius the Mede by J.C.
Whitcomb.)

Pusey, the source of so much sanctified common sense in Old Testament criticism, is seemingly somewhat indecisive on the issue but finally favors Darius, the Mede, as vice-king over Babylon under Cyrus the
Great. Rowley (Darius the Mede and Four World Empires) in 182 pages
comes to the conclusion that no such person as Darius, the Mede, ever existed. Rowley is the only author mentioned who has a low view of the inspiration of Scripture. Boutflower thinks Darius was Cambyses,[11] and
Wiseman that he was Cyrus, the Great, himself. The latter does not
sufficiently elaborate his position in his article in Christianity Today,

to do it justice.[12]

We have, then, the following options from the few authors quoted:

(1) Darius, as the successor of Belshazzar and Nabonidus, and the predecessor of Cyrus the Persian, whose two-year reign was so overshadowed by that of Cyrus that most secular writers overlooked it.

(2) Darius as vice-king with Cyrus as king.

(3) Darius as either Astyages or a brother of Astyages.

(4) Darius as Gubaru, a prominent general under Cyrus.

(5) Darius as Cambyses, son of Cyrus.

(6) Cyrus the Great himself, having Darius as his second name.

(7) Darius as fictitious character manufactured by Daniel for some unknown purpose.

All of these differing views depend for their information on a very few primary sources and the differences, then, are differing value judgments on the validity of these sources.[13]

In dating this chapter by the reign of Darius the Mede, Daniel is conforming to what seems to be his practice in the last six chapters of his book; that is, dating the events by the year of the reigning monarch.

As we have just indicated, theories relative to the identity of Darius, the Mede, that eliminate him from the king list (Rowley) or give him the status of governor only (Whitcomb) or identify him with Cyrus, the Persian, (Wiseman) should also give proof that Daniel is departing from his usual chronology. It seems to be the plain intent of Daniel to place Darius as the reigning monarch between Belshazzar, the Babylonian, and Cyrus, the Persian, though with no indication of the length of the reign.

Moreover, such theories should be prepared to invalidate the testimonies of Daniel, Jeremiah, Josephus and Xenophon and the implication of Aeschylus, and to show why they might be biased. That the name Darius is not a lapse, scribal or otherwise, is indicated by its continued use throughout the chapter (sixteen times) always in the context of kingship and in the added implications in Darius' proclamation *"unto all the peoples, nations, and languages that dwell in all the earth"* (not in "all the province"). This is the language of a king, not a governor. When we remember that Darius is never called a governor and Gobryas is never called a king in any ancient document and that there is no slightest hint that Daniel confuses Darius with Cyrus, it seems the part of caution at least, to place a very large burden of proof on those who disagree with Josephus.

Whitcomb has given a most able defense of the Gobryas viewpoint. Wiseman has not elaborated his viewpoint sufficiently and there is still much to be said for the validity of Josephus' explanation.

Rowley in his "Darius the Mede" and the "Four World Kingdoms of the Book of Daniel has, in 182 pages, packed a very impressive erudition. He comes to the conclusion that Darius, the Mede, was a fictitious character; that a nonexistent Daniel bore witness to a nonexistent Darius. He bases this on the following points:

(1) Darius is not Cambyses, son of Cyrus,

(2) Darius is not Gobyrus,

(3) Darius is not Astyages and

(4) Darius, the Mede, is not Cyaxeres II, son of Astyges.

With the first three of these propositions, we can thoroughly agree, though not necessarily on all of the same grounds. With his fourth point, which is the real point of debate, we must take issue and consequently disclaim his conclusion; namely, that there was no such person. I think we may rightly question whether Professor Rowley has used up all his options or that he made sufficient allowance for the bias of his sources.

Rowley's first objection, that the names Cyaxeres and Darius are non-equatable, is not a particularly valid objection. Many kings, ancient and modern, are often known by more than one name; e.g., Tiglath Pileser III is known among the Hebrews both as Jareb (Hosea 10:6) and as Pul (II Kings 15:19) even as Jehoahaz was also called Shallum (Jeremiah 22:11-12). When we consider that kings are sometimes known by one of several of their own names and sometimes by a name adopted from some famous ancestor (e.g., Tiglathpolesar III), this argument should not be impressive.

His second objection, that Xenophon could not be brought into agreement with the story of Daniel, again does not quite deal properly with what Xenophon does say. Xenophon speaks of Darius as king, of Cyrus as the conqueror of Babylon but pictures Cyrus as still not succeeding to the Persian throne at the time of the conquest of Babylon and still accountable to his father and to the Persian elders.[14]

This, Rowley concedes but says that Cyrus assumes the style of a king on the capture of Babylon. This is even as any conquering general would do until such time as it was necessary to turn over his conquest to higher authority. (General MacArthur was not king of Japan though he told the Emperor what to do.)

If we assume a gap of two years from the conquest of the city to the inscribing of the Cyrus Cylinder, this would give time for the brief reign of Darius (he was 62 years old at the taking of Babylon), the death of Cyrus' father Cambyses and Cyrus' first year of reign over the combined kingdoms of Media, Persia and Babylon. The term "first year of Cyrus," however, does not give us an absolute chronological fix.

The third objection is Rowley's inability to see any historical reality in the Cyropaedia but he fails to see the fatal deficiencies in any material emanating from the Babylonian priesthood; viz., the Nabonidus Annals, the Cyrus Cylinder, Herodotus' account and subsequent authors who depended upon these sources.

Keil, who should be read thoroughly on this subject, says:

"On the other hand, the account given by Xenophon regarding Cyaxeres so fully agrees with the narrative of Daniel regarding Darius the Mede, that, as Hitzig confesses, 'the identity of the two is beyond a doubt.' If, according to Xenophon, Cyrus conquered Babylon by the permission of Cyaxeres and after its overthrow not only offered him a "residence" there (Hitzig), but went to Media, presented himself before Cyaxeres and showed him that he had appointed for him in Babylon *oikos kai archeia*, in order that when, according to the Eastern custom, he changed his residence he might have a royal palace there, so, according to Daniel, Darius did not overthrow the Chaldean kingdom but received it (Ch. VI. 1) and was made king (...hamlak) by Cyrus, who, according to the prophecies of Isaiah, was to overthrow Babylon, and according to Dan. VI.29 succeeded Darius on the throne.

"The statement, also, that Darius was about sixty-two years old when he ascended the throne of the Chaldean kingdom, harmonizes with the report given by Xenophon, that when Cyaxares gave his daughter to Cyrus, he gave him along with her the kingdom of Media, because he had no male heir, and was so far advanced in years that he could not hope to have now any son.

"Finally, even in respect of character the Cyaxares of Xenothon resembles the Darius of Daniel. As the former describes the conduct of Cyrus while he revelled in sensual pleasures, so Darius is induced by his nobles to issue an edict without obtaining any clear knowledge as to its motive, and allows himself to be forced to put it into execution, however sorrowful he might be on account of its relation to Daniel.

"After all this, there can be no reason to doubt the reign of Darius, the Mede. But how long it lasted cannot be determined either from the Book of Daniel in which (see Ch. IX.1) only the first year of his reign is named or from any other direct source. Ptolemy, in his Canon, places after Nabonadius, the reign of Cyrus, the Persian, for nine years. With this, the words of Xenophon, to *hebdomon epi tes hautou arches*, which by supplying the world, *etos*, after *hebdomon* are understood of seven years reign, and thence it is concluded that Cyaxares reigned two years. But the supplement of *"etos"* is not warranted by the context.

"The supposition, however, that Darius reigned for two years over Babylon is correct. For the Babylonian kingdom was destroyed sixty-eight years after the commencement of the Exile. Since, then, the seventy years of the Exile were completed in the first year of the reign of Cyrus (II Chron. XXXVI.22f.; Ezra 1.1), it follows that Cyrus became king two years after the overthrow of Babylon and thus after Darius had reigned two years."[15]

Since tradition says that Darius reigned but two years and since Daniel speaks definitely of only the first year of Darius (which implies a second year) and both the Cylinder and the Annals speak of Cyrus as actual king succeeding his father, Cambyses (and his uncle, Darius or Cyaxeres II), there is no conflict actually between Xenophon's account and our other two sources.[16] At the death of his uncle and his father, Cyrus becomes the king of an integrated kingdom of Medes and Persians.[17]

The outstanding difference between the biblical account (also that of Josephus) and that of Xenophon is, of course, the status of Cyaxeres II (i.e., Darius) who, in the biblical account is described as actual and sole ruler of both Medes and Persians while Xenophon gives him a more nominal status though still the actual ruler of the Medes and overlord of the Persians. We need only mention Herodotus' complete omission of Nebuchadnezzar, the greatest king of them all, to absolve him of infallability. It is only fair to say that both authors probably erred because of their sources of information.

That Herodotus should fail to mention Darius when he omitted the names of Nebuchadnezzar and all of his descendants, needs explanation. When two obscure princesses are substituted to fill the gap, foul play may be suspected. He does mention Labynetus in passing probably meaning Nabonidus.

The priests of Marduk seem to be the source of Herodotus' information relative to Babylonian history. He speaks of the "Chaldeans, the priests of this god" (Belus; i.e., Marduk), "I relate what the Chaldeans report," "The Chaldeans told me," and so forth.

When this source fails to mention the whole dynasty of Nebuchadnezzar and no member of his family or of his descendants is so much as referred to, a dynasty under which Babylon's greatest achievements were accomplished, are we unduly suspicious in questioning other information from this same source? To add insult to injury, to fill a gap of sixty-five years with two hypothetical queens (Semiramis and Nitocris) and a non-Chaldean (Nabonidus-Labynetus), none of whom had any important hand in the great building enterprises of Babylon, we realize that history is being manufactured, not reported.

The same reasons and bias would seem to obtain with reference to Darius, who also is omitted. We have ample reason to think his short reign would be especially offensive to the same Chaldean priests, many of whose confreres (tools) have been destroyed by Darius in retaliation for their cabal against Daniel. On the contrary, so far as we can see, neither Daniel, Joseph, Xenophon or Aeschylus had any reason to manufacture the story of a nonexistent and unnecessary king.

Moreover, dismissing Xenophon's Cyropaedia with the wave of the hand as a historical romance does not explain why no one has yet proven that Xenophon's characters were fictitious. A good historical romance would seem to satisfy us insofar as it takes known personages and known facts of history and attempts to give vividness and plausible interpretations to them. Aside from Xenophon's gaffe in substituting a later episode for the bloodless and peaceful conquest of Babylon under Cyrus, he seems to have been better informed than was Herodotus.[18]

This is not to invalidate Herodotus. Anything that he can see for himself or hear from reliable sources, he painstakingly reports. If he has reason to doubt his source, he says so. In this case, he seemingly had no way of knowing the bias of the Chaldean priesthood.

Herodotus tells us, "Cyrus had captured this Astyages who was his mother's father, and kept him prisoner, for a reason which I shall bring forward in another part of my history."[19]

Following this statement, there is the legend of Harpagus, the dream of Astyages regarding his daughter, Mandane; the supposed exposure to the wild beasts of her infant son, Cyrus; the story of Astyages' revenge upon Harpagus by giving him the flesh of his own son to eat; and Harpagus' betrayal of Astyages' army in counter revenge.

This story with variations, has its parallels in the folk myth of other nations and is yet apparently the basis for the alleged capture of the Median kingdom and monarchy by Cyrus and of the story of Astyages' capture and death without a successor. This story has much more the marks of romance than anything found in the Cyropaedia and is the one reason for much of the modern confusion about Darius the Mede.

Herodotus goes on to say:

" Thus after a reign of 35 years, Astyages lost his crown and the Medes, in consequence of his cruelty, were brought under the rule of the Persians. Their empire over the parts of Asia beyond the Halys had lasted one hundred and twenty-eight years, except during the time when the Scythians had dominion. Afterward, the Medes repented of their submission and revolted from Darius but were defeated in battle and again reduced to subjection. Now, however, in the time of Astyages, it was the Persians who under Cyrus revolted from the Medes, and became henceforth the rulers of Asia. Cyrus kept Astyages at his court during the remainder of his life, without doing him any further injury."[20]

Albert Barnes says:

"The existence of such a person as Cyaxeres has been indeed denied because, according to Herodotus (i. 109) and Justin (i, 4, 7), Astyages had no son. But it should be remarked that the latter of these writers only copies from the former and what Herodotus states respecting Astyages has so much the appearance of a fable that no reliance is to be placed upon it."[21]

Whether Ctesias (400 B.C.) borrowed from Herodotus or used the same sources, at any rate, he also makes Astyages the last of the Median line (Persiae, 2, 5). We know their sources; unfortunately, it was the biased Chaldean priesthood. Since these sources were Babylonian (i.e., as to the Persian and Median information), we could question validity.

If the sources had been Persian, the viewpoint would be Persian rather Median with a natural tendency to glorify anything Persian. As against the implications of Herodotus and Ctesias and those who used them as sources, we have the testimony of Daniel, Josephus, Xenophon, Aeschylus, Megasthenes and, furthermore, that of the prophet Jeremiah who implies that a Mede was involved in the capture and rule over a captured Babylon. Isaiah implies the actual capture of Babylon was by Cyrus (Isaiah 45:1-2).

All of the records (Daniel, Josephus, Xenophon, the Cyrus Cylinder and the Annals of Nabonidus) can be brought into some degree of conformity if we assume a hiatus of approximately two years between the taking of Babylon and the inscribing of the two tablets; i.e., the Cylinder and the Annals. By then, Darius would have died (possibly Cambyses, father of Cyrus, also) and Cyrus would have become king of the Medes and the Persians for both the Cylinder and the Annals speak of Cyrus as king which he was not at the taking of Babylon according to Daniel and Xenophon and Josephus, the title being given retrospectively.

As to Gubaru, Xenophon gives him sufficient prominence to make his elevation to the governship of Babylon natural after the death of Darius. With the death of Darius, Cyrus might well have allowed Gubaru actually to function as a sub-king without the kingly title since the empire, comprising as it did Medo-Persia, Babylonia, Assyria, Lydia, Cyria, Palestine, Phoenicia, etc., had been made up of that many kingdoms.

Even though later appointed by Cyrus, Gubaru might even have been selected by Darius as one of the three presidents mentioned in Daniel. Of course, there is no hint of this in Scripture since there are no other names given but Daniel's. The significance of having three presidents may have been either one of establishing checks and balances in governmental affairs or, on the other hand, the empire of Darius and later that of Cyrus, could have been divided into three great supervisory districts. For example:

(1) the areas east of the Tigris (Media, Persia, Elam, etc.),

(2) Mesopotamia (Babylonia and Assyria) and

(3) the territories beyond the river (Syria, Lydia, Palestine, Phoenicia, etc.) which may have been administered by Gubaru. That area beyond the river could even have included Mesopotamia as the second district with Lydia and Asia Minor being the third district.

Dr. Whitcomb seems to be on very safe ground in magnifying the importance of Gubaru but on ground not so certain in equating him with Darius. One would have to have very adequate facts to counter the implications of Jeremiah 51 and of Daniel when the latter dates his visions and his historical chapters presumably according to the year of the reigning monarch. When we add the picture given us in Daniel 6 of the reorganization of the kingdom by Darius with the implication that the power to do so rested with him, we would seem to need even stronger grounds. When we add Josephus' clear and precise statements, it would seem to take more than a hypothesis to counter such testimony. This is especially true with reference to Josephus when we remember his great familiarity with secular historians preceding him and his careful quoting of authorities to the number of fifty- eight in his various works. I know of no writer, or at least few writers of antiquity, who refer to so voluminous a bibliography.[22] It cannot be asserted, therefore, that Josephus merely reiterated Bible facts and gave his own interpretation of them. He speaks as if he were an eyewitness of the tower in Ecbatana and may not only have visited that capital but may have had access to its records concerning Darius though he does not say so.

We have, therefore, bias in some of the primary records - those emanating from Babylon. Let us ask this question: Is it only coincidence that ancient authors who derive their information from Babylonian sources should, with one exception, omit mention of Nebuchadnezzar, Darius and Belshazzar while those from Persian sources should include these?

Is it also coincidence that none of the names and circumstances surrounding the most unusual events connected with these same individuals (which, if given, would discredit the Marduk priesthood) should also be softened or omitted? Herodotus, who apparently received his information from the Babylonian priesthood (the Chaldeans), entirely omits the name and exploits of Nebuchadnezzar, the name of Belshazzar and his unusual end as well as the minor personages of Avil Marduk, Darius (Cyaxeres) and Gubaru. This is unusual and significant since he visited Babylon less than eighty or ninety years after its surrender in 539 B.C.

The Cyrus Cylinder mentions Nabonidus and Cyrus but no mention of Belshazzar or Gubaru. The whole of the Cylinder is evidently written from the standpoint of the Marduk priesthood and might well be an alibi for the priesthood, provided they needed one.

Xenophon, on the contrary, who could most reasonably have received his information from Persian sources, refers to Cyaxeres II (Darius) and Gubaru but, of course, does not go back in his record to the days of Nebuchadnezzar since that is foreign to his purpose. Xenophon wrote his Cyropaedia sometime after 394 B.C. having undoubtedly made his Persian contacts in the expedition of the ten thousand in 401 B.C. possibly even from Cyrus the Younger himself. He does not mention Belshazzar by name, however, and gives a contradictory account of the taking of the city and the alleged storming of the palace.

When we come to Josephus, we have the following statements: "Against him (Baltasar) did Cyrus King of Persia, and Darius king of

Media make war" (Antiquities, p. 317) and again quoting, "But when Babylon was taken by Darius and when he and his kinsman Cyrus had put an end to the dominion of the Babylonians, he was sixty-two years old. He was the son of Astyages and had another name among the Greeks" (pp. 318-319).

Although his spelling is at variance with the usual, Josephus mentions the whole line of Neo-Babylonian kings: Nebuchadnezzar, Belshazzar, Avil Marduk, Labosordacus (Labashi Marduk), Naboandelus (Nabonidus), Neriglissar and Belshazzar. He mistakenly equates the name of Belshazzar with that of Nabonidus instead of calling them father and son in the passage, "And when he was dead (i.e., Labashi) it (i.e., the kingship) came to Baltasar who by the Babylonians was called Naboandelus" (p. 317).

To sum it up, Herodotus, the Nabonidus Annals and the Cyrus Cylinder are really all from Babylonian sources; hence, they are subject to Babylonian and priestly editing. Xenophon obviously gets his facts from Persian sources. Josephus had Babylonian, Persian and Greek sources to draw from and while he is convinced of the truth of the Hebrew Scriptures, he is neither blind nor unreasoning in their defense.

Nabonidus' dream, as reported in his Annals, is an exception to the studies' avoidance of the exploits of Nebuchadnezzar even to the mention of his name. His deified presence is evoked and his prestige called upon to bolster Nabonidus' unpopular and irregular kingship.

Xenophon's picture of the Darius-Cyrus situation is that of an incompletely integrated kingdom, a sort of dual alliance: the Medes under Cyaxeres II; the Persians under Cambyses, father of Cyrus (the latter having not yet succeeded to the Persian throne). Cyaxeres seems to be nominally, if not actually, Cyrus's superior, as well as his uncle and father-in-law (Cyropedia, VIII, V. 17, 18, 19). The family ties between the two royal houses and the nominal suzerainty of Cyaxeres (Darius?) does not hide the waning fortunes of the Median house and the rising fortunes of the Persian, according to Xenophon (Cyropedia, V, V, 1, 3ff). Whether this was the actual situation or whether in his desire to magnify the importance of Cyrus, Xenophon presumes to take liberties with the actual relationship, is not entirely clear. For when he wrote (ca. 394 B.C.), the Persians were the dominant race and his informants were doubtless Persian with the usual human tendency to magnify their own national deeds and importance. Xenophon is undoubtedly giving us the gospel according to Cyrus, the Persian. At least we get the following facts:

(1) Astyages did have a son, Cyaxeres II (Cyro.,I,IV,20 and V,2).

(2) He is pictured as older than Cyrus though there is no statement as to how much older (Cyro., VI,I,6). He was old enough, however, to be his father-in-law.

(3) Cyrus, as the son of Cambyses and as crown prince, is presented to us as conqueror of Babylon in cooperation with Cyaxeres, the Mede (Cyro., VIII, V, 22).

(4) Gubaru is made governor of Babylon, not king (Cyro. omits mention but gives him high status). Annals states this (op. cit., 170); the Cyrus Cylinder makes no mention of it.

(5) At the taking of Babylon, Cyrus is still not king of Persia and is still responsible to his father and the Persian council of state (Cyro., VIII, V, 22, 26). If the Cyrus Cylinder was written two or more years after the taking of Babylon (539 B.C.), Cambyses may have died, making Cyrus king in his father's place.

(6) In the light of the above, the Cyrus Cylinder picturing Cyrus as king may have been inscribed some years after the capture of Babylon (Cyrus Cylinder, Assyrian and Babylonian Literature, p. 173; Nebonidus Annals, p.168). Both sources speak of Cyrus as king of Anshan though he is not yet king in 539 B.C.[23]

Finally then, who is Darius? In terms of the evidence offered, we believe him to be Cyaxeres II, son of Astyages, king of the Medes and Persians who reigned two years after the capture of Babylon (539-537 B.C.). If as Josephus says, he was 62 years old at the capture of Babylon, he would have been born about 601 B.C. and would have died 537 B.C. He was uncle and father-in-law of Cyrus, the Persian, who succeeded him in 537 B.C. and who, himself, had a brief reign of seven years, dying, according to tradition, in a battle with the Scythians, 530 B.C.[24]

CHAPTER VIII

THE FOUR EMPIRES OF THE END TIME
THE VISION OF THE ANCIENT OF DAYS
THE EVERLASTING KINGDOM
THE LITTLE HORN

(Daniel 7)

Dr. Culver has rightly entitled his book, "Daniel and the Latter Days," for out of the more than one hundred sixty verses in the prophetic portions of Daniel, seventy-two verses seem to be prophetic of the latter days, the end time. This would be forty-seven percent of the total. Actually, aside from the historic chapters (1-6), all of the rest are implicitly concerned with the end time in type or antitype.

The setting and context of Chapters 7, 9, and 12 especially can be most meaningfully so interpreted as we will try to show elsewhere. In Daniel 8:17, we have the more specific statements: *"At the time of the end shall be the vision"*; in 10:14, *"What shall befall thy people in the latter days"*; in 11:35, *"Even to the time of the end"*; and in 11:40, *"At the time of the end."*

All of these quotations seem to specifically indicate that these chapters are prophetic of the end time. We could, of course, quibble over the phrase "the time of the end" and other phrases mentioned above but in the absence of any of other specified end time, the end time can hardly have reference to other than the end of the age. This is further confirmed by such phrases as "The last end of the indignation . . . for at the time appointed the end shall be" (8:19), *"for yet the vision is for many days"* (10:14), and *"shall prosper til the indignation be accomplished"* (11:36).

The cumulative effect of all these phrases together with the contextual impact of Daniel 2:31-35, 2:40-45, 7:1-28, 8:23-26, 9:24-27 and 12:1-13, make these portions predictive of the future rather than an epitome of the past. As we have indicated elsewhere even those areas that have had a measure of historical fulfillment may also have significance for things yet to come involving, as they may, geographic and ethnic identifications.

In every chapter (7-12, inclusive) therefore, either by direct statement or by setting, we are made to understand that at least part of the chapter concerns itself with the time of the end. In Chapter 7, where the four beasts are before us, the fourth is judged and destroyed, the other three have their dominion taken away but their lives are prolonged. Very obviously, this is the end time as we see by the context. In Daniel 8:17, we have the statement, *"For the time of the end shall be the vision"* and *"in the last end of the indignation."* In Daniel 9:24-27, the usual interpretation involves the time from the first appearance of Messiah to the time of Antichrist (the seventy weeks).

In Chapter 10, verse 14, we have the statement, "Now I am come to make thee understand what shall befall thy people in the latter days." Since Chapters 10, 11 and 12 are part of the same vision, they are in part at least, concerned with the latter days.

In Daniel 11:35 and 40, we have the two statements, "Even to the time of the end" and "at the time of the end." If we were not previously so informed, the setting in Chapter 12 is eschatalogical - such statements as "at that time . . . a time of trouble such as never was" (verse 1) and "the time of the end" (verses 4 and 9) would clue us in to the time. We question, therefore, whether the earlier parts of Chapters 8 and 11 which were prophetic to the scene nearer to Daniel's time, may not also be the geographic and ethnic setting for the end time. In this first of Daniel's own visions, the end time must be in our thoughts as we attempt its interpretation.

In this prophetic part, the following considerations seem to be applicable:

(1) While much prophecy (as viewed from the time of the prophets and even from our own time) seems to be understandable in broad outline, the full meaning and specific details of much of Daniel's prophecy, with exceptions noted later, must await their fulfillment. Some of the details are written, apparently, only to be completely understood when they have come to pass. However, it does not seem to be God's purpose to hide from us His main future actions in a world of men.

(2) While old friends and enemies of Israel are no more, their descendants and successors in the same geographic areas are apparently involved with Israel's destiny. After years of relative unimportance and even impotence, these ethnic groups are appearing front stage. Because of sudden and unexpected financial power (oil) as well as strategic location, they are once again assuming significance especially since more powerful nations find them convenient tools.

(3) Since the world has become increasingly one world, interrelated through commerce, communication and mutual interdependence, we should certainly expect that new nations and new peoples would appear on the prophetic scene and would have a vital relationship to Israel, God's focus of attention. The oft-repeated phrase with reference to the prophecy of the last days, "all nations," would seem to me just that. Sin is a worldwide phenomenon, so therefore is judgment even as is the offer of salvation. But it would be reasonable to think that the prophetic picture that is presented to us in Daniel is there because of Daniel's people and involves nations either antagonistic or friendly to Israel.

(4) Since the message of salvation went out from one center, Israel, it should not seem strange to us that God is bringing all nations who refuse that salvation back for judgment to the place where it all started, to finish their transgression and to meet their judgment.

(5) In Daniel, we are introduced in a more vivid and complete way to a person and a people who will appear at the end of the age and who will be given worldwide authority, the Roman Empire and the Antichrist. The old Roman Empire is gone but will be revived. It will become the seat and center of control for the Antichrist (the beast of Revelation 13, the little horn of Daniel 7). His area of control and influence is worldwide but he is not alone in the exercise of his power for we also have the second beast of Revelation 13. And we shall see later that he, Antichrist, will meet opposition from the East, the North and the South, indicating other great powers.

(6) These ten horns are evidently in the area of the revived Roman Empire and the Antichrist (who is the eleventh) is pictured as plucking up by the roots, three of the ten. We do not have overt descriptions of the seven remaining horns in Daniel but we do have in Revelation 17:12-13 ten kings who may not be identical to those in Daniel 7. For areas outside the empire, we turn to the three other beasts of Chapter 7 which, as we shall try to show, may be the British Empire, Russia and an Arab hegemony. These three do not have their present culture types distinctly Latin or Roman.

(7) While these three may involve only those countries proper, could it be within the purview of prophecy to include those areas culturally or ethnically related? For example, could the first beast include the English-speaking countries of Canada, United States, Australia, New Zealand and South Africa?

Could the second beast include the Slavic countries proper? And could the Arab world and its dependents be involved in the third beast? If we take this attitude, then the revived Roman empire might thereupon include not only the Latin countries of the old Roman areas but Mexico, Central and South America and those countries having Latin speech, literature and psychology, as well as having Latin blood ties.

(8) This view is not a complete one since it leaves several great groups, nearly half of mankind, out of the prophetic picture. The kings of the east (Revelation 16:12) might be China, Japan and India. Black Africa is not specifically mentioned and the Scandinavian block could only be included vaguely in the Russian coalition. We find little or no prophetic mention of these groups in the Book of Daniel, especially those relating to the reign of Antichrist.

(9) We must admit at once that we are offering only tentative and suggestive interpretation for which there are only a few biblical hints. This view is offered that we may be alerted to the possibilities inherent in a

worldwide dominion of Antichrist. While we do not have to account for this on purely natural grounds since the reign of Antichrist is satanically engineered, it may also help to account for the human side of his worldwide dominion. We know that sin and depravity are universal; hence, judgment is also universal but we also know that ideas motivate and spread from cultural sources to peoples related in language, race and psychology. So there is such a thing as an English-speaking world, a Latin world, an Arabic world and a Slavic world. We get the picture that the Antichrist will conquer both by force and also by the force of ideas. Surely by this time, we have learned about the power of lying propaganda.

(10) Elsewhere, we refer to the East-West divisions of the old Roman Empire with the likelihood that the symbolism of the two feet involves a dual, revived empire that will also be an East-West affair. It is apparent in studying the prophetic portions of Daniel that we have two ethnic settings involved, one Roman and one Greek. Daniel 7:8, 24, and 25 and Daniel 9:27 have a Latin setting while Daniel 8:23-25 and possibly Daniel 11:36-45 are Greek.

History tells us that the Western half of the empire was Latin in speech (though Greek became a second tongue), in culture and in psychology; the Eastern half, Greek linguistically and culturally. In the time of Diocletian, the empire was divided because of the difficulties of administering so large an area. The Western capital was located at Milan while the Eastern capital was at Nicomedia and later at Byzantium (Constantiople). The imperium, the center of governmental control, was at first at Nicomedia under Diocletian while Maximian, the co-emperor, ruled at Milan. The empire in Diocletian's time (285 to 305 A.D.) consisted of one hundred twenty-one provinces grouped into thirteen dioceses which in turn were grouped into four prefectures each of which was administered by an emperor or a Caeser and they acted collectively in the signing of edicts, though administratively largely independent.

(11) We have this question, then, in interpreting these prophetic portions: Does Daniel, in his descriptions of the personalities involved in Daniel 7, 8, and 11, anticipate the two beasts of Revelation 13, two individuals of diverse background but similar psychology and purpose? Both are Antichrist in spirit; proud, presumptious, satanically-motivated and empowered, depending upon force and persecution and the lie, and hating God's people with a deadly hatred. Many interpretations by evangelical writers merge all of these descriptions into one great personality, the Antichrist. It is much easier to do this than to bring two such individuals into conformity with the two beasts of Revelation 13 but since Revelation 13 is the last word on the question, it somehow seems necessary to do this even with the difficult fact that in Daniel, we seem to have at least two great rulers while in Revelation it is easy to think of the first beast as universal ruler and the second beast as his prophet as indeed he is called in Revelation 17:11 and 19:10.

In the following pages, we shall try to clarify somewhat an unclear situation, obscure because of assumptions which we have grown up to accept. It may be psychologically difficult to accept the interpretation given for three of the four beasts of Chapter 7, especially in the light of so many orthodox commentators who feel that in Chapter 7 we have a recapitulation and parallelism with the dream image in Chapter 2.

As we shall try to show, the beasts of Chapter 7 are not successive but contemporary, the key being verse 12 of the chapter. From a logical standpoint, why should it seem strange that two of the most bitter foes of Israel, Russia and the Arab countries, come into the prophetic picture and that England, the source of the Balfour declaration which made possible the present state of Israel, should also be mentioned? Let us see what Daniel has to say in this seventh chapter.

THE FOUR BEASTS

In the first year of Belshazzar, king of Babylon, Daniel had a dream and visions of his head upon his bed; then he wrote the dream, and told the sum of the matters.(1)

This is the only verse in which Daniel indicates that he took immediate notes, writing the vision down at the time of its occurrence. We cannot assume that this was his custom. He may have mentioned it as an exception or as a clue to his usual procedure.

Daniel spoke and said, I saw in my vision by night, and, behold, the four winds of heaven strove on the great sea.(2)

Some have interpreted the "great sea" literally as meaning the Mediterranean and as indicating that the action in the vision will take place around this sea. Others regard it as symbolic of humanity at large; i.e., the nations. There may even be a double reference here since there is no incompatability between these two meanings. The action may, indeed, take place around the "great sea" and involve all nations.

And four great beasts came up from the sea, diverse from one another. (3) The first was like a lion and had eagle's wings; I beheld til its wings were plucked and it was lifted up from the earth, and made to stand upon the feet as a man; and a man's heart was given to it. (4)

Here we come to a series of symbols that indeed are most certainly descriptive of nations or peoples. Either these are particular nations and these symbolic descriptions are somehow characteristic traits peculiar to each one or they are traits characteristic of mankind divided into classifications. It is most probably the former since God has usually chosen in prophecy to deal with nations or peoples as such. We will discuss the interpretations later.

And, behold, another beast, a second, like a bear, and it raised up it-

*self on one side, and it had three ribs in the mouth of it between its teeth;
and they said thus unto it, Arise, devour much flesh. (5)*

A variant translation, suggested by Rabbi Nathan and concurred by
Kranichfeld and Anderson, would translate the phrase "and it established
a dominion," instead of A.V. "raised up itself on one side." Keil, Young
and Leupold follow the A.V. and, fortunately, the basic interpretation of
the verse is not compromised either way. This animal is much more vora-
cious than the lion. It seems insatiable in its thirst for blood.

*And after this, I beheld, and, lo, another like a leopard, which had
upon its back four wings of a fowl; the beast had also four heads, and
dominion was given to it. (6)*

While this leopard or panther is a beast of prey, it is not specifically
stated that it was a killer, as was the bear. Dominion was given it, implying perhaps that it had not itself achieved dominion. A design or action
not its own was responsible for it.

*After this I saw in the night visions, and, behold, a fourth beast, dread-
ful and terrible, and strong exceedingly, and it had great iron teeth; it
devoured and broke in pieces, and stamped the residue with its feet; it was
diverse from all the beasts that were before it, and it had ten horns. (7)*

The description of this terrifying animal is incomplete (see Revelation
13:2) since we do not know what its body is like. It is just unlike the other
three. Its outstanding characteristic is its fearfulness, its destructiveness,
its ability to completely demolish anything in its path. We note that both
the leopard and the fourth beast appear after the other two but as we shall
see in verse 12, while they are described in sequence, they are ultimately
contemporary; the first three beasts finally surviving the fourth beast. We
will save the interpretation for the following pages. The vision now shifts
to the ten horns of the fourth beast which becomes the focus of our attention.

*I considered the horns, and, behold, there came up among them
another little horn, before which there were three of the first horns plucked up by the roots; and, behold, in this horn were eyes like the eyes of a
man, and a mouth speaking great things. (8)*

In Bible symbolism "eyes" are indicative of intelligence as well as
vigilance. The little horn, the eleventh, has eyes like the eyes of a man -
human intelligence of the highest sort but by implication, with nothing
divine in its makeup. In ways that we will try to explain later, this little
horn not only dominates the ten but abolishes three of the ten. There is a
contrasting scene that now shifts to the heavenlies.

*I beheld til the thrones were placed, and the Ancient of Days did sit,
whose garment was white as snow, and the hair of His head like pure*

wool; His throne was like the fiery flame, and His wheels as burning fire.(9)

Here Daniel uses an Aramaic phrase, *"Ancient of Days"* (yahtiq yomeen), not used elsewhere in Scripture by any other prophet (though used by Daniel again in 7:13-22). There is no exact Hebrew equivalent used in referring to Jehovah. Probably the closest is the Mosaic Psalm 90 where he uses the phrase *"from everlasting thou art God."* The phrasing only (not the idea) is new. It is a peculiarity of Daniel that the covenant name, *"Jehovah,"* is used only in the ninth chapter.

A fiery stream issued and came forth from before him; thousand thousands ministered unto him, and ten thousand times ten thousand stood before him; the judgment was set, and the books were opened.(10)

How does one describe the indescribable? What words can convey to earthly senses the awesome majesty and beauty of Him whose garments were light itself and whose court was the shining angelic host? And as is the beauty and majesty of this great assize so is its terror to those guilty ones who stand before it with no advocate to plead their cause and no righteous substitute as an offering for sin.

I beheld then because of the voice of the great words which the horn spoke; I beheld even til the beast was slain, and its body destroyed, and given to the burning flame. (11)

Individually and collectively, the beast and his kingdom (all who worship him) will be judged according to their works and disappear from the earthly scene forever. Evil must be allowed fruition else man cannot see how awful evil is and can be deceived as to its capacity for ruin.

As for the rest of the beasts, they had their dominion taken away yet their lives were prolonged for a season and time. (12)

This is the key verse to our understanding of this chapter. There are four beasts. The fourth is judged and destroyed. The first three have their lives prolonged after the destruction of the fourth beast. They are contemporary kingdoms as we shall see later in this chapter.

Once more we are referred to the heavenly judgment and the Ancient of Days,

I saw in the night visions, and, behold, one like to the Son of man came with the clouds of heaven, and came to the Ancient of Days, and they brought Him near before Him. (13) And there was given Him dominion and glory, and a kingdom, that all peoples, nations, and languages should serve Him; His dominion is an everlasting dominion, which shall not pass away, and His kingdom that which shall not be destroyed. (14)

The Jewish leaders of Jesus' day rightly considered the Son of man, sitting on the right hand of power and *"coming in the clouds of heaven,"* as not only Messianic but as referring to deity to whom it was blasphemy to liken oneself. Why then, was it so impossible to their blind eyes to give Jesus the place that was His? Possibly, for the very reason that Daniel's son of man appears in a heavenly scene of glory and Jesus of Nazareth appeared as the meek and lowly one of Zechariah 9:9; possibly also because of what they were, morally and spiritually. It was not given them to see the Transfiguration on the Mount, the Resurrection, the risen Christ of the forty days and the Ascension. They had no eyes to see His moral grandeur, they saw only their threatened leadership. Only in judgment will they ever see Jesus as the Glorified One. Perhaps it had been better that Annas and his line had never been born, they who led Israel down the path to ruin. Judas was only their tool and this was his obituary also; i.e., that he should never have been born.

I, Daniel, was grieved in my spirit in the midst of my body, and the visions of my head troubled me. (15) I came near unto one of them that stood by, and asked him the truth of all this. So he told me, and made me know the interpretation of the things. (16)

THE INTERPRETATION OF THE VISION

From here on, we are interested in the meaning of the vision. We are confronted with the following questions:

(1) Who are the four kings or kingdoms?

(2) Who or what are the ten horns?

(3) Who or what is the little horn?

(4) If he is a man, what is his relationship to, and his program with regard to the saints?

There has been so much confusion and controversy relative to the identity of the four kings or four kingdoms that, of necessity, this question will occupy a large portion of the chapter.

The question of the identity of these four kingdoms will guide our interpretation of the chapter as a whole. Here we enter an area where there seems to be an unanimity of opinion among conservative scholars of all millennial views but which we cannot share.

With few exceptions, it is held that the four beasts of Chapter 7 represent the four kingdoms of Chapter 2. Men like Tregelles, Barnes, Pusey, Leupold, Young, Walvoord and Culver all subscribe to this interpretation. Even Montgomery takes this view. William Kelley also subscribes to this view but with a special interpretation of his own.

Against such formidable opposition, Hitzig and Bonnar stand almost alone. They consider such an interpretation to be incompatible on grounds which we will discover in the following paragraphs.

One other scholar of great weight, Sir Robert Anderson, joins them in rejecting the parallel viewpoint.

Keil, whose scholarship has so long been the mainstay of Old Testament conservatives, joins the majority. In discussing the four world kingdoms of Daniel 7, he gives us the following:

"Almost all interpreters understand that these two visions are to be interpreted in the same way. The four kingdoms or dynasties which were symbolized (ch. 2) by the different parts of the human image, from the head to the feet, are the same as those which were symbolized by the four great beasts rising up out of the sea.

"This is the view not only of Bleek, who herein agrees with Auberlen but also of Kranichfeld and Kliefoth and all church interpreters. These four kingdoms according to the interpretation commonly received in the church, are the Babylonian, the Medo-Persian, the Macedo-Grecian and the Roman. In this interpretation and opinion Luther observes, 'All the world are agreed, and history and fact abundantly establish it.' This opinion prevailed til about the end of the last century, for the contrary opinion of individual earlier interpreters had found no favor."[2]

Even the Scofield notes of the A.V., representing as they do the combined judgment of many able and well known conservative scholars, agree in the following words,

"The monarch vision of Nebuchadnezzar (ch. 2) covers the same order of fulfillment as Daniel's beast vision but with this difference: Nebuchadnezzar saw the imposing outward power and splendor of 'the Time of the Gentiles' (Luke 21:24; cp. Rev. 16:19 note) whereas Daniel saw the true character of the gentile world government as rapacious and warlike, established and maintained by force. It is remarkable that the heraldic insignia of the gentile nations are all beasts and birds of prey."[3]

In the following pages, we shall find it necessary very reluctantly, to take our stand with the minority, Bonner and Anderson, and try to show reasons for our disgreement with so many great and good Christian scholars.

The similarities between Chapters 2 and 7 which the Scofield notes consider "the same order of fulfillment," are as follows:

(1) There are four world governments pictured.

(2) The fourth government, the last of each of the series, seems to be without doubt, the Roman empire.

(3) Both series of governments end in catastrophe through divine agency.

(4) This catastrophe ends the Time of the Gentiles and ushers in the millenial reign in both chapters.

(5) There are ten toes in Chapter 2 and ten horns in Chapter 7, though

nothing in Chapter 2 about three horns being plucked by the little horn.

It could be true that Chapter 7 gives the inner nature of the same four in Chapter 7; namely, their beastliness. The details would not have to necessarily conform in every respect.

Having said this, there are evident serious difficulties in such an interpretation relative to the following:

(1) The symbolisms involved in both chapters are not suitably characteristic.

(2) The fact that in Chapter 2 we have a succession of kingdoms already a part of history; in Chapter 7, kingdoms that seem to be contemporary with one another, existing at the same time. The added difficulty that the head of gold was not a kingdom but a person, Nebuchadnezzar, who had been dead perhaps ten years and this is a chapter of prophecy.

(3) The related fact that all four kingdoms in Chapter 7 are extant at the end time and have maintained separate identities.

(4) The survival of the first three beasts after the death of the fourth in Chapter 7 is distinctly not hinted as in Chapter 2.

(5) The historical circumstances already in the past fit Chapter 2 but do not fit Chapter 7, interpreted as a recapitulation of Chapter 2.

(6) The fact that the vision (Chapter 7) looks to the future whereas Nebuchadnezzar, the head of gold, has been dead nearly ten years.

(7) It is impossible to give a satisfactory interpretation of Chapter 7 as involving two well-known, contemporary kingdoms, England and Russia, and a still future time when the third and fourth kingdoms appear; namely, a fourfold Arab kingdom or hegemony and the revived Roman Empire.

It has not seemed strange to some commentators that there was a wealth of prophecy in the Old Testament relative to nations and events at the first advent of the Messiah and no extended prophetic purview of the nations and events just preceding the time of the second coming; this with special reference to Daniel. If we are to regard Chapter 7 as a recapitulation of Chapter 2, it would seem that there is this lack. The dominating gentile powers preceding Christ's first coming are delineated but the contemporary powers in existence at the time of the revived Roman Empire are not given, if so be that Chapter 7 is merely a recapitulation covering the same ground as Chapter 2. Also, to say that the four beasts in Chapter 7 reveal the inner nature of the kingdoms of Babylon, Persia, Greek and Roman dominions would seem to miss the reason for using beasts for symbols.

Until Darwin, men largely thought of themselves as men, good or bad but many more and more, now think of themselves as related to the beasts by descent and by basic nature. Even as the beasts know nothing of God so far as we can see so this age seems to be in the process of repudiating Him. Beasts could properly be used as symbols for a generation that proclaims and practices its identity with the animal world. Even more significantly, the nations at the end time are marked with the mark of the beast. And as the Scofield note suggests, wild animals are the insignia of modern nations. Finally, the moral condition of man at the End Time will be beastly.

With reference to the four beasts, it is evident that the fourth beast is properly identified with the fourth kingdom; that is, the revived Roman Empire but there is little except the fact of the number three, to identify the first three beasts with the three empires embodied in Chapter 2. Babylon, Persia, Greece and Rome are probably correctly identified in Chapter 2 with a hiatus between ancient Rome and future Rome not indicated. Descriptively, Chapter 7 describes a Roman Empire that never was. But it would seem that there are too many straws in the wind pointing to the differences between the two chapters: symbols, historical discrepancies, redundancies in a book not given to redundancies and above all, the fact that Daniel himself does not recognize any similarities between the parts of the image and the four beasts. All of these things militate against giving a common identity to the two visions.

No names are given to these beasts. Could it be, as we have indicated elsewhere, that these are not identified because at that time the kingdoms (if kingdoms they are) did not exist? And hence, if named by their subsequent names, would cause confusion and cast doubt on the prophecy as a whole? If this be granted for the time being at least, we must then identify them if at all, by the symbolism used and by descriptive marks. (It would be well to assume that all of these beasts are delineated here because of their significance to Israel and to Israel's land.)

Now symbols attach themselves to persons and events and in this case especially to peoples, in one of several ways. First, a symbol might be that by which the nations or peoples refer to themselves.[4] We have a case in point when we speak of the U.S. as "Uncle Sam" or Britain as "John Bull." Secondly, it could have been given either by way of identification or of reproach by others. During the First World War, the British spoke of the Germans as "Huns" and the Americans as "Yanks." Thirdly, it could involve a description of a nation or person in terms of some outstanding characteristic or some striking analogy; e.g., "Scotch thrift" or "Yankee ingenuity". We have the case of Nebuchadnezzar's second dream in which he is identified as the tree whose branches reach to heaven and we will also recall that this symbolism of a tree is used elsewhere in Scripture. For example, the first Psalm speaks of the righteous man as a symbol of a tree planted by the rivers of water.

Finally, we recall other symbols that are used characteristically in Scripture. In Isaiah, the Assyrian is spoken of as a *"rod"* of chastisement.

Jerusalem is given the symbolic name of Ariel and she is also spoken of as a *"virgin daughter."* The Antichrist is a *"wild beast."* And Christ is spoken of as *"our rock," "cornerstone,"* and *"rock of offense."*

In the interpretation of these beasts, we may be dealing either with contemporary or with past events. In subsequent chapters (i.e., Chapters 8 and 11), identifications are given as we believe, because there are two horizons (a near and a far event) involved in each one of the symbols, the future event possibly involving the same geographical areas, the same ethnic groups or perhaps the same group characteristics with reference to Israel as the nearer events listed. In Chapters 8 through 11, names can be given at least in part because these nations were contemporary and had identity and name known to that age with the possibility of future involvement in the affairs of Israel. To continue with the interpretation:

This chapter then, is the first of Daniel's own visions and as a good civil servant, he gives us the date in terms of the year of the reigning monarch, the first year of the reign of Belshazzar.⁵

As we have already indicated, the various interpretations of commentators while nearly unanimous, may overlook the temporal clue given us. It is entirely possible for us all to overlook the guidelines in the chapter which will provide some sort of certainty. Whether we are to consider the beasts as persons (as some do) or as kingdoms (which is more common) will appear later. The symbolism of wind is again, a point of disagreement. Is it the Spirit of God? Is it the Prince of the power of the air with the resulting turmoil and anarchy? This is a more likely view.

Let us consider Daniel's vision:

In his vision, he is standing by the sea. The winds are stirring up great waves, a valid description of the present state of nations of the earth if there ever was one, most especially applicable at this time in history. From this sea, which in other Scripture is interpreted as mankind in general, arise four great beasts, diverse from one another. We have the picture of the first beast in verse 4. It was like a lion, a lion with eagle's wings. Daniel says,

I beheld till the wings thereof were plucked, and it was lifted up from the earth, and made to stand upon the feet as a man, and a man's heart was given it.

The heading of this section in the A.V. (Scofield notes) identifies this as the Babylonian Empire but we find a lack of symbolic evidence to support this view.

To be sure, the lion was used as a motif for decorating the Sacred Way in Babylon,⁶ but the lions pictured are not winged lions. Furthermore, as we read Nebuchadnezzar's own account of his building of the city, he tells us that at each of the hundred gates a bronze bull and a bronze serpent were placed.⁷ The bull was to indicate strength, the serpent to indicate wisdom or subtlety presumably. Certainly, one could hardly consider the lion as a symbol of Babylon any more than the bull and the serpent or the sirrush (dragon). The serpent probably, or the bull possibly, but certainly not the lion. Neither are the figures on the Ishtar gate, lions but wild bulls and dragons. Neither was lion-heartedness peculiar to Babylon. Scripture speaks of them as a bitter, hasty nation but not lion-like.[8] As we continue to look for similarities, there is nothing entirely apropos in Babylonian history to the plucking of the feathers of the lion's wings nor to giving it a man's heart. To be sure, her feathers were plucked after conquest. She lost her national identity completely and was incorporated into the Persian Empire. But so far as we know, it was without change of heart and as to plucking feathers, that would hardly be a felicitous term to use to describe its incorporation in the Persian empire.

The second symbolism (verse 5) is that of a bear. And again the bear, so far as we know, was not a symbol used by the Persians themselves nor by Scripture nor by any classical writers. Instead of devouring much flesh, the Persian empire was a relatively tolerant and merciful empire so much so in fact, that the Jews seem to have given it a rather complete loyalty up to and including the time of its conquest by Alexander.[9] Certainly, it did not devour much flesh; that is, above any other empire. Since so far there is no solid indication as to what the three ribs were (though there have been numerous suggestions), we need not bring that into the present discussion though Egypt, Lydia and Babylonia are often assumed to be the ribs other Persian conquests being omitted.

When we come to the symbolism of the leopard (7:6), again we are at a loss. The description begins with *"after this."* After the appearance of the lion and the bear, this new beast appears. This has been thought of as quite descriptive of the Macedonian empire with the four kingdoms into which it broke after Alexander's death. But if one will consider that the four wings of the animal certainly would not have been characteristic of any of these empires after Alexander's death; that is, if wings are to symbolize either rapidity of action or extent of empire and the four heads, while they could indicate the four divisions of the kingdom, are still attached to one body and are not separate beasts (or kingdoms) as were the successors of Alexander, their being attached to one body would seem to indicate some commonality of identity or quality or characteristic not found in the four kingdoms (possibly Arabic language and religion). The chief objection to the whole symbolism is that the leopard was never considered a symbol of Greek or Macedonian nationality so far as we know now, and is not peculiarly descriptive of it.

The fourth beast is by a large number of commentators rightly considered to be Rome but if so, the characteristics described here would have to fit the revived Roman empire under the Antichrist rather than the old Roman empire. Under the republic or under the Caesars, Rome was terrible in war and that part of the description might fit but it brought the

"Pas Romana" and political order to those that it conquered. It did not break in pieces nor stamp the residue by any stretch of the imagination. All over the empire, men were proud of their Roman citizenship whenever it was granted and even the Apostle Paul claimed its privileges. Again, the ten horns do not correspond to anything sufficently significant in ancient Roman history. It could not refer to the twelve caesars or their imperial successors. Then ten Decemvirs were hardly characteristic or important enough. It could not refer to the two consuls annually elected whose number would total many times ten. This symbolism may refer to the ten horns elaborated in Revelation 13 and 17 or the number ten may be purely coincidental. Either way, they must be thought of as belonging to the Seventieth Week and to the revived Roman empire. It would seem that we could easily miss the significance of these symbolic beasts if we miss the temporal significance of the setting. As we see later, all four beasts are extant in the Seventieth Week.

Let us turn for a moment to the ninth verse of the seventh chapter which tells us that,

I beheld til the thrones were cast down (placed) and the Ancient of days did sit, whose garment was white as snow, and the hair of his head like the pure wool.

But following this *"placing"* of thrones, we have the fate of the fourth beast in the eleventh verse,

I beheld even til the beast (fourth) was slain, and his body was destroyed and given to the burning flame.

Now, if these verses (9 and 11) mean anything that can be discovered from the overt statement, they mean that the beast was slain and in a setting that is somehow involved with the Messianic appearance; i.e., "until the Ancient of Days came and judgments were set." If that be granted, we find the key to the chapter in the twelfth verse.

As concerning the rest of the beasts (that is, namely, the first three), they had their dominion taken away yet their lives were prolonged for a season and a time.

Prolonged after what, is the question. Obviously, after the destruction of the fourth beast (verse 11). Therefore, if these four beasts are representative of four kingdoms, they are contemporary and not successive and they exist and function, presumably at the time of the revived Roman Empire and survive its destruction. The thirteenth verse states, "*that he beheld one like the Son of Man who came with the clouds of heaven. . .*" and in the fourteenth verse,

There was given him dominion, and glory, and a kingdom, that all people, nations, and languages, should serve him: his dominion is an everlasting dominion, which shall not pass away, and his kingdom that which

shall not be destroyed.

The whole picture is only meaningful when placed in the setting of the Seventieth Week and terribly confusing otherwise.

There is confusion then, in any interpretation that assumes the historical existence of four beasts which have already succeeded one another, especially if there is an attempt to think of the symbolism as a recapitulation of the image in Chapter 2.

Such a view overlooks the very plain hint that these four beasts will all be in existence at the time of the coming Messiah and will be contemporary and not successive. If we take this view, I am sure that the following interpretation offers fewer difficulties:

What then do these four beasts represent? Let us go back to the fourth verse and see if we can discover symbolisms that would be at all appropriate.

If we were to ask anyone in Western Europe or America the symbols commonly used for England, they might first think of John Bull but certainly the British lion would be equally remembered. In what way has this lion with his far-flung empire, had his wings plucked? Winston Churchill said that he did not propose to preside over the liquidation of the British Empire but nevertheless, he did see it rather thoroughly liquidated and I do not know of any more fitting way of describing its partial disintegration than to say that its wings; its power of empire, its widespread interests and control, though not all of its influence, are like wings that have been plucked. When we consider the significance of a man's heart being given to this beast, our first thought is that this is a step up, that it is a psychological promotion, that which was beastly in its character has now become human.

There is also another way of looking at it. Anyone who can remember the days of either the First World War or the Second cannot but be struck with the lionheartedness of the British people under conditions that were, humanly speaking, almost impossible. Could this symbol then refer to a loss of this quality of lion-like courage and not refer to a humanizing of a beastly quality? Certainly, either interpretation is far more apropos than to try to make the history of Babylon fit such a picture.[10] We remember that England's creation of the Jewish state through the Balfour Declaration brings England into special relationship with Israel. Since we are looking for international involvement and what people have had a special relationship to Israel, what greater significance could we expect to find than the national instrument through which Israel was reestablished in the land of her destiny?[11]

Turning now to the fifth verse, we have the symbolism of the bear. The first thought that comes to one when Russia is mentioned is the Russian bear. For generations, this animal has been used to designate this vast, ungainly country. Can any one country on the face of the earth be so aptly described as having devoured much flesh? Even Hitler, with his demonic lust for power and willingness to shed much blood, cannot equal the human loss of Russia in the First World War, the Russian Revolution, the prison camps of Siberia (20,000,000), the Volga famines (6,000,000), the murders and liquidations that took place under Stalin (wholesale murder of Polish officers) and the human loss during the Second World War. How could anyone describe Russia in better terms? She has indeed devoured much flesh and given the chance, will probably do so again.[12] We must remember too, that this symbolic creature seems to be contemporary with the first beast and with the others. And her relationship to Israel? For generations past, she has been a persecutor of Israel and the present instigator and supporter of Arab opposition to Israel.

If we still insist that Chapter 7 is a recapitulation of Chapter 2, we must remember that Babylon was conquered by Persia and incorporated as a part of the empire. Persia was conquered by Alexander the Great and again became a part of his empire until it broke up. Rome in her conquests, absorbed the conquered peoples of the Hellenic world and in no sense could the four (later three) divisions of Alexander's empire be considered contemporary with the old Roman Empire inasmuch as they completely lost their own identity as empires. But in this chapter, one beast does not devour the others as in Pharaoh's dream (Genesis, Chapter 41) and all are extant on the destruction of the fourth beast. The significance of the three ribs is indeed a difficulty. There were the three Baltic states. But Russia's conquest of Hungary, West Germany and Czechoslovakia as well as her domination of central Europe in general, certainly would not limit the ribs to three.[13] So we must leave this as a significance not presently evident. Let us emphasize again however, that this bear survives the destruction of the fourth-named beast.

In verse 6, we come to the symbolism of the leopard. This verse begins with *"after this"* which also applies to verse 7; that is, after the second beast presumably; or after the first and second (since they seem to be contemporary), comes the leopard. This is a symbolism that has no present, obvious counterpart. We seem to be confronted with one body and with four heads as we first see the beast (not after some catastrophe). We do not know what these may be. One commentator holds that India, Burma and Pakistan might be included in the answer because the leopard is indigenous to these countries. If we consider however, some of the other chapters (notably the eleventh), there arises a very strong feeling that this animal is closer home; that is, closer to Israel than to the distant countries of Burma and India for so far as we can see, these countries do not come within the purview of sacred writ and have no special relationship to Israel though they may be included in the kings of the East (Revelation 16:12). So far as we know, there is no present or past empire that fits this symbolism of the leopard and it may be that the words *"after this"* may have a significance indicating that as yet or up to the present moment, this four-headed, four-winged kingdom has not yet arisen just as similarly the revived Roman empire has yet to appear.

Could the leopard be an alliance of the Arab nations? Most especially those that are closer to the old Babylonian world and which are found in the areas now designated as Iraq, Syria, Jordan, Egypt, Libya and Arabia? Some of these Arabian states in North Africa belonged to the old Roman empire in its greatest extent and might conceivably belong to the new one but not necessarily so. There are also the Moslem countries of Sudan and Pakistan. While there are many more than four Arab states, it would be a miracle indeed if any more than four could cooperate in any solid alliance even against Israel. Until these have consolidated into four, affiliated kingdoms or until some other more obvious combinations appear, they will not fit the symbolism. But that some fourfold federation could rather suddenly appear in the Arab world should not seem too far-fetched or impossible. The following are the secular reasons for regarding the third beast of Daniel 7 as being some part of the Arab world:

(1) There are 150,000,000 Arabs situated on three sides of Israel.

(2) Any attack or invasion of Israel must necessarily involve Arab acquiescence of the conquest.

(3) Arab countries have risen from poverty and political impotence to oil wealth and through it, to political power with a fierce determination to use this power against Israel and her friends.

(4) Oil blackmail can be used against nations favoring Israel. We are presently getting the taste of the degree of Arab enmity.

(5) Russia's schemes of control of the Mediterranean and the Suez Canal make her a party to, and a supporter of these Arab nations. If they are unable to achieve unity in any other way, Russia could be the unifying catalyst.

(6) There is a traditional enmity between Arab and Jew, in abeyance at times, going back to the time of the patriarchs.

(7) There is a present, increased enmity based on Israel's possession of territory long held by Arabs. Some of this territory cannot well be relinquished by Israel without jeopardizing her existence.

(8) The situation is further exacerbated by Israel's possession of an Arab holy place, the Mosque of Omar, the third most holy place of the Arab world.

(9) The four beasts must reasonably have their significance in reference to Israel.

(10) There is no other alternative interpretation available if we reject the Arab nations, considering the contiguity, the traditional involvement with Israel, the psychological factors and basic interests of both groups.

When the federation does appear, it will survive the destruction of the fourth beast. Moreover, if we were to ask what ethnic group or congeries of peoples whose impact on Israel is presently of overwhelming importance, the answer would be the Arab world. And in this respect history is repeating itself, for as Paul says (Galatians 4:29), *"He that was born after the flesh persecuted him that was born after the Spirit."* The descendants of Hagar are even now continuing their antagonism toward the seed of Israel and while we know the danger of interpreting prophecy in the light of what is presently obvious, certainly the age-old enmity must ultimately come up for judgment.

There is far less question about the identity of the fourth beast. The description of the fourth beast as given by Daniel, coincides with other biblical records concerning the world dominion of Antichrist and involves a revived Roman empire. Even now we seem to see forces at work, arranging alliances and creating an atmosphere for this great and terrible event. Present trends are in the direction of the destruction of old values, old concepts of truth, old patterns of life and in the direction of a general anarchy, political, social, moral and spiritual which the Antichrist will reorganize for his own purposes and into his own world order.

The picture then, that we get from this vision is that at the end time (the Seventieth Week of Daniel 9) just preceding Messiah's return in power and glory and judgment, there will be four great governmental or ethnic entities of great significance to the Jewish state:

First, Great Britain and possibly the English speaking people (Canada, Australia and possibly America). Their significance to Israel is one of friendliness but probably impotence.

Second, Russia and her satellites which, if we accept Ezekiel 38 and 39 as belonging to this particular situation, would include Persia, Ethiopia, Libya, Gomer with all his bands and the house of Togarmah. Russia has been and is, the persecutor of Israel.

The third beast may possibly be some part of the Arab world; in fact, four parts of it, with its unity of religion and speech but politically having its four heads of government.

The fourth beast is less questionable and is without doubt the revived Roman Empire, no longer an order-producing, civilizing force as at its first incarnation but an oppressive, tyrannical and intolerant government, demonic in its origin and its purposes.

When we come to consider the ten kings; that is, the ten horns of Daniel 7, we seem to discover that they are not hereditary kings if we identify them with those of Revelation, for they have *"received no kingdom as yet but received power one hour with the beast"* (Revelation 17), if they are the same ten kings as some hold. Actually, this identification is extremely doubtful. When the little horn of Daniel 7 comes up, three of them fall before him, apparently because they are opposed to him or he cannot manipulate them. He subdues these three horns and apparently can and does, dominate the other seven even though they precede him. *"He shall be diverse from the first."* Whether this difference is in his character, his power or his Satanic backing, we can only guess. It is possible that it is because he claims to be god and they do not; possibly because his power extends for forty-two months and theirs for only one hour. Whatever the difference, his power seems to rest upon Satanic enduement, theirs on his will.

It will be seen at once that there are obvious difficulties in any inter- pretation involving the revived Roman Empire that assumes the ten toes to be ten areas within the greatest former boundaries of that empire (East and West), especially if we assume the third beast to be the Arab states. How could the Arab states, occupying areas formerly a part of the east- ern empire, be a separate third beast, assuming the fourth beast to be the Roman Empire?

The most plausible solution would be to assume that neither the east nor the west of the revived empire would occupy areas of their greatest expansion.[14]

We have not so far, given variant or supporting viewpoints, though most are worthy of respect. However, space only permits the following. In an attempt to establish a parallel between Chapters 2 and 7 in Daniel, William Kelly considers verse 12 to mean as follows:

"Of the remains of the Chaldean, or of the races that were called so, we have still, Persia which abides as a kingdom and the Greeks who have lately become one. They exist therefore, though not as imperial powers. We have these races of men, more or less, representing those powers; smaller, it is true, and no longer having dominion as empires. That is the meaning of verse twelve."[15]

In a way, this is a plausible explanation but explains neither the sym- bolism nor the historical realities sufficiently and certainly not Daniel's unfamiliarity with these beasts and his lack of recognition of any relation- ship with what had gone before in Chapter 2.

However, let us examine more closely this viewpoint since it does at least recognize verse 12 as presenting us with kingdoms contemporary with the revived Roman Empire.

First, as to symbols: The head of gold was not Babylon as interpreted in Daniel 2, but was Nebuchadnezzar himself. This is not only stated but stated emphatically. But if we somehow by metonymy, assume the country to be symbolized by the king, then the present kingdom of Babylon would be Iraq which occupies the approximate territory of old Babylonia. If we attempt to equate modern Iraq with the first beast of Daniel 7:4, we see nothing symbolic in modern Iraq; nothing lion-like, no wings, no change of heart. Its flag consists of horizontal bars; red, white, and black with three green stars on the white bar. Nothing in the flag symbolizes the first beast. As to the nature of the government or people of modern Iraq, nothing is lion-like. What the country is chiefly noted for is oil and a rigid dictatorship which followed the murder of a progressive and benevolent king.

Modern Persia, on the other hand, does have the lion symbol on its flag but if it were to symbolize the second beast, we would expect it to be a bear. There is nothing in modern Persia, moreover, in the least bear-like either as to its government or its people. It has not devoured much flesh. It is rapidly becoming an industrial nation.

Modern Turkey and modern Syria occupy some of the area once controlled by the Seleucidae or what was called Syria. There is nothing suggesting a panther, neither the four heads nor the four wings. Therefore, for symbolic reasons alone, we must reject Kelly's interpretation.

If on the other hand, we try to identify these modern countries by their descriptions of people or government or in terms of significant events, again we draw a blank. As we have said above, there is nothing lion-like; no wings of empire, no change of heart for Iraq; no devouring much flesh for Persia; and as to the four-winged, four-headed leopard, no dominion has been given it (i.e., Greece) sufficient to cause biblical comment. It would be no more profitable for us, were we to take more space to particularize, since we would find far more disparities than similarities in the picture. I do not think that we are assuming too much to expect the biblical writer to have given outstanding characteristics of these beasts rather than some minor traits that could be twisted into conformity with the symbols and the descriptions.

If we follow Anderson's suggestion that the great sea is the Mediterranean and at least some of the beasts are contiguous to it, Turkey and some of the Arab states come immediately to mind when we try to identify the third beast. Turkey seems out of the picture, if the revived Roman empire has at least part of its eastern half; i.e., occupied at present by Turkey which has nothing to correspond to the symbols of the four heads and the four wings. The probabilities lie therefore, with some future, fourfold hegemony of Arab states. (See Anderson, The Coming Prince, App. II, p. 277.)

It has sometimes been assumed that there is only one reasonable, premillennial interpretation of this chapter (i.e., Daniel 7 as a recapitulation of Daniel 2) but this is not so. James Bonnar, writing in 1871, takes an entirely different and thought-provoking interpretation of the chapter in his book, "The Great Interregnum." We quote in part:

"We cannot but observe that Daniel's commentators seem to have found their way to the interpretation of this vision far more easily than Daniel himself. The 'undoubted parallelism' and identity of these two first visions (i.e., Daniel 2 and Daniel 7) seems not in the very least to strike the prophet himself. . . . It seems to us that so far from recognizing a subject already known, he feels himself transported into the midst of scenes and subjects strange, and painful as they are strange. He is the most anxious to know the meaning of all this. . . . For these foregoing reasons then; first because the four beasts, all of them, come up out of the great sea; secondly, because the four beasts, all of them, come up consequently to the date of the vision; thirdly, because the beasts, especially the fourth beast, do not symbolically correspond to the four empires in the received interpretation; fourthly, because the first three beast kings prolong their lives after their dominion is taken away which is in no sense true of the corresponding dynasties in the interpretation; fifthly, because the prophet's own entire feeling regarding the vision seems to speak expressly of a new world of mystery laid open to him; for all these foregoing reasons, we feel constrained decisively to reject the current interpretation of the vision of the four beasts. And what now then, with respect to the authentic interpretations of the visions? Two elements alone toward the interpretation we can at present note; that is the two termini. The closing terminus is simple and clear; it is the End. As to the commencing terminus of the vision, it is when 'the four winds of the heavens strove upon the great sea.' And at what hour then of the world's day or night, may we say, is it when the spirits of the East and the West, of the North and the South begin to strive upon the stormy sea of the European West? When did this western world begin to be the grand arena of this universal conflict of principles and fashions, the battlefield of all the spirits that it has now for so long been; waxing evermore upwards to the culminating Armageddon, when the kings of the earth and of the whole world shall be gathered together for the battle of that great day of God Almighty? At an hour, we may certainly say not earlier than the dawn of our modern era, than the inauguration of the cycle of Christian civilization."[16]

Sir Robert Anderson in *"The Coming Prince"* suggests grave difficulties in equating Daniel 7 with Daniel 2. He says,

" First, Daniel II and Daniel VII are both in the Chaldee portion of the book and are therefore bracketed together, and separate from what follows. This strengthens the presumption therefore, which would obtain in any case, that the latter vision is not a repetition of the earlier one. Repetition is very rare in Scripture.

"Second, the date of the vision of the seventh chapter was the first year of Belshazzar, and therefore only some two or three years before the fall of the Babylonian Empire. How then could the rise of that empire be a subject of that prophecy? Verse 17 appears definite that the rise of all these kingdoms was to be future.

"Third, in the history of Babylonia there is nothing to correspond with the predicted course of the first beast, for it is scarcely legitimate to suppose that the vision was a prophecy of the career of Nebuchadnezzar, whose death had taken place upwards of twenty years before the vision was given. Moreover, that transition from the lion with the eagle's wings to the human condition, though it may be taken decline in power, plainly typifies a signal rise morally and intellectually.

"Fourth, neither is there in the history of Persia anything answering to the bear-like beast with that precision and fulness which prophecy demands. The language of the English version suggests a reference to Persia and Media; but the true rendering appears to be, 'it made for itself one dominion' instead of 'it raise itself up on one side.'

"Fifth, while the symbolism of the sixth verse seems at first sight to point definitely to the Grecian Empire, it will appear upon a closer examination, that at its advent the leopard had four wings and four heads. This was its primary and normal condition, and it was in this condition that 'dominion was given to it.' This is surely very different from what Daniel VIII.8 describes, and what the history of Alexander's Empire realized; viz., the rise of a single power which in its decadence continues to exist in a divided state.

"Sixth, each of the first three empires of the second chapter (Babylon, Persia, Greece) was in turn destroyed and engulfed by its successor: But the kingdoms of the seventh chapter all continued together on the scene, though 'the dominion' was with the fourth (Daniel VII.12). Verse three seems to imply that the four beasts came up together, and at all events there is nothing to suggest a series of empires each destroying its successor, though the symbolism of the vision (in contrast with that of Chapter II) admirably adapted to represent this. Compare the language of the next vision (Daniel VIII.3-6).

"Seventh, while the fourth beast is unquestionably Rome, the language of the seventh and twenty-third verses leaves no doubt that it is the Roman Empire in its revived and future phase. Without endorsing the views of Maitland, Browne, etc., it must be owned that there was nothing in the history of ancient Rome to correspond with the main characteristics of this beast unless the symbolism used is to be very loosely interpreted. To 'devour the earth,' 'tread it down and break it in pieces' is fairly descriptive of other empires, but ancient Rome was precisely the one power which added government to conquest, and instead of treading down and breaking in pieces the nations it subdued, sought rather to mold them to its own civilization and polity. All this, and more might be added, suggests that the entire vision may have a future reference."[17]

Anderson considered the great sea to be the Mediterranean, "the lion possibly typifys England whose vast naval power may be symbolized by eagle's wings," and says further, "if the British lion has a place in the vision, the Muscovite bear can scarcely be omitted." He does not offer any confident suggestion as to the third beast. We must remember that he wrote nearly two generations ago, as would be noted by his suggestion to England's far-flung navy. Jerome's comment on this chapter is as follows,

"We should therefore concur with the traditional interpretation of all the commentators of the Christian Church that at the end of the world when the Roman empire is to be destroyed, there shall be ten kings who will partition the Roman world among themselves. Then an insignificant eleventh king shall arise who will overcome three of the ten kings; that is, the king of Egypt, the king of (North) Africa and the king of Ethiopia as we shall show more clearly in our later discussion. Then after they have been slain, the seven other kings also will bow their necks to the victor. . . . And behold, their eyes like unto human eyes in that horn. Let us not follow the opinion of some commentators of the human race, in whom Satan will wholly take up his residence in bodily form. . . and a mouth uttering overweening boasts . . . (cf. II Thess. 2). For this is the man of sin, the son of perdition, and that too, to such a degree that he dares to sit in the temple of God, making himself out to be like God."

In closing this chapter, we must call particular attention to the three verses (24, 25, and 26) which introduce to us not a kingdom only as they do in Daniel 2 but to a person, the eleventh horn that shall arise out of the fourth kingdom. He is described as different from the ten and shall subdue three of the ten. He is characterized as follows:

(1) *"He shall speak words against the most high."* He is anti-God and aggessively so.

(2) *"And shall wear out the saints of the most high."* He is both anti-Jew and anti-Christian and finds means to persecute and to destroy them.

(3) *"And think to change times and laws."* This would seem to mean moral and spiritual laws and even as the French revolution in its antitheistic view changed even the months of the year from their traditional nomanclature so this individual will try to abolish all traditional customs, usages and even memories of the true faith.

(4) *"And they shall be given into his hand until, a time, times and the dividing of times."* This is usually interpreted as applying to the last three and a half years of the Great Tribulation.

(5) *"But judgment shall sit, and they shall take away his dominion to consume and destroy it to the end."* In this one sentence we have the final judgment, the final destruction of Antichrist and the final destruction that pertains to his kingdom.

This sinister person sounds very much like the Antichrist of Christian tradition in that he rules over a dominion that is godless, intolerant, revolutionary and after a period of cooperation with Israel, breaks alliance with them and becomes their enemy. We shall keep these three verses in mind for evaluation when all other evidence is in since we have three, somewhat similar descriptions in Daniel 8, 9, and 11 and these in turn must be equated with John 5:43, II Thessalonians 2:3-10, Revelation 13:1-10 and Revelation 17:8-18. It will be well to keep in mind the Roman background of this man since some of the subsequent descriptions seem to be Greek as to ethnic source.

This chapter closes with a paean of victory for the saints of the Most High. Their kingdom is a universal kingdom, "under the whole heaven," given them by the Most High who reigns eternally. Even as Bonnar pointed out elsewhere in this chapter, Daniel does not in any way recognize this vision as the one interpreted to him in Daniel 2 for we read, "as for me, Daniel, my cogitations much trouble me and my countenance changed in me; but I kept the matter in my heart."

If we object to the second beast as being Russian, we seem to have a confirmation in Ezekiel 38 and 39. This is somewhat generally interpreted as equating Magog with the country of Russia and the cities Moscow and Tobolsk as being the equivalents of the two Hebrew words used, Meshech and Tubal. If these two chapters cannot be thus interpreted, there is no very logical interpretation of them given by commentators. If we accept this interpretation, we have identified the second beast and the fourth beast. For an amillennial view, they have the following,

"In recent times another interpretation has been making its appearance. This interpretation is known generally as dispensationalism. It is to the effect that the fourth monarch represents not only the historical Roman Empire, but a revived Roman Empire, which will come to an end by a sudden catstrophic judgment, after which the kingdom of God (i.e., the millennium of Revelation 20:1-6) will be set up. The destruction of the gentile world power, according to this view, occurs not at the first coming of Christ, but at his second event."[18]

Young could more correctly have said not the gentile world power but all gentile world powers since the destruction of the image is to be followed by the setting up of the universal kingdom of Christ. A view of the present world scene would lead one to doubt that Christ's kingdom has come on earth as it has in heaven or that there is any demonstrable change for the better to demonstrate any presence of Christ's kingdom on earth. Further, the premillennial viewpoint is as old as the Christian church.

If we may sum up the interpretation of this part of the chapter, the following points seem pertinent,

(1) Verse 12 of the chapter precludes any identification of any of the four beasts with the Babylonian, Persian, Macedonian and old Roman Empires (as in Chapter 2) since the destruction of the fourth beast is followed by the survival of the three other beasts.

(2) The third beast is not clearly identified biblically but the phrase

"after this," with reference to this beast and the same phrase relative to the fourth beast presents us with a temporal sequence. Even as the revived Roman Empire has not yet appeared so the fourfold third empire may also be yet in the future. It seems reasonable to think that this beast may have some positive or negative, special relationship to Israel and we have suggested that it may conceivably arise out of the Arab world and take on its fourfold organization at a later time. Israel is surrounded on three sides by Arab nations. It is almost inconceivable that anything could happen to Israel that would not involve these nearby nations.

(3) As the fourth beast clearly is involved with the Antichrist and the whole picture from verse 13 to 27 seems to be a clear picture of the Seventieth Week and the tribulation period, if the other three beasts survive the fourth, then all are contemporary with the events of the Seventieth Week. This would be impossible if Chapter 7 recapitulates Chapter 2.

(4) The symbolisms involved are consistent with the end time and the modern nations of England, Russia, etc., but confusing when applied to the four historic empires in Chapter 2.

(5) We must admit difficulties when we try to equate the third beast with the Arab world if we assume, first, that all the Arab nations are involved or, second, that the eastern Roman Empire as revived will cover the greatest territorial extent of the old empire. To avoid this large geographical overlapping, we will have to assume that either the whole Arab world will not be involved or a constricted eastern empire is meant or the western half represents the former total area. The fact that the Arab and Moslem world is anything but monolithic makes the first option somewhat preferable even though it is hard to see how most of the Asiatic (not including Turkey) and the North African Arab states could be left out of such a coalition. However, so fluid and unpredictable are the alliances in the Arab world that almost anything could happen.

(6) It is entirely conceivable that some other four-headed power is meant but territorially and ethnically, any other solution removes us from areas and racial groups traditionally involved with Israel.

(7) The description of the first and third beast contains nothing openly sinister. This does not particularly support our proposed interpretation of the third beast as an Arab coalition. At present, the Arab world (and her Russian ally) is Israel's most bitter foe and while the statement "dominion was given it" certainly could describe the revived importance of these oil rich countries yet there is nothing in the description to describe the bitter antagonism toward Israel. Actually, we have nothing good or bad. Again, this might be predictive of the futility characteristic of the Arab opposition but certainly not descriptive of its deep enmities. Is this perhaps because the Arab is also of Abraham's seed according to the flesh?[19]

(8) The second beast is characterized by bloodthirstiness and no other

western government, past or present, so truly fits this description as Russia. The fourth beast is the most extensively described in ten verses; i.e., a third of a chapter which emphasizes its importance. The description does not essentially give us a true picture of the old Roman Empire which with all its faults, brought law and order, established centuries of Roman peace, eliminated international rivalries and was a predictable and stable influence. This is not the picture given us in the ten verses of Daniel 7. It is a renewed Roman Empire that is described.

The suggested solution has obvious difficulties, but there seems to be a lack of reasonable alternatives. What past or present, ethnic or geographical groups or areas contiguous to Israel are offered as a substitute solution?

CHAPTER IX

THE KING OF IMPUDENT VISAGE
THE FALSE PROPHET

(Daniel 8)

In the second vision, we are given the time (the third year of Belshazzar, possibly 553 B.C.) and the place where the vision occurred (Shushan, the palace in the province of Elam by the River Ulai). From here on to the end of the book, Daniel writes in Hebrew; hence, with particular significance to the Jewish nation.

It will pay us to give attention to the outline of this eighth chapter since by following this, we will avoid confusing the vision and its details with the interpretation and its details. The chapter may be divided, roughly, into seven sections,

(1) The setting; i.e., time and place of the vision (verses 1-2).

(2) The historical background portion of the vision; namely, the contest between the ram and the goat (verses 3-8).

(3) The main theme of the vision; i.e., the little horn, possibly with the person of Satan as his inspirer (verses 9-14).

(4) The theophany and ministry of Gabriel together with dating of the vision; the end time, the 2,300 days (verses 15-19).

(5) The interpretation of the background portion of the vision: Medo-Persia and Greece (verses 20, 22).

(6) The interpretation of the main vision in which the little horn is interpreted as the king of fierce or bold or impudent countenance (verses 23-26).

(7) The personal note; Daniel fainted and was ill and perplexed over the vision. His astonishment precludes any identification of Chapter 8 with Chapter 7 - "none understood it."

Let us take these sections in order. In verses 1 and 2, we read,

In the third year of the reign of king Belshazzar, a vision appeared unto me, even unto me Daniel, after that which appeared unto me at the first. And I saw a vision; and it came to pass, when I saw that, I was at Shushan in the palace, which is in the province of Elam; and I saw in a vision, and I was by the river Ulai.

Daniel does not tell us why he is no longer in Babylon and since we have no particular certainty that Elam was a part of the Neo-Babylonian Empire at that time (more probably it was a part of Persia), it is possible that he may have been an envoy of some sort for verse 27 tells us that he was still a civil servant; i.e., *"he did the king's business."* We do know that at the taking of Babylon, he was once more in that city so whether permanently located at Susa or merely a special envoy, we can easily believe that Belshazzar would find it much more comfortable to have a man of Daniel's religious convictions at some distance from the royal court. As we read the record, both the king and his father are committed to a polytheistic reaction; the monotheistic influence of a man of Daniel's moral and personal stature would be particularly unwelcome. However, as a servant of outstanding talents and integrity, he is too valuable to lose. We read on:

Then I lifted up mine eyes, and saw, and, behold, there stood before the river a ram which had two horns; and the two horns were high, but one was higher than the other, and the higher came up last. (3) I saw the ram pushing westward, and northward, and southward, so that no beasts might stand before him, neither was there any that could deliver out of his hand, but he did according to his will and became great. (4)

And as I was considering, behold, a he goat came from the west over the face of the whole earth, and touched not the ground; and the goat had a notable horn between his eyes. (5) And he came to the ram that had two horns, which I had seen standing before the river, and ran into him in the fury of his power. (6) And I saw him come close to the ram, and he was moved with anger against him, and smote the ram and broke his two horns; and there was no power in the ram to stand before him, but he cast him to the ground and stamped upon him; and there was none that could deliver the ram out of his hand. (7) Therefore the he goat grew very great; and when he was strong, the great horn was broken, and for it came up four notable ones toward the four winds of heaven. (8)

These six verses (3-8) give us the background out of which the little horn springs and whatever its meaning, we are given a picture of great vividness. Whether this is a dream or more likely, a waking vision with the River Ulai as its link with the world of physical reality, we cannot be sure. We note that the beasts are symbols (as in Daniel Chapter 7) but here they are not beasts of prey but aggressive, domestic animals whose ordinary functions are to provide food and raiment for man. These verses were future to Daniel but they are now history to us.

They give us a thumbnail sketch of:

(1) the rise and fall of the Persian Empire, vignettes of selected, significant portions, and

(2) the enormous conquests of Alexander the Great, the notable horn of the he goat; conquests extending from India and beyond, westward and southward to Greece and Egypt. Alexander's premature death, at the age of thirty-three, is the *"great horn that was broken."* His enormous empire

was divided among his generals, the Diodochi; i.e., successors (his two sons being bypassed)who finally became heads of four great kingdoms, namely,

(1) Macedonia and Greece under Cassander,

(2) Thrace and Asia Minor under Lysimachus,

(3) Syria, Babylonia and India under Seleucus and

(4) Egypt, Palestine, and Arabia under Ptolemy. It is of these last two; the king of the north (Syria) and the king of the south (Egypt), with whom Daniel later (Chapter 11) concerns himself since Israel lies between these two ambitious kingdoms. The kingdoms of Cassander and Lysimachus are not contiguous to Israel and apparently do not enter into the prophecy. As in this and other chapters, only certain episodes and persons are presented. Intervening history not pertinent to the Spirit's purpose, is left out.

That Alexander's conquests and the Hellenizing effect upon Israel seem to have been a part of God's plan for a universal language (Greek) and the penetration of all cultural boundaries by Greek culture and thinking as a desirable prelude to the spread of Christianity, it is not given Daniel to see. Neither is there any hint that all of this was calculated not to destroy but to extend and fulfill the mission of Israel; to make outgoing that which otherwise would be ingrowing. What is perfectly clear is that all of this takes place according to the foreknowledge and by the determinate counsel of God. What is also clear is that Israel is a part of God's purposes and love to the end of the age.

The following verses (9-14) are properly described by the Scofield notes (older edition) as "confessedly the most difficult in prophecy, a difficulty increased by the present state of the text."

This section, often thought to refer to Antiochus Epiphanes (the little horn), if it does refer to him and him alone, the language used is utterly incongruous and exaggerated. It is the most gross hyperbole to speak of Antiochus as *"casting down some of the host of heaven"* and equating this host with the Jewish nation or again, equating the *"prince of the host"* with the Jewish high priest; there being no host, nor he its prince.

Scripture continues:

And out of one of them came forth a little horn, which grew exceedingly great, toward the south, toward the east, and toward the pleasant land. (9) And it grew great, even to the host of heaven; and it cast down some of the host and of the stars to the ground, and stamped upon them. (10) Yea, he magnified himself even to the prince of the host, and by him the daily sacrifice was taken away, and the place of his sanctuary was cast down. (11) And a host was given him against the daily sacrifice by reason of transgression, and it cast down the truth to the ground; and it

*continued and prospered. (12)   Then I heard one saint speaking, and
another saint said to that saint who spoke, How long shall be the vision
concerning the daily sacrifice, and the transgression of desolation, to give
both the sanctuary and the host to be trampled under foot? (13) And he
said unto me, Unto two thousand and three hundred days; then shall the
sanctuary be cleansed. (14)*

Thus ends the main burden of the vision; the introduction of the little
horn and his activities.

Were the vision to end here, we would be at a loss to identify the little horn. As we have suggested, he cannot be the little horn of Daniel 7:8.
But have we a new and possibly a similar character introduced? Out of
the obscurity of language so far, we cannot understand the when, where,
or what of these six verses. However, help is near and we are introduced
to those who are able to interpret the vision for with the vision come the
interpreters.

*And it came to pass, when I, even I Daniel, had seen the vision, and
sought for the meaning, then, behold, there stood before me one having
the appearance of a man. (15) And I heard a man's voice between the
banks of the Ulai, who called, and said, Gabriel, make this man to understand the vision. (16) So he came near where I stood; and when he came,
I was afraid, and fell on my face; but he said unto me, Understand, O son
of man: for at the time of the end shall be the vision. (17) Now as he was
speaking with me, I was in a deep sleep on my face toward the ground,
but he touched me, and set me upright. (18) And he said, Behold I will
make thee know what shall be in the last end of the indignation; for at the
time appointed shall the end be. (19)*

In these verses, we have presented to us the interpreters, but who are
they? One, a Voice; the other, the angel Gabriel who is the one actually
interpreting. Since the Voice is the authority by which Gabriel acts, it
would seem that in the Voice, we have an invisible presence of deity, especially so since in Daniel's fourth vision and under similar circumstances
we manifestly have a Theophany.

THE TIME SETTING

With the interpreters comes the key to the time significance of the
vision: "for the time of the end shall be the vision" (verse 17) and again
in verse 19, "what shall be in the last end of the indignation." The vision
concerns itself, therefore, with the Seventieth Week, the time of God's indignation and the time of the Seals, the Trumpets and the Bowls of the
Book of Revelation and the time of Israel's trouble of Daniel 12:1. The
time indicator is repeated in order that we do not miss the point.

THE IDENTITY OF THE LITTLE HORN

If we consult some of the most able commentators, we get a somewhat mixed result. Appropos of Daniel 8:9, Barnes says:

"There can be no doubt the Antiochus is denoted here. All the circumstances of the prediction find a fulfillment in him. Again, a few expositors have supposed this passage refers to Antichrist; what will not expositors of the Bible suppose? But the great body of interpreters have understood it to refer to Antiochus."[2]

Again, Walvoord, with reference to verses 9 and 10, says:

" As a result of his military conquests the little horn, representing Antiochus Epiphanes, is said to grow great 'even to the host of heaven.' He is pictured as casting some of the host and the stars to the ground and stamping on them. This difficult prophecy has aroused many technical discussions, as that of Montgomery which extends over several pages (J.A. Montgomery, The Book of Daniel, pp. 332-340). If the Mythological explanations such as identifying stars with heathen gods or the seven planets are discarded and this is considered genuine prophecy probably the best explanation is that this prophecy relates to the persecution and destruction of the people of God with its defiance of the angelic hosts who are their protectors, including the power of God Himself. To this may be added Daniel 12:3 where a starlike glory is held out to those who 'turn many to righteousness.' Compare also Matthew 13:43. If the world calls those men and women stars who excel in one or another department of human activity, why should not a similar statement be still more appropriate with reference to God's people?

"Leupold considers the host and stars in apposition, that is, 'the host even the stars.' That Antiochus blasphemed God and heavenly power as well as persecuted the people of Israel, the people of God, is all too evident from history. Even Driver states, 'the stars are intended to symbolize the faithful Israelites'; c.f. Enoch XLVI, 7."[3]

Contrariwise, Keil says:

"This horn raised in its might even to the Prince of the host, sar hatzavol, the Prince of the host of heaven is obviously not the high priest, Onias (Grotius) but the God of Heaven and the King of Israel, the Prince of Princes, as he is called in verse 25. "higdheel" (He magnified himself to) is repeated in verse 25 (He will stand up against). Wherein this rising up against God consisted, the second half of the verse indicates in the statement that the (daily sacrifice) was taken away, and the building of His sanctuary was destroyed. This verse does not record a part of the vision, but is a further development of that which was seen in prophetic words. Hence we may not, with Ebrard, refer its contents to heavenly events, to the putting away of the sacrifice from before the throne of God and a destruction of a heavenly sanctuary. On the contrary, Kliefoth has well remarked that it is 'without example in Scripture that men penetrated into heaven to insult God; what men do against God is done on the earth.'"[4]

Not against God personally but seducing angels and trying to make himself equal to God was a heavenly event by Satan. The final clause of verse 11 is even more difficult than verse 10 and utterly impossible to equate with any action by Antiochus, for here we are not describing a defilement but a destruction of the sanctuary. The statement that the "place of the sanctuary was cast down" by the little horn would imply the destruction of the temple. The Hebrew hushlak-michohn-mikdahsho means just that[5] But we have no destruction of the temple by Antiochus, only its pollution. Neither Nebuchadnezzar nor Titus, each of whom did destroy it, is a possible candidate. So whoever else the little horn may be, he is not Antiochus, and we must look to a future temple and a future destroyer.

This difficult chapter has usually one or two, or three, interpretations regarding the horn. He is regarded either as (1) Antiochus, (2) Antichrist or (3) Antiochus as type and Antichrist as antitype. Young says, "The little horn of Chapter 7 is Antichrist; the horn of Chapter 8 is Antiochus."[6]

Walvoord takes the other line, "But the verses 23-27 of the chapter before us have to do with 'a king of fierce countenance' who shall appear in the 'latter time' (verse 23) and he is none other than the Antichrist who is to come."[7]

Keil makes him Antiochus: "The king that rises up is Antiochus Epiphanes (cf. 1 Macc. 1. 10ff), hard of countenance; i.e., impudent, unashamed in trampling down, without fear of God or man."[8]

Tregelles: "The conclusion from all of this appears to be inevitable, that the horn of Chapter 7 and Chapter 8 are one and the same person."[9]

Talbot agrees with Walvoord: "But verses 23-27 of the chapter before us have to do with the king of fierce countenance who shall appear in the latter time (verse 23) and he is none other than the Antichrist who is to come."[10]

Kelly interprets this as a double reference type and antitype, "No doubt this was the person (Antiochus Epiphanes) meant historically by the 'little horn.' But he shows the same kind of features, which will reappear in another great leader of the last days."[11]

As does Pentecost:

"But this passage in Daniel 8 is speaking not only of Antiochus in his desolation and his desecration of the temple; it is looking forward to the great desolator who would come, the one who is called the little horn in Daniel 7. In Daniel 8:23 we read of this one and his ministry."[12]

For an excellent statement of the somewhat common view, William Kelly has this to say:

"Here, then, we find that this little horn 'waxed great even to the host of heaven: and it cast down some of the host and of the stars to the ground, and stamped upon them.' Thereby is meant, I apprehend, those that were in a position of honor and glory before the Jewish people. Thus stars are used, in the new Testament, as the symbol of those who are set in a place of authority in the Church. Just so, I conceive, 'host of heaven' here alludes to persons that held a place or authority in the Jewish polity. It is the keynote to all this part of the prophecy. The importance of all that affects Israel is now more and more coming into view. Hence the force of an expression used that may seem strong, 'the host of heaven.' But we must not be surprised at this. God takes the utmost interest in His people.[13]

This explanation is not in the least fantastic and has much to recommend it but the language is at variance with Daniel's usually restrained descriptions.

Whether the vision was, all of it waking or sleeping or part of each, the first contact with the heavenly personages was when he "was in a deep sleep upon my face toward the ground."

In the following verses (20-22), we have the identities of the ram as the kings of Medo-Persia and the rough goat as king of Grecia, Alexander the Great. The horn (Alexander) being broken (by his death), the four kingdoms; Macedonia, Asia Minor, Syria, and Egypt, were formed out of Alexander's empire but their rulers, the Diodochi (the successors), did not rule in his power.

In what follows (23-26), we leave the background verses (9-14) and are given the interpretation of the main thrust of the vision for which verses 20-22 have prepared us. Our attention now shifts to a particular individual somehow related in the latter days to one of Alexander's successors,or the someone rising up out of what was his kingdom. We read,

And in the latter time of their kingdom when transgressors are come to the full, a king of fierce countenance, and understanding dark sentences, shall stand up. (23) And his power shall be mighty, but not by his own power; and he shall destroy wonderfully, and shall prosper, and continue, and shall destroy the mighty and the holy people. (24) And through his policy also he shall cause deceit to prosper in his hand; and he shall magnify himself in his heart, and by peace shall destroy many; he shall also stand up against the Prince of princes, but he shall be broken without hand. (25) And the vision of the evening and morning which was told is true; wherefore shut up the vision; for it shall be for many days. (26)

Again, we note the time label: *"it shall be for many days."*

How shall we interpret this main portion of the vision? Rather, What does the interpretation given us mean? Obviously, the interpretation in verses 23-25 given us by Gabriel, is an explanation of verses 9-14. Furthermore, since the little horn is the main character in the vision and the king of fierce (bold, shameless) countenance is center stage in the interpretation, they must be the same person and/or related to the same situation. This little horn then, cannot be Antiochus Epiphanes as some allege since the description in verses 23-25 in no way fits him. Part of the difficulty with this chapter, however, arises from the apparent lack of complete harmony between the items in the vision and those in the interpretation, even though the overall effect is the same; the image of a blasphemous, egotistical, ruthless leader who fears neither man nor God and who uses any and all means; diplomacy, deceit, treachery, war, to destroy all opposition especially Jewish opposition.

If we were not specifically told that the interpretation belongs to the vision, we would be tempted to consider that two individuals rather than one were in view.

The obscurity, however, clears up when we see that the points of disparity have reference to two separate aspects of the same activity. Verses 9-14, largely emphasize the religious and spiritual aspects and motivation while verses 23-25 refer to the means by which opposition to God and to God's people is visibly accomplished. There are enough identical elements in each description to link them but enough disparity to emphasize two points of view, the heavenly (verses 10-11, especially) and the earthly (verses 23-25); i.e., the viewpoint of that minority who suffered under his rule. For example, in verse 10, do we not have hints with reference to satanic rebellion as that of Ezekiel 28:13-17? Do we not have the vision giving us the satanic source of the little horn's power and blasphemous attitude, Satan embodying himself in the little horn? It seems utterly impossible to think that the language used; i.e., *"grew great even to the host of heaven"* and *"cast down some of the host and of the stars to the ground"*, could possibly refer to Antiochus (or any other human being even demonically activated) in his dealings with the high priest or with any other circumstance of Jewish oppression. In view of the characteristically restrained language of Scripture and of Daniel especially, even symbolic language could hardly go so far.

In the prophecy against Tyre (Ezekiel 28), the prophet gives, it seems to me, a clue that might unlock this passage in Daniel which is rightly considered by many (see Scofield notes) as one of the most difficult in the book. At least the following gives us an alternative viewpoint:

In his prophecy against the ancient city of Tyre, Ezekiel first gives a description of the Prince of Tyre; proud, incredibly rich, impressed with his own wisdom and ready to bestow upon himself divine honors and immortality (verses 2-9). This is the human, visible ruler.

Following this, we have a lamentation on the King of Tyre (verses 12-19) described in terms that could not possibly refer to any mortal. He is obviously Satan, *"the anointed cherub," "full of wisdom and perfect in beauty until iniquity was found in thee."* Why do we have these two passages in juxtaposition and both identified with rule over Tyre? For the reason, of course, that back of the prince and kingdom of Tyre (and of all the kingdoms of this world) is the prince of this world system.

The real king of Tyre is not the man who sits upon the throne but the one who heads *"the principalities, powers, rulers of darkness of this world";* Satan, who motivates and empowers kings. He is this world's king of kings. He is the god of this age. This relationship was particularly true of Tyre as a type.

But how does this passage in Ezekiel furnish us light on Daniel 8? It would seem that in Daniel, we have an analogous situation except that the order is reversed. First, the image of the god of this age, Satan (Daniel 8:10), is interpolated in the description of a satanically-inspired person, the little horn but with this difference also; verse 9 identifies with the little horn, not with Satan who is obviously spoken of in verse 10.

We might paraphrase the passage in this way:

Out of one the notable horns came forth a little horn which grew exceedingly great toward the south, and toward the east, and toward the pleasant land. And it grew great, even to the host of heaven, even as his master Satan who cast down some of the host of angels and stars from the ground and stamped upon them. (Revelation 12:4)

There is this difference also that in Ezekiel, the two personalities are clear-cut and separate while in Daniel there is an intermingling. In verses 9-12 both personalities are in view. That there should be a double reference is not unusual in prophetic writings in general as well as in Daniel. This may or may not be the way out of the difficulty of this passage but it would seem more realistic than to make the high priest, Onias, the prince of the host which he was not (there being no host nor he a prince of it) or to bring in Antiochus as one answering to the description of the king of bold countenance *"who by peace destroyed many"* when war was Antiochus' mode of destruction.

Whether or not this view helps us understand the vision, this much is clear, the *"king of fierce countenance"* in Chapter 8 is not Antiochus, for:

(a) verses 9-12 are the vision;

(b) verses 23-25 are the interpretation of the vision, as indicated by verses 16 and 19;

(c) the interpretation (verses 23-25) does not delineate the historical facts of the person, methods, or characteristics of Antiochus;

(d) neither does this description conform to the scriptual picture of Antichrist who will be a man of war (Daniel 1:38,Revelation 13:7).

In view of the great importance given to the false prophet in Revelation 13:11-18, it at least is not absurd to expect some inkling of him in Daniel. Since the false prophet arises out of the land (Revelation 13:11) interpreted by some as indicating his Jewish origin, it should not be strange to find mention of him in that part of Daniel slanted toward the Jew.

There is, moreover, in verse 13, a statement that has no explanation in the interpretation given us in verses 23-25, though it would seem to belong there. It is an explanation not by Gabriel but by a holy one (A..V.) in response to a question by another holy one.

Then I heard one saint speaking, and another saint said to that certain saint that spoke, How long shall be the vision concerning the daily sacrifice, and the transgression of desolation, to give both the sanctuary and the host to be trampled under foot? And he said unto me, Unto two thousand and three hundred days; then shall the sanctuary be cleansed.

Many commentators have assumed that this verse has to do with the defilement of the temple and altar under Antiochus Epiphanes for a period of 2,300 days. If we take this number literally, we have a period of a little over six years, whereas Josephus tells us that the time of defilement under Antiochus was three years to the day.[14] And to make matters worse, Antiochus does not otherwise appear in the interpretation of this vision. This little horn does not fit what we know of Antiochus; moreover, we get nowhere if we regard the 2,300 days as symbolic. Symbolic of what? If we think of 2,300 days as year days, there is again no conformity to history or prophecy that seems at all feasible. Keil has an extended discussion of this (pp. 301-308) and gives various viewpoints, none of which are satisfactory.

If we put these verses in the setting where they belong not of Antiochus but of some future great opponent of God, then we are dealing with a defilement of an altar yet to be built, defiled after the analogy of the defilement under Antiochus. This will be accomplished by the desolator or by his prophet for the whole vision after verse nine, definitely refers to the time of the end.

We still do not know what to do with the 2,300 days, except that these are somehow identified with "the last end of the indignation." Somehow and in some way, the six years and 110 days (2,300 days) must have some significant relationship to the seven years, to Daniel's seventieth week and to the defilement of the temple by Antichrist; i.e., by his image as described in Revelation 13:15. The desolation continues not for seven years (2,520 days) as we might expect nor even for three and a half years (1,260 days) after Antichrist breaks his covenant with Israel and causes the *"sacrifice and oblation to cease,"* but for 2,300 days.

It would help us greatly if we could know (a) exactly when the temple of the seventieth week would be rebuilt and the daily sacrifices begun, (b) when the Antichrist begins his seduction of Israel, and (c) when he begins to use the temple and the sacrifices for his own worship.

Since we are dealing 2,300 days, the defilement can hardly commence at the beginning of the final 1,260 days; i.e., three and a half years, and it must not begin earlier than the first part of the seventieth week unless his break with the Jews still leaves him in charge of the temple worship or unless he, Antichrist himself, destroys the temple (verse 11).

There is possibility that the temple sacrifices begin with the commencement of the seventieth week and that Antichrist comes 220 days later. This is assuming that so significant a happening must begin the seventieth week or at least be contained within it. But we hasten to say that there may be other significance to the 2,300 days which will become more evident as the time approaches for their fulfillment.

Walvoord sums up very succinctly, prevailing view of premillennial expositors:

"It may be concluded that many premillennial expositors find a duel fulfillment in Daniel 8: some of them achieve this by a division of the first part of the chapter as historically fulfilled and the last part prophetically future; some regard the whole chapter as having, in some sense, a dual fulfillment, historically as well as in the future; but most of them find the futuristic elements emphasized, especially in the interpretation of the vision.

"A variation of the view that the last part of the chapter is specifically future is found in the interpretation which has much to commend itself. This variation regards the entire chapter as historically fulfilled in Antiochus, but to varying degrees foreshadowing typically the future world ruler who would dominate the situation at the end of the Times of the Gentiles. In any case, the passage intentionally goes beyond Antiochus to provide prophetic foreshadowing of the final gentile ruler."[15]

Anderson states:

"That the career of Antiochus Epiphanes was in a special way within the scope and meaning of this prophecy is unquestioned. That its ultimate fulfillment belongs to the future time, though not so generally admitted, is nevertheless sufficiently clear. The proof of this is twofold. First, it cannot be but recognized that its most striking details remain wholly unfulfilled. I allude to the 2,300 days of verse 14 and to the statement of verse 25, 'He shall also stand up against the Prince of princes, but he shall be broken without hand.' And, secondly, the events described are expressly stated to be 'in the last end of the indignation,' which is the great tribulation."[16]

The difficulty of so many and varied explanations is not only their disagreement with one another but also some lack of appropriateness. To build up in our mind a type, significant to be sure, but falling so far short of the significance of the anti-type and using language inappropriate for the type, leaves us with uneasy feeling that somewhere we have missed the trail. Some expositors compound the difficulty by assuming that the person spoke of in verses 9-14 is a different one than the character described in verses 23-27 whereas we are definitely told that verses 23-27 are an interpretation of the vision of verses 9-14. We see, from the above quotations, that the chapter is variously interpreted: (1) as Antiochus only, (2) as Antichrist only, (3) as Antiochus and Antichrist and (4) as Antiochus as a type of Antichrist. Others have even suggested the king of the north. One view, noticeably lacking, is that of equating both descriptions in the chapter with the false prophet of Revelation Chapter 13. That this person answers the description of the false prophet in the main, seems much more appropriate than any of those mentioned above. We present it as follows:

Whereas Daniel Chapters 7, 9, and 11 picture a conqueror using war for his purposes, the little horn of Daniel 8 does not necessarily feature conquest by war but "by his policy he shall cause deceit to prosper in his hand" and "by peace shall destroy many." He is a conqueror but specifically not by warlike methods.

One of the objections, among several, to this interpretation is that the little horn is a king and in Revelation 13, he is not so designated. But a careful reading of verses 11-18 of Revelation 13 shows that the false prophet "exerciseth all the power of the first beast before him," has power of life and death and appears to be king in everything but name and may actually be a king even as the first beast does not have this title. Since he seems to be subordinate to the first beast, do we have here an emperor in the first beast and an associate Caesar in the second beast, the false prophet? Would this be after the analogy of the later Roman Empire?

In summing up the characteristics of the little horn, alias *"the king of the bold countenance,"* we have the following:

(1) He comes at a time when the ten kingdoms are in a condition of great wickedness. *"In the latter time of their kingdom when transgressors are come to the full"* (verse 23). Does this not place this situation at the end time? And does not *"come to the full"* indicate the time of the final judgment?

(2) He, the little horn, is a king of fierce countenance; i.e., bold, impudent, shameless (verse 23). This is not said historically of Antiochus.

(3) He understands dark sentences; i.e., mysteries (verse 23). This sounds very much like the false prophet and his miracles, not at all like Antiochus.

(4) His power shall be mighty but not by his own power (verse 24). Does this refer to his being satanically empowered?

(5) *"He shall destroy wonderfully"* (verse 24), *"in an astonishing wonderful way"* (Keil).[17]

(6) *"He shall prosper and practice"* (verse 24). In the time allotted him, he shall know nothing but success.

(7) Both Daniel and Zechariah proclaim his conquest over Israel. *"He shall destroy the mighty and holy people"* (verse 24). *"And it shall come to pass that in all the land, saith the Lord, two parts in it shall be cut off and die; but the third part shall be left in it"* (Zechariah 13:8).

(8) *"And through his policy he shall cause deceit to prosper in his hand"*; he will be a master of deceit and cunning, being indwelt, as he is, with the father of lies (verse 25).

(9) *"He shall magnify (himself) in his heart,"* or, according to Young, *"in his heart he shall do greatly."* As his power comes from Satan so does his presumption reminding us of Isaiah 14:14. *"I will ascend above the heights of the clouds; I will be like the most high."*

(10) *"By peace shall destroy many"* (verse 25). He will be a diplomat after the order of Machiavelli's Prince. There is no mention at all of war as his means of control.

(11) *"He shall also stand up against the Prince of princes"* (verse 25). Also, *"he spoke like a dragon"* (Revelation 13:11). Even as Satan is the great opponent of God, so does the false prophet stand up against Messiah.

(12) *"He shall be broken without hand"* (verse 25). His destruction shall come about by divine rather than human means.

If we compare, in somewhat tabular form, Daniel 8 and Revelation 13:11-18, we get the following comparisons:

Daniel 8:23	Revelation 13:11-18
A king	Kingship not stated but posits kingly power
Fierce countenance	Not stated
Understands mysteries	Power to give life to the image of the beast
Power mighty	Causes all to receive mark of the beast and causes to be killed non-worshipers of first beast
Borrowed power	Exercises all power of the first beast
Destroys with wonderful works	Doth great wonders, fire from heaven
Through cunning casts down truth to the ground; causeth deceit	Deceiveth earth dwellers

to prosper	
By peace destroys many	By economic control can prevent buying of food . . . starvation
Stands up against the Prince of Princes	Exalts first beast; causes all to worship first beast
Destroyed without hand	Taken prisoner at Armageddon (Revelation 19) and finally cast into the lake of fire with Antichrist

There are several descriptive statements in Daniel 8:9-12 for which there are no corresponding ones in Revelation 13:11-18 none however that is a great exegetical problem with the exception of verse 10. We may sum them up as follows:

(1) Whatever else this little horn is, he is not a military conqueror.

(2) Since he is not a military man per se, he cannot be the Antichrist. The person described accomplishes by miracles and peace, his will.

(3) It cannot possibly be Antiochus who also was a military man. He used war, not peace.

(4) There is nothing to identify the little horn with either the king of the north or the king of the south.

(5) There are no real incompatibilities between Daniel 8:23-27 and Revelation 18:11-18 which describe the false prophet.

(6) There are several congruities:

    (a) Understands mysteries (Daniel); has power to give life to the image of the beast (Revelation).

    (b) Destroys wonderfully; i.e., by wonders (Daniel); doeth great wonders (Revelation).

    (c) By peace, destroys many (Daniel); without the mark 666 no one can buy or sell (Revelation).

    (d) A king of fierce countenance (Daniel); has all the power of the first beast (Revelation)

    (e) Causes deceit to prosper (Daniel); deceiveth them that dwell on the earth (Revelation).

(7) The language of verse 10 could be literally true of Satan. What we are told here could be a way of saying that the little horn is Satan incarnate emphasizing his pre-incarnate activity while verses 23-25 emphasize his actions through the false prophet. The old Scofield notes suggest a commingling.

(8) If we interpret verse 10 as figurative applying it to the high priest and the righteous remnant, the language is inappropriate and highly exaggerated, even if symbolic.

(9) Furthermore, since verses 23-25 are said to be an interpretation of verses 9-12, we must somehow spiritualize verses 23-25 to fit the high

priest and the Jewish righteous in their dealings with the king of bold countenance.

(10) The apparent incongruity between Daniel and Revelation; i.e., one little horn in Daniel and two in Revelation, may be explained by the thought that Daniel is relating his personage to the former realm of the 'one-horned' Alexander and John to an imitation Messiah.

At first glance, verse 25 seems to describe the self-deification of the little horn (as Daniel 11:36-37 so delineates the willful king). This is further strengthened by the italicized introduction of *"himself"* into the text indicating that it is the thought of the interpreters that this is needed to make complete sense.

However, if, instead of *"he shall magnify himself in his heart"* of the A.V. version, we give the equally accurate translation of Young; viz., *"in his heart he shall do greatly,"* we avoid the temptation of identifying these two individuals as identical and can more easily meet, in the person of the little horn, the description of the false prophet of Revelation 13:11-18.

This verse (25) is more easily understood in the Hebrew where the Hiphil is used which is causative in force as contrasted with Daniel 11:36-37 where the reflexive Hithpael is used and is properly translated *"he shall exalt himself."* There is therefore no valid reason for introducing the word "himself" into the text.

We are not here quibbling over a minor issue for if we are to interpret this chapter as referring to the false prophet, it must not be in basic conflict with Revelation 13:11-17 where the false prophet no matter how much he is impressed with himself and the powers given him, exalts the first beast, the Antichrist, and causes all men *"to worship the first beast whose deadly wound was healed."*

In Chapter 11 where the willful king (presumably, the first beast, Antichrist) is described, the Hebrew properly uses the reflexive Hithpael in both verses 36 and 37 to indicate that it is himself that he magnifies to the point of self-deification, placing himself above every god.

Of all four descriptions of the kings in Daniel 7:8, 24-25, 8:23, 9:27, and 11:36-45, the one in Daniel 8 is the only one at all suitable as a description of the false prophet. But we may ask, Why attempt to find a description of the false prophet in Daniel? The obvious answer is that a character so closely associated with Antichrist (the first beast of Revelation 13) could reasonably be expected to appear in Daniel who has so much to say about Antichrist. In Revelation, Antichrist's success or at least his success as a god appears, in some measure at least, to be due to the false prophet with his miracles, his economic controls, his power of life and death. That no hint of this should appear in Daniel seems very strange, indeed; improbable, though not impossible.

Of course, what we expect to find is not evidence unless we do find it. This much we can say, If we compare the two passages (Daniel 8 and Revelation 13), there are few incompatabilities. In fact, in addition to the only one already mentioned (the matter of kingship), there seems to be only one other of importance. In Daniel 8, we have one little horn; in Revelation 13, we have two horns, *"like a lamb."* Both descriptions give us an account of a wonder-working individual, destroying many by peaceful means, not operating in his own power and each having the power of life and death. While each account has details not found in the other, there is nothing in either that negates the other with one exception: the one identifying mark we might expect to indicate identity would be the horns. One explanation may be that in Daniel, the little horn may be used to identify the ethnic source of the man; in Revelation, the two horns are of the lamb, the symbol (in this case deceitful) of innocence and peace and an imitation and travesty of the Lamb of God.

If this seems farfetched, compare the picture of Daniel's Antichrist in II Thessalonians and in Revelation 13:1-10 of the same person. While the overall identification is established, there is nothing in Daniel about seven heads or deadly wounds or about being worshipped in the temple of God.

It seems that we must choose, at least in part, on the basis of appropriateness as to whether this chapter deals with the false prophet or the only other feasible alternative, the Antichrist himself. The one thing that needs to be emphasized is the impossibility of separating the vision from the interpretation thus making the chapter descriptive of two persons, where only one is really described. And if that be conceded, verses 23-26 cannot possibly be a description of Antiochus Epiphanes. The evidence points either to the false prophet or to Antichrist himself and it is definitely inappropriate as a description of Antichrist.

In summary:

(1) The description cannot be Antichrist. It does not fit.

(2) The description cannot be Antiochus, for the same reason.

(3) Hence it cannot be Antiochus as a type of Antichrist.

That the little horn of Chapters 7 and 8 are not identical seems evident. If the vision had anything in common with that of Chapter 7 and at all recognizable to Daniel, why after the explanation by Gabriel does he still say "none understood it"? And why his astonishment? Is it unthinkable to him that the Antichrist of Chapter 7 should have a false prophet and yet more, a Judas from among the holy people, a spiritual Benedict Arnold? Daniel understood his Chapter 7 vision so why is he so confused about the vision of Chapter 8 except that somehow the persons and situations are unthinkable and different?

In the time of spiritual declension, Israel was plagued with an epidemic of false prophets who told the people what they wanted to hear, having no mandate or message from Jehovah. In the Northern Kingdom, they were almost the rule, especially in the time of Ahab. There were 400 in the day when Elijah discomfited them on Mount Carmel.

Will it stagger our imaginations then, to believe that the false prophet might very well be a Jew? That Amaziah, the false prophet in the days of Amos, Zedekiah and Ahab in the times of the exile, should have their antitype in the days of the Antichrist should not be a matter of much amazement. We like to think and rightly, of the Jewish people in spite of their present blindness to the claims of Jesus their Messiah as merely temporarily estranged and in the future as being again the holy people of the Book of Daniel. But we must remember that out of the godly Edward's line in America came Aaron Burr, the seducer and traitor. Out of heaven itself, the anointed cherub became Satan who, entering into one of the twelve apostles, caused him also effectively to betray his Master. In fact, some commentators have interpreted Scripture to the effect that Judas, himself, will be reincarnate and will become either Antichrist or the False Prophet.

Finally, as we compare the overall picture given us in Daniel Chapter 8 with Revelation 13:11-18, we find the following:

(1) In both accounts, we get a person of great effrontery, impudence, bold countenance. This is in Daniel. In Revelation, he speaks like a dragon; i.e., with effrontery.

(2) In Daniel, he is a great destroyer. In Revelation, he kills all who do not worship the beast.

(3) He does not do this by war. In Daniel, he destroys many by peace; in Revelation, no one can buy or sell without the mark of the beast (that is death by starvation).

(4) In Daniel, he destroys in a wonderful way; in Revelation, he does great wonders, making fire come down from heaven.

(5) In Daniel, his power is mighty but borrowed; in Revelation, he exercises all the power of the first beast (again, possibly borrowed).

(6) In Daniel, he causes deceit to prosper; in Revelation, he deceives those that dwell upon the earth.

(7) In Daniel, he has one horn, possibly indicating his Greek affiliation or his origin from a part of the former Greek empire; in Revelation, he has two horns, possibly an imitation of the Lamb; that is, a false Christ.

(8) The Daniel account was first written for the Jewish saints; that of Revelation was written for gentile Christians. Each was written that this fearful deceiver should be identified by the respective groups.

(9) Neither one pictures the individual as using warlike methods but gaining his ends by cunning, deceit and economic control.

(10) If Daniel 8 refers to Antichrist, we have an unnecessary and inexplicable redundancy, even considering the importance of the subject.

CHAPTER X

DANIEL'S PRAYER OF CONFESSION
SEVENTY WEEKS OF ISRAEL'S DESTINY

(Daniel 9)

As to chronology, Chapter 9 is written the first year of Darius, the Mede, 539 B.C. The language is Hebrew. Since Daniel does not specify any other location, he is probably in Babylon. This chapter stands out as a Jewish-oriented chapter being almost entirely concerned with Israel. Chapter 12 has this same characteristic. In 9:1-6 we read,

In the first year of Darius, the son of Ahasuerus, of the seed of the Medes, who was made king over the realm of the Chaldeans; In the first year of his reign I, Daniel, understood by the books the number of the years, concerning which the word of the Lord came to Jeremiah, the prophet, that he would accomplish seventy years in the desolation of Jerusalem. I set my face unto the Lord God, to seek by prayer and supplications with fasting, and sackcloth, and ashes; And I prayed unto the Lord, my God, and made my confession, and said, O Lord, the great and awesome God, keeping the covenant and mercy to them that love him, and to them that keep his commandments, We have sinned, and have committed iniquity, and have done wickedly, and have rebelled, even by departing from thy precepts and from thine ordinances; Neither have we harkened unto thy servants, the prophets, who spoke in thy name to our kings, our princes, and our fathers, and to all the people of the land.

In these words, Daniel begins his confession and merely continues the indictment given by Elijah centuries before when he complained, "I have been very jealous for the Lord God of hosts, because the children of Israel have forsaken thy covenant, thrown down thine altars, and slain thy prophets with the sword" (I Kings 19:14).

That this was the characteristic condition of Israel rather than the exception, centuries later Jesus bore witness to the same purport, when he said in Luke 11:47, 49-51,

Woe unto you! For ye build the sepulchers of the prophets, and your fathers killed them. Therefore also said the wisdom of God, I will send them prophets and apostles, and some of them they shall slay and persecute, That the blood of all the prophets, which was shed from the foundation of the world, may be required of this generation; From the blood of Abel unto the blood of Zechariah, who perished between the altar and the temple.

What the Jewish establishment did to the prophets in the Old Testament was not so remote from what religious establishments, as well as pagan governments, have done through the centuries. Pagan Rome persecuted Christians. In medieval Europe, alleged Christians persecuted alleged heretics. Such names as Savonarola, Huss and Jerome of Prague are a few out of myriads. When Cortez conquered Mexico, he found to his horror, the Aztecs offering human sacrifices by the simple process of tearing out their living hearts and offering them to their god, Huitzilopochili. The Spain that he had just left was not quite so merciful; there they burned their sacrifices (called "heretics") by a slow and painful *auto-de-fe*. The difference between the two was merely one of ideology, not of humanity. Prophets and dissidents in all ages have had a hard time of it.

O Lord, righteousness belongeth to thee but to us confusion of face, as at this day; to the men of Judah, and to the inhabitants of Jerusalem and unto all Israel, that are near, and that are far off, through all the countries to which thou hast driven them, because of their trespass which they have trespassed against thee. (7) O Lord, to us belongeth confusion of face, to our kings, to our princes, and to our fathers, because we have sinned against thee. (8) To the Lord, our God, belong mercies and forgivenesses, though we have rebelled against him; (9) Neither have we obeyed the voice of the Lord, our God, to walk in his laws, which he set before us by his servants, the prophets. (10) Yea, all Israel has transgressed thy law, by departing, that they might not obey thy voice; therefore, the curse is poured upon us, and the oath that is written in the law of Moses, the servant of God, because we have sinned against him. (11)

Daniel, in the last verse, is referring to that terrible 28th chapter of Deuteronomy in which, after having enumerated the blessings that would come to Israel by obedience, the solemn curse is pronounced for disobedience, in particular, the threat that "*the Lord shall bring thee, and thy king whom thou shall set over thee, unto a nation whom neither thou nor thy fathers have known, and there shalt thou serve other gods, wood and stone*" (verse 36). Pursuant to that prediction, Israel is in Babylon in slavery and, as was predicted, is an astonishment and a byword. Not yet had the prediction of the 64th verse come to pass, "*and the Lord shall scatter thee among all people, from the one end of the earth even unto the other.*" It is this prediction and the rest of the 28th chapter, that the Spirit of God will bring to the mind of Daniel. Even though Israel was even now under God's displeasure, woe be to that nation or that people that should deal harshly with her. The statement of Zechariah 2:8 is still true: "*for he that toucheth you toucheth the apple of his eye.*" Babylon will soon discover this.

From verses 12-19, Daniel pleads with Jehovah for forgiveness for

Israel, not for the sake of their own righteousness or his own righteousness (*"for we do not present our supplications before thee for our own righteousness, but for thy great mercies"*). Daniel again calls the role of Israel's sins,

And he hath confirmed his words, which he spake against us, and against our judges that judge us, by bringing upon us a great evil: for under the whole heaven hath not been done as hath been done upon Jerusalem. (12) As it is written in the law of Moses (Deuteronomy 28:36), all this evil is come up on us: yet made we not our prayer before the Lord our God, that we might turn from our iniquities, and understand thy truth. (13) Therefore hath the Lord watched upon the evil, and brought it upon us: for the Lord our God is righteous in all his works which he doeth: for we obeyed not his voice. (14) And now, O Lord our God, that hast brought thy people forth out of the land of Egypt with a mighty hand, and hast gotten thee renown, as at this day; we have sinned, we have done wickedly. (15) O Lord, according to all thy righteousness, I beseech thee, let thine anger and thy fury be turned away from thy city Jerusalem, thy holy mountain: because for our sins, and for the iniquities of our fathers, Jerusalem and thy people are become a reproach to all that are about us. (16) Now, therefore, O our God, hear the prayer of thy servant, and his supplication, and cause thy face to shine upon thy sanctuary that is desolate, for the Lord's sake. (17) O my God, incline thine ear, and hear; open thine eyes, and behold our desolations, and the city which is called by thy name: for we do not present our supplications before thee for our righteousness, but for thy great mercies. (18) O Lord, hear; O Lord, forgive; O Lord, hearken and do; defer not, for thine own sake, O my God: for thy city and thy people are called by thy name. (19)

If ever a prayer showed full appreciation of a sinning people, of a merciful God, of a spiritual and moral cause and effect and if ever a prayer acknowledged the majesty, the righteousness and the power of Jehovah, it is this prayer. This prayer, even as the prayer of Moses, calls upon God for his own sake to forgive and to restore, not because of the righteousness of Israel or Daniel's own righteousness but for *"thy own great mercies"* ... *"for thine own sake."*

Daniel's prayer of confession and intercession might well have been offered by the high priest on the great day of atonement. Once a year, and *"not without blood,"* the high priest made confession and intercession, first for himself and then for the people.

It is written in Leviticus 23:27,

Also on the tenth day of the seventh month there shall be a day of atonement; it shall be a holy convocation unto you; and ye shall afflict your souls, and offer an offering made by fire unto the Lord.

And in Leviticus 16:11-13, we read,

Aaron shall bring the bullock of the sin offering which is for himself, and shall make atonement for himself, and for his house, and shall kill the bullock of the sin offering which is for himself. And shall take a censer full of burning coals of fire from off the altar before the Lord, and his hands full of sweet incense beaten small and bring it within the vail: And he shall put the incense upon the fire before the Lord, that the cloud of incense may cover the mercy seat that is on the testimony that he die not.

We are further told that, after slaying the sin offering for the people, there is that unique ceremony of confessing the sins of the people upon the live goat (Leviticus 16:21), as follows,

And Aaron shall lay both his hands on the live goat, and confess over it all the iniquities of the children of Israel, and all their transgressions in all their sins, putting them on the head of the goat, and shall send it away by the hand of a fit man into the wilderness.

But Israel in exile in Babylon has no temple, no altar, no sacrifice, no scapegoat and there is no mention of a high priest; hence, no atonement, no covering for sin. For seventy years, it will have been thus.

From a legalistic point of view, Daniel, a son of the tribe of Judah (not of Levi), would not be able to take the high priest's place; but in his prayer of confession, it would almost seem that he has done so, even though we do not know that this prayer was made on the Day of Atonement (Yom Kippur). No month or day is given.

But the prophets of Israel had long before spelled out the truth that God has more interest in the condition of the heart than formal symbols, *"for to obey is better than sacrifice and to hearken than the fat of rams."* Daniel's prayer of humility, confession and penitence might well have been in lieu of the high priestly prayer on the Day of Atonement. Who shall say it was not efficacious? In reciting the sins of Israel, Daniel identifies himself not only with his people but with their sins (8-10).

In this prayer all that the high priest might have said, Daniel did say. While we are not told that the high priest normally receives any sign or acknowledgment from God that his prayer was heard and Israel's sins forgiven, Daniel does not have time to finish his prayer and to rise from his knees before the answer comes, for we read (20-23),

And while I was speaking and praying, and confessing my sin and the sin of my people, Israel and presenting my supplication before the Lord my God, for the holy mountain of my God; Yea, while I was speaking in prayer, even the man Gabriel, whom I had seen in the vision in the beginning, being caused to fly swiftly, touched me about the time of the evening oblation. And he informed me and talked with me, and said, O Daniel, I am now come forth to give thee skill and understanding. At the beginning of thy supplications the commandment came forth, and I am now come to show thee; for thou are greatly beloved.

This is the second time that Gabriel has appeared to Daniel (see 8:16). He appears by name twice more in Scripture (Luke 1:19 and 26); once when he appears to Zacharias to announce the birth of John the Baptist, the forerunner and again to Mary, to announce Messiah's conception and birth. He is Gabriel *("man of God")*, the announcer who stands in the presence of God. What honor is this that is vouchsafed to Daniel that he should be given the divine message twice from so high a source - through the same messenger that announces Messiah? He must indeed be greatly beloved. And the messages? They must also be of profound importance; indeed, that of Messiah's advent. Appropriately, the first has to do with Israel's destiny and the exact time of Messiah's appearance and rejection (Daniel 8:25-26).

The A.V. translates Daniel 9:24 as follows,

Seventy weeks are determined upon thy people and upon thy holy city, to finish the transgression, and to make an end to sins and to make reconciliation for iniquity, and to bring in everlasting righteousness, and to seal up the vision and prophecy, and to anoint the most holy.

Young translates a little more literally,

"Seventy sevens are decreed upon thy people and upon the city of thy holiness, for restraining the transgression, and completing sin, and covering iniquity, and for bringing in everlasting righteousness, and for sealing the vision and prophet and anointing the holy of holies."[1]

Keil gives an exegesis of verse 24 as follows,

"Accordingly, the *kethiv* alone is to be adopted as correct, and the first passage to be translated thus: to shut up the transgression . . . to arrest wickedness or shut it up does not mean to pardon it, but to hem it in, to hinder it so that it can no longer spread about (Hofm); cf. Zech. V:8 and Rev. XX:3.

"In the second passage, 'to seal up sin . . . ,' the figure of sealing stands here in connection with the shutting up in prison. But in this figure to seal is not equal to take away according to which Hgstb. and many others explain it thus; the sins are here described as sealed, because they are all together removed out of the sight of God, all together set aside. Hence more correctly Hofman and Kliefoth say, 'if sins are sealed, they are on the one side laid under custody, so that they cannot anymore be active or increase, but that they may thus be guarded and held, so that they can no more be pardoned or blotted out;' cf. Rev. 20:3.

"The third statement, 'to make reconciliation for iniquity,' is *terminus tech*, to pardon, to blot out by means of sin offering; i.e., to forgive . . .

The three expressions, it is true, all treat alike of the setting aside of sin, but in different ways. The first presents the general thought that the falling away shall be shut up, the progress and the spreading of sin shall be prevented. The other two expressions define more closely how the source whence arises the apostasy shall be shut up, the going forth and continued operation of sin prevented. This happens in one way with unbelievers, and in a different way with believers. The sins of unbelievers are sealed, are guarded securely under a seal so that they may no more spread about and increase, nor any longer be active or operative; but the sins of believers are forgiven through a reconciliation. The former idea is stated in the second member, and the latter in the third, as Hoffman and Kliefoth have rightly remarked.

" The bringing of eternal righteousness; i.e., a righteousness that shall never cease, carries on through Messiah's reign and is not interrupted by the final revolt of Armageddon, where righteousness is not only triumphant, but removes completely from the scene sin and unrepentent sinners in the new heavens and the new earth.

"The fifth expression 'to seal up the vision and prophecy' can best be understood if we recall that the 'testimony of Jesus is a spirit of prophecy': He to whom prophecy looked forward, will then be, and forever, the present king reigning visibly in glory. No need of proclaiming any longer his coming, he will be here."

The final and sixth expression, "to anoint the most holy" (Holy of Holies), refers to a place, not a person. This is the technical term for the inner sanctuary. The term was first applied to the inner room of the tabernacle behind the veil afterward to the similar room in Solomon's temple and finally, to the rebuilt, second temple and its reconstruction by Herod. The term could hardly refer to the anointing of the third temple which the Jews will build and which will be defiled by Antichrist but to the one to be built by the Messiah himself, foretold by Zechariah, who says (6:12-13),

Thus speaketh the Lord of hosts, saying, Behold the man whose name is the Branch; and he shall grow up out of his place, and he shall build the temple of the Lord; Even he shall build the temple of the Lord; and he shall bear the glory, and shall sit and rule upon his throne; and he shall be a priest upon his throne and the counsel of peace shall be between them both.

This reference in Zechariah has by some, been taken to refer to the second temple. The context, however, forbids this. The second temple was not built by Messiah, the Branch, and he did not at that time sit and rule in glory upon his throne. The statement "and the counsel of peace shall be between them both" has been variously interpreted but if we accept the picture of Messiah on the throne of David, governing the world, and David, the prince among them, as the resurrected David, ruler of Israel under Messiah, then the phrase *"between them both"* could refer to Messiah and David.

If the anointing of the holy place means rebuilding a temple to replace the one destroyed in 70 A.D., we are immediately confronted with the question as to who builds this third temple. At present, the Mosque of Omar stands where such a temple ought to be. Until it is removed, no Jewish temple could be built there. There are persistent rumors that the Jews do plan to build such a temple even though at present Israel would hardly care to risk an Arab *jihad* by destroying the Mosque. Of course with their usual recklessness, Arab commandos might purposely or accidentally do just that. But should a third temple arise on Mount Moriah, it would hardly be the one envisioned by Ezekiel. Not only from Old Testament sources but from New, such a temple is certain for we read in II Thessalonians 2:4 that the situation in which the man of sin, who *"as god sitteth in the temple of God showing himself that he is god,"* demands a temple. We ask then, whether this temple results from Israel's own initiative and resources or if it is a joint product with Antichrist who "covenants with many." We cannot say now.

From Zechariah 6:12 however, we know that Messiah "the Branch" will build the temple of the Lord which is presumably the temple of Ezekiel's vision. So in prospect, there will be a third and then a fourth temple. The third temple will be defiled by Antichrist, the "abomination that maketh desolate," which will be destroyed, undoubtedly, by the earthquake mentioned in Isaiah 2:19, 21 and Zechariah 14:4-5 or by war (Zechariah 14:2, 10) or by some other means not identified. That there will be a temple built by Messiah is predicted in Zechariah 6:12-13 and is described (we believe) minutely in Ezekiel Chapters 41 and 42. Ezekiel's temple does not resemble any previous Jewish temple and is frequently thought of as an idealization but the detailed description would make us doubt this.

The third temple must be in existence before Messiah's reappearance or else Antichrist could not profance it. It could not be the one built by Messiah who will not yet have reappeared.[3]

The diverse interpretations of verse 24, other than that of Keil's, are very happily condensed by Culver in the following passage:

"There are six infinitive clauses: (1) to finish transgression, (2) to make an end of sins, (3) to make reconciliation for iniquity, (4) to bring in everlasting righteousness, (5) to seal up the vision and prophecy, (6) to anoint the most holy.

"Three common views have been adopted among the believing commentators concerning the scope of these six clauses. The least acceptable one, advocated notably by Stewart, is that which views all six of these blessings as following the conclusion of the seventy weeks, which conclusion is said to be in the events connected with the destruction of Antiochus Epiphanes. The idea is that the seventy weeks specifically concerned the remaining years of Israel's submission to, and persecution by, gentile powers. This is thought to terminate with Antiochus. The six blessings are then said to be simply the Messianic kingdom, conceived in a Postmillennial fashion.

"Another, championed notably by Barnes among the Postmillennialists, by Young and Mauro among the Amillennialists and by Auberlen among the Premillennialists, regards the seventy weeks as terminating shortly after the death of Christ and the six blessings as being conferred within the seventy weeks.

"These men feel that 'it was by the cutting off of Messiah that the six predictions of verse 24 were to be fulfilled' (Mauro, "The Seventy Weeks," pp. 43-44). Mauro states the view succinctly, 'When our Lord ascended into heaven and the Holy Spirit descended, there remained not one of the six items of Daniel 24 that was not fully accomplished.' (Ibid., p. 53.)

"A third position, adopted by Thompson (Daniel, Pulpit Commentary) among the Postmillennialists, by Keil and Leupold among the Amillennialists and by almost all of the Premillennialists of the past seventy-five years (West, Anderson, Gaebelein, Kelly, Tregelles, Seiss, Ironside, McCain, Cooper, Brooks, Larkin, Chafer, Bauman and many others) is that these six blessings arrive in full only at the termination (immediately after) of the seventieth week. These men generally recognize that the basis was laid in the grand providence of God which took place at the death of Christ but contend that the full effecting of these blessings comes only at the second advent."[4]

With this latter view, we can wholeheartedly concur, for the following two reasons:

(1) This whole chapter (Daniel 9) is almost wholly centered on Israel, "*thy people and thy holy city.*" Can anyone really believe that these blessings have been or will be visited upon Israel until that day when there shall be "*a fountain opened to the house of David and to the inhabitants of Jerusalem for sin and for uncleanness*" (Zechariah 13:1)? The whole of Zechariah 12 is a part of this scene.

(2) As to the gentiles, undoubtedly the gentile church has had a foretaste of these blessings when each individual Christian makes an end of his own sins before God by the substitutionary atonement and, hence, is reconciled to God. But there is no visible evidence that all six of these blessings can accrue to an imperfect church in this dispensation even though potentially, they are hers. As to the gentile nations, it seems obvious that the sin problem has not been solved by a Christ-rejecting world nor will it be until after judgment of the nations and the setting up of the Messiah's kingdom. What is much more evident, so far as the nations are

concerned, is that they are reverting politically, morally and spiritually to the days of Noah when violence and wickedness were the norm and *"the earth also was corrupt before God and the earth was filled with violence."* More and more, the Judeo-Christian ethic as well as doctrine, is being rejected.

Surely the six blessings have not touched the gentile world today nor in the discernible past, the presence of the church and the Word and the Holy Spirit notwithstanding.

If we think that modern commentators differ so markedly in the matter of verses 24-27, we find this to be equally so in the days of Jerome. He quotes Afracanus, Eusebius Pamphilius, Hypolytus, Apollinarius of Laodicea, Clement of Alexandria, Origen, Tertullian and Hebrew sources, all different and at variance. In despair, Jerome says, as for himself,

"I realize that this question has been argued over in various ways by men of greatest learning, and that each of them has expressed his views according to the capacity of his own genius. And so, because it is unsafe to pass judgment on the opinions of the great teachers of the church, and to set one above another, I shall simply repeat the view of each, and leave it to be the reader's judgment as to whose explanation ought to be followed."[5]

We owe it to Sir Robert Anderson to clarify this whole matter of the seventy weeks, as it pertains to Messiah. He says, "Dismissing from our minds, therefore, all mere theories on this subject, we arrive at the following definitely ascertained facts,

(1) "The Epoch of the seventy weeks was the issuing of a decree to restore and build Jerusalem. Daniel IX.25.)

(2) There never was but one decree for the rebuilding of Jerusalem.

(3) That decree was issued by Artaxerxes, King of Persia, in the month Nisan in the twentieth year of his reign; i.e., B.C. 445.

(4) The city was actually built in pursuance of that decree.

(5) The Julian date of 1st Nisan 445 was the 14th of March.

(6) Sixty-nine weeks of years; i.e., 173, 880 days reckoned from 14th of March B.C. 445, ended on the 6th of April A.D. 32.

(7) That day on which the sixty-nine weeks ended, was the fateful day on which the Lord Jesus rode into Jerusalem in fulfillment of the prophecy of Zechariah IX.9 and when, for the first and only occasion in all his earthly sojourn, he was acclaimed as *'Messiah the Prince, the King, the Son of David.'*

"Though God has nowhere recorded the Bethlehem birthdate of Christ, no date in history, sacred or profane, is fixed with greater definiteness than that of the year in which the Lord began his public ministry. I refer, of course, to Luke III. 1,2. The first passover of the Lord's ministry was, threrefore, in Nisan A.D. 29 and we can fix the date of the Passion with absolute certainty as Nisan A.D. 32."[6]

Seventy weeks would, of course, equal 490 days. If we consider a week to be a seven-day period there is nothing in history to give significance to this 490-day period from the going forth of the commandment. The same is true if we use weeks or months as a unit of time. But there is tremendous significance in considering these days as years, 490 years in all, and most significantly with reference to the sixty-nine weeks leading up to Messiah's advent, his rejection and the destruction of Jerusalem. The hiatus between the sixty-ninth week and the seventieth while not stated, is obvious and is not the only place in Scripture where this type of prophetic phenomenon is used.[7]

Dr. Alva McClain whose book, "Daniel's Prophecy of the Seventy Weeks" has had so much to do with popularizing Sir Robert Anderson's interpretation of verse 25, makes the following points (pp. 18-19),

(1) "The entire prophecy has to do with Daniel's 'people' and Daniel's 'city;' that is, the nation of Israel and the city of Jerusalem (verse 23).

(2) Two different princes are mentioned, who should not be confused: the first is named 'Messiah the prince' (25); and the second is described as the prince that shall come (26).

(3) The entire time period involved is exactly specified as seventy weeks (24); and these seventy weeks are further divided into lesser periods: first, a period of seven weeks; after that a period of threescore and two weeks; and finally, a period of one week (25 and 27).

(4) The beginning of the whole period of the seventy weeks is definitely fixed at 'the going forth of the commandment to restore and to build Jerusalem'(25).

(5) The end of the seven weeks and three score and two weeks (69 weeks) will be marked by the appearance of Messiah as the 'prince' of Israel (25).

(6) At a later time, 'after three score and two weeks' which follow the first seven weeks (that is, after sixty-nine weeks), Messiah the prince will be 'cut off,' and Jerusalem will again be destroyed by the people of another 'prince' who is yet to come (26).

(7) After these two important events, we come to the last, or seventieth week, the beginning of which will be clearly marked by the establishment of the firm covenant or treaty between 'the coming prince' and the Jewish nation for a period of 'one week'(27).

(8) In the 'midst' of this seventieth week, evidently breaking his treaty, the 'coming prince' will suddenly cause the Jewish sacrifices to cease and precipitate upon this people a time of wrath and desolation lasting to the 'full end' of the week (27).

(9) With the full completion of the whole period of seventy weeks, there will be ushered in a time of great and unparalleled blessing for the nation of Israel" (24).

Dr. McClain, covering much the same ground as Anderson, repeats that there is only one decree in Old Testament history which apart from all expedience of interpretation, can by any possibility be identified as the *"commandment"* referred to in Daniel's prophecy. That decree is found in the book of Nehemiah. Let the student read carefully Nehemiah 1:1-4 and 2:1-8, noting several facts: First, that it was a report of the ruined condition of the *"wall"* and *"gates"* of the city that aroused the deep concern of Nehemiah, Jewish *"cup bearer"* to King Artaxerxes; second, that after earnest prayer, he dared to petition the king *"that thou would send me unto Judah, unto the city of my father's sepulchres, that I may build it"* (2:5); third, that his bold request by the grace of God succeeded as he tells us, *"and the king granted me according to the good hand of my God upon me"* (2:8). But, most important of all, we should notice how carefully Nehemiah, writing by divine inspiration, records the exact date of this decree: *"In the month Nisan in the twentieth year of Artaxerxes the king"* (2:1).[8]

For those who believe in biblical inspiration and the genuineness of predictive prophecy, it will be no surprise to learn that the date fixed by Nehemiah happens to be one of the best known dates of ancient history. Even the latest editon of the Encyclopedia Britannica, certainly not biased in favor of prophecy, sets the date of Artaxerxes' accession as 465 B.C. Therefore, his twentieth year would be 445 B.C. Since no day is given, according to the Jewish custom, the date (the month of Nisan) would be understood as the first. Hence, in our calendar, the date would be March 14, 445 B.C. Here we have the beginning of the seventy weeks.

In the last verse of this chapter (verse 27), we get the final action of Antichrist. His covenant with the many may be the result of their desperate need. Surrounded on all sides by bitter enemies, implacable in their determination to destroy them, what shall Israel do? To what friends shall she turn, especially since she is still alienated from Jehovah?

It is probably not a great exaggeration to say that we live in a world where no nation has friends. Nations are apparently motivated largely by self interest and when any nation ceases to be of use to any other nation, there usually ceases to be any talk of friendship. Even more, treaties between nations are more and more honored only so long as they are profitable to one or the other. From God's viewpoint, we live in a world increasingly morally shabby. It is very easy to believe that it is presided over by the god of this age, Satan, so that the judgment that hangs over the earth will be entirely justified.

If, therefore blinded by the god of this age, Israel could listen to the blandishments of Antichrist and be impressed with the intelligence and with the power and the apparent good fortune of one *"who comes in his own name,"* can we wonder? The whole earth does the same, including an apostate church. The only mystery in the situation is why the Antichrist should find an advantage in this alliance. Is it because of Israel's geographic position? Will it be that she will possess some military advantage or secret that he can use? Or, more terribly, does he make a covenant that he may ultimately destroy her? This is not as fantastic as it may seem since Auschwitz and other places of horror have made it abundantly evident that Satan hates every Jew and always has hated them and would destroy every Jew if he could even as he hates Christians and would destroy them.

So we do not know why his tool, the Antichrist, makes a covenant with Israel nor why, nor by whom the covenant is broken - probably by the Antichrist (*"he shall cause the sacrifice and the oblation to cease"*). The hint that we get in II Thessalonians 2:4, where Antichrist demands worship as god, may be the key. When the covenant was made, Israel could not know that they were expected to worship a false god when they made a treaty with this superman, the Antichrist.

When therefore, the Antichrist decides to become god and turned in fury to destroy a people who long ago had enough of idols and who refuse him worship, we then have the time of Jacob's Trouble spoken of in Daniel 12:1.

We could hope that America which has on many occasions shown unselfish friendships, could always be a true friend of Israel and that without enmity to an Arab world. They, too, are Abraham's seed.

Whether we will be seduced by Arab oil and by that oil betray the best interest of Israel, of America and even of the Arab world itself, cannot be foreseen. In the long run, the final issue will not be determined by fearful America, a deluded Islam or even by an embattled Israel but by Jehovah of hosts, by the return of Christ in power and glory (Daniel 7:13-14, 26-27). God always has the last word.

The fact that after threescore and two weeks (presumably, after the seven weeks), it is stated in most explicit language that Messiah shall be cut off and have nothing, foreshadows the crucifixion and the rejection of Messiah as given in Isaiah 53 (also in Zechariah 11:12-13, 13:7).

The 26th verse of Daniel 9 continues, *"and the people of the prince that shall come shall destroy the city . . ."*; i.e. the people of the prince that shall later appear shall destroy the city. The *"prince that shall come"* has usually been thought to be the Antichrist and for this reason, it is assumed that the Antichrist will be of Italian origin. The destruction of Jerusalem, of course, came about in 70 A.D. as predicted by Jesus and was accomplished by the Roman armies under Titus. The city was completely destroyed with a loss of perhaps a million and a quarter of Jewish lives. The temple was burned and even as Jesus had prophesied, not one stone was left upon the other (Matthew 24:2; Deuteronomy 28:49-58, 63-65).

Verse 27 refers to *"he"* and its antecedent can be none other than the prince that is to come. Titus did not conform to this description for there was no covenant made with the Jews in 70 A.D. so the prince that shall come cannot possibly be Titus. The verse goes on to say,

And in the midst of the week he shall cause the sacrifice and the oblation to cease, and for the overspreading of abominations he shall make it desolate, even until the consummation, and that determined shall be poured upon the desolate.

This is ordinarily thought to be the seventieth week of Daniel and in the midst of the week, that is after three and one-half years, *"he shall cause the sacrifices and the oblation to cease."*

There is no mention, as is so often true in Scripture, of the long hiatus between the destruction of the Jews at the end of the sixty-ninth week and the beginning of Antichrist's convenant with the Jews at the beginning of the seventieth week. It is usual to explain this statement by saying that the prophetic clock as far as Judaism is concerned, stopped at 70 A.D. During this interim in which Israel is alienated from Jehovah and his Christ, the promise given by the Old Testament prophets for the gathering in of the gentiles, is to be accomplished. In Isaiah 42:6, we read, *"I the Lord have called thee in righteousness, and will hold thine hand, and will keep thee, and give thee for a covenant of the people, for a light of the gentiles."* Again, in Isaiah 49:6 and in Isaiah 60:1-4, we have the glorious promise,

Arise, shine; for thy light is come, and the glory of the Lord is risen upon thee. For, behold, the darkness shall cover the earth, and gross darkness the people; but the Lord shall arise upon thee, and his glory shall be seen upon thee. And the gentiles shall come to thy light, and kings to the brightness of thy rising. Lift up thine eyes round about, and see: all they gather themselves together, they come to thee: thy sons shall come from far, and thy daughters shall be nursed at thy side.

Keil says,

"If we observe that the destruction of the city and the sanctuary is so connected with the *'Maschiach'* that we must consider this as the immediate or first consequence of the cutting off of the Messiah, and that the destruction shall be brought about by a Nagid (a prince), than by Maschiach, we can understand neither a secular prince or king or simply a high priest, but only an anointed one who stands in such a relation to the city and sanctuary, that with his being *"cut off"* the city and the sanctuary lose not only their protection and their protector, but the sanctuary also loses, at the same time, its character as the sanctuary, which the Maschiach had given to it. This is suitable to no Jewish high priest, but only to the

Messiah whom Jehovah anointed to be a priest-king after the order of Melchesedeck, and placed as Lord over Zion, His holy hill."

In Daniel 9:26 the clause, *"and the people of the prince that shall come shall destroy the city and the sanctuary"* has had various interpretations and will be dealt with more at length in the chapter on Antichrist. Let us remember, however, that whoever The Prince may be, the destruction of the city by a Roman army under Titus is a matter of history. It has been described by Josephus in horrible detail. *"The Prince that shall come"* is the focus of the verse but is not Titus. The 26th verse ends with the statement that can only be constructed as ending all hopes for an earthly utopia until Messiah returns. The literal translation is *"unto the end shall be war; desolations are determined."* To those who expect a gradual diminution of war, or wars, as we approach the end of the age, we might consider the following,

(1) From 1496 B.C. to 1861 A.D., that is, 3,357 years, there has been war in some part of the world in all but 227 years of that period. This would mean that during this time, only one year out of fifteen has been free from war (Colliers Encyclopedia, 1969, p. 235, article "War Cost and Casualties").

(2) If trends have any meaning, we could hardly look forward to a decrease either in the number of wars or in a softening of their impact. Every generation of Americans has had the tragedy and cost of war with a sudden crescendo in death toll and costs. The five major wars in which America took part prior to 1914 had a total death toll of fewer than 150,000 American dead. This, of course, did not include the casualties of the other side. However, the First World War had a death toll to all belligerents of 10,000,000 soldiers. 10,000,000 civilians and the dead due to epidemics and famine, 20,000,000.

The total cost of this war was $338,000,000,000. Twenty-five years later, the Second World War occurred with 17,000,000 soldiers dead. 43,000,000 civilian dead and a total cost estimated at $1,348,000,000,000. Since that time, we have engaged in a Korean war with over 33,000 American dead with many times that number of North Korean and Chinese casulaties. The Vietnam War finally ended with over 56,000 American dead, billions of dollars of expenditure and literally millions of North and South Vietnam civilians dead.

(3) A leading Western scientist writes, "I have checked with historians and military experts and find we all agree on this point: Never before in history has there been a deployment of troops of the magnitude of that along the Sino-Soviet border without a war taking place"(U.S. News and World Report, Worldgram, Sept.4,1972).

Since all the nations of the various continents, big and little, are arming to the teeth, the angel's pronouncement in Daniel seems obviously right. There is a cry of *"peace, peace"* and there is no peace.

CHAPTER XI
DANIEL'S FOURTH VISION THE THEOPHANY

(Daniel 10)

Chapters 10, 11 and 12 are all concerned with the last vision experienced by Daniel. The time is the third year of Cyrus, 534 B.C.; the location, somewhere along the Tigris River. No city is mentioned. *"Time appointed is long"* and provides a distant perspective.

This revelation was received by a man near the end of his pilgrimage. If he were seventeen or eighteen years of age when he was taken captive to Babylon (605 B.C.), he is now nearly ninety years of age. He has seen the rise and fall of the Neo-Babylonian Kingdom, the passing of Nebuchadnezzar probably not much older than himself, the brief reign of Evil Marduk his son, the reigns of Neglissar, of Labashi Marduk his son and finally, the seventeen-year reign of Nabonidus and Belshazzar. Daniel's friend, Darius, the Mede, is gone and his successor, Cyrus, the Persian, rules the vast domain of Persia. In his old age, he is about to be given the longest revelation of his long life as a prophet. In a sense, this last revelation comes also as a sort of climax. Consider the following:

(1) Nebuchadnezzar has a dream, the interpretation of which is revealed to Daniel in a night vision (603 B.C.). Daniel 2.

(2) Again, Daniel interprets a dream for Nebuchadnezzar, involving the king's mental breakdown and recovery. The date is not certain but possibly sometime during the thirteen-year siege of Tyre. Daniel 4.

(3) Daniel is brought in to interpret the handwriting on the wall during Belshazzar's feast (539 B.C.). Daniel 5.

(4) The first of the revelations and visions made to Daniel are of the four great beasts of Daniel 7 which Daniel is unable to interpret himself but is interpreted by an angel (possibly 554 B.C.). Daniel 7.

(5) In the third year of Belshazzar, Daniel has a vision in which there is a theophany in which the angel Gabriel interprets. This is a waking vision (possibly 551 B.C.). Daniel 8.

(6) In the first year of Darius, the Mede, Daniel has a waking experience or vision, with the angel Gabriel interpreting for him (539-538 B.C.). Daniel 9.

(7) We have the last, the most vivid and perhaps the most important of all Daniel's visions in the third year of Cyrus. There is theophany with from two to four angels as a part of the revelation, the man clothed in linen being deity. Daniel 10-12.

The chapter begins (10:2-3),

In those days I Daniel was mourning three full weeks. I ate no pleasant bread, neither came flesh nor wine in my mouth, neither did I anoint myself at all, til the three whole weeks were fulfilled.

Daniel does not tell us the why of his mourning. Since the statement was made at the beginning of the vision, it is not its content that causes him to mourn. Keil suggests that his sorrow was caused by the condition of affairs among the Jews who had returned to Jerusalem (Ezra 4).

This then, is the fourth of Daniel's own visions appearing to him in the third year of Cyrus who by the way, has only four more years to reign. Ezra tells us (Ezra 1:1), *"The Lord stirred up the spirit of Cyrus king of Persia."* The record goes on to state, *"Thus saith Cyrus king of Persia: The Lord God of heaven hath given me all of the kingdoms of the earth; He hath charged me to build Him a house at Jerusalem which is in Judea"* (Ezra 1:2).

It is Cyrus who has been moved by God to befriend Israel, to permit their return to their own land, once more to rear a temple and to inhabit their own city. He does this in a kingly way as we read in Ezra 1:7, *"Also Cyrus, the king, brought forth the vessels of the house of the Lord, which Nebuchadnezzar had brought forth out of Jerusalem, and had put in the house of his gods."* In verse 9, we read further,

And this is the number of them: thirty platters of gold; a thousand platters of silver; nine and twenty knives; thirty basins of gold; silver basins of a second sort, four hundred and ten; and other vessels a thousand. And all the vessels of gold and of silver were five thousand and four hundred.

This was truly a royal treasure to give back to a captive people who could do nothing for him in return. May he be numbered among the blessed.

Two years have passed; the city of Jerusalem is again inhabited but the walls have not been rebuilt and the city is open to enemies and mis-chief- makers. The temple has been begun and an altar of sacrifice reared but the older men who had seen Solomon's temple wept when they saw the foundations of the new one even as they were to weep twenty years later when it was finished, so inferior was it to the grandeur of the old temple. Furthermore, almost immediately, adversaries appeared to hinder the building.

Is this the reason for Daniel's fasting and prayer for three weeks? Is it the apostasy of the Jews who went to Egypt (Jeremiah 44)? Is it the general, inglorious condition of a once glorious nation? Or is it the knowledge that the theocracy is ended until Messiah re-establishes it in the latter days? It may also have come home to him that at the end of the seventy years predicted by Jeremiah, never again will things be as they were and that when Messiah does come, *"He shall have nothing that is his, but shall be cut off."* This has been explicitly revealed to him in his previous vision, five years before.

Sorrow of heart was the portion of most of God's prophets who saw what might have been but were forced to face the reality of what was. Whatever the cause, we note that Daniel's three weeks of fasting and mourning corresponded to the twenty-one days of conflict between the angelic messenger and the prince of Persia. As we see, the prince of Persia has been defeated, and Michael and his angelic helper have prevailed.

Beginning with verse 5, we are given the vision featuring *"a certain man clothed in linen."* We read,

Then I lifted up mine eyes, and looked, and behold a certain man clothed in linen, whose loins were girded with the fine gold of Uphaz; His body also like the beryl, and his face like the appearance of lightning, and his eyes like lamps of fire, and his arms and his feet in color like polished bronze, and the voice of his words like the voice of a multitude.

If we compare this description with Revelation 1:13-16 where the person is identified as the risen Christ, we have the following parallel:

Daniel 10	Revelation 1
Man clothed in linen	Clothed in garment to feet
Loins gird with fine gold of Uphaz	Gird with golden girdle
His body like a beryl	
Face like lightning	Countenance as sun
Eyes like lamps of fire	Eyes a flame of fire
Arms and feet polished bronze	Feet like fine glass
Voice as the voice of a multitude.	Voice like sound of many waters

In substance, the two descriptions are so similar that we must be dealing with the preincarnate Christ since no angel is so described and the descriptions are what we would expect from two persons describing the same sight. The ineffable glory of the vision deprives Daniel of strength and speech and his companions, while not seeing the vision, flee in mortal terror (sensing, if not seeing) and hide themselves.

Therefore I was left alone, and saw this great vision, and there remained no strength in me; for my comeliness was turned in me to corruption, and I retained no strength.(8) Yet I heard the voice of his words; and when I heard the voice of his words, then I was in a deep sleep on my face toward the ground.(9)

Some have supposed this whole experience to have been a dream so vivid as to seem a waking experience. Dreams, however vivid, do not cause bystanders to be terror-stricken. Daniel's description of the vision was a waking one, we believe, but so overpowering in its effect that he describes it as a sleeping condition in which the first words of the angelic messenger are heard as in a dream. This condition does not last for we read,

And, behold, a hand touched me, which set upon my knees and upon the palms of my hands,(10) And he said unto me, O Daniel, a man greatly beloved, understand the words that I speak unto thee, and stand upright; for unto thee am I now sent. And when he had spoken this word unto me, I stood trembling.(11) Then said he unto me, Fear not, Daniel; for from the first day that thou didst set thine heart to understand, and to chasten thyself before thy God, thy words were heard, and I am come for thy words.(12) But the prince of the kingdom of Persia withstood me, one and twenty days; but, lo, Michael, one of the chief princes came to help me; and I remained there with the kings of Persia.(13)

The following verse 14, may be said to be the key not only to this chapter but the the remainder of the book (Chapters 11 and 12),

Now I am come to make thee understand what shall befall thy people in the latter days; for yet the vision is for many days (14).

We understand then that what follows in Chapters 10, 11 and 12 (that is, Daniel's fourth vision) specifically concerns *"Thy people"* (that is, Israel) and whatever characters or nations that are later introduced are there because of their significance to the Jewish people. While Jewish affairs are basic, they only dominate Chapters 9 and 12.

The second point that he emphasizes is the chronological setting. The occurrences listed are to be concerned with the latter days. While background material will be introduced, the focus of the chapters is the end time. Anything in this or the following chapters that on first glance seem obscure, must be there because it concerns *"thy people in the latter days"* with whatever background is necessary to give full meaning to these two objectives. But even though we recognize this, it is sometimes difficult to distinguish between the type and the antitype, between background data and the main thrust of the passage especially when we have them mingled in the same verse or verses. This seems to be especially true in Daniel 11:21-35. To turn our attention again to Chapter 10,

And when he had spoken such words unto me, I set my face toward the ground, and I became dumb.(15) And, behold, one like the similitude of the sons of men touched my lips; then I opened my mouth, and spoke, and said unto him who stood before me, O my Lord, by the vision my sorrows are turned upon me, and I have retained no strength.(16) For how can the servant of this my Lord talk with this my Lord? For as for me, straightway there remained no strength in me, neither is there breath left in me.(17)

Again, we have the similarity to the apostle John's experience in Revelation 1:17, *"And when I saw him, I fell at his feet as dead, and he laid his right hand upon me, saying unto me, Fear not; I am the first and the last."* Except as He diminished His glory and majesty, no man could see God and live whether it be the Father or the Son or the Holy Spirit. These earthly bodies must be changed and put on immortality before God can dwell familiarly with us in the New City.

Then there came again and touched me one like the appearance of a man, and he strengthened me.(18) And said, O man greatly beloved, fear not; peace be unto thee, be strong, yea, be strong. And when he had spoken unto me, I was strengthened and said, Let my Lord speak; for thou hast strengthened me.(19)

Again, we have a theophany in verses 16 and 17. In the following two verses, the accompanying angel addresses Daniel as *"greatly beloved."* No other Old Testament character is given this appellation. Abraham, the *"friend of God"* and Moses, the *"servant of God,"* were also beloved but in Daniel, it seems in my opinion, that we have a reflection of the coming Messiah himself; holy, harmless and undefiled. He is a person that we ourselves can love, without reserve, though in a lesser degree than the Messiah himself.

The angelic spokesman is not named though he could be Gabriel who is named in the previous chapter (Daniel 9:21). This cannot be assumed since the four visions of Daniel do not have a continuous chronology, there being a gap of perhaps three years between the first and second vision, of twelve years between the second and third visions and of five years between the third and fourth visions. The angel in this chapter, moreover, does not appear alone as in all cases where Gabriel is named but gives his message in the presence of the one from whom the message originates, the preincarnate Christ.

We come to verse 20, *"Then said he, Knowest thou why I have come unto thee? Now I will return to fight the prince of Persia; and when I am gone forth, lo, the prince of Greece shall come."* Keil paraphrases this as follows.

"Now shall I return to resume and continue the war with prince of Persia, to maintain the position gained (ver. 13) beside the kings of Persia; but when (while) I thus go forth to war; i.e. while I carry on this conflict, lo, the prince of Javan shall come ("henay" with the participle "bah", of the future) then shall there be a new conflict."

This last thought is not, it is true, expressly uttered but it appears from verse 21. The warring with the prince; i.e., the spirit of Persia hostile to Israel, refers to the opposition which the Jews would encounter in the hindrances put in the way of their building the temple from the time of Cyrus to the time of Darius Hystaspes, and further under Xerxes and

Artaxerxes til the rebuilding of the walls of Jerusalem by Nehemiah as well as at a later time on the side of the Persian world-power, in the midst of all which difficulties the Angel of the Lord promises to guide the affairs of His people. *"Sar javan"* is the spirit of the Macedonian world kingdom which would arise and show as great hostility as did the spirit of Persia against the people of God.[1]

It is a frightening thing to realize that every nation on earth, apparently, has a resident prince of darkness, a demon personality, influencing the thinking and actions of kings and rulers and governments. Scripture treats with respect these demonic powers, calling some of them princes, fully recognizing their power for evil and their capacity for influencing the affairs of nations. This seems, usually to be influence though there ocassionally arises a ruler where there seems to be actually demonic possession.[2] It seems impossible to think of Hitler or Stalin in any other way. This is the way Antichrist will be empowered except, instead of the prince of Persia or Greece or of some other country, the evil prince of princes, Satan himself, will exercise his acknowledged world dominion and possess in person the Antichrist. He will in this way, make the dominance of evil a universal and unopposed thing for his allotted time, *"for he that letteth will let until he be taken out of the way."* The kingdom of evil will have complete sway.

What Daniel spells out, Paul sums up in Ephesians 6:12 at least as this applies to the Christian believer, *"for we wrestle not against flesh and blood, but against principalities, against powers, against the rulers of the darkness of this world, against spiritual wickedness in high places."*

To return to Daniel, it is entirely apropos for Daniel to introduce us to the spiritual forces that will increasingly operate as we come to the seventieth week of Daniel and which will be consummated in the unopposed reign of Satan through his Antichrist, his false prophet and his demon host.

Here in verse 13, an angel of God *"excelling in strength"* seems unable to cope with Satan's ambassador to Persia. The stalemate is only resolved when Michael, the archangel, comes to his aid. Here in these two verses (59 words), we glimpse briefly the terrific power struggle going on in the supernatural world for the minds of kings.

In the hierarchy of angels, good and evil, is the decision decided on the basis of rank subject, of course, to the final fiat of God himself? Does the archangel, Michael, outrank a prince of Persia whereas the first angel who entered the contest did not?

Satan, the anointed cherub, whose power and influence were great enough to seduce the angels of God and lead them in rebellion apparently had in his number, angels of the highest rank: princes. These and others, we are told here and in Ephesians, are the powers back of this world system. They have influenced or controlled kings, possessed false prophets and oracles, inspired authors, contrived false doctrines and heresies, made war on the saints and in every way blasphemed the good name of God. Satan, himself, personally engineered the death of the Son of God since he could not seduce him.³ Such presumption must necessarily be based on a consciousness of power; power within the permissive will of God (Job 1:10, 12, etc.). Since this malice and presumption did not exclude the Son of God himself (e.g., he was tempted of Satan), we should not be surprised to see it operating against the angels of God.

It seems that men must be influenced by the Word and Spirit or by default, by the forces of evil. In the long run, there is no position of permanent neutrality. In our present study, it is the mind of Cyrus the Great that is the battleground. Of him, Isaiah wrote,

That saith of Cyrus, He is my shepherd, and shall perform all my pleasure; even saying to Jerusalem, Thou shalt be built; and to the temple, Thy foundation shall be laid. Thus saith the Lord to his anointed, to Cyrus, whose right hand I have held, to subdue nations before him; and I will loose the loins of kings, to open before him the two-leaved gates; and the gates shall not be shut.

I will go before thee, and make crooked places straight; I will break in pieces the gates of bronze, and cut in sunder the bars of iron; And I will give thee the treasures of darkness, and the hidden riches of secret places, that thou mayest know that I, the Lord, who called thee by thy name, am the God of Israel,

*For Jacob my servant's sake, and Israel mine elect, I have even called thee by thy name; I have surnamed thee, though thou hast not known me.*⁴

Though we see from Isaiah's account that Cyrus was ordained to perform *"all my pleasure,"* there is still the invisible battle for his mind and will. Though victory is sure, the contest is nonetheless sharp.

Xenophon in his Cyropaedia has tried to pass on to his readers something of the reverence and idolization with which Cyrus was regarded by the Persians. While he makes Cyrus talk like an Athenian, he has at least caught something of the fairness, the vigor, and even the genius of the king. He does not and undoubtedly could not, give us any clue to the spiritual side of Cyrus and certainly no inkling that he was a choice tool in Jehovah's hand. This, we find only in Scripture. Terms such as, *"His anointed"* and *"My shepherd"* are most unusual. They are used of no other gentile king not even of Nebuchadnezzar. They are the terms formerly used of David. The phrase, *"though thou has not known Me"* could be best understood if we added *"heretofore"* to the sentence, for in the previous verse, we have the statement *"that thou mayest know that I, the Lord, who called thee by thy name, am the God of Israel."*

This chapter closes with the angel's words applicable to all the remaining chapters of the book, *"But I will show thee that which is noted in the scripture of truth.*" This, seemingly, should refer to what follows in Chapters 11 and 12 but we look in vain for any biblical quotation, reference or even ground covered by previous scripture. What does he mean? Keil says,

"The 'scripture of truth' is the book in which God has designated beforehand according to truth, the history of the world as it shall certainly be unfolded"(cf. Malachi 3:16, Revelation 5:1).[5]

Barnes says,

"The 'scripture of truth' means the true writing and the reference is doubtless to the Divine purposes or decrees in this matter for (a) there is no other writing where these things were then found; (b) the angel came to make known what could be known in no other way, and therefore what was not yet found in any book to which man had access; (c) this language accords with the common representations in the Scriptures respecting future events. They are described as written down in a book that is in the hands of God, in which are recorded all future; the names of those that shall be saved and all the deeds of men." Compare Deuteronomy 32:34, Malachi 3:16, Psalm 139:16, Revelation 5:1.[6]

If we think of this tenth chapter as a separate vision (which it is not) and unrelated to what follows, we should take another look. All the endless strife pictured in Chapter 11 and the tremendous happenings of Chapter 12 have as their visible explanation the perverted wills of kings and rulers, their desire for power, for land, for fame. This is but a front for the real contests, invisible but terribly real. The king of the north, the king of the south, the false prophet and above all, "The King" are but subject to the god of this age whose unknowing tools they are. It is not that they do not have wills of their own; they are deluded and seduced by the Great Seducer who is using them for his own purposes. Caiaphas and Annas merely thought they were protecing their own interests and those of their Sadducean party; instead, they were committing Israel to twenty centuries of persecution and loss.

However noble the thoughts and high desires of men, the Great Manipulator bends them all to his purposes. There is a refuge and a recourse from his wiles only to be found in the shadow of the Almighty and in the intercession of his Messiah. So as we read the following chapters, we have in this chapter been given the clue to the realities and forces controlling the gentile world and find its culmination in a final revolt against the only One in the universe who truly loves man as he ought to be loved; the One whose fiats are based on the ultimate good found in the spiritual, moral and physical realties of the universe. He alone knows how it was made and what must eternally belong to it, if the ultimate good which he had planned for it is to be worked out.

CHAPTER XII

DANIEL'S FOURTH VISION
CONFLICTS OF THE GENTILE NATION
THE KING

(Daniel 11)

As we begin Chapter 11, we will avoid much confusion if we keep in mind Daniel's word to us that the chapter has to do primarily with the *"end of years"* (Daniel 11:6) and equally must we not assume, *a priori*, that Daniel spends thirty-five verses devoted to background and only ten verses relating to future prophecy; i.e., the end time.

Keil warns us:

"All that the angel says regarding the Persian and Javanic world kingdoms and the wars of the kings of the north and south has its aim to the end time and serves only briefly to indicate the chief elements of the development of the world kingdoms til the time when the war that brings in the end shall burst forth, and to show how, after the overthrow of the Javanic world kingdoms, neither the kings of the north nor those of the south shall gain possession of the kingdoms of the world." North - Seleucus / South - Ptolemy

As the angel oriented Daniel at the beginning of the vision, the prophecy is for *"thy people"* and *"in the latter days."* Let us keep this in mind as we consider these last two chapters (11 and 12). Since Daniel 11:5-20 is usually thought of as past history, we give Keil's paraphrase of these verses. He says,

"If we now, before proceeding further in our exposition, attentively consider the contents of the revelation of verses 5-20 so as to have a clear view of its relation to the historical fulfillment, we shall find the following to be the course of the thoughts exhibited: After the fall of the Javanic world kingdom (verse 4) the king of the south shall attain to great power, and one of his princes shall find (verse 5) a yet greater dominion in the north. After a course of years they shall enter into an agreement, for the king of the south shall give his daughter in marriage to the king of the north so as to establish a right relationship between them; but this agreement shall bring about the destruction of the daughter, as well as of her father and all who cooperated for the effecting of this marriage (verse 6).

"Hereupon a descendant of the south shall undertake a war against the king of the north, victoriously invade the country of the adversary, gather together great spoil and carry it away to Egypt, and for years hold the supremacy. The king of the north shall, it is true, penetrate into his kingdom, but he shall again return home without effecting anything (verses 7-9). His sons also shall pass over the kingdom of the south with a multitude of host, but the multitude shall be given into the hand of the king, who shall not come to power by casting down myriads. The king of the north shall return with a host yet more numerous; against the king of the south many, also faithless members of the Jewish nation, shall rise up and the king of the north shall take the fortified cities without the king of the south having the power to offer him resistance (verses 10-15).

"The conqueror shall now rule the conquered lands after his own pleasure, and set his foot on the Holy Land with the intention of destroying it. Thereupon he shall come with the whole might of his kingdom against the king of the south, and by the marriage of his daughter seek to establish a right relationship with him, but he shall only thereby bring about the destruction of his daughter. Finally, he shall make an assault against the islands and the maritime countries of the west: but he shall be smitten by his chiefs and be compelled to return to the fortresses of his own land, and shall fall (verses 16-19). But his successors, who shall send taskmasters to the most glorious regions of the kingdom, shall be destroyed in a short time (verses 20).

"Thus the revelation depicts how, in the war of the kings of the south and of the north, first the king of the south subdued the north but when at the summit of his conquest he sank under the power of his adversary through the insurrections and revolt of an apostate party of the Jews; whereupon, by an assault upon the west in his endeavor after a firmer establishment and wider extension of his power, he brings about his own overthrow, and his successor, in consequence of the oppression of his kingdom, comes to his end in a few days.

" Now, since the king who comes into his place (verse 21f) after he has become strong raises himself up against the holy covenant, takes away the daily worship in the temple of the Lord, etc., is, according to the historical evidence found in the book of the Maccabees, the Seleucidan Antiochus Epiphanes so the prophetic announcement (verses 5-20) stretches itself over the period from the division of the monarchy of Alexander among his generals to the commencement of the reign of Antiochus Epiphanes in the year 175 B.C. during which time there reigned seven Syrian and six Egyptian kings, but in the prophetic revelation there is mention made of only four kings of the north (one in verses 5-9; his sons, verses 10-12; a third, verses 13-19 and a fourth, verse 20) and three kings of the south (the first, verses 5-6; the branch, verses 7-9 and the king, verses 10-15) distinctly different, whereby of the former, the relation of the sons (verse 10) to the king indefinitely mentioned in verse 11, is admitted, and of the later kings of the south, it remains doubtful whether he who is spoken of in verses 9-15 is different from or identical with 'the branch of her roots' (verse 7).

"This circumstance shows that the prophecy does not treat individual personages, but only places in view the king of the south and the king of the north as representatives of the power of these two kingdoms."[2]

Keil goes on to say,

"But yet all these specialties do not establish the view that the prophecy consists of a series of predictions of historical facts, because even these features of prophecy which find their actual fulfillments in history do not coincide with the historical reality."[3]

But if they do not coincide, is the fault that of the prophecy or perhaps a lack of knowledge or understanding on our part? Keil thus leaves us with the difficult question of why so detailed and so large a part of the chapter should seemingly lack the accuracy that we should have had the right to expect. Are we dealing here with inspirational fiction? If so, to what end and for whom? Is it possible that our secular sources are inaccurate with notable errors of omission and commision?[4]

In the nature of things, this is not provable but also not likely, for the sources we have seem largely in agreement, though imcomplete. Is it not more likely that we have here again, a double horizon - that while roughly, verses 5-20 correspond to the Seleucid and the Ptolemaic conflict, there will be a replay of these conflicts in the end time that will rectify the seeming inaccuracies of the first horizon? This would seem to be a far safer course in view of the long history of alleged, historical inaccuracies of the Old Testament subsequently discovered to be verifiable history. Our present interest, however, is to discover whether we are dealing with history, good or bad, or with prophecy yet to be fulfilled.

Keil, in the context quoted above, points out that eleven of the first thirty-five verses of Daniel 11 have no counterpart in history and three others are corroborated only in part. On the other hand, verses 36-45 are completely prophetic; i.e., future, without the slightest corroboration in past history.[5]

For an opposite viewpoint, Walvoord feels that Keil has made concessions to the critics though perhaps is it not possible that the concessions are actually made to the facts of history? He says,

"In making this concession to the critics, Keil concedes far more than the record requires. If the text is properly interpreted, the alleged historical errors fade; and Daniel's record stands accurate and complete, although not without problems of interpretation such as are true in any prophetic utterance. The expositor of this portion of Scripture has no convenient compromise between the two diverse views. Either this is genuine prophecy or it is not. The fact that it corresponds so closely to history should be, instead of a basis for criticism, a marvelous confirmation that prophecy properly understood is just as accurate as history. As has been previously pointed out the attack on the prophecies of Daniel always fall short. The fulfillment of the complete revelation anticipates a situation yet future and could not be considered history even from the point of view of an alleged second century Daniel.

" In attempting the different exegeses of this portion, the general principle should be observed that prophecy as far as it goes is accurate, but that prophecy is selective. The revelation does not contain all the history of the period nor name all the rulers. It is not always possible to determine why some facts are included and others excluded. But the total picture of struggle and turmoil which characterized the period of the third empire is portrayed by special reference to Antiochus Epiphanes, who is given more space than any other ruler in this chapter because of the relevance of his activities to the people of Israel."[6]

Walvoord has expressed very clearly the present, prevailing conservative view. But his "problems of interpretation" are really the points at issue. It seems possible, however, to hold the same high regard for prophecy by considering that we are dealing with a double reference. After all, if the picture given us of Antiochus IV is typical of Antichrist, why cannot the conflicts between the Seleucidae and the Ptolemies be a type in accurate detail of the conflicts of the end time? The geographic and ethnic possibilities are there. To the protagonists, the king of the north and the king of the south, we need add only the king (the Antichrist), the head of a revived Roman empire already foreshadowed in the reference to the *"ships of Chittim"* in Daniel 11:30.

Instead of regarding the phrase in verse 6, *"in the end of years,"* as referring to events prior to 63 B.C., why not consider the term as having reference to both the Maccabean period and to the end time? It will, of course, be objected that persons not historical patterns, are types; that history does not repeat itself. But it can be answered that a type would hardly be a type without the factual and even historical setting that brought out the typical qualities. Abraham minus the circumstances of his sojourn in the land of promise (his willingness to offer Isaac and so forth) would not be a type, so is it too farfetched to think of a historical pattern as a type of Christ the Messiah with His exaltation and glory and also, equally, the Suffering Servant? How could they reconcile these two things until the sufferings actually occured?

Leupold has a very pertinent suggestion, apropos of this section,

"Let this yet be said about the first part of the chapter: There is another deeper reason why such details as these are worthy of the work of the Spirit of prophecy, and that is that what is foretold here is in reality, with minor variations, the pattern into which all history falls. Is there not an appalling sameness about this business of leagues and pacts between rival nations, of disagreements, of wars of alliances, of political marriages, of recriminations, of treachery, of temporary ascendancy, of defeat and utter downfall, of recovery through some aggressive leader and the same thing all over again with a slightly different sequence of events? From this point of view there is a drab sameness about history which allows us to say that, in addition to being a prophecy of a particular period of Syrian and Egyptian history, this may be regarded as a panoramic view of all history in a picture that is idealized, at least to some extent."[7]

In verses 36-45, we have the same protagonists that we have met heretofore; the king of the north, the king of the south and the central character, the king; the first two directing their attacks against the latter. There is a possibility that the king of the north refers to a king farther north than was previously identified.

Verses 6-20 have this designation in common with verses 21-25: (1) There are contests between the north and the south.[8] (2) There is Jewish division (a majority party and a minority) and some sort of alliance with the apostate Jews and their alliance with Antichrist of his type. (3) There is persecution of the faithful remnant. (4) There is the same antagonism to the Holy Covenant. (5) There is pollution of the sanctuary. (6) The details that belong peculiarly to the future world of the revived Roman Empire can only be determined negatively. All verses that conform to past historical events should, of course, be interpreted as belonging to Antiochus as a type of Antichrist. All others refer to Antichrist himself. (7) A chief stumbling block in the path of the modern student of prophecy, in accepting such a viewpoint, is the apparent unlikelihood that the present governments of the north (Syria) and the south (Egypt) would be at war with one another rather than with Israel, though even this sometimes seems possible.

But if we move the king of the north a little farther north, as far as Turkey or even Russia, our difficulties are mitigated. Is it thinkable that Turkey can be left out of a future conflict or that Russia would be quiescent in any final conflict? While Turkey is Moslem, she is not Arab. Also, she has a history of military prowess and military involvement. Suppose that, under a competent and aggressive leadership, she should again attempt to reassert her former sovereignty over Egypt, Lebanon and Palestine. Equally postulate an Egypt backed by the oil billions of Saudi Arabia and Libya both egged-on by Russia for her own, ultimate purposes. Let us further assume that Antichrist, the king of the west, has made a covenant with the Jews for the purpose of controlling the strategic landbridge occupied by Israel even though the bulk of his kingdom is in Europe. He might further have the religious goal of using the ancient city of Jerusalem as the center of his own deification.

Why is this, or some similar pattern, so hard for us to accept? The answer is that while we know anything can happen, we do not expect it to happen. Only until the pieces of the jigsaw puzzle finally fall into place and we see precisely and in detail what could only previously be seen in general outline and somewhat vaguely, will we be sure of the picture in all its details.

It seems unimaginable to the student of Bible prophecy that any nation on earth will be neutral or unattached in the final maelstrom and that those nearest the vortex, Israel, should escape involvement. That all nations will try to solve their unsolvable problems by war seems to be the message of prophecy, as well as that of history.

In commentating on Daniel 11:6-36, Keil considers that of the thirty verses in this section, eleven are not verified by history, four are corroborated in part and three are ambiguous. If he is correct in this, the eleven unverified verses must, of necessity, require a still future fulfillment as, of course, must verses 36-45 since they do not conform to what we know of Antiochus. Are we then, presented with a double horizon, a type and antitype?

Walvoord, on the other hand, seems to find a complete fulfillment, or at least one sufficiently close, in these verses and sees in them the fulfillment of the struggles of the Seleucidae and the Ptolemies, their mutual invasions and political maneuvers. Both writers have access to the same, non-biblical authorities, Josephus, I and II Maccabees, Polybius, Appian and Livy. Many premillennial writers take this latter view; i.e., that we are dealing only with fulfilled history and with one horizon and this, of course, greatly simplifies the problem but leaves it in the air.

Since Antiochus Epiphanes is rather commonly considered to be the subject of verses 21-35 perhaps a brief summary of his life might be in order since, whatever his secular standing, his horrible persecution of the Jews and their religion gives him special importance from the biblical point of view.

Antiochus IV (175-164 B.C.), self-styled Epiphanes (illustrious or manifest deity) was the younger son of Antiochus III, called the Great. After the Battle of Magnesia (190 B.C.) in which Antiochus III was defeated by a Roman army, his son Antiochus Epiphanes was taken to Rome as a hostage where he spent fourteen years, later spending a year in Athens where he became enamored of everything Greek. While there, his elder brother, Seleucus IV, called Philopator, died and Antiochus with the aid of Eumenes II (King of Pergamum) secured his father's throne over the better claim of his brother's son, Dematrius (his brother having been murdered by Heliodorus, a claimant for the throne). He killed Heliodorus, poisoner of his brother, thus establishing his own position.

Pagan writers (Polybius, Livy, Appian) picture him as able but eccentric; Jewish writers picture him as almost demonic in his hatred of the Jewish God and the orthodox way of life. Scripture gives him no better rating, speaking of him as both furious and precipitate to the point of madness. As many rulers before and after, he regarded religious unity as a desirable basis for political unity. This, along with his great admiration for classical Greek culture, his almost fanatical devotion to the Greek Zeus (Jupiter), the large amount of Hellenization already at work in Israel, coupled with an affront offered by the Jews at the false rumor of his death, made him one of the great persecutors of Israel. At the beginning of his reign, he was asked to arbitrate a dispute between the incumbent high priest, Onias, and Jason, his brother, concerning the high priesthood. He settled the office on Jason, a Hellenizer, who paid a large sum for the position. Later, Jason was deposed in favor of Menelaus who offered an even larger sum of money and under whom the temple ritual finally ceased. Jason, however, hearing that Antiochus had died while on his campagin against Egypt, besieged Jerusalem but was defeated upon Antiochus' return. The city was recaptured and the temple plundered. There was a general massacre of all orthodox Jews and their wives and children were sold into slavery.

On Antiochus' third expedition against Egypt, he was met by a Roman consul, Gaius Popilius Laenas, who ordered him to evacuate occupied Egyptian territory or face war with Rome. Antiochus vented his spleen upon his return to Judea, on everything Jewish. He sent his general, Apollonius, with twenty thousand men to wipe out the city and its inhabitants and recolonize it with Greeks. Apollonius attacked on the sabbath; the Jews refused to fight on that day. Most of the males were killed and the women and children sold into slavery. He garrisoned the city with Syrian troops.

Antiochus now issued a decree prescribing the death penalty for anyone found circumcising a male child, anyone keeping the Sabbath or anyone found in possession of the Torah or who kept the Jewish dietary laws. An altar to Olympian Zeus was erected on the place of the altar of sacrifice and a sow offered. During this period, many Jews were martyred for their faith.

A drastic turn of events came through the courage of a priest, Mattathias of Modin near Jerusalem, who killed the official of Antiochus sent to enforce his demands and fled to the hills with a few followers to wage guerrilla warfare. At first, they refused to fight on the sabbath; later, after much loss, they fought whenever attacked. Mattathias died (166 B.C.) and was succeeded by his son Judas, called Maccabeus, an able and zealous leader who was not satisfied with guerrilla tactics but boldly put into the field a small army. He first defeated Appolonius, later another general, Seron, and captured Jerusalem, reestablishing the temple worship.

Antiochus, during this time, was absent from the scene of fighting being occupied with revolts in Parthia and Armenia. Upon hearing of Judas' successes, he sent his general, Lysias guardian of his son, with orders to deal ruthlessly with the Jewish rebellion. Lysias in turn, delegated the campaign to his three generals; Ptolemy, Nicanor and Gorgias, with a large army which was surprised and defeated at the Battle of Emmaus. The whole Syrian army fled. Lysias, at the head of an even larger army, was thoroughly defeated at the battle of Beth-Zur, the only Syrians left being the garrison in the citadel in Jerusalem. The temple worship was restored, an altar of hewn stones was erected and sacrifice resumed on the 25th Chisleu, 165 B.C. (according to Josephus, three years to the day from its desecration). Antiochus was enraged but powerless since his affairs were not prospering in the east. Being short of money, he attempted to pillage the rich temple of Manea in Elymas but was unsuccessful. Tradition has it that he became really insane in Persia where he spent his last year, dying in 164 B.C.[10]

While his war against the Jews was a lesson in futility, he actually recovered much of the territory elsewhere lost by his father after the battle of Magnesia. In his dealings with Israel, he might very properly be a type of Antichrist.

While the antagonist featured in Daniel 8 destroys many by peace, our willful king is a warrior and conqueror. War is his life, war is his method, war is his god. This does not mean that he would lack qualities of intelligence of a high order, a gift for diplomacy and a mastery of statesmanship, or that he might be able to recognize and utilize all the scientific resources of our modern age. He might indeed be Superman, the man on horseback (Revelation 6:2).

Let us see him through Sir Robert Anderson's eyes,

"What is it that all Europe is looking for? It is the king of men, the great head of the Hellenic race (like Agamemnon), the man whom a thousand galleys and a hundred thousand men submitted to on a simple recognition of his personal qualities and obeyed for ten long years. . . . The realization of this dream will be the fulfillment of prophecy. . . . True it is, that popular movements characterize the age, rather than the power of individual minds. It is the age of mobs. Democracy, not despotism, is the goal toward which civilization is tending. But democracy in its full development is one of the surest roads to despotism. First the revolution; then the plevescite; then the despot. The Caesar often owes his sceptre to the mob . . . and the true king of men must have an extraordinary combination of great qualities. He must be a scholar, a statesman, a man of unflinching courage and irrepressible enterprise, full of resources and ready to look in the face a rival or a foe. The opportunity, too, must synchronize with his advent. But the voice of prophecy is clear; that the Hour is coming , and the Man."[11]

What Anderson observed and quoted in 1876 is much more true today as it is much nearer the event. We have more mob reactions, more anarchy, more democracy run amuck and perhaps an even greater longing for peace. It would seem that the world is becoming more and more weary with small men trying to meet great issues and with less prospect of success. And over all hangs the shadow of the atomic bomb.

Relative to the identity of the king, "ha-melek", in verse 36, we find an excellent discussion in Keil. Whereas the introduction of the king seems abrupt and unconnected with what has gone before, Keil holds that this same individual has already been the subject of discussion in verses 21-35. He says,

"The nonmention also of the descruction of this enemy (Antiochus) in verses 32-35 is not justified by the remark that this was already known to Daniel from Chapter 8, and that in verses 36-45 a duration of Antichrist is also omitted (Klief). For the verses do not treat of the duration of the precedings of the enemy of God but of his end or his destruction. The destruction of the enemy at the time of the end is, however, expressly declared in verse 45. This would also have been stated in verses 32-34 if the king in verse 36 had been a different person from the one previously described, "*ha-melek*", with the definite article, undeniably points back to the king whose appearance and conduct are described in verses 21-33. The definite article neither denotes that the Antichrist of Chapter 7 and 11:26f was known to him (Klief), nor is it to be emphatically interpreted in the sense of the king simply (Geier).

"This is only so far right, that that which is said regarding this king, verses 36-39, partly goes far beyond what Antiochus did, partly does not harmonize to what is known of Antiochus, and finally, is referred in N.T. expressly to Antichrist; cf. verse 36 with II Thessalonians 11:4, and 12:1 with Matthew 24:21.

"These circumstances also are not satisfactorily explained by the remark that the prophecy regarding Antiochus glances forward to the Antichrist, or that the image of the type (Antiochus) hovers in the image of the anti-type (Antichrist); they much rather show that in the prophetic contemplation there is comprehended in the image of one king what has been historically fulfilled in its beginnings by Antiochus Epiphanes, but shall only meet its complete fulfillment by the Antichrist in the time of the end."[12]

Keil agrees with Jerome, Theodoret, Luther, Oecolampadius, Osiander, Calovius, Geier and at length Kliefoth in interpreting verses 36-45 (and 12:1-3) as a direct prophecy of Antichrist (p. 461) and seemingly, it could be no other, but if we concede this and insist with Keil that verses 22-35 are talking about Antichrist in type or in part, it would seem then, that we must also place the ethnic origin and the activities of Antichrist in the Eastern Empire (revived).

One way of solving the apparently conflicting views of the ethnic source of Antichrist is given us by Sir Robert Anderson. He says,

"That Antichrist is to arise from the eastern part of the Roman Empire, and from that part of the east which fell under the rule of Alexander's successors, is rendered unquestionable by this chapter (i.e., Chapter 8). But seeing in the eleventh chapter he is mentioned as conflicting with the king of the north (i.e., the king of Syria) and also with the king of the south (i.e., the king of Egypt), it is plain that he does not arise either from Egypt or Syria. He must, therefore, arise either from Greece or from the districts immediately contiguous to Constantinople. It is true that if he arose from the latter, or indeed from either of the four, he would be esteemed Greek in origin, because all four were divisions of a Greek empire; but it seems far more probable that Greece proper will be the place of his rise. He is described as waxing great toward the south and toward the east and toward the pleasant land; that is, toward Egypt, Syria, and Palestine; a description that would geographically suit the position of one who was supposed to be in Greece. Moreover, "*a little horn*" (an emblem not of that which he is as an individual but of that which he is as a monarch) is a symbol that well suits one who should arise from one of those petty principalities which once abounded in Greece and have even til their memorial in the throne of the sovereigns of Montenegro."[13]

If we could identify the king with the Antichrist, we would have the picture of global involvement portrayed in the great day of Armageddon. We would thus have the Antichrist as the head of the revived Roman Empire in opposition to any program of strategic encirclement contemplated by Russia and in a contest for world resources against both Russia and China. It would not be necessary to assume that the prince of Rus and the kings of the East were acting in conjunction. Both have global goals, both are involved in a mutual struggle for the control of earth's resources which will become more and more of a necessity as expanding population pressures make these resources more and more insufficient.

Again, the king of the south on the present chess board would seemingly have to be someone who has finally consolidated the Arab countries (possibly part of Arabic Africa) into a hegemony of four heads discussed in Chapter 7. This might be inferred from the mention of Egypt, Libya and Ethiopia with other Arab countries (possibly Arabia and other North African states). This is not hard to believe at the present time for from Morocco to Saudi Arabia, a ferment is working and whoever can synthesize the fervor of the Moslem faith with the social pressures resident in the Arab world and can have control over the oil billions recently at their command, such a one could be no mean antagonist to the king with his original resources of western Europe.

But suppose the king of the north is not Russia but Turkey for it is inconceivable that any great conflict could take place in the Near East for any length of time without Turkish participation for, as we have indicated elsewhere, Turkey is both Moslem with its tradition of conversion by the sword and has its history of possession of Palestine, Lebanon and Egypt. These areas would be very much worth fighting for again. Or are we to assume that, willingly or unwillingly, Turkey becomes an ally of Russia?

This part of Chapter 11 has other interest for us: the scriptural prospect that all of the fighting and conquest takes place on the west side of the

Jordan thus leaving Transjordan unconquered; the prospect (not now evident) that Egypt will suddenly come into great wealth of some kind and equally, the king's conquest over Egypt, together with the Libyans and Ethiopians.

All of what we have said is postulated upon the possibility that the present world order or present world forces are operant at the time of the end. In fact, much of our interpretation of Daniel 7 involves this viewpoint. But if not, what then? Then, it will be necessary to find if possible, biblical substitutes or to ask why there is no mention of peoples and nations so obviously and significantly related to the problems of Israel in these latter days. How do we account for the fact that twenty- eight verses should be devoted in Chapter 7 to an elaboration of verses 40- 45 of Chapter 2 if these are not significant actors at the climax of prophecy?

The six verses, Daniel 11:40-45, give a brief description of the exploits of the willful king, probably the Antichrist, the subject of these verses being he throughout. The other actors; *"king of the north," "king of the south"* and the phrases *"tidings out of the east and the north"*, are not so easily identifiable probably at best, only conjecturally.

The countries Egypt and Libya seem clearly identified but we cannot be even sure that Ethiopia is the Ethiopia of old (the modern Sudan) or is the modern Ethiopia. There are signifcant stirrings in modern Ethiopia which might be prophetic.

This much does seem clear,

(1) He will have to defend himself against the kings of the north and the south who will come at him with fury, with chariots and horsemen and many ships. By ships, we can only conjecture whether at that future time they will be air ships or naval vessels - or their primitive successors if the great earthquake has occurred.[14] If the former, we might ask, Who, of the possible opponents, has a substantial navy? There are many small navies in the world, a few of second rank (England, France and so forth) but only two great naval powers, America and Russia. If the kings of the north and the south are Arab countries, they do not at present have significant navies or any in prospect but Russia does, and Russia has identified herself closely with the Arab world.

(2) He seems to be victorious; "many countries shall be overthrown." This seems to include Egypt.

(3) Apparently, the whole (or a large part) of Transjordan shall escape; i.e., even Edom, Moab and the Chief of Ammon.

(4) Egypt, seemingly, will have treasures not presently evident and these will be at his disposal. A discovery of oil in the Egyptian desert is a possibility. Or does this refer to some Egyptian mineral strike?

(5) The Libyans and Ethiopians (Lubim and Cushim) shall be in his train; i.e., at his heels. While all these Arab countries have one thing in

common, their anti-Jewishness, the tensions between these nations themselves is almost as great as those between Arab and Jew. These tensions could, however, result in internecine conflict and consequent consolidation of the numerous Arab states into a hegemony of four as represented by the four heads and four wings of the third beast.

In verse 41, Edom and Moab and the chief of Ammon will escape (i.e., the present kingdom of Transjordan which, so far at least, has been less anti-Israel than the others and, hence, might reasonably be expected to escape the consequences visited up on the others). The chapter speaks of the king, the Antichrist, as having power over all the precious things of Egypt and having the Libyans and the Ethiopians at his heels.

The eleventh chapter ends with the statement: *"He shall plant the tabernacles of his palace between the seas in the glorious holy mountain; yet he shall come to his end, and none shall help him."* This verse may find its clarification in Revelation 19 but there are some discrepencies. The passage in Revelation 19:19 describes, apparently, a joint action of the beast and the kings of the earth against the Faithful and True of verse 11. There is no hint of disunity. In Daniel, there is furious conflict between the king and the king of the south and the king of the north with no hint of their combined action against Jerusalem. It may be that there needs to be a re-evaluation of Ezekiel 38 and 39, Zechariah 14, Daniel 9:26- 27, Revelation 14:14-20, Revelation 16:12-16 and Revelation 19:11-21.

At the time of the end, apparently as a part of the great battle of Armageddon, we have the following personalities to deal with: (1) the king, (2) the king of the north, (3) the king of the south, (4) the kings of the east, (5) Gog and (6) the False Prophet (or king of fierce countenance; i.e., the little horn of Daniel 8).

The statement "*but tidings out of the east and the north shall trouble him, and he shall go forth with great fury to destroy and to utterly sweep away many"* is not entirely clear to us at this time for presumably, the king of the north and the king of the south have already been subdued (verse 41).

Do we have here reference to Ezekiel 38 and 39? And is the invasion of Gog and the hordes of Magog the tidings that are spoken of? And is the tiding out of the east the invasion by the kings of the east (i.e., beyond the Euphrates mentioned in Revelation)? It is not said that they destroy him or that he destroys them. This fits the description in Ezekiel 38:19-23 where hints of earthquakes, internal fighting in Gog's host, pestilence and blood, rain, great hail stones, fire and brimstone are the agencies for destruction, yet controlled by God himself. We are told that only a sixth part will be left of all the great host. The whole defeat of Gog's hordes will be done in such a way that there shall be no doubt that it is a divine act. *"They shall know that I am the Lord"* (Ezekiel 38:23, 39:6).

So far as we can see, there is no evidence that the kings of the east cause Gog's downfall. Because their way is prepared by the drying up of the Euphrates River (Revelation 16:12), they must have a very significant part to play in the great, final conflict. Their way would not be *"prepared"* except for the possibility of future action involving their overthrow. But so far as the record goes, they are apparently merged with the other kings of the earth in the great Battle of Armageddon. Zechariah says, *"I will gather all nations against Jerusalem to battle. . . Then shall the Lord go forth and fight against those nations as when he fought in the day of battle"* (Zechariah 14:2-3).

The chapter ends,

And he shall plant the tabernacles (tent) of his palace between the seas and the glorious holy mountain; yet he shall come to his end, and none shall help him (Daniel 11:45).

While there are several personalities involved in the final, great conflict, is it not probable that while all the above references are speaking of the same general event, it is undoubtedly a series of battles and an extended campaign, ending in a single, colossal battle (i.e., a series of conflicts that are phases of a single culminating event rather than just one titanic conflict)? Daniel tells us that wars are determined to the end, not just at the end; even as the great earthquake, the great plagues and so forth may be the culmination of a series.

This view would resolve some of the apparent discrepancies, or lacunae, in Ezekiel, Zechariah, Daniel and Revelation.

While the battles involved would thus be spread over a greater period of time and geographic area, it would seem that they might well all come within the final three and a half years; the final battle of Armageddon because of its colossal magnitude and terrible death toll, alone being pinpointed and highlighted.

"Between the seas" could mean either between the Sea of Galilee and the Dead Sea (that is, somewhere in the Jordan Valley) or between the Dead Sea and the Mediterranean. However, the latter must be meant since his tent is located in *"the glorious holy mountain;"* that is, in or near Jerusalem. If Antichrist's religious capitol is located in Jerusalem, we do not quite see why the word *"tabernacle"* (oh'hel or tent), was used. The term *"tent of his palace"* (oh'hel-ap-peh-do), gives us a picture of the luxurious tent of an oriental monarch.

The final phrase *"he shall come to his end and none shall help him"* (literally, *"shall not be a helper to him")* dismisses Antichrist without fanfare and almost with the wave of God's hand. He is not even given a lengthy obituary. The evil that he exerted was his own evil nature; the ability to impose it on others was due to a power not his own, regardless of his personal endowments.

With the passing of Antichrist, there is final victory for Israel through the faithfulness of Him whom they have pierced (Zechariah 12:10). Isaiah tells us in unforgettable language, *"Speak ye tenderly to Jerusalem, and cry unto her, that her warfare is accomplished and her iniquity is pardoned; for she hath received of the Lord's hand double for all her sins."*

Were I a Jew, conservative, liberal, reformed or especially orthodox, I would be tormented by two questions, the first being: Do I really believe that God is good; or if good, powerless? The second: If I believe that God is good and is not powerless, what great sin, or sins, has Israel committed that for two millennia she has been left without a king, without a prince, without a sacrifice, without an image, without an ephod and without a teraphim? (Hosea 3:4.) That sin is the basis of disaster for Israel was predicted by Moses (Deuteronomy 28-30). Moreover, Israel who seeks salvation by the law, can no longer keep the law since she has no Levitical priesthood, no altar and no temple. And since this is so according to the law, she has no covering for sin.

Why has a good God who is not powerless, made impossible the ritual atonement for the sins of the people, unless perchance all other possible sins were relatively insignificant as compared to the rejection of Messiah, Jesus Christ, and unless He was the atonement that they rejected foretold by all the prophets, especially Isaiah (Chapter 53, *"when thou shalt make his soul an offering for sin"*)?

For two thousand years, Israel has had no temple, no priesthood, no morning and evening sacrifice and while the day of atonement is celebrated, it cannot be celebrated according to the Levitical law for there is no temple, no Holy of Holies, no sacrificial altar and no high priest to enter the Holy of Holies on this day. And, of course, there is no Shekinah glory.

Much of Israel according to the flesh, is still alienated from the God of her fathers (according to reports from Palestine) and from Messiah the prince but thank God, there will shortly come a day when *"They shall look on me whom they have pierced, and they shall mourn for him as one mourneth for his only son, and shall be in bitterness for him as one is in bitterness for his firstborn"* (Zechariah 12:10).

CHAPTER XIII
PORTRAIT OF THE ANTICHRIST

Our earliest intimation of a future *"man of sin"* is in Genesis 3:15 where we read, *"And I will put enmity between thee and the woman and between thy seed and her seed."*

That the woman should have seed is the God-given order of nature but what about the serpent's seed? So far as we know, Satan neither creates nor procreates.

How then may he have seed? In a sense, we may speak of the children of the devil as we speak of the children of God, as those who choose Satanic leadership as against those who have accepted Christ; between those who are motivated by a fallen nature and demonic influence operating therein and those in whom the incorruptible seed of the Holy Spirit dwells and guides. But it would seem that our analogy in this passage means much more.

Is it possible that Satan may beget seed by a process of incarnation or even a type of spiritual procreation? Jesus, who never uses language carelessly, speaks of *"the son of perdition"* and again, speaking of Judas, *"one of you is devil* (diabolos)." Paul again speaks of *"the son of perdition," "the man of sin."*

Now if you or I were to use such terms (as loosely as we speak at times), this language could merely mean that such an individual was doing works of the devil perhaps in an unusual way. But do we not have here a more technical use of the language pointing to a unique individual, from a unique source, fulfilling prophecy in an altogether new and supernatural way? Our minds are still further stirred by Revelation 17:8 where we read, *"the beast that thou sawest was, and is not, and shall ascend out of the bottomless pit, and go into perdition, and they that dwell on the earth shall wonder . . . when they behold the beast that was, and is not, and yet is,"* and again similar words are used in Revelation 17:10-11, referring to the eighth king.

A piece of Christian fiction written some years ago, presents us with an individual conceived by a woman and purportedly begotten by Satan himself. This is one way out of the problem but we are told by Jesus that the angels of heaven *"neither marry nor are given in marriage"* and we would need very definite evidence that Satan who was once the anointed cherub, had been given powers not common to the angelic host. In the absence of such assurance, we would have to believe in some form of incarnation or some form of reincarnation. Whatever our interpretation, the utter uniqueness of Antichrist and possibly the false prophet, seems evident.

The early church fathers thought of a resurrected Nero as the beast of Revelation 13:1-10. Newell expresses it in the following,

"The voice of history and tradition calls to us that the Antichrist and the last Roman emperor are to be identical. Victorinus, voicing an impression that was very common in early Christian centuries, says, 'Nero will be raised from the dead, appear again at Rome and persecute the church once more, and finally be destroyed by Messiah.' Augustine first mentioned this idea concerning Nero. Even Tacitus, the Roman historian, spoke of many believing rumors about Nero's possible return (Hist. 11, 8, 1 & 2). Sulpicius Severus said, 'It is current opinion among many that he (Nero) is yet to come as Antichrist.' Note carefully that we are not insisting at all that Nero will be Antichrist but that early Christians believed that a Roman, imperial persecutor, possibly Nero, would be the Antichrist."[1]

While Daniel tells us in more detail about the personality and characteristics of the mysterious person or person of evil than any other Old Testament writer, he is not the first to do so. In Genesis 3:15, we have not only the adumbration of the Christ but equally of the Antichrist; the seed (singular) of the woman, the seed (singular) of the serpent. Symbolically, for this epitome of evil is not called Antichrist in the Old Testament, he is given titles such as *"the seed of the serpent"* (Gen esis 3:15), *"the Assyrian"* (Isaiah 10:5-6, 14:24-27, 30:27-33), *"the king of Babylon"* (Isaiah 14:4, 14:9-11), *"the king"* (Isaiah 30:33). Ezekiel designates him as a type, *"the prince of Tyre"* (Ezekiel 28:12-19) while Daniel sees him under the title of *"the little horn"* (Daniel 11:36-45). One more Old Testament writer speaks of *"the idol shepherd"* (Zechariah 11:15-17) whose identity would be greatly in doubt except for Revelation 13:3.

With the advent of Christ comes also a clarification of Antichrist. Christ himself speaks of *"one that shall come in his own name"* (John 5:43) and *"the son of perdition"* (John 17:12) where we may have a double reference: the immediate one to Judas Iscariot, the more distant to Antichrist, for the term *"son of perdition"* is applied to Judas in John 17:12 and to Antichrist in II Thessalonians 2:2-3. The definite article being used in both cases is *"the"* son of perdition, not *"a"* son.

In Revelation, we have the rider on the white horse (Revelation 6:2), the beast (Revelation 11:7, 13:1-10), etc. The question may be rightly asked as to whether all these references are speaking about one person or two, or several. All have the spirit of Antichrist. In Revelation 13, it is obvious that we are speaking of the two beasts, the Antichrist and the False Prophet. No other New Testament reference makes this distinction though John speaks of many Antichrists (I John 2:18).

The question then arises, Do we have in the Old Testament the equivalent of the two beasts? And do we have any light on the many Antichrists that John says shall come? Whether they be one or many, in

Daniel's descriptions and in the Old Testament, all are characterized by pride, presumption, blasphemy, opposition to God and to God's people, self will, temporary success, ultimate destruction and above all, opposition to faithful Israel.

There are also clashing characteristics. In Daniel 8, the little horn conquers by peace while in Daniel 11:36-45, he is pictured as a warrior par excellence. In Daniel 7:8, 24-25 and 9:26-27, the little horn and the prince that shall come seemingly derive from the fourth kingdom (the Roman Empire revived), whereas in Daniel 8:9-14 and 8:23-25, his source is Greek as also may be implied in Daniel 11:36-45. Are they then not speaking about two individuals?

Therefore, it is not unreasonable to expect that Daniel is presenting us with the same two personalities we have in Revelation 13; the little horn (Daniel 7) and the prince that shall come (Daniel 9) and possibly the king (Daniel 11) as Antichrist; while the second beast, the False Prophet, may be portrayed in Daniel 8:9-14 and 8:23-25. This is what we should expect since there should be no conflict between Daniel and Revelation and no omission of so important a character. But is this assumption correct?

Daniel presents us with four personality descriptions, one of which (Daniel 11:21-35) may possibly be of double entendre, referring to Antiochus as a type and to a later anti-type. These persons have certain characteristics in common, as follows:

1. All four descriptions (Daniel 7,8,9, and 11) state or imply that these individuals are rulers or kings. In Daniel 7:24, 8:23, and 11:36, they are all called kings *(melek)*, one (Daniel 9:26) calls him *(nagidh)* prince and one (Daniel 8:9-14) implies kingship, seemingly.

2. All of these personalities are anti-God. In Daniel 7, the individual *"speaks great words against the most high"*; in Daniel 8:9, he *"magnifies himself to the prince of the host"*; in Daniel 8:23, he *"stands up against the prince of princes"*; in Daniel 11:36, he *"speaks marvelous things against the God of Gods."*

3. Most of these individuals are anti-Semitic; that is, anti-Jew. In Daniel 7:25, it is said that *"he made war against the saints."* In Daniel 8:11, we are told that *"the place of the sanctuary was cast down"; in* Daniel 8:23, *"he destroys the mighty and holy people"*; in Daniel 9:27, *"he causes the sacrifice and oblation to cease"*; in Daniel 11, there is no specific anti-Semitism.

4. Each of these individuals has unusual power given. In Daniel 7:25, we have the phrase *"they shall be given into his hand"*; in 8:12, "a *host was given him"*; in Daniel 8:24, *"his power shall be mighty though not by his own power. "* There is no statement in Daniel 9:27 of this kind but it is implied. In Daniel 11:36, *"he shall prosper til the indignation be*

accomplished," implying a limit to his power, making him subject to control.

5. All of these individuals are pictured as being willful and egotistical.

6. They are all pictured as being lawless. In Daniel 7:25, the individual *"thinks to change times and laws"*; in 8:12, he *"cast down truth to the ground"*; in 8:25, he *"causes deceit to prosper"*; in 9:27, he breaks his covenant with Israel; in 11:36, he *"does according to his will."*

With all these similarities in mind, there are sufficient notable differences. And we question furthermore, whether Daniel would repeat himself four or five times if all of these descriptions refer to one person. His style is so succinct and compact that before we accept this solution, we should consider all of the options.

They seem to be as follows:

1. Perhaps we are dealing with one great personality, the Antichrist, described four times but with somewhat different emphasis in each separate description. Of course the main argument for this viewpoint is the obvious similarities mentioned above but there is very serious objection to this view. A Roman origin is described to two of these individuals; namely, in Chapters 7 and 9 but the context in Chapter 8 implies a Greek origin for this personage. The ethnic background of the individual of Chapter 11 is doubtful but seemingly Greek. In the New Testament, it is fairly evident that the first beast out of the sea in Revelation 13, is Roman or at least gentile, while the second out of the earth seems to have a different origin, thought by some to indicate a Jewish background (he comes out of the land). Paul in II Thessalonians 2:3-9, does not give the man of sin a nationality but speaks of him as *"the son of perdition."* It seems likely then, that one person only is described in II Thessalonians.

2. If we postulate these descriptions as covering two persons, we have the advantage that at least two ethnic origins are involved, Roman and Grecian. But the New Testament features one person, the Antichrist (the first beast of Revelation 13), with no stated regal authority for the second beast though he exercises all the power of the first beast, whereas all four men of Daniel are rulers. To be sure, the second beast of Revelation 13 exercises unlimited economic power but is called a prophet not a king and furthermore, seems to depend upon the first beast for his authority.

3. If we interpret these descriptions as involving three persons, we do find that Daniel speaks specifically of the king of the north, the king of the south (in the Septuagint, Egypt) and the king, against whom these kings made war. Since these are all rulers and kings, one difficulty is removed but there is nothing in the four personality descriptions to link any of them to these two kings. Though the king of the north may come out of a Grecian background, the king of the south could hardly be thought

of as Roman. Conversely, these two kings are more or less lay figures without sufficient importance to need other elaboration. They are merely opponents of the king. The three kings plucked up by the roots by the little horn of Daniel 7 do not qualify for particular notice.

4. This leaves us with a final option. If the Roman Empire should be revised after its pattern in the time of Diocletian; namely, with two emperors and two Caesars, members of a tetrarchy, each of which would rule one prefecture as king, we have the possibility that the four descriptions (not including 8:9) refer to these four rulers; all however, as in Diocletian's day, under his imperium. That these kings would have similar characteristics and attitudes should be expected, being satanically inspired. They would be, of course, anti-God, anti-Christian, anti-Jewish, and anti-Judeo-Christian in morality. But if we accept this solution, what would we do with the ten horns, three of which were plucked up (that is, the seven plus the little horn) who have apparently been otherwise anonymous? Perhaps the solution may be found in Revelation 17:12-13 where we learn that these ten kings *"received power as kings one hour with the beast"* but have received no kingdom as yet. But we look in vain in Scripture for any word that they ever receive any kingdoms and we ask, What is a king without a kingdom? Who are these honorary kings? The only obvious answer is that these individuals are not political rulers of the Roman Empire but may be kings of finance, propaganda, scientific achievement, economic control, psychological manipulators, generals, engineers, inventors; in other words, super experts which the Antichrist will use to achieve political control, a sort of political bureau of experts with the false prophet as the brain and the will that bends all these diverse resources to the will and worship of Antichrist. Perhaps this is what is meant by Revelation 17 in referring to these kings, *"These have one mind and shall give their power and strength unto the beast."*

In each of the four visions, we have the continuing theme of either the Antichrist or one having many of his characteristics such as (we think) the False Prophet:

1. Antichrist's source, his uniqueness, his blasphemies, his persecutions, the length of his reign and his final downfall (Daniel 7:20-26, five verses in all).

2. The greatness of a similar person possibly the false prophet, the extent of his domain described as casting down some of the host of heaven, magnifying himself against the prince of the host, stopping the daily sacrifice, continuing and prospering, and the length of the desolation, 2,300 days (Daniel 8:9-14).

3. We have a king of fierce countenance (again, the False Prophet), understanding dark sentences, mighty in borrowed power, destroying wonderfully, prosperous through deceit, magnifying himself, destroying the mighty and holy people, destroying many by peace, standing up

against the Prince of princes, being broken without hand (Daniel 8:23-25).

4. A person who confirms the covenant with many for one week, in the midst of the week causes the sacrifice and oblation to cease because of the overspreading of abominations, he makes it desolate to the consummation of that which is determined shall be poured out on the desolator - again the Antichrist (Daneil 9:27).

5. And finally a character called the king, who does *"according to his will," "exalts himself above every god," "speaks marvelous things against the God of Gods,"* prospers until the end of the indignation, does not regard his father's God nor the desire of women nor any god, magnifies himself above all, honors the god of fortresses, he honors his god with the gold and silver and precious stones and the pleasant things, he does this in strongest fortresses with a foreign god which he shall acknowledge and increase with glory, shall cause them to rule over many, shall divide the land for a gain; the Antichrist in all of his characteristics (Daniel 11:36-40).

6. *"This same king shall enter into countries, shall overflow and pass through, shall enter the glorious land, many shall be overthrown but Edom, Moab and the chief of the children of Ammon shall escape out of his hand. He shall stretch forth his hand also upon the countries and Egypt shall not escape; he shall have powers over the things of silver and gold and the precious things of Egypt; Libyans and Ethiopians shall be in his train. He shall be troubled by news out of the east and north; he shall go forth with great fury to destroy and utterly sweep away many. He shall plant the tabernacles of his palace between the seas in the glorious holy mountain; yet he shall come to his end, and none shall help him;"* the final passage concerning Antichrist (Daniel 11:40-45).

In these less than twenty verses, Daniel gives us a picture, if we have properly identified him, of the Antichrist which (together with the four verses from Zechariah) is as complete and specific in the description of his traits and character and activites as any other Scripture, Old and New. Ten verses are devoted to the false prophet.

The few words that Christ gives us of the *"one who shall come in his own name"* John 5:43), the ten or so verses in II Thessalonians 2:1-10 and the descriptions of the beast in Revelation 13, 14, 17 (about twenty-five verses in all) would be far less significant without Daniel's detailed description.

The three verses in Zechariah (11:15-17) in which he contrasts the Good Shepherd with the idol shepherd, *"who shall not visit those cut off, neither seek the young, nor heal that that is broken, nor feed that which standeth still; but shall eat the flesh of the fat and tear their claws in pieces,"* seems to belong here. Zechariah goes on to say, *"Woe to the idol shepherd that leaveth the flock! The sword shall be upon his arm, and upon his right eye; his arm shall be completely dried up, and his right eye shall be utterly darkened."* How else shall we understand Revelation 13:3 as the deadly wound that was healed? Furthermore, his image (idol) is worshipped.

In no other Scripture except Daniel do we have so complete a picture of Satan fulfilling himself in a man whether under the *nom de plum* of the Assyrian, the idol shepherd, the king of fierce countenance, the Antichrist, the Beast.

One stumbling block to an understanding of the three or four references in Daniel that seem to be descriptive of Antichrist has been our determination to make him an Italian. This is the way we usually interpret Daniel 9:26, *"the people of the prince that shall come shall destroy the city."* We somehow do not realize that ultimately, to be a Roman citizen might cover any inhabitant from Britain to Babylon. We also have a tendency to forget that the Hebrew word, *"am" (ahm)* may be capable of a broader interpretation. Could it not refer to any of the peoples or nations within the whole Roman Empire, east or west?

Girdlestone says,

"If *"goi"* denotes a nation regarded from without, *"am or ahm,"* signifies a people as viewed by one of themselves . . . It is often brought into direct relationship or contrast with *goi*. . . A word which occupies a less definite position than either *"goi"* or *"am"* is *"lom"*, a race. *"Ummah,"* a *"tribe"* or *"family,"* literally those sprung of one mother, is rendered *"people"* in Numbers 25:15 and Psalm 117:1 and *"nations"* in Genesis 25:16, Ezra 4:10 and throughout the book of Daniel.

For whatever significance it may have, Daniel does not use either *"lom,"* a race, or *"ummah,"* a tribe. If, therefore, *"ahm"* could be inclusive of all those to whom Roman citizenship had been given and in contrast with all nations as *"goi"* outside the Roman Empire, some of the difficulties of our interpretation might be removed. The territory involved that might claim Roman citizenship would then cover Syria, Egypt, Greece, Turkey, Yugoslavia, Spain and France as well as Italy; all territory west of the Euphrates, south of the Danube and west of the Rhine plus all of northern Africa. Whether all the nations contained in this area considered themselves one people or not, three of the greatest Roman emperors were not of Italian blood; Theodosius, Constantine, Justinian. Two of them were Dalmatians (Yugoslav) and one was an Iberian, that is a Spaniard, yet they were accounted Roman emperors of the Roman people.

While the Hebrew use of the words *"ahm"* and *"goi"* is not sufficiently precise on which to rest any great conclusions unless supported by other data, it does not forbid the suggestion made above.

Are we, then, to include in the word *"ahm"*[4] those to whom Roman citizenship was granted? Or is it to be restricted to those of Italian blood?

It should be remembered that the citizens of Constantinople, largely Greek in blood and language, thought of themselves as Romans and their city as new Rome. Saul of Tarsus, a Hebrew of the Hebrews, could proudly say, *"Civis Romanum Sum."* Provided we give the wider meaning to the word *"ahm"* (people), the sections referring to those kings having characteristics of Antichrist but who appear to come out of Greek background become eligible for consideration for Antichrist (Daniel 8 and 11).

This still leaves us with the greater problem of redundancy. Why should four chapters, with great overlapping, be used to describe the same individual? However, provided that these descriptions can be shown to include both Antichrist and the False Prophet, we have more manageable data. It is still possible, though seemingly improbable, that these descriptions include others; e.g., the king of the north and the king of the south.

Conservative Bible scholars are somewhat in agreement as to the nationality of Antichrist. He must be a member of the Roman Empire and probably a gentile. As to the False Prophet, there is less agreement some holding him to be an Assyrian Jew some considering him a gentile, more considering him a Jew because of the covenant made with the Jewish people to be broken in the middle of the week (Daniel 9:26). It is reasoned that a Jew will be a necessary intermediary between Antichrist and the Jewish people; that a gentile could hardly possess religious influence enough to bring about such an unusual alliance. In taking this view, many seem to be guided by the way in which ancient Israel used to think and believe but do not take into account the way in which a majority of the people of Israel may think and believe at the present time. According to reports, orthodox Jews are not now in a majority in Israel. The old Messianic promise to Israel and to the house of David must seem to many not only impossible of fulfillment but perhaps not intended to be taken as a literal fulfillment. In fact, many would hold that it is no longer possible of fulfillment. Messianic and Davidic promises are to be spiritualized at best and at the worst, regarded as merely wishful thinking. To many a Jew, a God that has not prevented Auschwitz and all its predecessors for 1,900 years is not likely to do for Israel anything that she cannot do for herself. As to Messiah and His universal reign . . . can they really expect a literal fulfillment?

With this as a spiritual and psychological backgound, are a people who did not recognize Messiah in 27 A.D. likely to discern the false one coming in his own name; a counterfeit in these latter days? Parenthetically, it is also questionable whether some of the Christian church of today would recognize their Messiah if He came again as He came 1,900 years ago.

To return to our major theme, Does Antichrist have to be a Jew to be accepted as a Messiah by the Jews? The first beast out of the sea (Revelation 13), if the symbolism means anything, is not a Jew. The second beast, out of the land, is probably a Jew. The question is, Could the False Prophet, if a Jew, sell the gentile first beast to Israel as a Jewish Messiah?

In proclaiming the first beast as the promised Messiah, could not the False Prophet say the following?

1. The hope of a Messiah from the house of David is vain. There is no visible house of David and no man could prove Davidic descent.

2. Two thousand years have passed and no Messiah. The Davidic promises are a part of a biblical system to be abandoned as useless and untrustworthy.

3. In terms of the miracles done by the False Prophet and the spectacular conquests of Antichrist, what could a Davidic Messiah do and be, that the Antichrist and his prophet have not already done? Miracles, fire from heaven, a speaking image of the Antichrist, his resurrection from a fatal wound; what more could you ask? Both the carrot and the stick will be used. The carrot, the miracles; the stick, economic controls; most of all, the Antichrist's backing at a time and in a world where Israel has few reliable friends.

4. See what this man-God is going to do for you. Could any Jew do more for you?

It is said that Herzl once offered Abdul Hamid, sultan of a now defunct Turkish Empire, Messiahship of the Jewish people in return for their occupancy of the land of Palestine. After all, the statement that "*no Jew could be made to believe that any other Jew is God*" is probably apropos here. That a majority of Jews will make a "*covenant with death,*" we find in Isaiah 28:15, but we should also remember, on the contrary, that in every age there has been a faithful remnant who are the true children of faithful Abraham.

Another view as to the identity of Antichrist, making him a Jew, is given us by A.C. Gaebelein. He says in part,

"The personal Antichrist and the northern invader, that other Antiochus Epiphanes, are therefore not the same being. The personal Antichrist, the man of sin, will be a Jew. He takes his seat in the temple when the first beast breaks his covenant with the Jews; he works lying miracles. He is the false Messiah claiming to be king over the Jewish people, a very incarnation of Satan. He demands divine worship. But the one described in Daniel 8 is an external foe. And who will he be? From where will he come? . . . The prophecy in the chapter before us makes it plain that this desolator will arise from one of the divisions of the Grecian Empire. That territory is now held by Turkey. When the time of the end comes, the greatest upheavals will take place both in Asia Minor and in the surrounding countries. . . . But it seems clear that the king with a fierce countenance will act under the instructions of a superior, for we read, '*his power shall be mighty but not by his own power*' . . . The third person is the king of the north. He is the little horn of Chapter 8 and is typified by Antiochus Epiphanes. According to Daniel 11, he emanates from the north and enters into the glorious land where he shall find a miserable end. He is the Assyrian of Isaiah and Micah, the one from the north in Joel's prophecy. He is the great external foe of the restored Jewish people."[6]

In spite of the prestige of Dr. Gaebelein, many do not find this an acceptable solution.

What is the source of Antichrist's power? Daniel himself does not give us the source nor indeed the mystery of his personality. We need to turn to Paul for a hint when in II Thessalonians 2:3-9, he calls him the Son of Perdition; not "a" son but "the" son which deepens the mystery. We get another hint from Christ's own words in two references that He makes to Judas in John 6:70. Christ calls him the Son of perdition. Later, he speaks of Judas in more scathing terms, when he says, *"Have I not chosen you twelve and one of you is Diabolos (devil)."* If we look at these verses alone, we could say that the Son of Perdition of II Thessalonians and Christ's words concerning Judas could make Judas a candidate for Antichrist, for the beast that ascends out of the bottomless pit (Revelation 11:7 and 17:8) or more appropriately, the person of the second beast, the False Prophet. But in Revelation 17:8-11, we are given to understand that the first beast is a reincarnation of a Roman emperor, according to some interpretations, for we read, *"There are seven kings: five are fallen, and one is, and the other is not yet come; and when he cometh he must continue a short space. And the beast that was and is not, he is the eighth, and is of the seven, and goeth into perdition."*

Domitian was the emperor ruling during John's stay on Patmos and is counted the sixth and any one of the subsequent emperors, especially one of the great persecutors, could be the seventh.

Fathers of the early church felt that Nero was the beast because of the terrible persecutions that he initiated as well as because of his depraved character but even more terrible atrocities were committed under Diocletian, whose self-deification exceeded the usual worship demanded by Roman emperors. It is possible to make a case for the first beast to be a former Roman emperor reincarnate and to make of Judas, reincarnate, the False Prophet. Whether these are the meanings intended in Scripture or whether we are reading into Scripture something that is not there, it is difficult to say. But there is nothing inherently repugnant to our thinking should we admit the first beast as the reincarnate Roman emperor and to interpret the second beast as Judas brought again into the scene of a second betrayal.

In interpreting Daniel 7:8-11 and 24-26, the most obvious way of looking at the matter would be to suppose a Roman Empire (revived) consisting of ten subdivisions each under the jurisdiction of a king or a dictator; each dictator or king functioning as ruler in charge before the coming of the little horn; the little horn finally subduing three of the ten and finally bending all the others to his will. But to think of a situation this way seems to be in direct conflict with Revelation 17, where there are two phrases that are difficult to reconcile with ten kings ruling in their own right or indeed ruling at all before the coming authority of the Antichrist. The first phrase, *"ten kings which have received no kingdom as yet,"* seems to deny a previous regal authority; i.e., before the appearance of the beast. Furthermore, their power is received and they are given power one hour with the *"beast,"* not seven years or even three and a half years. Putting it simply, they are not the original and only source of the beast's power though they have *"one mind and shall give their power and strength to the beast."*

The temporal sequence (Revelation 17) is:

(1) The beast, who is the eighth king (Revelation 17:11);

(2) the ten horns which are ten kings who have received no kingdoms as yet (verse 12);

(3) but received power as kings (without a kingdom) one hour with the beast (verse 12);

(4) having one mind, they give their power and strength to the beast (verse 13);

(5) the ten horns; i.e., kings, hate the whore and destroy her after having been used of her and also using her for their own ends (verse 16);

(6) God has put it in their hearts . . . and give their kingdom unto the beast (verse 17). Nothing is said of the ten kings or what happens to them after the beast is destroyed. There is no statement that the ten kings ever receive their kingdoms, though that may possibly be implied.

Of course, we must always be cautious in describing a temporal succession to situations where items are described one after another. Things happening simultaneously must necessarily be described in some sort of order but here we seem to have a true temporal sequence, no less obviously so in Daniel 7:24. However, confusion occurs when we think of these ten kings as political rulers. What sort of power and strength can kings with *"no kingdoms as yet"* give to the beast? Certainly, they do not seem to be in a position to give political power for they have none. The answer must be in the more likely realm of influence and in powers non-political; their influence and their achievements in fields contributing to political power, such as wealth, scientific knowledge, control of news media and communication, psychological knowledge and propaganda *"know how."* An Antichrist, who could have the complete loyalty and support of kings of finance, propaganda, science, wealth and even religion, would be in a position to exert complete control over men. He might then reward these individuals with brief, political status or honorary kingships.

But when we speak of kings, are we not talking about political power? Usually this is true, although we do speak of kings of finance, etc. But kingdoms are also kingdoms and these kings have none. What kind of a king is it that has no kingdom?

In offering this suggestion tentatively, as a way out of the dilemma we realize that there are other possibilities and as we refer back to Daniel 7, there is difficulty in solving the problem this way. In Daniel 7, we seem to be dealing with ten political rulers and we naturally interpret the phrase *"out of this kingdom"* as meaning made up of segments of this kingdom.

There is another solution to the problem given by Bleek as quoted by Keil, page 255,

"We are induced, as Bleek justly observes by verse 8, where it is said of the little horn that it would rise up between the ten horns, to think of the contemporary kings, or rather kingdoms existing along with each other, which rise out of the fourth kingdom."

Since Daniel 7:24 is an interpretation of Daniel 7:8, we would then be dealing with kingdoms not persons, with no need of harmonizing Daniel 7:24 with Revelation 17:12; the number 10 in each case being purely coincidental or the ten kings of Revelation 17 arising from the ten kingdoms of Daniel 7 but not ruling over them.

As we summarize Daniel 8:26-27, we have in more detail Antichrist's program with reference to Israel. It is an amplification of Daniel 8:25.

1. The Antichrist shall confirm the covenant with many for one week. Whether the Jewish nation does this out of desperation, lacking other powerful friends, or is seduced by his blandishments is unsure. Scripture does not say.

2. In the midst of the week, he shall cause the sacrifice and oblation to cease. The implication here is that the temple has been rebuilt, sacrifices resumed and Antichrist claiming deity, shall begin his persecution of the Jews (II Thessalonians 2:3-4).

3. He makes the place of sacrifice desolate spiritually and while we do not have the statement in Daniel in the same language as we do in II Thessalonians 2:4 *("so he as God sitteth in the temple of God showing himself that he is God")*, this could hardly be any other than the abomination of desolation (compared to which, Antiochus' pollution of the temple was insignificant).

4. *"And that determined shall be poured out upon the desolator"* (Daniel 8:27). This is another way of saying that he shall be broken without hand.

When we come to Chapter 11 (verses 36-45), we have further amplification of Antichrist's exalted ego,

a. *"The king shall do according to his will"* (36).

b. *"Shall exalt and magnify himself above every God"* (36).

c. *"Shall speak marvelous things aginst the God of Gods"* (36).

d. *"Shall prosper until the indignation be accomplished"* (36).

e. *"He shall not regard the God of his fathers nor the desire of women nor any god"* (37).

f. *"For he shall magnify himself above all"* (37).

g. *"For he shall honor the God of forces"* (38).

Whether this is a war god or the forces of nature with himself as representative man at the peak of the evolutionary series or whether he has become master of some super hydrogen bomb or death ray, we can only guess.

After this description of Antichrist as a person, we have a description of his final activities as follows:

At the time of the end shall the king of the south push at him; and the king of the north shall come against him like a whirlwind, with chariots, with horsemen and with many ships; and he shall enter into the countries and shall overflow and pass through. (40) He shall enter also into the glorious land, and many countries shall be overthrown, but these shall escape out of his hands, even Edom and Moab and the chief of the children of Ammon. (41) And he shall stretch forth his hand also on the countries, and the land of Egypt shall not escape. (42) But he shall have powers over the treasures of gold and silver, and over all the precious things of Egypt and the Libyans and the Ethiopians shall be at his steps. (43) But tidings out of the east and out of the north shall trouble him and he shall go forth with great fury to destroy and utterly to sweep away many.' (44) And he shall plant the tabernacle of his palace between the seas in the glorious holy mountain, yet he shall come to his end and none shall help him. (45)

That not only Scripture but secular sources are proclaiming the advent of a world dictator is brought home to us in an article in Christianity Today, quoting the Columbia Forum,

"Two hundred years ago Alexander Tytler discussed democracy in a book devoted to the Athenian republic. He said because of the eventual greed of citizens, no democracy could survive:

"'A democracy cannot exist as a permanent form of government. It can only exist until the voters discover that they can vote themselves largesse from the public treasury. From that moment on the majority always votes for the candidates promising the most benefits from the public treasury, with the result that a democracy always collapses over a loose fiscal policy, always followed by a dictatorship.'

"Reinhold Niebuhr, a socialist and a founder of Americans for Democratic Actions and certainly no apologist for capitalism, had a word to say about the threat of communism over against democracy,

""That evil (Communism) is a pretentious scheme of world salvation, a secularized religious apocalypse, which foolishly divides the world between good and evil classes and nations, predicts the final triumph of the hosts of justice against those of injustice, and destines one class, the "proletariat," to become the masters of the whole historic process, by taking the "leap from the realm of necessity to the realm of freedom." If this absurb religious apocalypse should ever be implemented on a large scale, and should master the destinies of all the nations, mankind would face not only totalitarian government, but a dangerous effort to press all the vitalities and forces, the hopes and aspirations of many nations, the cultural and ethical aspirations of sensitive individuals into the restrictive and confining pattern of its scheme of world salvation. The Communist danger is, in short, much more grievous and perilous than we assume it to be if we define it merely as despotism ... Communist dictatorship ... is but the product and instrument of a religio-political dogmatic system with a fantastic ambition to master all the variegated processes of history and press all its themes into one mold, and which promises redemption from all social evil.'"[8]

What Alexander Tytler said is, in my opinion, being carried out before our own eyes in our own country and Niebuhr's statement about communism again shows us the forces working to finally bring about the rider on the white horse, the superman, the Antichrist.

In many ways, the Russia of today offers us a blueprint of the principles and methods by which any dictator could gain and maintain control,

1. He could, as did the Bolsheviks, create and spread confusion by subversion and propaganda, taking advantage of all existing antagonisms and spreading distrust even among members of the same family.

2. He could organize the anarchy that would follow by force, treachery, propaganda and by pitting one group against another, using prison and jail deliveries of desperate men as his original means of coercion.

3. By control of food and economic sources and means of production, he could consolidate and perpetuate his control (the mark of the beast-- 666).

4. By terror and by savage repression of any real or fancied opposition and by seeking out and eliminating potential leaders, he could still further consolidate his gains.

5. All police states must have spy systems and Gestapo-like police forces, such forces to have preferred treatment. This has been not only peculiar to Russia and Nazi Germany but would be necessary for Antichrist.

6. A rigid passport system would be used to control travel. There would be no escape and, if his rule was worldwide, no place to go to safety.

7. All civilians would be deprived of firearms or other means of resistance.

8. There would be complete control of all news media, control of all educational institutions.

9. Since a police state is not equipped to offer as a common motive the power of love, propaganda will be used to create a common fear and hate toward whatever objects seem to be in opposition. Therefore the church, God or any other object on which people can lay their own fancied wrongs will be used as scapegoats.

10. He will destroy all religious faith and replace it by a cult of the state or a personality cult and some form of secular religious system, a la Hitler.

11. By every means possible, there will be discredit of institutions, organizations, potential political leaders, with special attention to demoralizing family loyalties and ties; taking control of children's lives by mobilizing their mothers for work forces and placing their children in brain washing nurseries.

What Russia has found successful, the Antichrist will undoubtedly employ, since these are the principles that Satan has found useful in dealing with the human race throughout the ages. The offer of bread and circus as per the Roman Empire will be supplemented by these modern devices.

The biblical description of the Antichrist's methods, while brief are as follows,

1. Destruction of faith in God (Daniel 7:25).

2. Destruction of the believing remnant (Daniel 7:25).

3. Change all standards, times and laws (Daniel 7:25).

4. The use of the big lie; that is, propaganda (Daniel 8:25).

5. Establishment of a personality cult (Daniel 11:36).

6. Phony or real, demonically produced miracles (Revelation 13:14-15).

7. Economic control (Revelation 13:17).

8. A living passport system (Revelation 13:16).

We can see how the Antichrist and his collaborators could take over the revived Roman Empire and indeed the world by the control of the press, the food supply, communication, education, travel and all means of livelihood.

William Shirer has given us a brief, but very clear, picture of the way in which the religious forces of Germany were seduced, cajoled, betrayed and by force rendered powerless to function as a moral and spiritual force in a country at least nominally Christian. He gives us a sample of the thirty articles drawn up by Rosenberg, an outspoken pagan, for the moral and spiritual guidance of the country. When we remember that out of the total population of 68,000,000, there were 45,000,000 members of various Lutheran denominations alone, to say nothing of a strong Catholic minority, we realize that the absolute control which the Nazi party finally exerted over all the religious life in Germany was really exerted over a majority of the whole population, occasionally with consent, more often without.

Some of the thirty articles as given by Shirer are as follows,

1. The national Reich of Germany categorically claims the exclusive right and the exclusive power to control all churches within the borders of the Reich; it declares these to be national churches of the German Reich. . . . .(numbers 2-4 omitted here)

5. The National Church is determined to exterminate irrevocably . . . the strange and foreign Christian faiths imported into Germany in the ill-omened year 800. . . .

7. The National Church has no scribes, pastors, chaplains or priests but National Reich orators are to speak in them. . . .

13. The National Church demands the immediate cessation of the publishing and dissemination of the Bible in Germany . . . .

14. The National Church declares that to it, and therefore to the German nation, it has been decided that the Fuehrer's Mein Kampf is the greatest of all documents. It . . . not only contains the greatest but it embodies the purest and truest ethics for the present and future life of our nation. . . .

18. The National Church will clear away from its altars all crucifixes, Bibles and pictures of saints.

19. On the altars there must be nothing but Mein Kampf (to the German nation and therefore to God the most sacred book) and to the left of the altar a sword. . . .

30. On the day of its foundation, the Christian Cross must be removed from all churches, cathedrals and chapels . . . and it must be superseded by the only unconquerable symbol, the swastika."[9]

That wealth and propaganda and political organizations wield great power will come as news to no one but the extent to which psychological controls are now being exerted over men's minds is not often realized by the lay public. Our interest in quoting the following is to show how these psychological principles in the hands of an evil agency could powerfully affect not only individual lives and decisions but mass reactions in a social world. Dr. Carl Rogers, an eminent psychologist, has given us a list of capabilities open to the modern psychologist, many of which are usefully employed but which also are capable of perversion. The list is as follows:

1. We know how to set up conditions under which many members of a group will report judgments which are contrary to the evidence of their senses (i.e., induced hallucinations).

2. We know a great deal about how to establish conditions which will influence consumer responses and/or public opinion (suggestion).

3. We know how to influence the buying behavior of individuals by setting up conditions which will provide satisfactions for needs of which they are unconscious but which we have been able to determine (suggestion).

4. We know how to predict which members of an organization will be troublesome and delinquent (personality profiles and analysis).

5. We know how to provide conditions in a work group, whether in industry or in education, which will be followed by increase of productivity, originality and morale (mass control).

6. We know how to provide conditions of leadership which will be followed by personality growth in the members of the group as well as by increase of productivity and improved group spirit.

7. We know how to provide psychological conditions in the classroom which will result not only in the learning of academic content but in improved personal adjustment as well.

8. We know how to provide interpersonal relationships with qualities such that it enables the individual to meet stress with more security and less anxiety.

9. We know the attitudes which, if provided by a counsel or therapist, will be predictably followed by certain constructive personality and behavior changes in the client.

10. We now know how, I believe, to disintegrate a man's personality structure, dissolving his self confidence, destroying the concept he has of himself, and making him completely dependent on another.

11. We know how to provide psychological conditions which will produce vivid halucinations and other abnormal reactions in a thoroughly normal individual in the waking state.

12. We know how to influence psychological moods, attitudes, and behaviors through drugs.

13. We know the psychological conditions of family life which, if established in a home, will tend to produce emotionally secure children with many socially valuable characteristics the contrary characteristics can also be produced."[10]

As will be noted in this list, numbers 10, 11, and 12 of these capabilities on the part of the psychologist can be constructive but could also be manipulated by conscienceless individuals for sinister purposes. The point which we are trying to make is that psychological science, along with other fields of knowledge, could be another weapon for the control of the many by the few. The Antichrist, either himself or through those controlled by him, would undoubtedly use such a weapon in his mastery of universal control. One of the ten kings of Revelation 17 would certainly be a master psychologist.[11]

CHAPTER XIV

END OF THE TIMES OF THE GENTILES
THE TRIBULATION
THE JEWISH RESURRECTION

(Daniel 12)

Daniel 12 is the conclusion of the vision begun in Chapter 10 and it begins with the statement *"at that time"* which links it chronologically to the previous two chapters. It is the time of the end, the seventieth week.

"And at that time shall Michael stand up, the great prince which standeth for the children of thy people" (1).

Here again, as in Chapter 10, we have Michael identified as the great spiritual protagonist of Israel. His help is needed for a beleaguered Israel, for at that time, *"there shall be a time of trouble, such as never was since there was a nation even to that same time."*

This is the time of Jacob's trouble. But we ask ourselves, How, with all that Jacob has already gone through, could there be any greater trouble? How could anything exceed the extermination camps of Auschwitz? Still, this is the greater tribulation that shall come upon all the earth and equally upon Israel. This is the time pictured in Revelation Chapters 11 to 18 and Isaiah Chapters 24 to 27.

It is customary with many premillennial writers to consider the seventieth week of Daniel as divided into two parts of three and a half years each; the first half of the week (3 1/2 years) to be a time of tribulation and the last half, an overwhelming intensification of judgment to be thought of as the great tribulation. Biblically, of course, the week is divided by the broken covenant between Antichrist and Israel (Daniel 9:27) and by the death of the two witnesses (Revelation 11:3).

The events of the first three and a half years are somewhat as follows, and perhaps we should say, the status quo at the beginning of the week:

1. There will be four great empires or governmental hegemonies in the purview of prophecy if our interpretation of Daniel 7 is correct; England or the English speaking peoples, Russian and her allies, a four-headed Arabic coalition and a revived Roman Empire.

2. The absence of the true church, the body of Christ, raptured before the beginning of the tribulation (Romans 5:9, I Thessalonians 1:10, 5:9, Revelation 3:10).

3. The Holy Spirit has been taken out of the way; that is, no longer prevents a completely diabolical government but still operative in the world for the salvation of millions (II Thessalonians 2:7, Revelation 7:4-17).

4. The appearance of Antichrist and the false prophet and his covenant with the majority of the Jewish people (Daniel 9:27, Revelation 6, 13, etc.).

5. The building of the third temple in Jerusalem later to be defiled by Antichrist (II Thessalonians 2:4).

6. The possible rebuilding of a great commercial city on the old site of Babylon (Isaiah 13:20-21, Jeremiah 50:40). Also see Larkin, "The Book of Revelation," pp. 156-158.

7. The preaching of the gospel of the kingdom and salvation by the blood of the Lamb possibly inspired by the two witnesses (Revelation 11:9-17).

8. The appearance of ten kings who are somehow identified with the revived Roman Empire, three of whom are displaced by the little horn who will control the other seven (Daniel 7:24).

9. The apostasy of the visible church (II Thessalonians 2:3, Luke 18:8).

10. The sealing of the 144,000 Jews, sealed to escape destruction during the tribulation (Revelation 7 and possibly 14).

11. Ten kings who give their power and strength to the beast but who have received no kingdom as yet (Revelation 17).

12. Finally, the preaching of the two witnesses to end with their death in the middle of the week and their resurrection at the end of three days (Revelation 11:3-12).

The last three and a half years of the week will include all of those events described from Revelation 11 to 19 from the sounding of the seventh trumpet to Revelation 20. The period begins with the breaking of Antichrist's covenant with the Jews and with the flight of Israel; that is, *"the woman,"* into the wilderness for a time, times and a half time, and somewhere in this period, the following:

1. The fall of ecclesiastical Babylon (Revelation 17:1-6).

2. The fall of political Babylon (Revelation 18:2-8).

3. The great earthquake predicted in Isaiah 2:19-21, Zechariah 14:4-5, Ezekiel 38:20, Revelation 16:18).

4. The great hail coming upon a wicked world when there are no buildings and no shelters for protection, these having been leveled by the great earthquake (Revelation 16:21).

5. The plagues mentioned in Revelation 11 to 18.

6. The drying up of the Euphrates River and the descent of the kings of the east with their hordes (Revelation 16:12).

7. The great battle of Armageddon possibly preceded by a series of battles involving all four of the nations mentioned in Daniel 7 (Ezekiel

38:39, Zechariah 14:2, Revelation 19:17-21, Daniel 11:40-45).

8. The Jewish resurrection which could be neither the rapture of the church coming before the Revelation nor the white throne judgment, the latter being at the end of the reign of Messiah (Daniel 12:2).

9. The powers of heaven shaken Mt 24:29, Luke 21:26.

10. The sign of the Son of Man in the heavens and His coming in glory (Matthew 24:30).

11. The destruction of the great armies at Armageddon by Christ himself and the judgment of the nations (Zechariah 14:3, Revelation 19, Matthew 25:31-46).

12. The conversion of multitudes of every nation and their probable martyrdom (Revelation 7:9-17).

Verse 1 tells us that *"at that time shall Michael stand up, the great prince who standeth for the children of thy people."* In II Thessalonians 4:16 and in Jude 9, he is called an archangel. Here he is called the great prince and in Daniel 9:13, we have the term *"one of the chief princes,"* implying others of equal rank. His name and presence would indicate that events of great moment were about to take place even if we did not have them specifically mentioned in the following verses. Daniel continues: *"And there shall be a time of trouble such as never was since there was a nation even to that same time."* Even though we know from other Scriptures that this is a worldwide event, our context here is Israel and Israel's trouble with Michael as Israel's protector.

We who have seen Hitler's attempt to exterminate all Jews in what was the most notorious and perhaps the greatest single diabolical effort in history, are reminded that this is only one of many previous attempts and as we see, it will not be the last. Even so, we wonder how anything more terrible could happen to Israel. From the Maccabean persecutions, the million or more killed in the capture of Jerusalem, the five or six million done to death in Auschwitz and other horror camps, we wonder how there could be survivors of the nation at all. Harried and robbed and tortured during the Middle Ages, the victim of pogroms in tsarist Russia within recent memory and still persecuted in communist Russia, how could a people endure more and survive? Indeed, only a remnant does survive, for *"at that time thy people shall be delivered, everyone that shall be found written in the book."* That this is a minority, is indicated in Zechariah 13:8, where we read, *"In all the land . . . two parts shall be cut off and die, but the third shall be left therein."* Ezekiel 20:38 testifies to the same thing. This would seem to be the final judgment on national apostasy and is horrible to contemplate but not more horrible than that which will happen to the gentile world. In fact, if we read Ezekiel 38 and 39 aright, of the great gentile armies invading Israel, only one-sixth will return.

Daniel 12:2, *And many of those who sleep in the dust of the earth shall awake, some to everlasting life, and some to shame and everlasting contempt.*

After objecting rightly, to Gaebelein's statement that the physical resurrection is not taught in this passage, Culver says,

"Now, granting with the almost unanimous support of all believing interpreters that physical resurrection is here predicted, to what resurrection does it refer? Biederwolf . . . has classified the views as follows:

1. 'To the general resurrection at the end of all things.

2. To a limited resurrection immediately after the tribulation, and prior to the last and general resurrection, and one confined to Israel.

3. To a resurrection of the righteous just before Christ's second coming, and of the wicked at the end of time, no notice being taken by the angel of the hiatus between them.

4. To a resurrection of all that sleep in the dust after the time of great tribulation; the good, at that very time (immediately after), and the wicked later, at the end of all time, with no notice taken by the angel of the hiatus or intervening time.'"

Culver chooses the second option largely on the basis of the Hebrew language used. As we view this passage with which we heartily agree, there could be added to Dr. Culver's cogent arguments: (1) the argument of type and antitype, (2) the passages referring to the millennial reign of David over Israel and the inappropriateness of equating the prince of Ezekiel 40-48 with Messiah (this objection is brought forward by Feinberg).

In discussing this resurrection verse (verse 2), we have several interrelated problems with which to deal. We need answers to the following questions:

1. Is the resurrection which is spoken of before the setting up of the Messianic kingdom, during the kingdom age, or at its end?

a. If before, is it a part of the rapture of the church?

b. Or is it a separate resurrection of the Old Testament saints, limited to them, after the analogy of Matthew 27:52? In other words, is it a strictly Jewish resurrection (Zechariah 14:5)?

2. If this resurrection is during the Messianic age, is it limited to Jews? Or is there ambiguity here?

3. If at the end of the thousand years, is it a part of the general judgment scene where Jew and gentile alike are to be judged before the great white throne?

4. If we assume a special Jewish resurrection, does it include both righteous and unrighteous Jews at the same time?

Before answering these and related questions, we should recall that

Scripture pictures:

First, Christ as king over all the earth upon the throne of David as prophet, priest and king (Isaiah 25:23, Daniel 7:14, etc.).

Second, in Ezekiel Chapters 40 to 48, together with a rebuilt temple and an officiating priesthood, we have a Prince (*Nahsee*) with headquarters in Jerusalem with no mention of a throne for the Prince, no priestly functions attributed to him and no statement that his jurisdiction extends beyond the boundaries of Israel.

Third, in Matthew 19:28, Christ tells his apostles that in the regeneration, they will sit upon twelve thrones judging the twelve tribes. Does this word *"regeneration"* have reference to the kingdom age as per Scofield notes and others? If so, is their resurrection due only to their position in the church? Or is it also due to their Jewish heritage. (This function at least is tribal.)

Fourth, thus involved in the total problem is the identity of the Prince for if there should be a special resurrection of Jewish saints, there is reason to interpret those verses which speak of a resurrected David as individual and not generic as David himself, not Messiah his son (descendant). The prince of Ezekiel then, would not be Messiah but David himself. Conversely, if these verses refer to a resurrected David, it is reasonable to suppose a special Jewish resurrection.

There are six very interesting verses that would seem to have a bearing on, and relation to a Jewish resurrection. They have reference to David. The first two are in a setting of judgment and are as follows (Ezekiel 34:22-24),

Therefore will I save my flock, and they shall no more be a prey; and I will judge between cattle and cattle. And I will set up one shepherd over them, and he shall feed them, even my servant, David; he shall feed them, and he shall be their shepherd. And I, the Lord, will be their God, and my servant, David, a prince among them; I the Lord have spoken it.

When we ask how this is to be accomplished since David has been dead these many centuries, we turn to Jeremiah 30:9,

But they shall serve the Lord their God, and David, their king, whom I will raise up unto them.

The context, again is found in verse 7 of the same chapter:

It is even the time of Jacob's trouble.

The length of David's reign, who has been raised up for Israel as a prince, is found again in Ezekiel 37:24-25,

And David, my servant, shall be a king over them, and they all shall have one shepherd; they shall also walk in mine ordinances, and observe my statutes, and do them. And they shall dwell in the land that I have

given unto Jacob, my servant, in which your fathers have dwelt; and they shall dwell in it, even they, and their children, and their children's children forever; and my servant David shall be their prince forever.

This is perpetual rule and if the text means anything, it refers to a future time when Israel will be reconciled to Jehovah permanently. There is one more reference that should be considered, Hosea 3:5. After pointing out the long hiatus in Israel's relationship with Jehovah where she shall be without a prince, etc., Hosea says,

Afterward shall the children of Israel return, and seek the Lord, their God, and David, their king, and shall fear the Lord and his goodness in the latter days.

The sum total of these verses is, in my opinion, very impressive and if they do not indicate the personal resurrection of David, not one of his descendants and not Messiah especially, then the whole group of references must be spiritualized with accompanying confusion.

It would seem that this problem of a special resurrection for the Jews then, is bound up with the identity of the Prince in Ezekiel 34:23-24, 37:24-25, etc. and in Jeremiah 30:9, Hosea 3:5 and possibly Amos 9:11. For if there is a special resurrection of Israel at the initiation of Messiah's reign, then the term *"David the prince"* can properly refer to a resurrected David. If not, we are at sea relative to his identity and must interpret the term David as being generic, referring to some presently unknown descendant of David (Feinberg).

We may approach the problem in any of three ways. The first has to do with typology.

In Leviticus 23:10-11, we have the feast of the firstfruits, the wave sheaf:

Speak unto the children of Israel, and say unto them, When ye come into the land which I give unto you, and shall reap the harvest thereof, then ye shall bring a sheaf of the firstfruits of your harvest unto the priest; And he shall wave the sheaf before the Lord to be accepted for you.

Paul makes the application of this prophetic symbol and type in I Corinthians 15:23: *"Christ the firstfruits; afterward they that are Christ's at his coming."* If we interpret *"those that are Christ's"* as restricted to the church, we have problems with Matthew 27:52, where we read, *"And the graves were open and many bodies of the saints which slept arose and came out of the graves after his resurrection and went into the holy city and appeared to many."* These, of course, were Israelitish saints, the wave sheaf. We might reasonably expect if the sheaf be Israel, the harvest will also logically be Israel. Also, Jeremiah 2:3 speaks of Israel as firstfruits: *"Israel was holiness unto the Lord and the firstfruits of his increase."*

But perhaps Daniel 12:2 refers to the Rapture and includes righteous

Jews. Since there seems to be nothing in Scripture that definitely links the Old Testament saints with the Rapture of the church, it follows that the resurrection spoken of in Daniel 12:2 must either be the final Great White Throne judgment at the end of Messiah's reign or a special Jewish resurrection. Since it is very difficult (actually impossible) to connect the Old Testament saints with the final judgment, our alternative would seem to be their resurrection at the beginning of Messiah's reign. We must concede that, had we no other indications in Scripture, this argument would hardly be conclusive. There are, however, Scriptural hints given us, the cumulative effect of which is much more conclusive. For example, what does Isaiah mean when he says, *"Then the moon shall be confounded and the sun ashamed when the Lord of hosts shall reign in Mount Zion and in Jerusalem and before his ancients gloriously"* (Isaiah 24:23)? Is this a heavenly scene? It would not seem so, since the context is not that of a new heaven and a new earth but of Mount Zion and Jerusalem. If this is so, who are the ancients? Neither angels nor the gentile church nor the surviving remnant of Israel fit this terminology. Who, then, if not the resurrected Old Testament saints? The answer is seemingly found in Zechariah 14:5: *"The Lord thy God will come and all the saints with thee."*

There is a second approach to the problem that involves the identity of the prince in Ezekiel 34:23-24 and 37:24-25. That the prince is not Messiah is clear from:

(a) the absence of any priestly functions, in that sin and peace offerings are offered for him, instead of by him;

(b) that his sons are to be given land from his own oblation and

(c) that there is no mention of a throne for him.

If he were Messiah, would he not be pictured as sitting on the throne of his father David and would that throne not have been mentioned? Furthermore, should he not have been called king *(melek)*, not prince *(nahsee)*? There are verses that speak of *"David their king"* (Jeremiah 30:9, Ezekiel 37:24) and other verses that speak of *"David their prince"* (Ezekiel 34:24, 37:25). Those calling him king could possibly refer to his past status in retrospect; those calling him prince, to his future status. Ezekiel uses the term *"prince"* in Chapters 40 to 48. But we are told that the Lord will be king over all the earth (Zechariah 14:9) and upon the throne of David (Isaiah 9:7). It seems therefore that we get the following picture:

First, Messiah the son of God and the son of David reigning upon the throne of his father David over all the earth (Zechariah 14:9);

Second, David the resurrected prince reigning in Palestine over Israel under Messiah;

Third, the twelve apostles sitting upon twelve thrones and judging the twelve tribes according to the promise (Isaiah 1:26, Matthew 19:28).

Thus, in Messiah's reign, we have combined simultaneously, all the governmental economies through which Israel passed: (a) the theocracy - this time a visible one (Messiah, Christ); (b) judges - the twelve apostles; (c) the kingdom of Israel with David their prince.

The third approach is a negative one. If we reject the suggestions just made, what answers do we give to the following questions?

1. If Israel does not have a special resurrection, are we to suppose that God's earthly people of the Old Testament dispensation are to be absent from the fulfillment of all of Israel's hopes and promises and that only a living remnant, together with the gentile survivors as survivors of the tribulation, are to partake of the glory for which the Old Testament saints and prophets faithfully endured but never experienced?

2. If there is not a special resurrection of Old Testament saints, do we connect their resurrection with either the rapture of the church or with the last judgment? If not, what are the alternatives?

3. If references to *"my servant David," "David a shepherd over them,"* etc., are to someone other than the real David, whom do we suggest? Not Messiah, as we have shown. If we do not concede a special Jewish resurrection, Dr. Feinberg has made the only sensible suggestion: a scion of the house of David. But, here again, it is difficult to conceive of any Jew living or yet to be born who could achieve such eminence and a worthiness sufficient for such an exalted position. There is no hint that it would be one of the survivors of the tribulation or either of the two witnesses of Revelation and certainly it would be inappropriate for any gentile Christian to inherit the throne of David since, in every reference quoted, the setting is Jewish.

As we have said above, it would seem that the identity of the prince and a special resurrection of the Old Testament saints are interrelated. Dr. Feinberg's suggestion would seem to be the one alternative left us if there is no speical premillennial resurrection. For this reason, therefore, the solution presented above rests upon such a presupposition.

Walvoord says,

"What is presented here is that those who have died will be raised from the dead to join those living in this period of restoration. Israelites surviving the tribulation, and who are the objects of the divine deliverance prophesied in Romans 11:26, will be joined by the Old Testament saints who are raised from the dead. This will occur after the Great Tribulation at the second coming of Christ. Actually, there is no passage in Scripture which teaches that the Old Testament saints will be raised at the time the church is raptured, that is, before the final tribulation. It is preferable, therefore, to consider their resurrection as occurring at the same time as the restoration of the living nation with the result that resurrected Israel and those still in their natural bodies who are deliverd at the second coming of Christ, will join hands and ministries in establishing Israel in the land in the millennial kingdom which follows the second advent . . . . At the same time, those who have died in the Great Tribulation just preceding will also be raised as taught in Revelation 20:4-6."[4]

It is admittedly contrary to our usual thinking to conceive of the righteous dead as being resurrected to a continued earthly existence. We think of them as raised up to an eternal life with a new heaven, a new earth and a new city as their final habitat. Why, then, should they return, even temporarily, to the imperfections of a ruined earth? The answer is that that is exactly what Christ himself will do. It may be that his *"ancients"* will be needed and will also return to serve.

The chapter continues,

They that be wise shall shine like the brightness of the firmament, and they that turn many to righteousness as the stars forever and ever (3).

Keil says,

"Then shall they who in times of tribulation have led many to the knowledge of salvation receive the glorious reward of their faithfulness."[5]

The setting is the tribulation; further therefore, the emphasis is Jewish primarily. The reference could be to those who are responsible for the salvation of the 144,000 of Revelation 14 and for that innumerable company who are saved in the great tribulation.

The testimony of the two witnesses of Revelation 11 and all of those Jews who had not previously accepted their Messiah but who responded to their preaching, could be the agency of their conversion. Those Jews who in this church age are members of the body of Christ will, of course, have been raptured.

Some have supposed that the agency for the salvation of this innumerable multitude is the nominal members of the Christian church, not worthy of the Rapture but who turn to the true faith as a result of the tribulation. This does not seem to be indicated here.

And thou Daniel, shut up the words and seal the book until the time of the end, many shall run to and fro, and knowledge shall be increased (4).

The first part of this verse has been used to proclaim the novel idea that the book of Daniel was not intended to be understood, that the purpose of revelation was not to reveal but for some mysterious reason, to be secret. Secret documents have often been the stock in trade of heretical groups, not of God's people. *"If our gospel be hidden, it is hidden to them that are lost"* (II Corinthians 4:3). It is undoubtedly true that from age to age, the Christian church ought to achieve a fuller and more complete understanding of Scripture. But this does not excuse us in viewing Daniel as a book full of hidden meanings not to be understood until that understanding would be too late to be of any use to the church or to believing

Jews. Young gives us the following,

"To Daniel is given the injunction to shut up (i.e., guard, preserve, protect, as in 8:26) the words which have just been revealed to him (i.e., 10:2-12:3) and to seal (for the sake of preserving) the book (the book in which these words were found). Kliefoth has well brought out the force of the words, 'A document is sealed up in the original text, and laid up in the archives (shut up) that it may remain preserved for remote times, but not that it may remain secret, while copies of it remain in public use.' The words, therefore, are the words which have just been revealed and which Daniel has written down, but the 'book' evidently includes more than these words. Else, why should this designation have been chosen? Evidently Daniel had written down his revelations, as he received them. This last revelation formed a conclusion, and the entire body, i.e., the book was now to be sealed."[6]

That *"many shall run to and fro"* in the modern manner, could not have been remotely envisioned even a hundred years ago. There have always been travelers and travel but largely travel by the wealthy few. It took a condition of great affluence by a large part of the population; leisure made possibly by the enormous production of all necessities by the industrial revolution; the invention and development of modern, rapid transit (railroads, autos, airplanes); added to this, the demands of organized labor, increasing the financial status of the many. All of these things provided the desire, the opportunity and the wherewithal to make possible this unique phenomenon. Psychological and spiritual factors were not wanting. As education increased, peoples' horizons and curiosities broadened. As spiritual contentment decreased, together with a loss of spiritual values, travel was a response to a restlessness and travel (anywhere) a means of escape from problems and self. The excitement of new scenes became an emotional necessity.[7]

That knowledge shall be increased is again a unique thing, if we consider its almost universal extension or the depth of its impact. There have always been centers of culture where books and scholars were found in large numbers. Some of their learning has come down to us but for a nation to make learning its biggest business and its greatest consistent investment is something very new. Compulsory education for every child up to the age of at least 14 and in some states as high as 18, is legally required in America and in most modern, industrial countries.

The educational pyramid which years ago characterized the diminishing numbers advancing from grade school to high school, from there to college and finally a few elite who enrolled in graduate and professional schools, has now become not a pyramid but an obelisk. Who in Daniel's day or even two hundred years ago, could have been imagined such a thing? Certainly, not Plato or even Comenius, nor even Horace Mann.[8]

And what are the enormous sums spent for our space program but a desire to increase our knowledge of the macrocosm even as we have searched out the microcosm?

And I heard the man clothed in linen, who was above the waters of the river, when he held up his right hand and his left hand unto heaven, and swore by him who liveth forever, that it shall be for a time, times, and a half; and when he shall have accomplished breaking of the power of the holy people, all these things shall be finished. (7)

Here again we have a theophany. The vision must have been a glorious one, involving as it did, Messiah and four angels. And as to the message, it concerns the last half of the seventieth week and is spelled out more explicitly in Zechariah 14:2,

For I will gather all nations against Jerusalem to battle: and the city shall be taken, and the houses rifled, and the women ravished; and half of the city shall go forth into captivity, and the residue of the people shall not be cut off from the city.

Israel's power will indeed be broken but when she has come to the end of herself, we read, *"Then shall the Lord go forth and fight against those nations, as when he fought in the day of battle."* This could not possibly refer to the capture of Jerusalem under Titus.

In this chapter as in all others, every phrase is pregnant with special significance, when we read (verse 10), *"But the wicked shall do wickedly."* We say, of course, that is what the wicked have always done. Why mention it? The student of Scripture will have noticed that in this chapter, we seem to have an intensification of human tendencies we have known previously; ceaseless travel, learning, the righteous turning many to righteousness, and wickedness . . .

Well, in the following special report from the U.S. News and World Report, we have the following,

"In a world largely at peace, terrorism and wanton brutality are cutting ever more deeply into lives of people and nations. No longer is it only governments and ruling classes that possess the power to inflict fear on large segments of humanity. Today it is the common man, acting alone or in groups, who is making terror a common event in common places; a downtown street, an athletic contest, an airliner high above the earth. Whether solitary criminals or terrorist gangsters, such persons are leaving a trail of death and desolation. This trail is widening over much of the world by assassination, skyjacking, rioting and random murder.

"Now moving into the foreground over the globe is the political terrorist; more so than at any time since the years leading to the Russian Revolution in 1917 . . . with the 'new terrorism' has come a 'new morality' that encompasses the willful murder of the innocent. Two years ago a spokesman for the Popular Front for the liberation of Palestine stated it clearly: 'There can be no political or moral limits to the operations of the peoples' camp. In today's world, no one is "innocent," no one is "neutral."' At one time, the wanton killer, criminal or political terrorist, was held to be 'possessed of devils,' a theory on which the Russian author, Feodor Dostoevski, a century ago constructed, 'The Possessed,' a classic novel of Nihilist terrorism."⁹

Perhaps this is not such an unreasonable explanation in view of the increase of spiritism, Satan worship and anti-God activities in general. We are reminded of the unclean spirit that went out of the man in Luke 1:14 but returned with seven spirits more wicked than himself. This is further emphasized by Paul in his first letter to Timothy (verses 1-2 of Chapter 4),

Now the Spirit speaketh expressly that, in the latter times, some shall depart from the faith, giving heed to seducing spirits, and doctrines of demons. Speaking lies in hypocracy, having their conscience seared with a hot iron.

Again, in his second letter, Paul is even more descriptive (2:1-4),

This know, also, that in the last days, perilous times shall come, For men shall be lovers of their own selves, covetous, boastful, proud, blasphemers, disobedient to parents, unthankful and unholy, Without natural affection, truce breakers, false accusers, incontinent, fierce, despisers of those that are good, Traitors, heady, highminded, lovers of pleasures more than lovers of God.

Until it comes to pass, we shall probably only approximate an understanding of the thirteenth verse wherein Daniel is told to *"go thy way till the end; for thou shalt rest and stand in thy lot at the end of days."* We are not told whether the end of days is the end of his own life or the end time. Does his rest refer to a heavenly one? Certainly, he has earned it. His prophetic visions and work have continued to the third year of Cyrus. He is probably over ninety years old. But, if we are correct about the resurrection of Old Testament saints, he will also be a part of that goodly company around Messiah's throne.

The word *"lot," (goral)*, is the same word used in the casting of lots. Is the angel speaking of his heavenly reward? Or could it be that Daniel will again see earthly service after his rest as one of those close to Messiah's throne?

Certainly, it could not have referred to his prophetic life in Babylon. All of his adult life was spent as a stranger in a strange land. He outlived Nebuchadnezzar, whom he seemed to have respected and even loved. He saw the end of the Babylonian empire.

There is no mention of his having a wife or child, if indeed he was not a eunuch. Never again did he see his beloved Jerusalem; perhaps this was a mercy.[10] He did live to see the captivity of his people ended. But he could look back over a prophetic career in which, as a vehicle of divine foreknowledge, he tells us in more detail some of the circumstances surrounding the end time than any other single prophet. We are equally intrigued with the theological insights and with the range of his prophecies. His prophetic scope includes,

1. The broad outline of world history as far as the gentile world is concerned in a series of vignettes from 605 B.C. to the end of the age. This includes the only sequence of world empires of which history speaks. The word pictures began with Nebuchadnezzar, the head of gold (Daniel 2) and ends with the revived Roman Empire (Daniel 2:40-43, 7:7-8, 19-21, 24, etc.). A supplementary view of great powers extant at the time of the end is given us in Chapter 7, if we interpret correctly.

2. The Jewish future is given us in broad outline particularly in Chapters 9, 11, and 12.

3. In Daniel 9:26, we have Messiah's appearance and rejection, the exact time of the triumphal entry (9:25) according to Anderson and the consequent destruction of Jerusalem.

4. In Daniel, we have a more detailed description of Antichrist, his nature, his activities and his relation to the Jewish people in 7:20-21 and 11:36-45.

5. The resurrection of the just which we interpret to mean the Old Testament saints (Zechariah 14:5). This is to take place just after the time of Jacob's trouble and at Messiah's return. This is uniquely specific especially in Daniel. It is a statement of fact, not a conditional promise. There is the later resurrection of the wicked probably at the end of the millennium (Revelation 20).

6. We have a clue in Chapter 10 of the forces back of history similar to that found in Isaiah 10:5-19 and Ephesians 6:12.

7. There is a short but poignant description of the Great Tribulation, The Time of Jacob's Trouble (Daniel 12:1).

8. We are given the end of the present gentile world order by the stone cut out without hands; i.e., Messiah (Daniel 2:34-35, 44).

9. The present explosion of knowledge was predicted in Daniel 12.

10. In the same chapter is the picture of ceaseless travel by so greater a portion of the world's population.

11. There was the more immediate prediction of the rebuilding of Jerusalem (Daniel 9:25) and its second descruction by the people of the prince that shall come.

12. Wars are predicted to the end of the age, no lasting peace til Messiah comes (Daniel 9:26).

13. Daniel predicts the millennial kingdom which shall not be

destroyed and which shall be given to the saints of the most high and all dominions shall serve and obey Him (Daniel 2:35, 44, 7:14).

14. God the Son, the Son of man, is revealed in Daniel 7:13-14 and in 10:5-6, possibly also in Daniel 3:25. The Jews in Jesus' time also recognized the deity of this reference to Messiah.

15. There are special revelations in more detail, concerning the empires of Persia, Macedonia, Syria, Egypt and Rome.

16. In Chapter 7, we believe, are descriptions of nations not then born nor heard of during the days of Daniel and, hence, no name given them. We have suggested England, Russia, the Arab countries and the revived Roman Empire as representing the four beasts of Daniel 7.

APPENDIX I

Chronological Summary, B.C. Some pertinent dates relative to historical and prophetic references in Daniel:

690 Destruction of Babylon by Sennacherib; city leveled and canals turned over the ruins.

680-678, Babylon partially rebuilt under Esarhaddon, who reigned 681-668.

668-648, Shamash shumukin, King of Babylon under Assyria, rebelled against Assyria; Babylon taken and partially burned (648).

668-626, Ashurbanipal, King of Assyria, ruled Babylon through a viceroy, Kandalu; plundered Thebes 661.

640-608, Reign of Josiah, King of Judah; last good king of Judah.

626-605, Nabopolassar, King of Babylon, gains independence from Assyria; begins a new dynasty and the Neo-Chaldean Empire.

612 Destruction of Nineveh under its king, Sin-shar-ishkun, by Nabopolassar and Cyaxeres I the Mede; possibly the date of the marriage of Nebuchadnezzar to Amytis, daughter of Cyaxeres.

609 Jehoahaz, King of Judah, reigns three months and is taken captive to Egypt where he dies.

609-598, Jehoiakim, King of Judah, reigns 11 years, rebels against king of Babylon. 605-562, Reign of Nebuchadnezzar, son of Nabopolassar; one of the greatest kings of antiquity.

605 Beginning of the servitude of the Jews to Nebuchadnezzar; Daniel taken to Babylon.

604 Nebuchadnezzar's first regnal year.

603 Nebuchadnezzar's first dream; second regnal year.

601 Battle with the Egyptian army under NechiII; result, a draw.

597 Jehoiachin reigns three months; exiled to Babylon.

597-586, Zedekiah, last king of Judah, reigns 11 years; Jerusalem destroyed (586); Zedekiah blinded and taken to Babylon with most of the population.

562-560, Avil Marduk succeeds Nebuchadnezzar his father; is assassinated by his brother-in-law, Neriglissar, after reigning two years.

560-556, Neriglissor, son-in-law of Nebuchadnezzar, reigns four years.

556-555, Labashi Marduk, son of Neriglissar, deposed and murdered after reigning nine months.

555-539, Nabonidus, a Babylonian noble and a non-Chaldean, usurps the throne.

554-c.539, Belshazzar, son of Nebonidus, made regent and joint king in absence of his father in Tema in Arabia. The date of the beginning of his regency uncertain, but absence of King Nabonidus from the seventh to the eleventh year documented; Daniel's vision of the four beasts of Daniel 7 in the first year of Belshazzar; Daniel's vision of the ram and the goat, Chapter 8, the third year of Belshazzar.

547 Destruction of Lydian kingdom of Croesus.

542 Destruction of the great Hadramaut dam and ruin of the spice country of Sheba.

539 Belshazzar's feast; captures of Babylon by Cyrus and Darius; Belshazzar slain; end of Neo-Babylonian Empire.

539-537, Probable reign of Darius; plot against Daniel; Daniel's vision of the seventy weeks; possible inscription of Nabonidus' Chronicle and Cyrus cylinder two years after this date.

537-530, Reign of Cyrus over the Persian Empire; Daniel's final vision in the third year 534.

536 End of the servitude of Judah; Cyrus decrees the return of the Jews.

530- 522, Cambyses succeeds his father, Cyrus, on the throne of Persia.

522-486, Darius Hystaspes becomes king of Persia; city of Babylon revolts twice, 522 and 521.

486-464, Xerxes I stirs up the Persian kingdom against Greece, invades Greece but is defeated; Babylon revolts, 478, and recaptured; Xerxes murdered, 464.

484-425, Herodotus, native of the Greek city of Halicarnasis in Asia Minor, called the father of History.

464-423, Artaxerxes I (called Longimanus), king of the Persian Empire.

445 Edict issued in Artaxerxes' 20th year; 1 Nisan for the rebuilding of Jerusalem; the count begins for the seventy weeks of Daniel 9; Herodotus given prize for his history of the Persian wars at Olympia.

425-404, Darius Nothus, King of Persia.

404-359, Artaxerxes, his defeat, and the march of his ten thousand Greek mercenaries described in Xenophon's Anabasis.

c. 397, The era of the Old Testament prophets ends with Malachi.

394 Xenophon wrote his Cyropaedia sometime after this date.

359-337, Artxerxes III (Ochus), King of Persia, murdered.

338-335, Arses, King of Persia, murdered.

335-331, Darius Codomanus, King of Persia, defeated by Alexander the Great and murdered by his own people; end of the Persian rule and empire and the beginning of the Macedonian Empire under Alexander the Great.

356-323, Alexander the Great reigns over the kingdom of Macedonia and, after 331, over the empire.

332 Surrender of Jerusalem to Alexander; high priest Jaddua shows the prophecy of Daniel to Alexander.

323-285, Ptolemy Soter, King of Egypt, one of the Diadochi (successors of Alexander).

312-281, Seleucus I (Nicator), King of Syria.

281-261, Antiochus I (Soter), King of Syria.

285-247, Ptolemy II (Philadelphia), King of Egypt (his daughter Bernice mentioned in Daniel 11:6).

c. 250 Translation of the Hebrew Old Testament law into Greek; the Septuagint.

246-222, Ptolemy III (Euergetes), King of Egypt (Daniel 11:7-8).

246-226, Seleucus II, King of Syria (Daniel 11:9).

226-223, Seleucus III, King of Syria (Daniel 11:10).

222-205, Ptolemy IV (Philopator), King of Egypt(Daniel 11:11,12, 14).

223-187, Antiochus III (The Great), King of Syria (Daniel 11:10,12-14,16-18).

187-175, Seleucus IV (Philopator), King of Syria (Daniel 11:20).

175-163, Antiochus IV (Epiphanes), King of Syria; persecutor of Jews and types of Antichrist (Daniel 11:21-35?).

168 Desecration of the Jewish temple and altar by Antiochus Epiphanes on 25 Chisleu; desecration lasted 3 years (Josephus).

165 Daily sacrifice restored by Judas Macabbeus, commemorated in the feast of Hanukkah.

142 Jewish independence under the Hasmoneans (Maccabees). This line was of the tribe of Levi and hence did not have complete divine legitimacy.

143-135, Simon Maccabeus murdered.

135-104, John Hyrcanus.

104-76, Alexander Janneus.

78-68, Queen Alexandra.

68-64, Aristobolus an Idumean, the end of independence for Judea and the beginning of Roman rule (Daniel 2:40).

64-63, Judea becomes a Roman province; Pompey the Great enters the Holy of Holies and finds nothing there; i.e., no Shekinah.

40-4, Herod the Great, son of Antipas and Idumean, made king over Palestine under Roman auspices. 27-14 A.D., Reign of Augustus Caesar over the Roman Empire.

6-4 A.D., Birth of Christ in Bethlehem; slaughter of the children by Herod.

4 A.D., Archelaus succeeds Herod the Great. 4-39 A.D., Herod Antipas.

Chronological Summary, A.D. Some pertinent dates relative to historical and prophetic references in Daniel:

14-37, Tiberius Caesar succeeds Augustus as Roman emperor.

29 Beginning of Christ's public ministry. This date debated.

32 Christ's triumphal entry (10 Nisan-April 6) as predicted in Daniel 9:25-26 (according to Sir Robert Anderson).

32 Crucifixion (14 Nisan-April 14) end of the 69th week of Daniel (Daniel 9:26).

32 Day of Pentecost; beginning of the Christian church.

54-68, Nero, Emperor of Rome and originator of first great persecution of Christians.

69-79, Vespasian, Emperor of Rome.

66-70, Roman army under Titus, son of Vespasian, carries on a war against the Jews.

70 Destruction of Jerusalem by Titus, with a loss of a million and a quarter Jews and Jewish dispersal (Daniel 9:26).

1917, Balfour Declaration, committing Great Britain to the creation of a Jewish state in Palestine.

1948, Formation of the State of Israel. Filson, ed. The Westminster Historical Atlas to the Bible.

APPENDIX II

Introduction

The book of Daniel has had a very hard time of it in modern encyclopedic literature. We have, for example, the following from the Universal Jewish Encyclopedia under the article of Daniel: "on the whole, however, Jewish thought has concerned itself but little with the predictions of the book; instead, it has become a series of stories for children, and a text book of absolute faith in the obedience to God."

While modern Judaism may not have any great interest in the book of Daniel, it was not so in times past.

Perhaps Abrabanel's greatest achievement was his defense of the Rabbinic concept of soteriology against the Christian claim that Jesus was the Messiah (appearing principally in his Migdal Yeshuot). Christian and Jew alike drew upon Scripture for evidence of the Messiah, and Abrabanel's brilliant exegesis gave strong support to the Jewish view. Particularly ingenius among these apologetics was Abrabanel's interpretation of the book of Daniel, which served to convince him that the Messianic Age would arrive in the year 1503. At that time the Jews would be revenged on their enemies, the dispersed Jews would return to Israel, the resurrection and judgment would take place, and all Jews would live in Israel under Messiah, whose rule would extend over all mankind. Thus the days of Messiah will begin.[1]

The following is a more detailed account of the alleged errors of Daniel, with the usual claim of unanimity of judgment of those holding this viewpoint:

Bible critics are unanimous in declaring that Daniel could not possibly have been written as it is claimed to have been.... They point out that the author uses the late form "Nebuchadnezzar" instead of the correct form "Nebuchadrezzar" (Nabu-Kudur-Uzur); that the siege of Jerusalem by Nebuchadnezzar did not take place in the third year of Jehoiakim, as reported in 1:1; that Belshazzar was not the son of Nebuchadnezzar as reported in 5:11, that there was no Median kingdom immediately following the fall of Babylon as the author believed, and no such king as Darius the Mede; that the statement that there were only four kings between Cyrus and the conquest of Persia by Greece (11:2-4) is erroneous; and that there are Greek words in the text, such as Karoza, "herald," (3:4) and sumponiah, "bagpipe" (3:5, 15).[2]

Protestant higher criticism has been equally unbelieving and much more vociferous and dogmatic. The new Catholic Encyclopedia has the following to say:

"The book's place in the Jewish Canon indicates a late date. The historical inaccuracies (a siege of Jerusalem in 605 B.C., Daniel 1:1-2; Darius the Mede, 6:1; Belsassar the 'son' of Nebuchodnosor and 'king' of Babylon, etc.) are scarcely conceivable in an exilic writer. The language and religious concepts of the book are postexilic and, in part, Machabean. The perspective of Chapter seven to twelve is clearly Machabean, and a revelation of the detailed course of history found there cannot easily be postulated."[3]

APPENDIX III

Chapter I

A sample of the "tender mercies" of an Assyrian king: Ashurbanipal had made his twin brother Shamash-shum-ukin governor of Babylon, and when the city under the leadership of his brother revolted, Ashurbanipal besieged the city and set it on fire. He reports as follows:

"At that time famine laid hold of the people of Akkad (Babylon) who had sided with Shamash-shum-ukin and had plotted evil, and they ate the flesh of their sons and daughters in order to satisfy their hunger, and they cut open their stomachs. "Ashur, Sin, Shamash, Ramman, Bel, Nabu, Ishtar of Nineveh, Queen of Kidmuri, Ishtar of Arbel, Ninib, Nergal, and Nusku, who went before me and subdued my foes, threw Shamash-shum-ukin, the hostile brother who had attacked me, into an abyss of burning fire and destroyed his life. But as for the men who had formed plans against Shamash-shum-ukin, the hostile brother, and had accomplished this wicked deed, who feared death, and whose life was precious in their own eye, so that they had not thrown themselves into the fire with Shamash-shum-ukin, their lord; who had fled from before the slaughter of iron dagger, hunger, famine, and burning fire, and had seized a place of refuge, the net of the great gods, my lords, from which there is no escape, overthrew them; not one escaped; not a rebel went forth from my hands; they (i.e., the gods) delivered them into my hands. They brought before me chariots, a state carriage, a canopy, his wives, and the property of his palace. I cut out the tongues of those soldiers in whose mouths was insolence because they had spoken insolence against Ashur, my lord, and had plotted evil against me, the prince who fears him; and I murdered them. As for the rest of the men who were alive, by the bull-colossi, where my grandfather, Sennacherib, had made a slaughter, there I at that time slew those men as a lamentation for him. I let dogs, swine, vultures, eagles, birds of the heavens, and fish of the ocean eat their flesh, which was cut off."[1]

APPENDIX IV

Chapter II

From "The East India House Inscription of Nebuchadnezzar II": (p. 138) "Imgur-Bel and Nimitti-Bel, the large walls of Babylon which Nabopolassar, King of Babylon, the father, my begetter, had made, but had not completed their construction; their moat he had dug, and by means of two strong walls with bitumen and burned brick he had strengthened their banks; a wall along the Arahtu canal he had made, and with the dike of burned brick on the other side of the Euphrates he had joined it, but had not completed the rest. From Du-azag-ki-nam-tar-re-e-ne, the shrine of Fates, as far as A-ibur-shabu(m), (p. 139) the street of Babylon, in front of the Gate of the Lady, I constructed a way with brick and tur-mi-na-tur-da stone as a procession street for the great lord Marduk.

"As for me, his first-born son, the beloved of his heart, Imgur-Bel and Nimitti-Bel, the great walls of Babylon, I completed. The sides of the wall of its moat, two strong walls, with bitumen and burned brick I built, and to the wall which my father had strengthened I joined it, and I surrounded the city for its protection with a wall of burned brick toward the east, and I constructed a wall about Babylon. A-ibur-shabu(m), the street of Babylon, I filled in with a high terrace as a procession street for the great lord Marduk, and partly with brick and tur-mi-na-tur-da stone, partly with brick and stone from the mountain, A-ibur-shabu, from Bab-Ella (the shining gate) as far as Nana-sakipat-tebisha, I macadamized for a procession street of his divinity; I joined it to what my father had built, and I constructed the boulevard Nana-sakipat-tebisha.

"The entrances of the city gates on both sides of Imgur-Bel and Nimitti-Bel, on account of the filling in of the street of Babylon, had become too low, and I tore down these gates and at the water's edge I firmly laid their foundation with bitumen and burned brick, and with burned brick and brilliant ugnu-stone, out of which the wild-bulls and the serpents are constructed, skillfully I built them.

"I laid in rows mighty cedar trees for their roof. I set in place in their gates the cedar doors, with a sheathing of copper, the thresholds and the hinges, made of bronze. I stationed at their thresholds strong wild-bulls of bronze and serpents standing erect. I filled with splendor these city gates for the astonished gaze (of all people). That the shaft of battle might not reach Imgur-Bel, the wall of Babylon, what no former king had done, for four thousand land cubits on the site of Babylon, afar off, to make approach impossible, I surrounded Babylon with a large wall toward the east. I dug its moat and strengthened its bank with bitumen and burned brick, (p. 140) and built a strong wall on its bank mountain high. Its wide city gates I put in position, and the doors of cedar, with a sheathing of copper, I set in place. That a terrible enemy might not push forward to the sides of Babylon, I surrounded the land with large bodies of water, like the volume of the sea; and that the plying (of ships) as on the raging sea or the briny gulf might not bring about a breach in their banks, I threw up against them a levee of mud, and surrounded them with a wall of burned brick. I skillfully strengthened the watch-tower, and made the city Babylon a fortification. Tabisuburshu, the wall of Borsippa, I built anew; I dug its moat, and strengthened its bank with bitumen and burned brick."[1]

APPENDIX V

Chapter III

Herodotus of Halicarnassus, so-called Father of History, describes the city of Babylon as being one hundred and twenty furlongs in length each way, so that the entire circuit of the city is four hundred and eighty furlongs. With the furlong or stadium approximately two hundred and two yards in length, this would mean that the walls were between fourteen and fifteen miles long on each side. He describes the height of the walls as two hundred royal cubits and its thickness as fifty royal cubits.

There were two main walls, an inner wall called Imgur Bel and an outer wall called the Nimitti Bel. The facings, at least, of these walls were of burnt brick, and there were twenty-five gateways on each of the four sides, making one hundred gates in all. At each gate, two bronze figures stood, one on either side of the doors, which were faced with bronze plates. On one side, also of bronze, stood an erect serpent, and on the other side, a bull.

Modern archeologists have questioned the size and length of these walls as exaggerations, reducing the length to a very few miles, since the excavations have failed, so far, to verify Herodotus's description. Since the portions that have been excavated are so much shorter in length than, say, the walls of Nineveh or Charchemish and since Herodotus, who saw the walls, pictures them as the wonder of Asia and greater than the walls of any other city that he knew and visited, we must assume that further excavations will verify his statements.

As stupendous as these masses of masonry were, they do not compare with the great wall of China, with its fifteen hundred miles of length, its height of fifteen to thirty feet, and its width, at the base, of twenty-five feet. Considering the stupendous labor force at Nebuchadnezzar's command, there is no improbability at all in Herodotus' description. We may believe also the accuracy of the description since (1) he visited the city and saw it with his own eyes, (2) his history was read to Greek audiences, many persons of which must also have visited Babylon, and (3) he is usually an accurate and truthful observer and falls into error only when he accepts information from sources that he can neither verify nor dispute (e.g., the story of Nitocris and Semiramis).[1]

k

APPENDIX VI

Chapter IV

Relative to the Maccabean dating (165 B.C.), there are the following overall objections:

1. As one of the Kethubim, if it had been written after Jesus Ben Sirach had considered the canon closed, it would have immediately been called in question as to its inspired nature. No such controversy has come down to us.

2. An author other than Daniel, at that time (165 B.C.) and under those circumstances, could hardly have remained anonymous.

3. Jaddua, the high priest, could hardly have shown Alexander the Great in the year 332 B.C. a prophecy of Daniel yet to be written. Josephus is not given to manufacturing such incidents.

4. The local color demands that the book shall have been written in Babylon or by someone miraculously informed concerning the Babylon of the sixth century. The Babylon of 165 B.C. was an entirely different city; in reality a ghost town, or something less than its ancient bustle.

5. Ezekiel mentions a Daniel fitting the spiritual description of the Daniel of the book. (One so eminent in righteousness as to be classed with Noah and Job would surely have found a place in sacred history.)

6. The predictions given have not yet all fulfilled, but enough of them have come to pass to give validity to those pending (e.g., Daniel 9:25 and 26). The unfulfilled ones are for the end time.

7. Doctrinally, predictively, and especially eschatologically, Daniel is consistent with the other prophets, which is not always chracteristic of pseudepigrapha.

8. Our Lord calls him *"Daniel, the prophet"* (Matthew 24:15 and Mark 13:14) and quotes from him, which would be unthinkable did He not consider Daniel as a part of Sacred Scripture.

APPENDIX FOOTNOTES

APPENDIX I

None.

APPENDIX II

1. Art. "Abrabanel," Encyclopedia Judaica, pp. 107-108.
2. Art. "Daniel," The Universal Jewish Encyclopedia, pp. 464-465.
3. Art. "Daniel," Catholic Encyclopedia, p. 635.   Remiel. Only Michael has biblical designation as archangel.

APPENDIX III

1. Assyrian and Babylonian Literature, pp. 109-110. Op. Cit.

APPENDIX IV

1. "The East India House Inscription of Nebuchadnezzar II, "Assyrian and Babylonian Literature, p. 3.

APPENDIX V

1. Herodotus, History (New York: Tudor Publishing Co., 1928), pp. 66-67.

APPENDIX VI

None.

FOOTNOTES

PROLOGUE FOOTNOTES

1. Personalities appearing in the book are both human and supernatural:

(a) The human actors of the historical portions: Nebuchadnezzar; Daniel; Hananiah; Mishael; Azariah; Belshazzar; Darius the Mede; Cyrus the Persian; the prince of Eunuchs; the Melzar; Arioch; the queen mother; Daniel's accusers. The only Palestinian personality is Jehoiakim, introduced for the purpose of dating the first chapter.

(b) There are supernatural personalities introduced to us: the God of Heaven; the Ancient of Days; the Son of Man, Messiah the Prince; One like the appearance of a man; a certain man clothed in linen; Gabriel; Michael; two other theophanies; two saints; four angels.

(c) There are certain unnamed actors in Daniel's visions: the Little Horn of Chapter 7; the Little Horn of Chapter 8; the King of Fierce Countenance; The King who does as he wills; the King of the North; the King of the South; ten kings unnamed and undescribed; certain kings of Persia; Alexander the Great; by implication and description the Diodochi, his successors; the Roman Prince to Come; Antiochus Epiphanes, by description; unnamed but identifiable rulers of Syria and Egypt.

2. If First Maccabees was written, as some aver, within thirty-five years of the pseudo-Daniel, how did the latter escape embodying the same spirit and the same patriotic elements? The best answer would seem to be that the temple was not mentioned because, in the time of Nebuchadnezzar, there was no temple; no call to patriotic action because there was no revolt; no glorification of Hasmonean leaders because they had not yet been born. When we add it all up and find that Daniel has no emphasis for the temple, no battle cry, no anti-Hellenism, no local color; in short, no hint of the purpose for which the book was allegedly written, we must conclude that there was no pseudo-Daniel and no book written in 165 B.C. purporting to be the product of an unknown patriotic zealot.

3. Zechariah 12:10 and 13:1.

INTRODUCTION FOOTNOTES

1. See Appendix for opposing arguments.

2. "The book of Daniel is especially fitted to be a battle field between faith and unbelief. It admits of no half measures. It is either divine or an imposter. To write any book under the name of another, and to give it out to be his, is in any case, a forgery, dishonest in itself and destructive of all trustworthiness. But the case as to the book of Daniel, if it were not his, would go far beyond even this. The writer, were he not Daniel, must have lied, on a most frightful scale, ascribing to God's prophecies which were never uttered, and miracles which are assumed never to have been wrought. In a word, the whole book would be one lie in the Name of God." (E.B. Pusey, Daniel the Prophet (Funk and Wagnalls, 1885).)

3. C.F. Keil, Bible Commentary on the Book of Daniel (Grand Rapids: Eerdmans), p. 20.

4. Montgomery, p. 90.

5. Note: An excellent introduction is found in E.J. Young's The Prophecy of Daniel, pp. 15-29.

6. "The right of the book of Daniel to canonicity was never called in question in the Ancient Synagogue." (Edersheim, Life and Times of The Messiah, Vol. II, app. V.)

7. As to the greatness of Daniel himself, as judged by his own people prior to modern times, we have the following from Pusey: "Josephus says, that he was 'one of the greatest prophets.' And whereas the Talmud mentions a saying, that 'Haggai, Zechariah, Malachi, had this above him, that they were prophets, and he was not a prophet,' yet they themselves explain this to mean 'that he was not sent to Israel for the office of prophecy'; i.e., as said above, that he had not the prophetic office. It was a part of the same saying, that, in another respect, 'he was greater than they, in that he saw the vision which they saw not.' And the Talmud says, 'if all the wise of the nations were in one scale of the balance, and Daniel in the other, he would outweigh them all.' And Abarbanel says, that 'he stood

in the secret of God and heard his words,' and assents to the Rabbins who, in the Seder Olam, metaphor, or of mission, but in the way of precision and truth.'" (Pusey, Daniel the Prophet, p. 309.)

8. Assuming that Darius reigned from 539-537 B.C., according to tradition, and   assuming that Cyrus began his reign immediately thereafter.

9. Keil, p. 90.

10. Robert D. Culver, Daniel and the Latter Days (Revell, 1954), pp. 98-99. (However, this is only partially true. Daniel 7, which offers ultimate deliverance and glory,is in Aramaic.)

11. R.K. Harrison, Introduction to the Old Testament (Grand Rapids: Eerdmans, 1969), pp. 1109-1110.

12. Romans 9:4-5.

13. We have no positive evidence as to when Belshazzar began his regency. It is certain that Nabonidus was absent in Tema from his seventh to his eleventh year (548-544 B.C.). It seems probable that Belshazzar's regency began much earlier, say 553 B.C.

CHAPTER I

1. Psalm 9:17.

2. Psalm 9:15.

3. Jeremiah 1:10; 25:15 and 16.

4. Jeremiah 25:27-29.

5. The following great cities met judgment; i.e., capture and some-times complete destruction, in the century and a half from 690 to 539 B.C. Some rose again to prominence, some remained only a heap of ruins. The following are some of the most prominent:

690 B.C. Old Babylon destroyed by Senacharib and canals turned over the ruins. Later rebuilt with greater size and magnificence.

676 B.C. Sidon destroyed by Esarhadden. Later rebuilt.

670 B.C. Egyptian Memphis captured by Esarhadden.

661 B.C. No-Amon (Thebes) captured and plundered by Ashur-banipal and never again recovered her former glory.

645 B.C. Susa captured and destroyed by Ashurbanipal. Later rebuilt and became the spring capital of the Persian kings.

612 B.C. Nineveh destroyed completely by Nabopolassar, king of Babylon, and Astyages, king of the Medes. It remained a heap of ruins.

605 B.C. Carchemish captured and completely destroyed by Nebuchadnezzar. Never rebuilt. (Present site of Jerablus.)

606 B.C. Jerusalem besieged by Nebuchadnezzar and tribute taken, including part of the temple vessels.

598 B.C. Jerusalem taken by Nebuchadnezzar's army but not destroyed.

586 B.C. Jerusalem taken and completely demolished by Nebuchad-nezzar. Most of remaining population deported to Babylon.

585-573 B.C. Tyre besieged and Paleo-Tyre captured by Nebuchad-nezzar. (The island citadel not captured.)

549 B.C. Sardis captured by Cyrus; the end of Croesus' Lydian Empire.

541 B.C. Destruction of great Hadramout Dam and ruin of four spice countries, vis., Minaea, Kataban, Hadramout, Sheba.

539 B.C. Babylon captured by Cyrus the Persian and Darius the Mede. No destruction and no pillaging. City became the winter capital of Persian kings. The seventy years of desolation of Jerusalem began 589

B.C., with seizure of city under Zedekiah and ended 520 B.C. when exiles under Ezra laid the foundation of the temple. City walls were rebuilt in 445 B.C.

6. Isaiah 20:1-6.

7. "Annal of Ashurbanipal," Assyrian and Babylonian Literature, pp. 99 and 700.

8. See Appendix for example of Assyrian atrocity.

9. Lewis Spence, art. "Wonders of the Past," Hammerstein, p. 769.

10. Ezekiel 32:24 and 25.

11. Jeremiah 49:36 and 37.

12. Assyrian and Babylonian Literature, pp. 114, 115, and 116.

13. Jeremiah 27:8.

14. In Ezekiel Chapter 27, we get something of the extent and richness of the caravan traffic of Ezekiel's day, which is also the day of Daniel and Nebuchadnezzar. While the merchandise is listed as that of Tyre, we must remember that both Tyre and the whole trading world brought its products to Babylon as a center, that caravans and ships came regularly from China, India, Africa, Arabia, Tyre, Asia Minor and Greece.

Exports:	Imports:
From Tyre: purple dye, glass-ware, and metal artifacts;	From Egypt: linen, blue and purple;
From Cyprus: copper;	From Cyprus: silver, iron, tin;
	From Tarshish(Spain and Sardinia): lead;
From Ugarit: bronze;	From Russia: slaves and brass;
	From Togarmah: horses (Cilicia);
	From Dedan: ivory and ebony.
From Lebanon (Byblos):cedars;	From Syria: emeralds, purple, broidered work, linen, coral, agate.
	From Israel: wheat, honey, oil, and a multitude of wares, wine of Helbon/white wool from Damascus.
From Egypt: linen.	From Javan or Greece: bright iron, cassia, and calemus;
	From Kedar (Arabia): sheep and goats;
	Sheba: spices, precious stones and gold.

In addition to Ezekiel's list:

From Cilicia: horses.	From China: silk, fine iron, and furs.
From Mohendaro and Harappa: copper, ivory, gold, cotton, and precious stones.	Clothing and wool.

15. II Kings 18:11.

16. Jeremiah34:32.

17. Ptolemy replaced the table for the shewbread with a copy at the time the Septuagint was translated. According to Josephus, Antiquities, Bk. XII, Ch. 11, Paras. 8-10.

18. Ibid.

19. Ezekiel 21:27.

20. Hosea3:4 and 5.

21. Jeremiah 25:11-14.

CHAPTER II

1. Romans 9:4.

2. Was Daniel a eunuch? In the prophecy of Isaiah (39:6 and 7), the prophet predicted to Hezekiah:

Behold, the days come, that all that is in thine house, and that which the fathers have laid up in store until this day, shall be carried to Babylon; nothing shall be left, saith the Lord. And of thy sons that shall issue from thee, whom thou shalt beget, they shall be taken away; and they shall be eunuchs in the palace of the king of Babylon.

Josephus, beginning his account of Daniel, says:

"But now Nebuchadnezzar king of Babylon, took some of the most noble of the Jews that were children and kinsmen of Zedekiah their king, such as were remarkable for the beauty of their bodies and the comeliness of their countenances, and delivered them to the hands of tutors, and to the improvement to be made by them. He also made some of them to be eunuchs." (Josephus, Antiquities, X, X.1.)

Whether Josephus was depending on oral tradition or on this hint in Isaiah, it is somewhat questionable as to whether he would introduce the matter at all unless it applied to Daniel. The implications here might apply to a broader use of the term "eunuch," which would be applicable to any high official in an oriental court.

3. Josephus, X, X, 1.

4. Josephus, X, XI.1.

5. See Appendix for Herodotus's description of Babylon.

6. Wiseman, Chronicles of the Babylonian Kings, pp. 46-47.

7. Daniel 5:19.

8. In discussing the terms used to designate the different ages of the male child, Edersheim gives us the following:

"Yeled, the new born babe, as in Isaiah 9:6; yoneq, the suckling in Isaiah 11:8; olel, the suckling beginning to ask for food, Lam. 4:4; gamul, the weaned child, Isaiah 28:9; taph, the child clinging to its mother, Jer. 40:7; elem, a child becoming firm; naar, the lad, young man literally, one who shakes himself free; and bachur, the ripened one, young man." (Edersheim, Life and Times of Jesus the Messiah, pp. 221 fn.)

But the word yeled seems to be more comprehensive and is used to indicate young men, as well, as in Genesis 4:23, I Kings 12:8, 10, 14; II Chronicles 10:8, 10, 14, Daniel 1:4, etc.

9. Josephus, Against Apion, p. 867.

10. Josephus, p. 317.

11. Grotefend, Inscriptions No. 150, Assyrian and Babylonian Literature.

12. Josephus, p. 317.

13. Of course, eminence is not to be measured primarily by space in "Who's Who," even the "Who's Who of Scripture," but non-entities would hardly be expected to capture much space in the biblical record. Nebuchadnezzar is referred to in the most unusual terms. He is called the *"head of gold"* (Daniel 2:38), *"my servant"* (Jeremiah 25:9) and in the God-given dream, the *"tree whose height reached to heaven"* (Daniel 4:20). Only Cyrus, *"anointed"* and *"Shepherd"* (Isaiah 45:1, 44:28), is given more honor.

14. The Dani-el of the Ugaritic texts could not be the Daniel of Ezekiel 14:14 (see E.J. Young, The Prophecy of Daniel, pp. 274 f.) any more than George Fox and George Washington could be identified as identical because of having the same first name. The Ugaritic Dani-el is of 1400 B.C.; the Daniel of Ezekiel, the sixth century. It is beyond all credibility that Ezekiel should include a Ugaritic character entirely unknown to Scripture, as the equal of Noah and Job.

15. Briefly, our basic knowledge of Daniel and his personal life is limited to the book of Daniel, quotations from Josephus, two passages in Ezekiel 14 and to our Lord's reference to him in Matthew 24:15. From these sources, we learn that:

(a) He was of noble or kingly lineage. (Josephus, X, X.1.)

(b) He was outstanding among three other companions as to his wisdom and knowledge of dreams. (Daniel 1:17; Josephus.)

(c) He was a civil servant all his life during the reign of Nebuchadnezzar and Nebuchadnezzar's successors, the brief reign of Darius, and to the third year of Cyrus.(Daniel 1:21, 10:1; Joesphus.)

(d) He was one of the first of the exiles to Babylon, living most of his adult life in that city. (Daniel 1:4, 6; Josephus.)

(e) He probably never saw Jerusalem again. (Josephus, X, XI. 7.)

(f) His piety and faithfulness classed him with Noah and Job.(Ezekiel 14:14, 20)

(g) He was greatly beloved of God.(Daniel 9:23, 10:11)

(h) His prophetic status was recognized by Christ himself.(Matthew 24:15)

(i) He was made for a few hours the third ruler in the kingdom of Babylon. (Daniel 5:29; Josephus, X, XI.4.)

(j) Under Darius, he was made the first of three presidents over the kingdom. (Daniel 6:2; Josephus.)

(k) He was the object of miraculous protection in the den of lions. (Daniel 6; Josephus, X, XI.6.)

(l) He was taken to Ecbatana by Darius, where he died (probably at an age of 90 or more). (Josephus, X, XI.7.)

(m) He built a tower that became the tomb of the kings of Persia. (Josephus. BK X, 497 S.370 Whiston Tr.)

(n) At least twice, he was apparently transferred out of Babylon: once to Susa (Daniel 8:2) and once to a location on the Tigris (Daniel 10:4).

(o) He was apparently unknown to Belshazzar. (Daniel 5:13.)

16. See Keil, Daniel, p. 80.

17. Whether the older code of Lipit Ishtar was still required reading, we cannot know.

18. Goodspeed, quoting Rawlinson, says:

"Hers was apparently the genius that excogitated an alphabet; worked out the simpler problems of arithmetic; invented implements for measuring the lapse of time; conceived the idea of raising the enormous structures with the poorest of all materials, clay; discovered the art of polishing, boring and engraving gems; reproduced with truthfulness the outlines of human and animal forms; attained to high perfection in textile fabrics; studied with success the motions of the heavenly bodies; conceived of grammar as a science; elaborated a system of law; saw the value of exact chronology; in almost every branch of science made a beginning, thus rendering it comparatively easy for other nations to proceed with the super structure. . . . It was from the East, not from Egypt, that Greece derived her architecture, her sculpture, her science, her philosophy, her mathematical knowledge; in a word her intellectual life. And Babylon was the source to which the entire stream of Eastern civilization may be traced. It is scarcely too much to say that, but for Babylon, real civilization might not even yet have dawned upon the earth." (Goodspeed, History of Babylon and Assyria, p. 365, quoting Rawlinson, Great Monarchies, III, pp. 75f.)

19. Wright and Filson, The Westminister Historical Atlas to the Bible, p. 69.

20. If we leave out the blessings of gunpowder, the printing press, and the steam engine, the Babylon of Nebuchadnezzar's day was hardly inferior technically to America 150 years ago, where an industrial revolution had not furnished, as yet, the luxuries and comforts that were commonplace among upper class Babylonians.

21. "The following table shows the approximate number of drugs in use:

Drugs	Species	Frequency of mention %
Vegetable	250	80
Mineral	120	10
Others	180	10

	550	

... without counting the various alcohols, fats and oils used as vehicles or solvent." (Cambridge Ancient History, III, Ch. XI. V, p. 241.) Comparing the 550 medicinal drugs with the 217 listed in the first American Pharmocopea of 1820, we realize the Empirical Medicine must have had a long tradition in Babylon.

22. The patient, then as now, had protection, for the code of Hammurabi provides the following penalties for malpractice:

"If a doctor has operated with a bronze lancet on a gentleman for a severe wound, and has caused the gentleman's death, or has removed a cataract with a bronze lancet, and has destroyed the gentleman's eye, they shall cut off his hand.

"The surgeon receives ten shekels of silver for the removal of a cataract and five shekels of silver for a broken bone." (R.W. Rogers, The Cuneiform Parallels to the Old Testament, 2d ed., pp. 447 and 448.)

23. The statement that Babylon was the greatest city of antiquity does not give us much solid ground on which to estimate its population, since whatever census lists may have been compiled by cities of antiquity, very few hints of population estimates have come down to us. In the case of Babylon, we may arrive at an estimate in a roundabout way. A city fourteen or fifteen miles square could conceivably house five or ten million people (it is estimated that Rome in Pliny's time had a population of 1,500,000), especially when we realize many Babylonian houses were several stories high. But if we remember that, undoubtedly, there were villas, canals, caravanseries with stockades for camels and other beasts of burden, we would need to reduce our estimates.

Another way of looking at it might be to list the number of temples and places of worship. We are told that there were fifty-three temples and places of the chief gods, fifty-five chapels of Marduk, three hundred chapels for the earth deities, six hundred for the heavenly deities, a hundred and eighty altars for Ishtar, a hundred and eighty altars for Nergal and Adad, and twelve for other gods; all these in addition to the temple of Marduk and its ziggurat (the former, fifteen hundred feet by eighteen hundred feet at the base).

An immense population must have resided within the walls of Babylon to have needed so many places of worship, but here again, we can only guess at the number of devotees who regularly worshipped at a single shrine. Nineveh had sixscore thousand persons; children who could not "discern between their right hand and their left hand" (Jonah 4:11). Babylon was incomparably larger and more populous.

24. Herodotus, History (New York: Tudor Publishing Co., 1928), pp. 72-73.

25. The majority of the bricks that are so numerous in the ruins of Babylon have the stamp of Nebuchadnezzar upon them. They read: "Nebuchadnezzar, king of Babylon, fosterer of Esagila and Ezida son of Nabopolassar king of Babylon." (RobertKoldewey, The Excavations at Babylon (Macmillan, 1915), p. 76.)

26. Ezekiel 29:12 and 19; Jeremiah 46:19, 24, and 26; II Kings 25:14.

27. See Appendix for East India House Inscription of Nebuchadnezzar

28. Ezekiel 22:27.

29. Ezekiel 22:26.

30. Ezekiel 22:25 and 28.

31. Ezekiel 22:29-31.

32. Jeremiah 5:30, 31, and 29.

33. Jeremiah 29:21-23.

34. Jeremiah 22:29 and 30.

CHAPTER III

1. The titles used for the interpreters:

(a) magicians, chartumim (scholars, scribes);

(b) astrologers, ashaphim (conjurors, chanters);

(c) sorcerers, choshiphim (magicians, sorcerers);

(d) Chaldeans, chasdim (priestly class of Chaldeans);

(e) astrologers, nahzreen (not included in this list).

See Keil, p. 88, and Leupold, pp. 84 and 85.

2. Who were the Chaldeans? Leupold quoting Haevernick, with approval:

"What is in itself more likely than that the Chaldeans as conquerors of Babylon made themselves masters of that group (Stand) that exercised the strongest influence in the state, the group to which the care of sacred things and of the very religion itself, was entrusted?"

Though this is conjecture, something of this sort must have happened, says Leupold. (Exposition of Daniel (Grand Rapids: Baker Book House, 1969), pp. 8485.)

3. Jeremiah6:14 and 8:11.

4. "The New York Inscriptionof Nebuchadnezzar II," Assyrian and Babylonian Literature.

5. The Grotefendinscription of Nebuchadnezzar II, quoted in Assyrian and Babylonian Literature, p. 150.

6. Why "God of heaven" rather than the covenant name "Jehovah"?

7. "Now Alexander, when he had taken Gaza, made haste to go up to Jerusalem; and Jaddua the high priest, when he heard that, was in an agony, and under terror, as not knowing how he should meet the Macedonians, since the king was displeased at his foregoing disobedience. He therefore ordained that the people should make supplications, and should join with him in offering sacrifice to God, whom he besought to protect that nation, and to deliver them from the perils that were coming upon them; whereupon God warned him in a dream, which came upon him after he had offered sacrifice, that he should take courage, and adorn the city, and open the gates; that the rest should appear in white garments, but that he and the priests should meet the king in the habits proper to their order, without the dread of any ill consequences, which the providence of God would prevent. Upon which, when he rose from his sleep, he greatly rejoiced, and declared to all the warning he had received from God. According to which dream he acted entirely, and so waited for the coming of the king.

"And when he understood that he was not far from the city, he went out in procession, with the priests and the multitude of the citizens. The procession was venerable, and the manner of it different from that of other nations. It reached to a place called Sapha, which name, translated into greek, signifies a prospect, for you have thence a prospect both of Jerusalem and of the temple.

"And when the Phoenicians and the Chaldeans that followed him thought they should have liberty to plunder the city, and torment the high priest to death, which the king's displeasure fairly promised them, the very reverse of it happened; for Alexander, when he saw the multitude at a distance, in white garments, while the priests stood clothed with fine linen, and the high priest in purple and scarlet clothing, with his mitre on his head, having the golden plate whereon the name of God was engraved, he approached by himself, and adored that name, and first saluted the high priest. The Jews also did all together, with one voice, salute Alexander, and encompass him about whereupon the kings of Syria and the rest were surprised at what Alexander had done, and supposed him disordered in his mind.

"However, Parmenio alone went to him, and asked him how it came to pass that, when all others adored him, he should adore the high priest of the Jews. To whom he replied, 'I did not adore him, but that God who hath honored him with his high priesthood; for I saw this very person in a dream, in this very habit, when I was at Dios in Macedonia, who, when I was considering with myself how I might obtain the dominion of Asia, exhorted me to make no delay, but boldly to pass over the sea thither, for that he would conduct my army, and would give me the dominion over the Persians; whence it is that, having seen no other in that habit, and now seeing this person in it, and remembering that vision, and the exhortation which I had in my dream, I believe that I bring this army under the divine conduct, and shall therewith conquer Darius, and destroy the power of the Persians, and that all things will succeed according to what is in my own mind.'

"And when he had said this to Parmenio, and had given the high priest his right hand, the priests ran along by him, and he came into the city. And when he went up into the temple, he offered sacrifice to God, according to the high priest's direction, and magnificently treated both the high priest and the priests. And when the Book of Daniel was showed him, wherein Daniel declared that one of the Greeks should destroy the empire of the Persians, he supposed that himself was the person intended." (Josephus, Antiquities of the Jews, Bk. XI, Ch. VIII, Paras. 4 and 5.)

8. Jeremiah 27:6-10.

9. For an excellent discussion of the symbolism, see: Robert Culver, Daniel and the Latter Days, pp. 118-121; Keil, Daniel Ch. II, pp. 103-107; J.F. Walvoord, Daniel: A Key to Prophetic Revelation, Ch. II (Moody Press, 1971), pp. 79-94.

10. With reference to the third empire, Jerome offers an interesting commentary. He says, ". . . and the third empire of bronze . . . shall rule over the entire earth. . . . This signifies the Alexandrian empire and that of the Macedonians, and of Alexander's successors. Now this is properly termed brazen,for among all the metals bronze possesses an outstanding resonance and a clear ring, and the blast of a brazen trumpet is heard far and wide, so that it signifies not only the fame and power of the empire but also the eloquence of the Greek language."

11. Scofield notes on Chapter 2, fn. 1 on verse 44.

12. Keil, p. 109 (see also Young, p. 77).

13. The following are true regarding this dream:

(a) This dream is unique and prophetic.

(b) No word in it could be construed to be of use to a people under persecution in the Maccabean age. There is no mention of Israel.

(c) It gives us the picture of a world in which gentile preeminence will continue until the God of heaven sets up a kingdom that shall never be destroyed, either an earthly or a heavenly one.

(d) The dream is apocalyptic; what will be, will be. There is no contingency and no appeal to action on the part of Israel.

(e) The kingdom set up by the God of heaven is not mentioned as being specifically Jewish, though to the Jewish mind, that might be implied.

(f) The dream has no word of condemnation for gentile oppression and no call to arms for a defense of the Torah, the temple or the Jewish way of life.

(g) On the other hand, the dream is a fitting answer to Nebuchadnezzar's hope of perpetual, universal sovereignty for his own dynasty.

(h) It emphasizes, however, the transitoriness of each gentile empire.

14. Ezekiel 40-48.

CHAPTER IV

1. Young, p. 85.

2. Herodotus,p. 67.

3. Montgomery, p. 90.

4. Boutflower, p. 246.

5. Pusey, p. 92.

6. Harrison, p. 1126. (For a list of Semitic words taken over into Greek, see Cambridge Ancient History, III, Ch. XI, VII, p. 249.)

7. M.A. Beek, Atlas of Mesopotamia (Nelson, 1962), p. 142.

8. Wiseman, pp. 36-37, 73.

9. "The East India House Inscription of Nebuchadnezzar II, King of Babylon (601-565 B.C.)," Assyrian and Babylonian Literature, p. 135.

10. "Inscription of Nabopolassar, King of Babylon (Hilprecht; 625-604 B.C.)," Assyrian and Babylonian Literature, p. 132.

11. "Indeed it is manifest on the face of the whole narrative that one great design, of all that occurred, was to proclaim the knowledge of the true God and to secure His recognition. That object was worthy of the divine interposition and the facts in the case show that God has power to induce princes and rulers to recognize His existence and perfections and His government over the earth." (Albert Barnes, Notes on the Old Testament: Daniel, Vol. II (Grand Rapids: Baker Book House, 1950), p. 28.

12. In his description of the building of the immense walls of Babylon, Herodotus fails to tell us what fuel was used to burn this immense number of bricks. He merely tells us they were burned, and modern excavations reveal that they were burned to a hardness comparable to the best modern brick. This necessitated, of course, an enormous amount of some kind of fuel. All the forests of Lebanon would hardly have sufficed, and the plains of Babylonia were practically treeless, except for date palms.

The only answer to the problem available at this distance in time would have to be the use of petroleum or asphalt. Perhaps both are included in the term "bitumen," which is the usual translation for the Semitic word translated "pitch." That such material was available, both ancient and modern authorities concur in affirming. Goodspeed writes the following:

"In both north and south (of Mesopotamia) a substance was found which made the region famous in the ancient world, this was bitumen. On the northern edge of the alluvium at the modern town of Hit, on the Euphrates were the renowned bitumen springs. A recent traveler describes them as follows:

'Directly behind the town are two springs within thirty feet of one another, from one of which flows hot water black with bitumen, while the other discharges intermittently bitumen, or, after a rain storm, bitumen and cold water . . . . where rock crops out in the plain about Hit they are full of seams of bitumen.' (Peters, Nippus 1, p. 160.)

"The less known bitumen wells of the north are on the plain east of the Tigres at the modern Karduk." (Goodspeed, A History of the Babylonians and the Assyrians, p. 11.)

We know that the walls of Babylon were cemented with this material which was undoubtedly asphalt or a heavy type of petroleum. It seems entirely possible that this might have been the material that also heated the kilns for burning the brick and, therefore, for heating the furnace for Meshach, Shadrach, and Abednego. Herodotus tells us that, in building the walls of Babylon, hot bitumen was used as a cement for the brick. He says:

"The bitumen used in the work was brought to Babylon from the Is, a small stream which flows into the Euphrates at the point where the city of the same name stands, eight days' journey from Babylon. Lumps of bitumen are found in great abundance in this river." (Herodotus, History, Bk. 1, p. 67.)

13. A Maccabean dating of this alleged pious fraud carries with it another incongruity; namely, the fact that the alleged hero of the story, Daniel, was not even present at this most unique and probably greatest of all Old Testament miracles and that minor characters, Shadrach, Meshach, and Abednego, were the heroes of this stupendous event. It would seem that anyone who had literary ability enough to fabricate a tale with such coherence and vividness would have been well advised to make Daniel the central figure. The overall effect of the chapter presents us with a reality of local color, psychological probability, and moral purpose that is difficult to reconcile with fiction. (See Appendix for list of objections to the Maccabean dating.)

14. Edersheim. Sir Robert Anderson says: "One point more. While books of great repute, such as Ecclesticus and 1 Maccabees, were absolutely excluded from the canon, and even canonical books, such as the book of Proverbs, Ecclesiastes and even Ezekiel, were challenged, the right of the book of Daniel to canonicity was never called in question in the Ancient Synagogue." (Robert Anderson, Daniel in the Critic's Den (London: James Nesbit and Co., 1909), p. 108.

15. C.S. Lewis in his book, Miracles, presents a philosophical defense of miracles that is most helpful.

16. Perhaps David Hume has put the question of miracles from the unbeliever's viewpoint most succinctly when he says:

"Miracles are violations of the laws of nature. But we learn from experience that the laws of nature are never violated. . . . For miracles we have the questionable testimony of a few persons . . . against them we have universal experience; therefore, this stronger testimony nullifies the weaker and more questionable."

We could put it in a different way: If a miracle happened, it didn't, because it couldn't since most people haven't seen miracles because they don't happen regularly. Furthermore, Hume's idea of universal experience has, a priori, left out that part of experience not shared by everyone must not be included, according to Hume, and it must happen regularly or on demand. The devil works his lying wonder on demand. God works according to His own righteous purpose, when and where He wills.

17. Christianity Today, Feb. 14, 1969.

18. The following appeal, in my opinion, is a reasonable statement of the facts pertinent to establishing the authenticity of this occurence:

a. The presence of the furnaces is entirely in keeping with the building operations of Nebuchadnezzar. It is not necessarily, at all, a normal mode of punishment.

b. The psychological fact of the jealous opposition of the Chaldean informers, given legal grounds for so doing.

c. The presence in Babylon of Greek influence is sufficient to account for the Greek names of musical instruments, if they were originally Greek (though such names do not in the least need to depend on local Greek influence).

d. The fact that names of musical instruments may have accompanied them to a new social environment without much cultural exchange, even though of foreign origin (the Greeks were in Babylon, then and earlier).

e. The political expedient of demanding religious unity as a means of producing political unity.

f. The presence of a few Persian words would be natural. In addition to the fact of common frontiers and political ties strengthened by inter-marriage between the two royal houses, there must have been also constant diplomatic exchange. Anyone at the center of government as was Daniel, would be likely to be at least tri-lingual. (Consider our modern use of such words as "detente," "politburo," and "fuehrer.") If Daniel wrote after 539, one wonders why there were not more Persian words and many more Greek ones.

Negative considerations:

a. The hero of the book is obviously Daniel. If the book is fictional, why was he not present as the hero?

b. In this chapter, there is no Palestinian local color, no slip of the pen, relating to the temple, no priest, and no prophet to invoke Jehovah's intercession, and no inadvertent reference to the Maccabean situation. As a pious fraud, it is badly staged.

c. Having created such heroic characters as Shadrach, Meshach, and Abednego as lay witnesses to Jehovah's faithfulness, why not use them as further participants and as examples of lay resistance to Greek persecution? The reader is referred to Sir Robert Anderson's The Silence of God.

19. The description of the apparel of these young men, as given in the Authorized Version, is clarified by Herodotus:

"The dress of the Babylonians is a linen tunic reaching to the feet, and above it another tunic made in wool, besides which they have a short white cloak thrown round them, and shoes of a peculiar fashion, not unlike those worn by the Boeotians. They have long hair, wear turbans on their heads, and anoint their whole body with perfumes. Everyone carries a seal, and a walking-stick, carved at the top into the form of an apple, a rose, a lily, an eagle, or something similar; for it is not their habit to use a stick without an ornament." (Herodotus. p. 73.)

20. C.S. Lewis, Miracles, pp. 107-110.

CHAPTER V

1. "As for Babylon, city of the great lord Marduk, his renowned city Imgur-Bel and Nimitti-Bel its great walls I completed at the entrances of the city gates, I built and stationed strong wild bulls of bronze and serpents standing erect, and what no former king had done the father my begetter, had thrown around the city the wall of its moat with bitumen and burnt brick and second time these mighty walls for the third time, the first joined with the second, I built with bitumen and burnt brick, and joined them to the wall which my father constructed, and laid their foundations in the bosom of the broad earth, and raised their battlements mountain high." ("Winckler Inscription of Nebuchadnezzar," Assyrian and Babylonian Literature (Appleton, 1901), pp. 144-145.

2. In addition to Nebuchadnezzar's tremendous fortifications, his devotion to things religious is shown by his building and restoration by 53 temples of the chief gods; 55 chapels to Marduk; 300 chapels to the earth deities; 600 for the minor heavenly deities; 180 altars to Ishtar; 180 for Nergal and Adad; and 12 for other gods. Above all, the restoration of the great temple of Marduk (1,500' x 1,800') and the great Ziggurat accompanying it.

We do not know the population of Nebuchadnezzar's Babylon, but such a large number of shrines and places of worship would seem to indicate a tremendous population, as well as a much more extended area for the city than some modern authors are willing to concede. For example, Martin Beek in his Atlas of Mesopotamia suggests a reconstruction of the city that approximates a plan of 1,000 yards and 1,500 yards, that is, less than a square mile in area; an area, by the way, that would hardly accommodate the temples and shrines mentioned, to say nothing at all about the population worshiping in them.Since Herodotus was an eyewitness of the city, and since he does not have to depend on hearsay, I think we can trust his testimony when he gives the description of the city as a square fifteen miles each way (1,200 stadia times 1,200 stadia).

3. Jeremiah 50:17.

4. Isaiah 47:6.

5. We have from Babylonian literature a prayer for a favorable dream:

"From my wickedness cause me to depart, and let me be saved by thee. Send unto me and let me behold a favorable dream. May the dream I behold be favorable, may the dream I behold be true. Turn the dream I behold into favor. May the god . . . the goddess of dreams stand at my head. Cause me to enter into Esagila, the temple of the gods, the house of life, unto Marduk, the merciful, commend me to his favorable hands for favor. So will I bow myself before thy greatness, will I glorify thy divinity. And the people of my city will praise thy power." (Quoted by King, First Steps in Assyrian, pp. 238-239, as quoted by R.W. Rogers in Cunieform Parallels to the Old Testament, pp. 185-186.)

6. Jeremiah 50:17, *"Israel is a scattered sheep; the lions have driven him away: first the king of Assyria hath devoured him; and last this Nebuchadnezzar king of Babylon hath broken his bones."*

7. Zechariah 2:8, *". . . for he that toucheth you toucheth the apple of His eye."*

8. "The new palace built by Nebuchadnezzar was prodigious in size, and superb in embellishments. Its outer wall embraces six miles; within that circumference were two other embattled walls, besides a great tower. Three brazen gates led into the grand area, and every gate of consequence throughout the city was of brass. The palace was splendidly decorated with statues of men and animals, with vessels of gold and silver, furnished with luxuries of all kings brought thither from conquests in Egypt, Palestine, and Tyre. Its greatest boast were the Hanging Gardens, which acquired, even from Grecian writers, the appellation of one of the wonders of the world.

"They are attributed to the gallantry of Nebuchadnezzar, who constructed them in compliance with a wish of his queen Amytis to possess elevated groves, such as she had enjoyed on the hills around her native Ecbatana. Babylon was all flat, and to accomplish so extravagant a desire, an artificial mountain was reared, four hundred feet on each side, while terraces, one above another, rose to a height that overtopped the walls of the city, that is, above three hundred feet in elevation.

"The ascent from terrace was made by corresponding flights of steps, while the terraces themselves were reared to their various stages on ranges of regular piers, which, formed a kind of vaulting, rose in succession one over the other to the required height of each terrace, the whole being bound together by a wall twenty-two feet in thickness. The level of each terrace or garden was then formed in the following manner: the tops of the piers were first laid over with flat stones, sixteen feet in length, and four in width; on these stones were spread beds of matting, then a thick layer of bitumen, after which came two courses of bricks, which were covered with sheets of solid lead.

"The earth was heaped on this platform, and in order to admit the roots of large trees, prodigious hollow piers were built and filled with mold. From the Euphrates, which flowed close to the foundation water was drawn up by machinery. The whole, says Q. Curtius (v. 5), had, to those who saw it from a distance, the appearance of wood overhanging mountains." (Barnes, Daniel, I, pp.265-266.)

9. Herodotus, Bk. 1, pp. 68-69.

10. J.C. Coleman, Abnormal Psychology and Modern Life, 2d ed. (Scott Foresman and Co., 1956), p. 289.

11. Ibid., p. 297.

12. Rosen and Gregory, Abnormal Psychology, p. 290.

13. Harrison, pp. 1116-1117.

14. Rawlinson says,

"Berosus appears to have kept silence on the subject of Nebuchadnezzar's mysterious malady ... It was not to be expected that the native writer would tarnish the glory of his country's greatest monarch by any mention of an affliction which was of so strange and debasing a character. Nor is it at all certain that he would be aware of it. As Nebuchadnezzar outlived his affliction and was again 'established in his kingdom,' all monuments belonging to the time of his malady would have been subject to his own revision, and if any record of it was allowed to descend to posterity, care would have been taken that the truth was not made too plain, by couching the record in sufficiently ambiguous phraseology.

"Berosus may have read, without fully understanding it, a document which has descended to modern times in a tolerably complete condition and which contained an illusion to the fact that the great king was for a time incapacitated for the discharge of the royal functions. In the inscription known as the 'Standard Inscriptions' of Nebuchadnezzar, the monarch himself related that during some considerable time, four years apparently, all his great works were at a stand: 'he did not build high places, he did not offer his sacrifice, he did not keep up the works of irrigation.'

"The cause of this suspension, at once, of religious worship and work of utility is stated in the document in phrases of such obscurity as to be unintelligible. Until, therefore, a better explanation is offered, it cannot but be regarded as at least highly probable that the passage in question contains the royal version of that remarkable story with which Daniel concludes his notice of the great Chaldean sovereign." (George Rawlinson, Historical Evidences of the Truth of the Scripture Records (Boston: Gould & Lincoln, 1868), pp. 136-137.)

15. Rawlinson, p. 133.

16. Goodspeed, pp. 342-343.

17. Wiseman, pp. 43-47. Other dates, commonly accepted. See New Bible Dictionary, Douglas, p. 873.

CHAPTER VI

1. "The Stele of Nabonidus," Assyrian and Babylonian Literature, pp. 159-160.

2. "Annals of Nabonidus," Assyrian and Babylonian Literature, pp. 168-169.

3. Harrison, p. 1120.

4. J. Finegan,Light From the Ancient Past, pp. 189-190.

5. Koldeway, The Excavations in Babylon (Macmillan, 1914), pp. 103-104.

6. Ibid., p. 104.

7. Josephus, Bk. X, Ch. XI, Para 2.

8. Ibid., Ch. XII, Para. 2.

9. Amytis, Nebuchadnezzar's wife, must have been a very exalted and beloved person. Even kings do not build Hanging Gardens indiscriminately. (See the case of Artemisia, where a queen built for a beloved husband, a tomb reckoned as a wonder of the world; the Mausoleum of Halicarnassus.)

10. Barnes remarks that Daniel seems to have been forgotten and his talents and former services seem to have passed from the recollection of those in power. It is true that Daniel gives us no slightest hint of the succeeding reigns of Avil Marduk, Nerglissor, Labashi Marduk, or Nabonidus; no record, in fact, of the change in Jehoiachin's fortune when Avil Marduk "lifted up his head" causing him to eat at the royal table.

The historical and biographical gap between Chapters 4 and 5 is complete except for the hints given us in Chapter 8 where, in the third year of Belshazzar, we find him at Shushan, the palace in the province of Elam over two hundred miles to east, and the item in Chapter 5 of his being apparently unknown to Belshazzar. The events in this gap of fourteen years or so, apparently are not significant to the purpose of Daniel's narrative. He does not explain his apparent loss of personal status, possibly even banishment. He apparently is not dismissed from the civil service.

11. Young, p. 126.

12. Josephus, Bk. X, Ch. XI, Para. 4.

13. Isaiah 47:5-6.

14. Isaiah 47:10, 12-13.

15. Goodspeed, pp. 374-375.

16. "Annals of Nabonidus," Assyrian and Babylonian Literature, p. 170.

17. See also Dionysius of Halicarnassus (Bk. 1. 1), Ctesias (2:5), Diodorus (11. 34), and other late writers who seem to get their information from Herodotus. Xenophon apparently does not depend on Herodotus but on Persian sources.

CHAPTER VII

1. Josephus says (Bk. X, Ch. 11, Para. 4): "Now after a little while, both himself (i.e., Belshazzar) and the city were taken by Cyrus the king of Persia who fought against him; for it was Baltasar, under whom Babylon was taken when he had reigned seventeen years, and this is the end of the posterity of king Nebuchadnezzar, as history informs us, but when Babylon was taken by Darius, and when he, with his kinsman Cyrus had put an end to the dominion of the Babylonians, he was sixty-two years old. He was the son of Astyages and had another name among the Greeks. Moreover he took Daniel the prophet and carried him with him into Media and honored him very greatly, and kept him with him; for he was one of the three presidents whom he set over his three hundred and sixty provinces, for unto so many did Darius part them."

The discrepancy in the number of provinces by Josephus does not necessarily impugn the accuracy of either author. It is possible that Daniel is discussing the divisions or satrapies of the newly conquered territory while Josephus refers to the empire as a whole. Another possibility is that Daniel's account is correct for the whole empire for that time (539 B.C.), and Josephus' account refers to subsequent records when the number of provinces was increased threefold.

2. It is probably a lie (unless this group is made up of Babylonians only and refers only to the reorganization of the conquered territory) because in spite of any and all false rumors spread by Daniel's enemies, it is hardly possible that satraps have a complete unanimity on any matter. That men old enough and experienced enough to be chosen as governors should be unacquainted with the possibilities of intrigue inherent in so preposterous a decree is most unlikely.

It may be significant that whereas the conspirators say "all," the rest of the record does not say all, but says "these men." The picture that we seem to get from the record is that of a well organized minority, moved by envy and able to play upon the envy of others but having also the deeper motives of religious antagonism not necessarily shared by the others.

If we may believe Herodotus when he says: "The customs which I know the Persians to observe are the following. They have no images of the gods, no temples or altars, and consider the use of them the sign of folly. This comes, I think, from their not believing the gods to have the same nature with men, as the Greeks imagine. Their wont, however, is to ascend the summits of the loftiest mountains, and there to offer sacrifice to Jupiter, which is the name they give to the whole circuit of the firmament. They likewise offer to the sun and the moon, to the earth, to fire, to water and to the winds."

This is somewhat at variance with the possibility of a complete monotheism, or even a dualism, but might be as close as polytheist could come to an understanding of nonpolytheistic religious practices.

3. This scene could have taken place in Babylon and Daniel's removal to Ecbatana (Ackmetha) might well have come later. While there is nothing in the chapter that could with certainty place the occurrence in either place, the conspiracy and the conduct of the conspirators smells of Babylon, and the priests of Marduk. The venom, the unanimity of the conspirators, the familiarity with Daniel's character and habits do not fit into a situation where there is a heterogeneous and newly formed officialdom for a newly reorganized empire and in a strange setting. Here we have at least a core of conspirators rather sure of themselves.

4. Perhaps we should consider what is involved a little more particularly. All told, from four to five hundred persons might have been thrown to the lions: men, women, and children (120 satraps, if all 120 were found guilty, with at least one wife and several children for each). Is this just? In answer, we must of course say that we do not have to defend Persian justice, and the book of Daniel does not try to, but consider the following:

(a) An innocent man has been framed and his murder attempted, a man of vice-regal standing.

(b) A king has been deceived and made to look foolish.

(c) The men who engineered this coup d'etat were to be put in charge of the lives and fortunes of millions. If they would so treat a man like Daniel, innocent by their own confession, what about their abuse of power later toward people more helpless within their satrapies?

(d) According to oriental ideas of justice, their families should not be publicly supported nor allowed the opportunity to retaliate for the death of their husbands and fathers.

(e) The greater the status of the criminal, the greater the crime and the greater the punishment because of his great opportunity for evil.

5. In contrast to the polytheism of Babylonian pronouncements in Chapters 2, 3, 4, and 5 of Daniel, there is no overt polytheism in Chapter 6. While Darius does not actually identify himself with Daniel's God, he does express confidence in His ability to deliver (verses 16, 20, 26, 27). Instead of saying He is a God of gods, he says He is the living God and stedfast forever.

This makes us wonder if the original basic monotheism of Zoroaster had already become a force in Persian society. If so, it might explain the generally good relations between Israel and the Persian government. If this view seems to be invalidated by the Cyrus cylinder, in which Cyrus seems to give praise and preeminence to Marduk, god of Babylon, the answer is an appeal to common sense. Does anyone really think that Cyrus, the Persian, really worshipped the gods of Babylon? The cylinder proclamation is cast in the language of official Babylon and probably permitted by a Cyrus who is tolerant of other religions. But the language and mode of expression is Babylonian and priestly from start to finish, in every way similar in religious tone to the Nabonidus stele.

Haug tells us: "Spitana Zarathustra's conception of Ahura Mazda as the supreme being is perfectly identical with the notion of Elohim (God) or Jehovah which we find in the Old Testament. Ahura Mazda is called by him 'creator of the earthly and spiritual life, the Lord of the whole universe in whose hands are all the creatures,' he is in possession of all good things spiritual and wordly, such as the good mind (vohu mano), immortality (amerated), health (haurvated), the best truth (asha valushta), devotion and piety (armasiti) and abundance of every good (khshathra vairya)." (Martin Haug, Essay on the Religion of the Parsees, Trubner OrientalSeries (London: Kegan Paul, Trench and Co.Ltd., 1878), p. 302.)

Whether this is entirely accurate or not, the subsequent dualism of this Persian religion is not too incompatible with monotheism. At least it is not polytheism.

6. Josephus, Bk. X, Ch. 11. 7, p. 370.

7. There are no names given us in Scripture of either the three presidents, other than Daniel's, or of any of the satraps. We have the following, however, from the Cyropedia, which gives a little of the organization of the empire but does not include Gubaru mentioned as satrap. It does give the names of other satraps chosen by Cyrus: "And then he (Cyrus) chose out from the number of his friends whom he saw eager to go on the conditions named and who seemed to him best qualified, and sent them as satraps to the following countries: Megabyzus to Arabia, Artabatas to Cappadocia, Artacamas to Phrygia Major, Crysantas to Lydia and Ionia, Adusius to Caria (it was he for whom the Carians had petitioned) and Pharnuchus to Aeolia and Phrygia and the Hellespont. He sent out no Persians as satraps over Cilicia or Cyprus, or Paphlagonia because these he thought joined his expedition against Babylon voluntarily; he did however require even these nations to pay tribute." (Cyropedia, VII, VI, 7.)

It is difficult to think of Xenophon going to the trouble (and danger) of manufacturing the names and assignment of all these satraps; i.e., danger of being discredited by those familiar with Persian history.

8. Haug, p. 299. On no circumstances can we assign him (i.e., Spitama Zarathushtra) a later date than 1000 B.C., and one may even find reasons for placing his era much earlier and making him a contemporary of Moses.

9. Boutflower, p. 130.

10. The following lines in Aeschylus, quoted by Barnes, seem to imply:

(a) That sovereignty of Persia came through two Median rulers directly to Cyrus;

(b) that this sovereignty did not involve joint rule or the conquest of Media by Cyrus;

(c) the picture of Cyaxeres, if he is the son referred to, is not that of a man ruled by his passions for, "whose reason was the helmsman to his spirit." The quotation is from The Persians, translated by S.G. Benardete.

"First was Medus leader of the host; next his son fulfilled the office well, whose reason was the helmsmen to his spirit; third was Cyrus, fortunate, whose rule brought peace to all."

Since Aeschylus lived in the last quarter of the sixth century, not far removed in time from the events, he writes as if to an audience familiar with the situation. If Astyages and Cyaxeres were not the Medes referred to, who else? His king list subsequent to Cyrus is correct, so we may assume his accuracy of that preceding Cyrus.

11. "Now when Cyaxeres heard of the plot and of the war like preparations of the nations allied against him, without delay he made what counter preparations he could himself and also sent to Persia both to the general assembly and to his brother-in-law, Cambyses, who was king of Persia and he sent word to Cyrus too, asking him to try to come as commander of the men, in case the Persian state should send any troops. . . . for Cyrus had by this time completed his ten years among the youths also and was now in the class of mature men. So Cyrus accepted the invitation and the elders in council chose him commander of the expedition to Media." (Cyropaedia, Bk. 1, V, 2, Loeb Cl. Lib., p. 77.)

12. Wiseman has this to say: "Nabonidus had won his own way, but not for long. 'The King of the Medes' in the tenth year of Nabonidus' reign can be no other than Cyrus the Persian for he had incorporated in the Province of Media in what became the greater province of Persia. We know that at the end of our seventy year period, in 539, Cyrus captured Babylon; both Nabonidus and Belshazzar died soon after the fall of the city and the Babylonian empire passed under the sway of the Acheamenian rulers. It now seems that in Babylonia, Cyrus used the title 'King of the Medes' in addition to the more usual 'King of Persia, King of Babylonia, King of the lands.' On the other hand, according to the book of Daniel, the conqueror of Babylon was an elderly Median named Darius who succeeded Belshazzar.

"The biblical text, if you remember, says: 'So this Daniel prospered in the reign of Darius, and in the reign of Cyrus the Persian.' There is no place in Babylonian or Persian history for any such predecessor of Cyrus, and attempts to identify this 'Darius' have been a source of controversy for years. In fact, the majority of scholars doubt his historicity. But this new text reopens the whole question. Is it too bold an hypothesis to suggest that the 'King of the Medes' of our Babylonian text may prove to be the 'Darius the Mede' of Daniel's day? Cyrus, at the age of 62, might well have taken another name as the king of the Medes and even have been the son of Ahasuerus, as was the biblical 'Darius' so obscure is his ancestry. The biblical reference can as easily be translated 'Daniel prospered in the reign of Darius, even in the reign of Cyrus the Persian.' ("The Identity of Darius," Christianity Today, Nov. 25, 1957.) Wiseman's reference is to a passage on Nabonidus Stele, where he is made to say that at the end of ten years' absence at Tema his subjects in Babylon were reconciled to doing the gods' will" (i.e., as seen by Nabonidus).

13. It will be seen then that Whitcomb, Boutflower, Wiseman, and of course Keil assume the integrity of the Scripture record. The point at issue being, in part, the equivalent name to Darius, the Mede. Rowley does not so assume and pins his faith to secular records, as he interprets them, as having at least the weight of greater numbers and hence greater authority. He seems, also, to have an uncritical faith in such records, investing them with an infallibility they do not deserve. He seems to make insufficient allowance for bias on the part of his authorities, not questioning the adequacy of their sources and not allowing for partisan editing.

14. Xenophon goes into the reorganization of Babylonian affairs after the conquest of the city, at great length and in great detail. He pictures Cyrus as accomplishing this before going back to Persia to make his report to his father, King Cambyses, and to the Persian elders. The reorganization, which he mistakenly attributes to Cyrus, could have been that carried out by Cyaxeres; i.e., Darius, and could have been subject to the same inaccuracies and due to the same misinformation that is so very obvious in his description of the means by which Babylon was taken. We merely substitute the name Darius for that of Cyrus. Cyrus has come back, and his father has called together the Persian elders and speaks to them:

"Then Cambyses assembled the Persian elders and the highest of the chief magistrates; he called in Cyrus also and then addressed them as follows: 'Toward you, my Persian friends, I cherish, as is natural, feelings of goodwill, for I am your king; and no less toward you, Cyrus, for you are my son. . . . For as long as I live, the Persian throne continues to be mine own. But when I am dead, it will of course pass to Cyrus, if he survives me.'"

In verse 28 of the same passage, we have further confirmation of Cyrus's relationship to Darius:

"When, on his way back he came to Media, Cyrus wedded the daughter of Cyaxeres, for he had obtained the consent of his father and mother. And to this day people still tell of her wonderful beauty. (But some historians say that he married his mother's sister. But that maid must certainly have been a very old maid.) And when he was married he at once departed with his bride for Babylon." (Xenophon, Cyropaedia, Ch. VIII, vs. 21-28, Loeb Cl. Lib., Vol. II, tr. by Walter Miller.)

15. Keil, pp. 198-199. Keil notes the marked agreement between Daniel and Xenophon. Since there is no likelihood of collaboration between these two men, nor likelihood that they appeal to the same sources, it is logical to assume that here we do not have an accidental agreement but that both must refer to the same factual material, that of Daniel being a firsthand experience and that of Xenophon filtering down through Persian sources.

16. See Keil, p. 198. ("The supposition, however, that Darius reigned for two years over Babylon is correct. For the Babylonian kingdom was also destroyed sixty-eight years after the commencement of the exile. Since, then, the seventy years of the exile were completed in the first year of Cyrus (II Chron.XXXVI. 22f.; Ezra 1.1), it follows that Cyrus became king two years after the overthrow of Babylon and thus after Darius had reigned two years.")

17. Albert Barnes gives us the following explanation: "The authority of Xenophon, who not only says that a Cyaxeres ascended the throne after Astyages, but that he was the son of Astyages (Cyropaedia, 1, 5, 2) and besides relates so much of this Cyaxeres(1, 4, 7; 111, 3, 20; VIII, 5, 19) that his Cyropaedia may be regarded as in a measure a history of him. Yea, Xenopon goes so far (VIII, 7, 1) that he recounts the years of the reign of Cyrus from the Cyaxeres II. Can anyone conceive a reason why Xenophon had a motive to weave together such an issue of falsehood as this, unless Cyaxeres II actually lived? If one should object, indeed, that he is so far to be reckoned among fictitious writers that he gives a moral character to the subjects on which he writes, and that he has passed over the differences between Cyrus and his grandfather Astyages, yet there is no reason why he should have brought on the stage so important a person wholly from fiction, as Cyaxeres. What a degree of boldness it must have required, if he, who lived not much more than a century after the events recorded, had mentioned to his contemporaries so much respecting a prince of whom no one whatever had even heard." (Albert Barnes, Daniel, Bk. II, pp. 8-10.)

18. "Xenophon, although writing a historical novel, may very possibly (like the great modern writers of 'the historical novel') have, in great points, known the historical truth and adhered to it. . . . But when almost all Herodotus' account of Cyrus is embellishment, and the evident object of Xenophon is to adorn his hero, they have no authoritative weight for any statement, unless they are supported from without. Probably those who quote Herodotus so freely against Holy Scripture would be surprised, if they made clear to themselves, what an almost nothing they themselves believe of the account which they so employ. He needs to be confirmed by Holy Scripture, not Holy Scripture by him." (Pusey, p. 159.)

19. Herodotus, p. 28.

20. Herodotus, p. 51.

21. Barnes, Vol, II, p. 8.

22. Writers from whom Josephus quotes:

(A) Acusilaus, Agatharchides, Alexander Bala, Alexander the Great (Epistle), Alexander Polyhistor, Andreas, Antiochus the Great (Epistle), Apion, Appolodorus, Aristeas, Aristophanes.

(B) Berosus.

(C) Caesar (Augustus), Caesar (Julius), Caerilus, Castor, Chaermon, Clearchus, Cleodemus.

(D) Demetrius (king), Diocles, Dius.

(E) Ephorus, Eupolemus.

(H) Hecateus, Helenicus, Hieronymus, Hermogenes, Herodots, Herod's Commentaries, Hesoid,He stiaeus, Homer, Hypsecrates.

(L) Lysimachus.

(M) Malchus, Manetho, Megasthenes, Menander, Mnaseas, Mochus.

(N) Nickolas of Damascus.

(O) Onias.

(P) Pausanias, Philostratus, Photius, Polybius, Posidonius, Ptolemy Lagi, Pyphagoras.

(S) Sothrabazanes, Strabo.

(T) Theodotus, Theophilus, Theophrastus, Timagenes, Titus Livius.

(Z) Zophyrion.

Fifty-eight authorities quoted by name. In addition, Josephus quotes numerous decrees, public documents, archives, and letters, including Cyrus's letters to Sissines, the Tyrian archives, etc. No one has yet accused Josephus of an injudicious use of his numerous sources. (Whiston, ed., pp. 1014-1020.)

23. Cyrus calls himself king of Babylon in the Cyrus Cylinder, but since Darius reigned only two years, it is possible that this tablet might have been inscribed after Darius' death. "I am Cyrus the king of the world, the great king, the powerful king, king of Babylon, King of Sumer and Akkad, king of the four quarters (of the world), son of Cambyses, the great king, king Anshan; grandson of Cyrus the great king, king of Ansham; great grandson of Teispis the great king, king of Anshan, of ancient seed royal." (Assyrian and Babylonian Literature, pp. 172-173.)

24. Barnes sums up the evidence for the correctness of Daniel's reference to Darius by quoting the following:

a. Xenophon, Cyropedia (I. 4. 7; III. 3. 20; I. 5. 28; VIII. 5. 19).

b. Aeschylus, Persae (VS 762).

c. Josephus, Antiquities (X. 11. 4).

d. Abydenus, quoting Megisthenes, who speaks of a Mede who in connection with a Persian overthrew the Babylonian kingdom.

e. Jeremiah, who threatens the Jews with punishment by a Median king (Jeremiah 51 :11, 28).

f. Isaiah, who says Chaldea will be destroyed by the Medes (Isaiah 13:17-18).

g. Isaiah, in extolling Cyrus, makes only obscure mention of his taking Babylon (Isaiah 44:28; 45:1-4).

With all these straws in the wind, with hints from four secular sources and from three biblical prophetic writings, there is a tremendous burden of proof required for those who would reject Daniel's plain statement. In light of the fact that so many so-called biblical, historical inaccuracies have, in the long run, been shown to be our own momentary ignorance, we must reject out of hand those who would question Daniel's statements. (See Albert Barnes, Vol. II, pp. 8-10, with reference to Chapter 6.)

CHAPTER VIII

1. We may think it strange that America, who thinks of herself as a super power and, presently, has so large a part in world affairs, should have no easily discernible place in prophecy, while we postulate in the prophetic picture England, Russia, and Arab states, and the revived Roman empire. Even though America's place in the present power struggle should later be relegated to a second or third rating, the very bulk of her population should entitle her to some mention. Even more, her significance as the home of nearly half the Jews in the world, as well as America's rather consistent support of Israel's claims to nationhood in the land, should at least give her honorable mention.

The answer seems to be that only as America is included in some total ethnic picture; that is, as a part of the English speaking world symbolized by the first beast, can she be included. As to our present importance, we need only to remember that it took England (an empire on which the sun never set) just one generation to lose her position as mistress of the seas and to become a second rate power. One generation could do for America what it did for England.

2. Keil, Daniel, p. 245.

3. Modern nations, not ancient nations (with the exception of Rome whose battle insignia were the eagles). Perhaps it is the modern nations of which Daniel is speaking.

4. Barnes, Vol. II, pp. 40-42.

5. However, we do not know in terms of absolute chronology whether Belshazzar was co-regent with his father near the beginning of his reign in 554 B.C. or whether this date indicates Belshazzar's complete charge of affairs in Babylon when, in the seventh year of his reign Nabonidus, his father, was reigning in, and rebuilding Tema (552 B.C.), in which case the date might be as late as 549 B.C.

6. Assyrian and Babylonian Literature.

7. "I set in place in their gates the cedar doors, with a sheathing of copper, the thresholds and the hinges made of bronze. I stationed at their thresholds strong wild bulls of bronze and serpents standing erect." ("India House Inscriptions," Assyrian and Babylonian Literature, p. 139.)

8. As for the lion as a symbol of Nebuchadnezzar (Jeremiah 4:7), we should remember that Nebuchadnezzar is dead, and this passage is a prophecy of the future. In Jeremiah 50:44, Babylon is referred to as a lion, but this is not a characteristic name.

9. The exception to the lenient treatment of the Jews by the Persian government occurred in the reign of Artaxerxes II (or III). A Jewish rebel-

lion was put down with great severity by the Persian general, Bagoses. The occasion for this severity was due to the high priest, John, who slew his brother, Jesus, in the temple, following which the Persian general, a friend of Jesus, entered the temple and punished the Jews seven years for the murder of Jesus. (Josephus, Bk. XI, VII, 1.) The episode given in the book of Esther was initiated by Haman, the Agagite, not by a Persian.

10. A serious objection to equating the first beast with the British commonwealth is the fact that England was once a part of the Roman empire, and, as we noted elsewhere, it continued to be Roman up to 395 A.D., possibly even to the breaking up of the empire (476 A.D.). The question is, How could the first beast be both a separate kingdom and a part of the fourth kingdom? The problem becomes more difficult when we view the current situation. The news media tells us that England has already joined the European common market, most of whose nations were once a part of the Roman empire. One is tempted to see this economic hegemony as a preliminary step to a political union later to be subject to the Antichrist.

There are five possible answers:

a. There is a possibility that England may subsequently withdraw from this common market or never actually join any political confederation, finding that she has more to lose than to gain. There is a great deal of opposition already in England, and the British have political traditions which they might not be willing to forego for the economic advantage obtained.

b. While the present special relations that she has with the United States seem about to vanish, at least temporarily, she may find that her commonwealth ties and the other advantages of the alliance cannot be thrown off so easily.

c. There is the third consideration, namely, that no other nation or peoples so nearly fits the description of the first beast, and, as we have already said, it is not necessary to consider the revived Roman empire as occupying the largest area of the first, merely that the core and organizational center be involved.

d .While Britain was once Romanized, succeeding Teutonic invaders so changed the cultural outlook and customs that England has never truly been a part of Western Europe in the same sense that France or Spain or even Germany have been.

e. Since all of these nations, as represented by the four beasts, are extant at the coming of Messiah, our solution must be in terms of the present and future national groups rather than nations existing in the past.

11. It would be difficult to include America in the picture of the first beast, even though at one time it was a part of the British empire, except for its involvement with Israel. Of the fourteen million Jews in the world, six million are citizens of this country. No other country has so large a Jewish population, and in no other country has there been less overt

anti-Semitism of a serious kind (the Ku Klux Klan got nowhere in its attempt). American Jews have, in the main, found more economic, educational, civic, and religious elbow room than most other countries. One could argue that with nearly half the world's Jewish population, with the real concern we have for the preservation of the Jewish state, and with our somewhat uncertain, but real, political backing, we might also be involved in this first beast.

12. The Gulag Archapelago by Solzhenitsyn spells out the terrible reality of the statement.

13. Part of the difficulty seems to lie in our failure to see the numbers involved; i.e., three ribs in the mouth of the bear, and later the number of wings and heads of the leopard could at some future time change to other numbers through consolidation of kingdoms.

14. Some writers on eschatology assume the revival of the Roman Empire to involve only its western half and look to find all ten toes in that western half. In Daniel, Chapter 2, there are two legs and two feet and ten toes, and while the ten toes are not specifically allocated five to each foot, that would be the natural inference. Historically, the Roman Empire as of the date 395 A.D. has the following dioceses, organized into four prefectures:

Western	Eastern
1.Britain	1.Egypt, with Libya
2.Gaul	2.The Orient, Palestine,
3.Spain	Pheonicia, Transjordan
4.Italy (north), with	3.Pontus (East Turkey)
Switzerland, Austria	4.Asia, West Turkey
5.Italy (south)	5.Thrace
6.Africa(from Libya west)	6.Macedonia
7.Pannonia(Austria,part)	7.Greece, Thessaly
Jugoslavia, Hungary	

If the ten heads and ten toes are to be ten kingdoms in the Roman Empire, we are confronted with the question as to whether or not these dioceses or kingdoms are to be consolidated into five each, or if they are to be eliminations, either east or west. If eliminations are to be made, are they subtracted equally? If the third beast involves part of the eastern kingdom that is part of the Islamic territories (as we shall explain later), that is, unequally, then it would seem that our interpretation must depend upon whether the revived empire is to be taken in its greatest extent or whether only the core of its holdings is involved. For the boundaries of the Roman Empire, east and west, varied significantly at various times, from Augustus to 476 A.D. in the west and from Constantine to 1453 A.D. in the east.

However, our problem is greatly simplified if we do not have to allocate these areas to ten kings (Revelation 17:12) and take the minimal extent of the two halves of the Roman Empire.

15. William Kelly, Biblical Commentary on the Book of Daniel (New York: Loizeaux Brothers, 1943), p. 128.

16. James Bonnzar, The Great Interregnum (Glasgow: Hugh Hopkins, 1871), pp. 27 and 28.

17. Sir Robert Anderson, The Coming Prince (Grand Rapids: Kregel, 1954), pp. 274-276.

18. Young, p. 75.

19. As we sum up the reasons for designating the third beast as some portion of the Arab world, we have on the positive side:

a.The tradtional ethnic enmity of the Arab nations toward Israel and the feeling of having wrongly been deprived of the land of Palestine.

b.The geographic proximity of these nations.

c.The fact that the clash of interests is likely to continue indefinitely.

The nation of Israel cannot only not forego her living space, but she has biblical grounds for not doing so. Contrariwise, Arabian enmity has become so fixed a psycholigical condition that no national leader is likely to resist the temptation to use it as a plea for leadership. Only a miracle of grace could change the situation. It would not change by another Arab defeat and certainly not with an Israeli defeat, in case the issue should be left to a decision by war.

CHAPTER IX

1. Of the eleven Hebrew words translatable as *"prince,"* the one that could indicate his office as priest,or Cohen, is not used. Therefore, though Cohen is used only twice to mean prince (II Samuel 8:18 and I Chronicles 27:5), it would, nevertheless, have been appropriate to have used this term if Onias, the high priest, had been meant in the phrase *"prince of the host."* Instead, the usual term, *sar,* is the term used.

Also, the high priest did not have an army, and *"host"* is not the proper designation for a nation. The word, *tsabah,* has military connotations, while the word for "nation" or *"people"* would be, preferably *lohm.* (See Girdlestone, Old Testament Synonyms (Grand Rapids: Assoc. Publishers & Authors, Inc., 1897), pp. 257-259.

2. Barnes, p. 108.

3. Walvoord, pp. 185-186.

4. Keil, p. 297.

5. Keil says, appropos of this clause, "The horn also overthrew the place of the sanctuary of Jehovah: to cast away, to cast forth; used of buildings, to lay waste." (Keil, p. 298.)

6. Young, p. 178.

7. Walvoord, p. 195.

8. Keil, p. 317.

9. S.P. Tregelles, Remarks on the Prophetic Visions in the Book of Daniel (London:The Sovereign Grace Advent Testimony, 1965), p. 83.

10. Louis T. Talbot, The Prophecies of Daniel, p. 143.

11. Kelly, p. 152.

12. J.D. Pentecost, Prophecy for Today, p. 83.

13. Kelly, p. 148. Notes on Daniel.

14. It is impossible to equate the 2,300 days of Daniel 8:14 with what Josephus has to say concerning the descration of the temple and the altar, so that, whatever it means, it cannot refer to that incident. Josephus says (Bk. XII, Ch. VII, Para. 6): "Now it so fell out, that these things were done on the very same day on which their divine worship had fallen off, and was reduced to a profane and common use, after three years' time; for so it was that the temple was made desolate by Antiochus, and so continued for three years. . . . and this desolation came to pass according to the prophecy of Daniel which was given 408 years before; for he declared that the Macedonians would dissolve that worship (for some time)." Three years; i.e., 360 days times three equals 1,080 days.

15. Walvoord, p. 196.

16. Andersons, The Coming Prince, p. 42.

17. *'pahlah'*, wonderful, marvelous, extraordinary, beyond one's power.

CHAPTER X

1. Young, p. 185.

2. Keil, pp. 342-343.

3. If Messiah's temple (Zechariah 6:12) is the one described by Ezekiel Chapters 40 to 48, it and its environs are too extensive to be located on Mount Moriah, over one mile square. The great earthquake described by Zechariah 12:4-5 would, and does, change the topography of the whole city, making it seems, a plateau much more commodious for a larger city. This is, at least one reason why the third temple will have to be different from Messiah's temple. The intervening earthquake destroys the one and makes room for the other. On the other hand, if Ezekiel is to be taken literally, and why not, this fourth temple will not be located in Jerusalem at all but in the midst of the Oblation (Eze. 45:1) at or near the old site of Shiloh, or 12 to 15 miles north of Jerusalem. See Larkin, C.

4. Culver, pp. 156-157.

5. Jerome, Commentary of Daniel, tr. by Gleason Archer (Grand Rapids: Baker Book House, 1958), p. 95.

6. Anderson, The Coming Prince, Preface v-vii.

7. The phrase "seventy weeks" is literally seventy sevens (shavium shivim). "The special account of the contents of the weeks can be adjusted with the year week alone; and the half week, verse 27, particularly appears to be identical in actual time with these three and a half times (years)," Ch. VII.25 (Keil, Daniel, p. 338).

"The overwhelming consensus of scholarship, however, agrees that the time unit should be considered years" (Walvoord, Daniel, p. 218).

8. Sir Robert Anderson in the Coming Prince, pp. 128-129 footnote, relates: "The 1st Nissan is the twentieth year of Artaxerxes (the edict to rebuild Jerusalem) and was 14th March, B.C. 445. The 10th Nissan in Passion Week (Christ's entry into Jerusalem) was 6th April, A.D.32. The intervening period was 476 years and 24 days (the days being reckoned inclusively, as required by the language of the prophecy and in accordance with the Jewish practice).

But 476 X 365 equals	173,740 days
Add 14 March to 6th April, both inclusive	24 days
Add for leap years	116 days
	173,880 days

Add 69 weeks of prophetic years of 360 days (69 X 7 X 360) and it equals 173,880 days.

It may be well to offer here two explanatory remarks. First: in reckoning years from B.C. to A.D., one year must always be omitted; for it is obvious, ex.gr., that from B.C. 1 to A.D. 1 was not two years but one year. B.C. 1 ought to be described as B.C. 0, and it is so reckoned by astronomers who would describe the historical date B.C. 445 as 444 (see note previous).

And secondly, the Julian year is 11m. 10.46s. or about 129th part of a day longer than the mean solar year. The Julian calendar, therefore, contains three leap years too many in four centuries, an error which had amounted to eleven days in A.D. 1752 when our English calendar was corrected by declaring the 3rd September to be the 14th September and by introducing the Gregorian reform which reckons three secular years out of four as common years; ex.gr., 1700, 1800 and 1900 are common years and 2000 is a leap year. "Old Christmas Day" is still marked in our calendars and observed in some localities on the 6th January and to this day the calendar remains uncorrected in Russia.

9. For a more detailed critical examination of Daniel 9:24-27, the reader is referred to the excellent following works: Culver, Daniel and the Latter Days, IV, pp. 135-160; McClain, Daniel's Prophecy of the Seventy Weeks; Sir Robert Anderson, The Coming Prince; Walvoord, Daniel, Chapter Nine. All of the above commentators are premillenial in their outlook.

10. Keil, p. 360, Op. cit.

11. The New York Times Almanac of 1970, page 722 says, "Very rough estimates indicate that since 1900, more than $4,000 billion have been spent on wars and military preparedness. If the current level of military spending should continue, this total will be doubled in twenty years. If the recent rate of increase in military spending continues, the arms race will consume another $4,000 billion in only ten years." This would be 7% of the world's gross product.

CHAPTER XI

1. Keil, pp. 422-423.

2. The same archangel, Michael, that great prince who is Israel's protector, we find, is obliged to treat Satan with respect, for we read in Jude verse 9,

Yet Michael, the archangel, when contending with the devil he disputed about the body of Moses, dared not bring against him a railing accusation, but said, The Lord rebuke thee.

The Mohammedan Koran, with its usual mixture of biblical names and theological error, speaks of "Satan who was stoned." Scripture speaks of him as the personification of evil but speaks of him with respect. After all, he was once the Anointed Cherub.

3. The Lamb was slain according to the preordained counsel of God; the event was carried out by Satan as the instrument.

4. Isaiah 44:48, 45:1-4.

5. Keil, p. 423- op. cit.

6. Barnes, II, pp. 104-205. Op. cit.

CHAPTER XII

1. Keil, p. 248. Op cit.

2. Keil, pp. 444-446. Op. cit.

3. Ibid., p. 446.

4. Jerome has given us a very full account and interpretation of the historical portions of verses 1-23 of this chapter, all of this in answer to Porphyry's attack on the validity of the book. When he comes to the twenty- fourth verse, he says:

"Up to this point the historical order has been followed, and there has been no point of controversy between Porphyry and those of our side (variant: and us). But the rest of the text from here on to the end of the book he interprets as applying to the person of the Antiochus who was surnamed Epiphanes, the brother of Seleucus and the son of Antiochus the Great. He reigned in Syria for eleven years after Seleucus, and he seized Judaea, and it is under his reign that the persecution of God's Law is related, and also the wars of the Maccabees.

"But those of our persuasion believe all these things are spoken prophetically of the Antichrist who is to arise in the end time. But this factor appears to them as a difficulty for our view, namely the question as to why the prophetic discourse should abruptly cease mention of these great kings and shift from Seleucus to the end of the world. The answer is that in the earlier historical account where mention was made of the Persian kings, only four kings of Persia were presented, following after Cyrus, and (712) many who came in between were simply skipped over, so as to come quickly to Alexander, king of Macedonians. We hold that it is the practice of Scripture not to relate all details completely, but only to set forth what seems of major importance.

"Those of our school insist also that since many of the details which we are subsequently to read and explain are appropriate to the person of Antiochus, he is to be regarded as a type of the Antichrist, and those things which happen to him in a preliminary way are to be completely fulfilled in the case of Antichrist.

"We hold that it is the habit of Holy Scripture to set forth by means of types the reality of things to come, in conformity with what is said of our Lord and Savior in the Seventy-first (i.e., Seventy-second) Psalm, a psalm which is noted at the beginning as being Solomon's, and yet not all the statements which are made concerning him can be applied to Solomon. For certainly he neither endured 'together with the sun and before the moon from generation to generation,' nor did he hold sway from sea, (p. 566) to sea, or from the River unto the ends of the earth; neither did all nations serve him, neither did his name endure before the sun; neither were all the tribes of earth blessed in him, nor did all races magnify him. But in a partial way these things were set forth in advance, by shadows as it were, and by a mere symbol of the reality, in the person of Solomon, in order that they might be more perfectly fulfilled in our Lord and Savior.

"And so, just as the Savior had Solomon and the other saints as types of His advent, so also we should believe that the Antichrist very properly had as a type of himself the utterly wicked king, Antiochus, who persecuted the saints and defiled the temple." (Jerome, pp. 129-130, Daniel Gleason Archer Translation.)

5. According to Keil, verses 10-20, inclusive, and verses 22 and 27 are without counterparts in history (verses 6, 11, 12, only in part). (See Keil, pp. 446-461.) In our own view, these, then, belong to the future. Sir Robert Anderson says in The Coming Prince (p. 195), apropos of Daniel 11:36-45 and 12:1:

"I'm inclined to believe that the entire passage from verse five in Daniel eleven will receive a future fulfillment, and I have no doubt of this as regards the passage beginning with verse twenty-one. See especially verse thirty-one. But the future application of the portion quoted in the text is unquestionable. Although the chapter in part refers to Antiochus Epiphanes, 'There are traits which have nothing to correspond to them in Antiochus, which are even the exact contradictory of the character of Antiochus, but which do reappear in St. Paul's account of the Antichrist to come.' I quote from Dr. Pusey."

He adds (Footnote, p. 93): "The image of the Antichrist of the Old Testament melts into the lineaments of the Antichrist himself. . . . One trait only of the anti-religious character of the Antichrist was true of Antiochus also: 'He shall speak marvelous things against the God of Gods.' Blasphemy against god is an essential feature against any god opposed to power or any individual. It belongs to Voltaire as much as to Antiochus, all besides has no place in him. . . . The characteristics of this infidel king are: (1) self exaltation above every god; 'He shall magnify himself above every god'; (2) contempt of all religion; (3) blasphemy against the true God; (4) apostacy against the God of his fathers; (5) disregarding the desire of women; (6) the honoring of a god whom his fathers knew not. Of all these six marks one only, in the least, agrees with Antiochus. The entire passage is valuable and the argument conclusive."

He quotes Pusey also as identifying this king with the second beast of Revelation 13 but disagrees on the ground that the second beast is not a king but is dependent upon the first beast. I'm not sure that this is a valid objection since all five descriptions in Daniel that might be applied to the two beasts seem to be descriptions of kings. After all, one king could conceivably be dependent upon another king.

6. Walvoord, p. 254. Op. cit.

7. Leupold, pp. 475-476. Op. cit.

8. For brevity, the following table, by Young (The Prophecy of Daniel , p. 303), concerning the Northern and Southern Kingdoms, according to the verses involved, will explain the historical illusions:

Syria--Northern Kingdom	Egypt--Southern Kingdom
The Seleucids	The Ptolemies
B.C.	B.C.
Seleucus I - Nicator - 312-280	Ptolemy I - Soter - 326-285,
Antiochus I - Soter - 280-261	Daniel 11:5
Antiochus II-Theos-261-246	Ptolemy II - Philadelphia -
Seleucus II - Callinicus -	Daniel 11:6
246-226, Daniel 11:9	Ptolemy III - Euergetes -
Seleucus III - Ceraunus -	246-221, Daniel 11:7-8
226-223, Daniel 11:10	Ptolemy IV - Philopator -
Antiochus III - The Great -	221-204, Daniel 11:12, 14
223-181, Daniel 11:10-18	Ptolemy Epiphanes-204-181
Seleucus IV - Philopator -	Ptolemy VI - Philometor -
187-175, Daniel 11:20	181-145
Antiochus IV - Ephiphanes -	
175-164, Daniel 11:21-35	
Antiochus V - Eupator-164-162	
Demetrs I - Soter - 162-150	
Alexander Balas - 150-145	

9. "Antiochus, sitting upon an ivory chair in the Roman fashion, would administer justice and adjudge disputes on the most trifling matters. And so incapable was his mind of sticking to any station in life, as it strayed through all the varieties of existence that it was not really clear either to himself or to others what kind of person he was. It was his habit not to speak to his friends, to smile at mere acquaintances in a most friendly way, and with an inconsistent generosity to make himself and others laughing stocks; to some, men of distinction who held themselves in high esteem, he would give childish presents, as food or toys; others who expected nothing, he would make rich.

"And so he seemed to some not to know what he wanted; some said he was playing childish tricks, some that he was unquestionably insane. Nevertheless, in two great and important respects his soul was truly royal; in his benefactions to cities and in honors paid to the gods. Of his magnificent ideas as to the treatment of the gods, the temple of Jupiter Olympius at Athens, the only one in the world which though unfinished, was designed to conform to the greatness of the god, can well be in evidence;

besides, he also adorned Delos with marvelous altars and abundance of statuary and at Antioch, he built a magnificent temple to Jupiter Capitolinus, which had not merely its ceiling panelled with gold, but also had its walls wholly covered with gilded plates; and many other things he promised in other places, but by reason of the very short duration of his reign he did not finish them.

"Also in regard to the splendor of his shows of every sort he surpassed earlier kings, his other spectacles being given in their own proper style and with an abundance of Greek theatrical artists; a gladiatorial exhibition after the Roman fashion he presented which was at first received with greater terror than pleasure on the part of men who were unused to such sights; then by frequent repetitions, by sometimes allowing the fighters to go only so far as wounding one another, sometimes permitting them to fight without giving quarter he made the sight familiar and even pleasing, and he aroused in many of the young men a joy in arms. And so, while at first he had been accustomed to summon gladiators from Rome, procuring them by large fees, finally he could find a sufficient supply at home." (Livy, Bk. XLI, 720.)

10. "In Syria, King Antiochus, wishing to provide himself with money, decided to make an expedition against the sanctuary of Artemis in Elymais. (Josephus, Antiquities Bk. XII, Ch. IX, Para. 1.) On reaching the spot he was foiled in his hopes, as the barbarian tribes who dwelt in the neighborhood would not permit the outrage, and on his retreat he died at Tabae in Persia, smitten with madness, as some people say, owing to certain manifestations of Divine displeasure when he was attempting this outrage on the above sanctuary." (Polybius, Bk. XXXI-III-9, p. 177, Loeb-Classical Library.)

11. Anderson, The Coming Prince, pp. 190-191, quoting in part the London Times, December 18, 1876.)

12. Keil, pp. 462-463. Op. cit.

13. Sir Isaac Newton, The Ten Kingdoms, p. 193, as quoted by Sir Robert Anderson, The Coming Prince, pp. 191-192.

14. Here, we would greatly desire to know more of the chronology of the events in the seventieth week, the Week of Antichrist. We read in Isaiah 2:19, 21, Ezekiel 38:20, Zechariah 14:4-5, and Revelation 16:18 of an earthquake, the like of which the world has never experienced. It seems to come in the last half of the seventieth week. It seems to be worldwide. We read that *"the cities of the nations fell,"* and general devastation resulted, but have we considered the concomitant circumstances in the practical realm?

We know that the modern world largely travels by a motor driven vehicle in air, land, or sea but these are dependent upon oil; and oil, upon oil wells. An earthquake of a magnitude and extensiveness of that described in Scripture would, undoubtedly, shut off all oil wells, all pipe lines, all refineries, and all storage tanks. Hence all cars, military vehicles, airplanes, motor driven machines of all kinds would come to a standstill, as would rail and bus transportation. Further, all factories will be destroyed.

So when we read of Gog's invasion with his hordes on horseback and armed with spear, sword, and bow, these may be actual conditions of warfare and not just symbolic; only, of course, if his invasion comes after the earthquake.

CHAPTER XIII

1. Newell, The Revelation, p. 200.

2. "The foolish shepherd is not Herod or Agrippa (Kimchi), nor all the rulers of Israel from the decline of the Maccabean period to the rejection of Christ (Lowe) nor the Roman Empire (Wright) but the personal Antichrist (Jerome, Pusey, Baron, Dennett, and others). In verse 15, we have the character of this shepherd; in verse 16 his works; in verse 17 his punishment. The adjective ewili is a hapaxlegomenon, the substantive of which is often used. Folly in the Old Testament is sin. Compare Psalm 14:1. He is foolish in the moral sense. (Charles Feinberg, God Remembers, p. 212.)

Keil aptly says: "If the Good Shepherd represented by the prophet in verses 4-14 is no other than Jehovah in His rule over Israel, the foolish shepherd who is raised up over the land in the place of the Good Shepherd, who had been despised and rejected, can only be the possessor of the imperial power, into whose power the nation is given after the rejection of the Good Shepherd sent to it in Christ, i.e., the Roman Empire, which destroyed the Jewish state." (Keil, "Zechariah," Minor Prophets, Vol. II, p. 378.)

3. Girdlestone, p. 257. Old Testaments Synonyms.

4. Daniel uses am ten times in the Aramaic portion and nine times in the Hebrew in the following verses: 2:44, 3:4, 7:29, 4:1, 5:19, 6:25, 7:14-27; in the Hebrew, translated as "people": 8:24, 9:6, 15-16, 19, 9:24, 26, 10:14, 11:14-15, 32-33, 12:1, 7. Goi is used in the following: 8:22, 11:23, 12:1, three times as "people" and two times as "nation" or "heathen." Ummah (Aramaic) is used six times: 3:4, 7:29, 4:1, 5:19, 6:25, 7:14, and translated "nations." Lohm is not used at all.

The A.V. consistently translated ahm as "people" and goi as "nation." The Septuagint translates laos as "people" and ethnos as "gentile" (sometimes "nations"). The ethnos is used in Daniel 9:27 in the LXX.

5. Newell, The Book of Revelation, p. 198.

6. A.C. Gabelein, The Prophet Daniel (New York: Our Hope Publishing Co., 1911), pp. 117-118.

7. Kings of the east, as viewed from present situations, could be China and India and could involve Japan and Korea. Which of these or all of these, we cannot at present determine.

8. Christianity Today, Nov. 24, 1972, p. 28.

9. William Shirer, The Rise and Fall of the Third Reich (New York: Simon & Schuster, 1960), p. 240.

10. Hartley and Hartley, Readings in Psychology, 2nd ed., p. 3.

11. In Revelation 13:2, we have a picture of the composite nature of the kingdom of the First Beast. If our interpretation of this is to be consistent with Daniel 7, as we have suggested, the leopard likeness and bear-like feet would seem to refer to the characteristic qualities of the animals, swiftness and brute force, rather than to ethnic or national origins.

CHAPTER XIV

1. The apocryphal book of Enoch (Enoch 20:1-7) speaks of six angels of power, apparently equal: Uriel, Raphael, Raguel, Michael, Zariel, Gabriel, and, possibly a seventh, Remiel. Only Michael has biblical designation as archangel. Gabriel is named but not designated as a chief angel. There is no biblical warrant for the other names.

2. Culver, p. 173. Op. cit.

3. The word "ancients," used over 170 times in the Old Testament and usually translated "elder," is the Hebrew word zahkehn. It is never, so far as we can discover, used of angels or heavenly beings for which the characteristic word is malahch, meaning "messenger." Neither is the word used of departed saints, for which the term would be kahdohsh, meaning "holy one." So the quotation in Isaiah 24:23, which pictures the Lord of hosts as reigning in Mount Zion and in Jerusalem and before his ancients gloriously, carries with it no connotation of another wordly scene. Nothing could more implicitly indicate a terrestial scene and the millennial setting.

4. Walvoord, p. 287. Op. cit.

5. Keil, p. 483. Op. cit.

6. Young, p. 257. Op cit.

7. Scripture is not characterized by exaggeration, but if ever there was an understatement, it is found in the two phrases "many shall run to and fro" and "knowledge shall be increased." Consider the first phrase, in terms of actual statistics for the United States, in the light of the following facts:

(a) As of January 1, 1970, there were over 105,000,000 registered motor vehicles in the United States, with 75% of the population licensed to drive them over 3,703,831 miles of public roads.

(b) In 1969, buses carried 380,000,000 passengers.

(c) In the year 1967, railroads carried 296,995,000 passengers.

(d) Airplane companies report for the year 1969, 125,414,212,000 passenger miles.

(e) Travel bureaus lure millions to ocean cruises.

(f) If we add to this the number of private airplanes owned, river and lake traffic, walking tours, and so forth, and all of this for a population of 265,000,000, it would almost seem as if the whole country is going somewhere most of the time. What is true of America is characteristic, to a lesser degree, for many parts of the world. Many are running to and fro. (Data from World Almanac, 1970.)

8. What shall we say then about the increase of knowledge? Since education in the United States is its biggest business, shall we consider the following:

(a) There are 45,000,000 elementary and high school pupils in the United States taught by 2,000,000 teachers at a cost of $40,561,997,000.

(b) Over 2,000 universities, colleges, junior colleges, and other institutions of higher learning enroll 6,000,000 at costs that are astronomical.

(c) There are research institutions and groups for medicine, technology, business, and so forth, all over America.

(d) At least 36 universities have libraries with a number of volumes ranging from 1,202,000 to 9,000,000 each.

(e) Out of the many public libraries in the country, 21 of them report their number of volumes from 1,235,000 to 7,202,000, and the Library of Congress lists 14,000,000 volumes.

Again, what is true of the United States is true, in a lesser degree, all over the world. Newly emerging nations in Asia, Africa, and the islands of the sea are establishing universal education and even founding universities.

There has never been any time in the world's history when so many knew so much about so many things and when there were so many opportunities for everyone to learn anything he wished. As one educator once put it, there has been an explosion of knowledge, an explosion something on the order of an intellectual hydrogen bomb. We hasten to say that it is hard to prove an equal explosion of wisdom; wisdom seems as scarce as ever. (Data taken from World Almanac, 1970.)

9. U.S. News and World Report, November 13, 1972, "Behind the rise in crime and terror."

10. Montgomery suggests that Daniel and his three companions returned to Jerusalem with Nehemiah, because these same names appear in Nehemiah's list; the name of Azariah in Nehemiah 3:24, Daniel in 10:6, Hannaniah in 10:23, Mishael in 8:4. (Montgomery, p. 90.)

Since these names are not uncommon and since they are neither grouped together nor given any distinction but are included in a general list, and, furthermore, since these men would have been over 170 years old at the time of Nehemiah's return, I find this difficult to believe. These men were taken as youths, perhaps 17 or 18 years of age, in 604 B.C., and Nehemiah's returned to Jerusalem, at least according to some authorities, in 445 B.C. This would leave a gap of 159 years which, added to their ages at the beginning of their captivity, would make them about 176 years old.

BIBLIOGRAPHY

Anderson, Sir Robert. The Coming Prince. 14th ed. Grand Rapids: Kregel, 1954.

———. Daniel in the Critic's Den. London: James Nesbit and Co., 1909.

Appian. Roman History: The Syrian Wars. Loeb Classical Library.

Assyrian and Babylonian Literature. Edited by R.F. Harper. New York: Appleton and Co., 1901.

Barnes, Albert. Notes on the Old Testament: Daniel. 2 Vols. Grand Rapids: Baker Book House, 1950.

Bonnar, James. The Great Interregnum. Glasgow: Hugh Hopkins, 1871.

Beek, Martin A. Atlas of Mesopotamia. Nelson, 1962.

Bosanquet, J.W. Messiah the Prince. 2nd ed. 1866.

Boutflower C. In and Around the Book of Daniel. 1923.

Brown, Driver, Briggs. Hebrew and English Lexican of the Old Testament. Oxford, 1951.

Cambridge Ancient History. Vol. 3. Cambridge University Press.

Coleman, J.C. Abnormal Psychology and Modern Life. 2nd ed. Scott Foresman and Co., 1956.

Culver, Robert D. Daniel and the Latter Days. Revell, 1954.

Diodorus, Siculus. Roman History. Loeb Classical Library.

Dougherty, R.P. Nabonidus and Belshazzar. Yale Oriental Series, Vol. 15. New Haven, 1929.

Edersheim, A. Life and Times of the Messiah. New York: Longmans, Green and Co., 1931.

Englishman's Hebrew and Chaldee Concordance. 5th ed. London: Samuel Bagster and Son Ltd., 1890.

Feinberg, Charles. The Prophecy of Ezekiel. Chicago: Moody Press, 1969.

———. God Remembers: Zechariah. New York: American Board of Missions to the Jews, 1965.

Finnegan, J. Light from the Ancient Past.

Gaebelin, A.C. The Prophet Daniel. New York: Our Hope Publishing Co., 1911.

Girdlestone. Old Testament Synonyms. Grand Rapids: Associated Publishers and Authors, Inc., 1897.

Goodspeed, G.S. A History of the Babylonians and the Assyrians. Charles Scribner and Sons, 1902.

Harrison, R.K. Introduction to the Old Testament. Grand Rapids: Eerdmans, 1969.

Hartley and Hartley, ed. Readings in Psychology. 2nd ed.

Haug, Martin. Essay on the Religion of the Parsees. Trubner Oriental Series. London: Kegan Paul, Trench and Co. Ltd., 1878.

Herodotus. History. New York: Tudor Publishing Co., 1928.

Hume, David. Treatise Human Nature

International Standard Bible Encyclopedia.

Jerome. Commentary on Daniel. Translated by Gleason Archer. Grand Rapids: Baker Book House, 1958.

Josephus, Flavius. Antiquities of the Jews. J.C. Winston and Co.

Contra Apion. J.C. Winston and Co.

Keller, Werner. The Bible as History,N.Y.:Wm. Morcwand Co., 1963.

Keil, C.F. Bible Commentary on the Book of Daniel. Grand Rapids: Eerdmans.

Kelly, William. Biblical Commentary on the Book of Daniel. New York: Loizeaux Brothers, 1943.

Kittel, Rudolf. Biblia Hebraica. Stuttgart: Wurttembergische Bibelanstalt, 1951.

Koldeway, Robert. The Excavations at Babylon. Macmillan, 1915.

Lewis, C.S. Miracles.

Leupold, H.C. Exposition of Daniel. Grand Rapids: Baker Book House, 1969.

Livy. Loeb Classical Library.

McClain, Alva J. Daniel's Prophecy of the Seventy Weeks. Grand Rapids: Zondervan Publishing House, 1968.

Montgomery, J.A. The Book of Daniel. ICC Series. Edinburgh: T. and T. Clark, 1926.

New Catholic Encyclopedia. Art. "Daniel."

Newell. W The Book of Revelation.

Noble, C.F. The Drama of the Ages. 1955.

Pentecost, J. Dwight. Things to Come. Grand Rapids: Zondervan Publishing House, 1970.

Prophecy for Today.

Polybius. Histories. Vol. 6. Loeb Classical Library.

Pusey, E.B. Daniel the Prophet. Funk and Wagnalls, 1885.

Rawlinson, George. Historical Evidences of the Truth of the Scripture Records. Boston: Gould & Lincoln, 1868.

Rogers, Robert W. Cunieform Parallels the Old Testament. Abigdon Press, 1926. (First published in 1912.)

Rosen and Gregory, ed. Abnormal Psychology.

Rowley, H. H. Darius the Mede and the Four World Empires in the Book of Daniel. Cardiff: University of Wales Press Board, 1959.

Sayce, A.H. Early Israel and the Surrounding Nations. New York: E.R. Herrick & Co., 1899.

Schaff. Herzog Religious Encyclopedia. Art. "Daniel."

Shirer, William. The Rise and Fall of the Third Reich. New York: Simon & Schuster, 1960.

Short, A.R. The Bible and Modern Medicine.

Scofield Reference Bible. New Edition.

Solzhenitsyn, Aleksandr. The Gulag Archipelaco. Harper Row; 1973-74.

Spence, Lewis. Hammerstein. Art. "Wonders of the Past."

Strabo. Lib. X & XVI. Loeb Classical Library.

Talbot, Lewis T. The Prophecies of Daniel.

Thiessen, H.C. Will the Church Pass Through the Tribulation? New York: Loizeaux Brothers, 1941.

Thompson, J.A. The Bible and Archeology. Grand Rapids: W.B. Eerdmans Publishing Co., 1968.

Tregelles, S.P. Remarks on the Prophetic Visions in the Book of Daniel. London: The Sovereign Grace Advent Testimony, 1965.

Universal Jewish Encyclopedia. Art. "Daniel."

U.S. News and World Report. Nov. 13, 1972.

Walvoord, J.F. Daniel: A Key to Prophetic Revelation. Moody Press, 1971.

Whitcomb, J.C. Darius the Mede. Philadelphia: Presbyterian and Reform Publishing Co., 1963.

Wiseman, D.J. Chronicles of the Chaldean Kings. Trustees of the British Museum, 1961.

"The Last Days of Babylon." Christianity Today, 11, No. 4, 1957.

Wright and Filson, ed. The Westminster Historical Atlas to the Bible.

World Almanac. 1970.

Xenophon. Cyropaedia. Loeb Classical Library.

Yamauchi, E.M. "Stones, Scripts and Scholars." Christianity Today, February 14, 1969.

Young, E.J. The Prophecy of Daniel. Grand Rapids: W.B. Eerdmans Publishing Co., 1953.

BIOLA HOUR SPECIAL EDITION

THE BIOLA HOUR, a half hour daily broadcast sponsored by BIOLA UNIVERSITY, La Mirada, California, is heard on a special network of radio stations across the United States and Canada.

Dr. David Hocking who wrote the Introduction to this book, UNLOCKING THE MYSTERIES OF DANIEL, follows a long tradition of speakers and Bible teachers who have been featured on the BIOLA HOUR.

When Dr. Louis T. Talbot became president of BIOLA and sensed that radio, though still in its infancy, held tremendous potential for future ministry, he began a daily radio broadcast on November 16, 1932, that was later to become the BIOLA HOUR.

It has continued ever since, making it one of the oldest daily religious radio broadcasts in the nation.

BIOLA UNIVERSITY in La Mirada, traces its beginnings to 1906, and continues to equip Christian young people through Bible-centered education. This training prepares them for productive lives in service for Christ as professionals, in the pulpit, on the mission field or in the work place.

For further information about the BIOLA HOUR, write:

BIOLA HOUR MINISTRIES,

13800 BIOLA AVENUE,

LA MIRADA, CALIFORNIA 90639